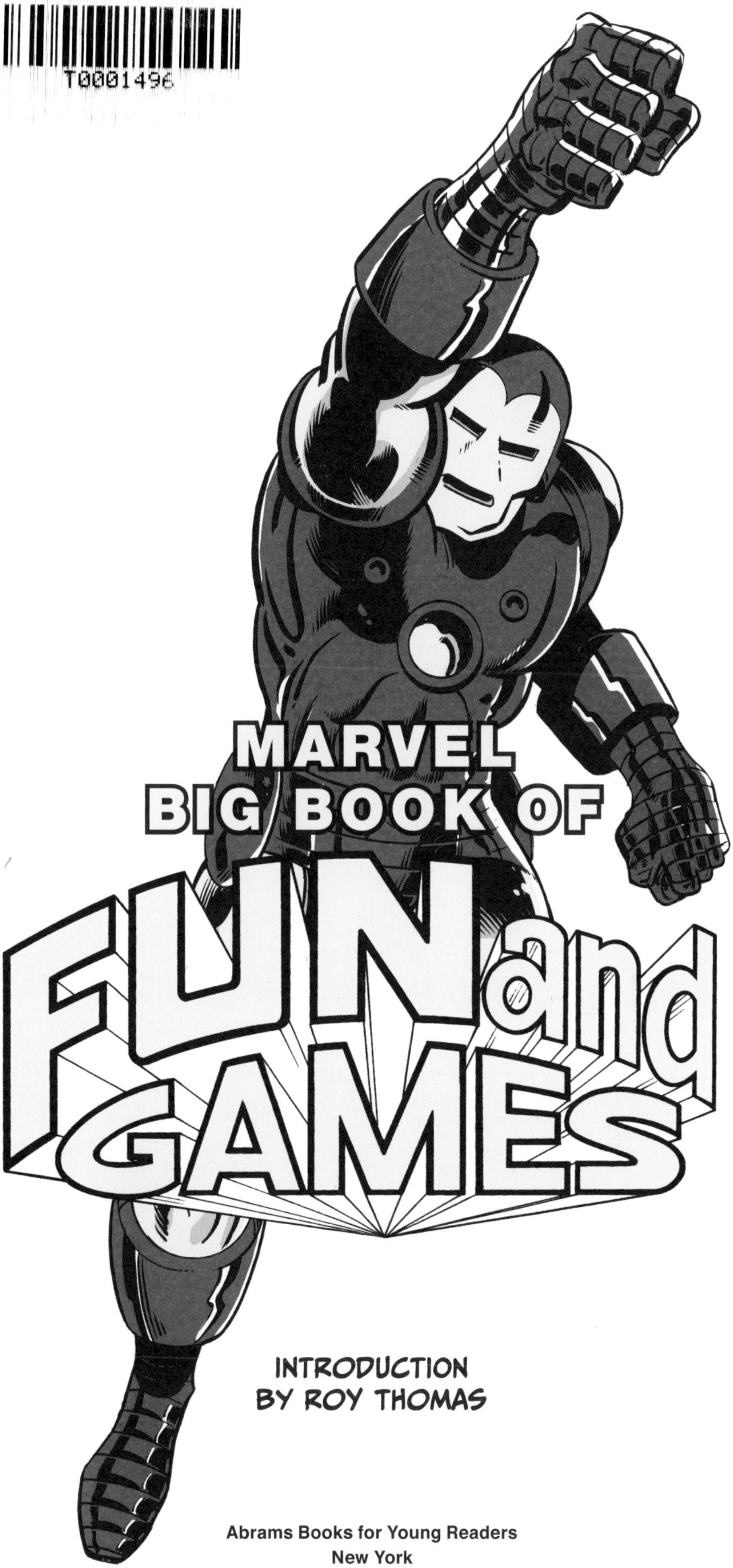

# MARVEL BIG BOOK OF FUN and GAMES

INTRODUCTION BY ROY THOMAS

Abrams Books for Young Readers
New York

ISBN 978-1-4197-6112-6

© 2022 MARVEL
ORIGINAL *FUN AND GAMES* ISSUES WRITTEN,
DRAWN, AND EDITED BY OWEN MCCARRON
INTRODUCTION TEXT BY ROY THOMAS
COVER ART BY DOALY
BOOK DESIGN BY LIAM FLANAGAN

PRINTED AND BOUND IN CHINA
10 9 8 7 6 5 4 3 2 1

ABRAMS BOOKS FOR YOUNG READERS ARE AVAILABLE AT SPECIAL
DISCOUNTS WHEN PURCHASED IN QUANTITY FOR PREMIUMS AND
PROMOTIONS AS WELL AS FUNDRAISING OR EDUCATIONAL USE.
SPECIAL EDITIONS CAN ALSO BE CREATED TO SPECIFICATION.
FOR DETAILS, CONTACT SPECIALSALES@ABRAMSBOOKS.COM
OR THE ADDRESS BELOW.

ABRAMS® IS A REGISTERED TRADEMARK OF HARRY N. ABRAMS, INC.

**ABRAMS** The Art of Books
195 Broadway, New York, NY 10007
abramsbooks.com

DAREDEVIL    NOVA    SPIDER-WOMAN    VISION    HULK    IRON MAN    THOR    HELLCAT

# INTRODUCTION BY ROY THOMAS

In a way, the title *Marvel Big Book of Fun and Games* is a redundancy. In a broader sense, Marvel was *always* about "fun and games," from the day in 1961 when writer/editor Stan Lee and artist/co-plotter Jack Kirby first produced *Fantastic Four* #1, leading to what Stan styled "The Marvel Age of Comics."

The day I first met Stan in July 1965, he was definitely "on," playing Marvel up to me—like I needed convincing—in what was technically a job interview. He quickly persuaded me that working at Marvel would be more fun than staying at DC Comics, where I'd been employed for the past two weeks. And, while being a writer and editor at Marvel was still a job, of course, and all jobs have their up and downs, I'd never claim he misled me. I truly enjoyed working for him and for Marvel, especially during the eleven years I lived in New York City, as I've never enjoyed any other work experience.

I was living in LA, still employed by Marvel, by the time Stan launched the magazine called *Fun and Games* in 1979–80. I had no direct contact with it, but it's easy to see why many folks feel a strong nostalgia for those thirteen issues. They were even the *size* of a comic book—only instead of stories, they sported games and puzzles festooned with Marvel's colorful panoply of Super Heroes. Hail, hail, the gang was all there: Spider-Man and the Hulk and Wolverine, the whole crew. It was a bit like having the Avengers and X-Men and F.F. all drop by your house to match wits with you. If you were familiar with the comic adventures of those stalwarts, you got even more out of the games—but you didn't need to be an expert on Marvel history to play.

Amazingly, the series' entire contents were written, drawn, and edited by Owen McCarron, a Canadian-born cartoonist who often doubled as publisher of comics-related material. He was a versatile artist, able to render Marvel's heroes very much as if they'd been drawn by Kirby, Steve Ditko, John Romita, and the rest of the super talented Marvel bullpen. For me, the test of a Marvel artist's versatility was always how they drew the ever-lovin' blue-eyed Thing. If the Thing approximated one by Kirby that Joe Sinnott inked, I knew the artist could handle any other Marvel hero thrown at them. And McCarron definitely did not disappoint.

Now, many of the "fun and games" of that baker's dozen of issues have been gathered in one color-splashed volume, so you can wander wide-eyed through "Prof. Xavier's X-citing, X-acting X-Maze," or groan to puns uttered by Groot, the tree that walks (and talks) like a man, or search for your favorite Marvel hero's name in rectangles chock-full of seemingly random letters, or even try your hand at drawing the right half of Spider-Woman next to a spot-on rendering of her left side.

You don't have to be an *actual* kid to enjoy this ultimate collection of Marvel's *Fun and Games*—because Owen McCarron and Marvel's ever-ebullient editors will bring out the kid *in* you, page by pulsating page. *Enjoy!*

*Roy Thomas* *has been a writer and often editor for Marvel for much of the time since that day in 1965 when he wandered into Stan Lee's Madison Avenue office—and never really wandered out again.*

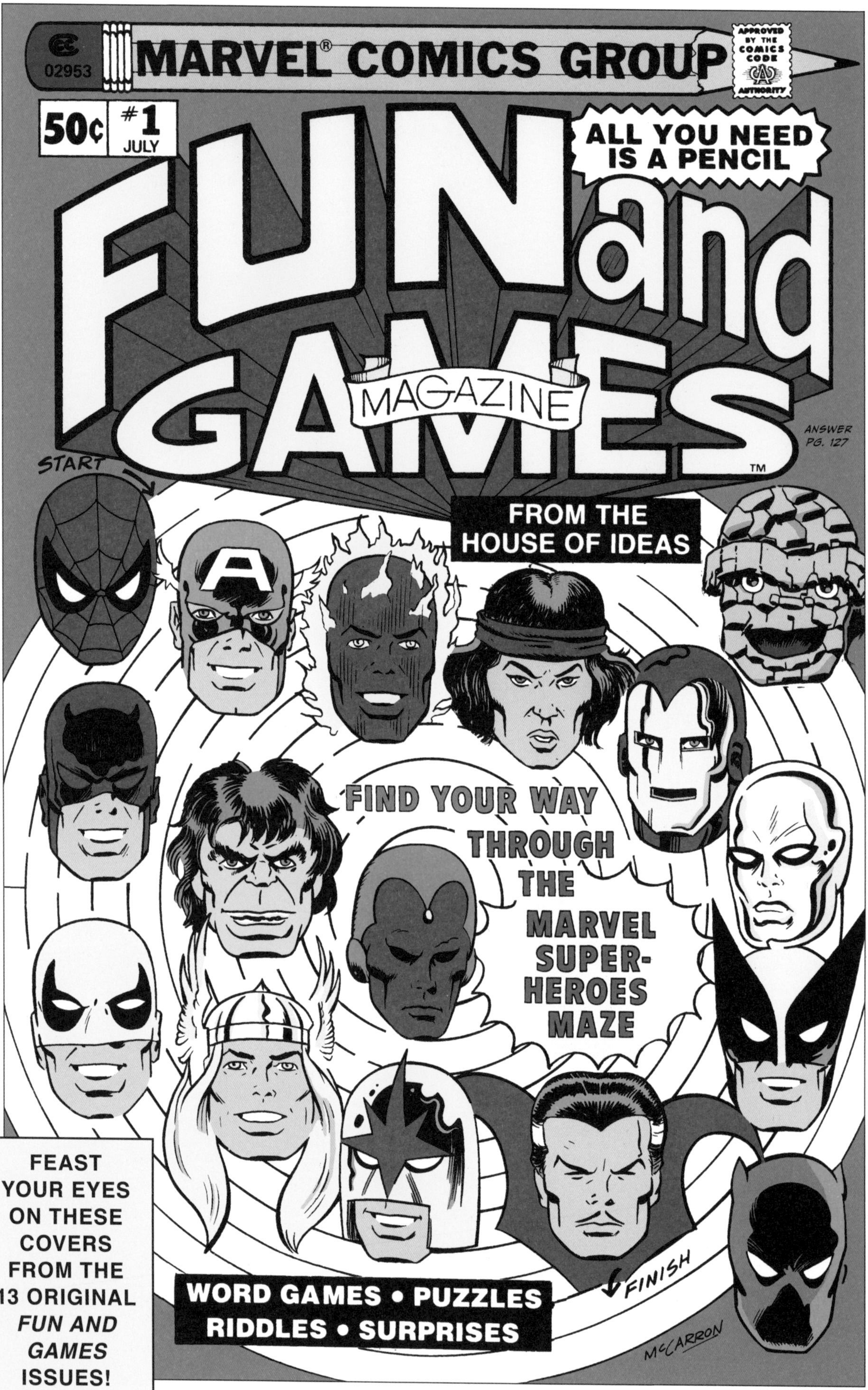

02953
MARVEL® COMICS GROUP
APPROVED BY THE COMICS CODE AUTHORITY
50¢
#1
JULY
ALL YOU NEED IS A PENCIL
FUN and GAMES
MAGAZINE
ANSWER PG. 127
TM
START
FROM THE HOUSE OF IDEAS
FIND YOUR WAY THROUGH THE MARVEL SUPER-HEROES MAZE
FINISH
WORD GAMES • PUZZLES
RIDDLES • SURPRISES
McCARRON


FEAST YOUR EYES ON THESE COVERS FROM THE 13 ORIGINAL *FUN AND GAMES* ISSUES!

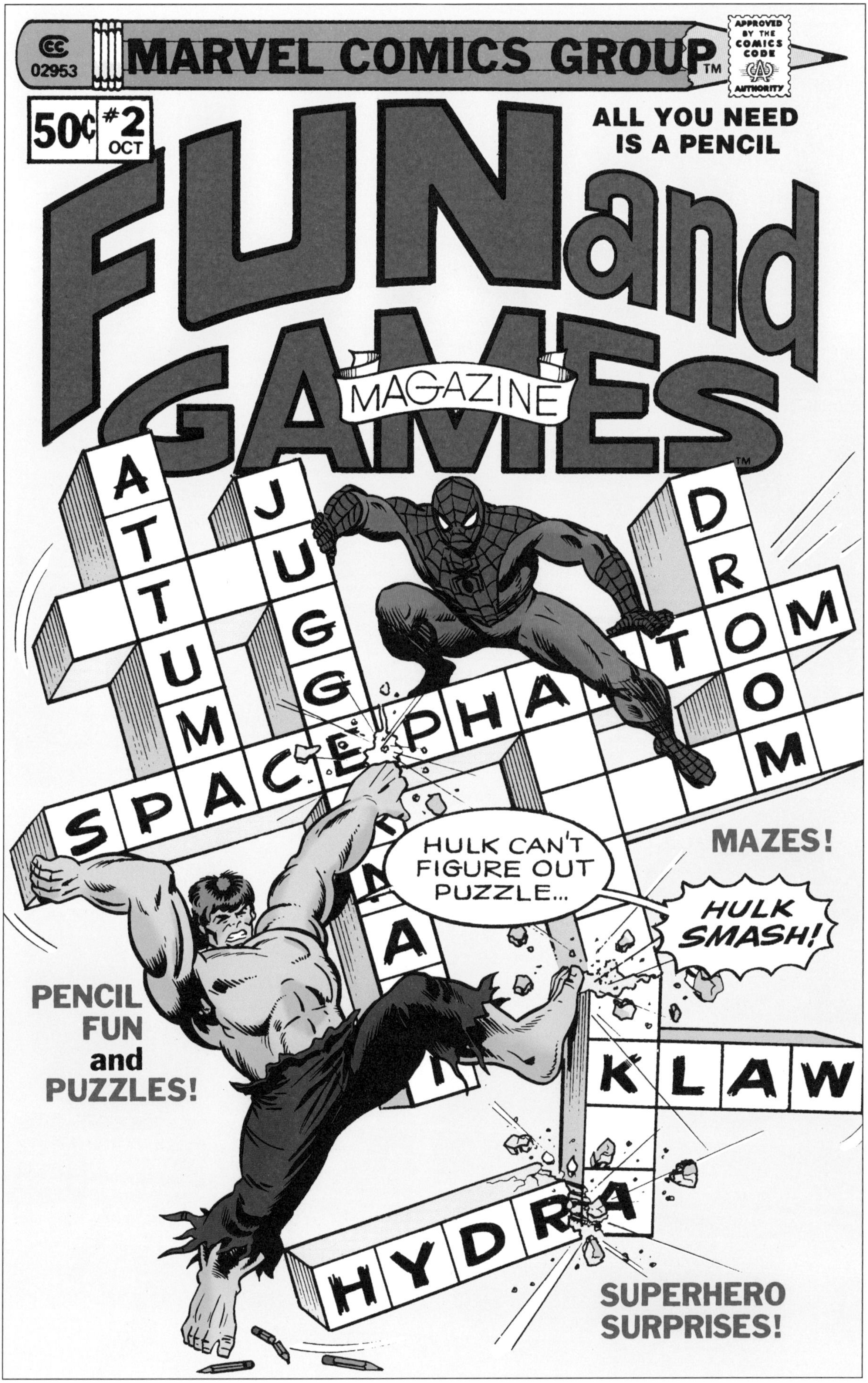

CC
02953
MARVEL COMICS GROUP™
APPROVED BY THE COMICS CODE AUTHORITY
50¢
#2
OCT
ALL YOU NEED IS A PENCIL
FUN and GAMES MAGAZINE™
HULK CAN'T FIGURE OUT PUZZLE...
HULK SMASH!
MAZES!
PENCIL FUN and PUZZLES!
SUPERHERO SURPRISES!

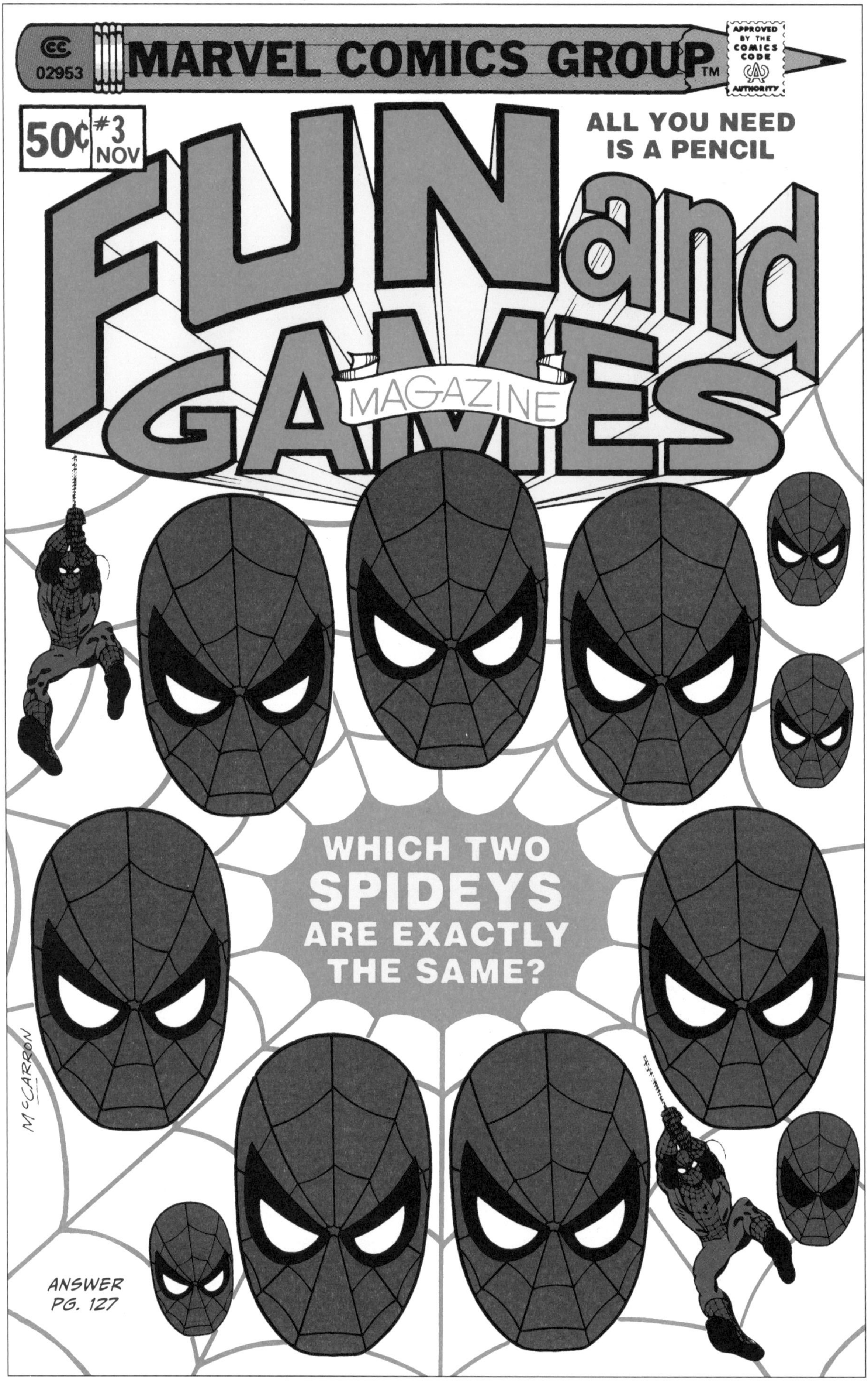

02953
MARVEL COMICS GROUP
APPROVED BY THE COMICS CODE AUTHORITY
50¢
#3 NOV
ALL YOU NEED IS A PENCIL
FUN and GAMES
MAGAZINE
WHICH TWO SPIDEYS ARE EXACTLY THE SAME?
MCCARRON
ANSWER PG. 127

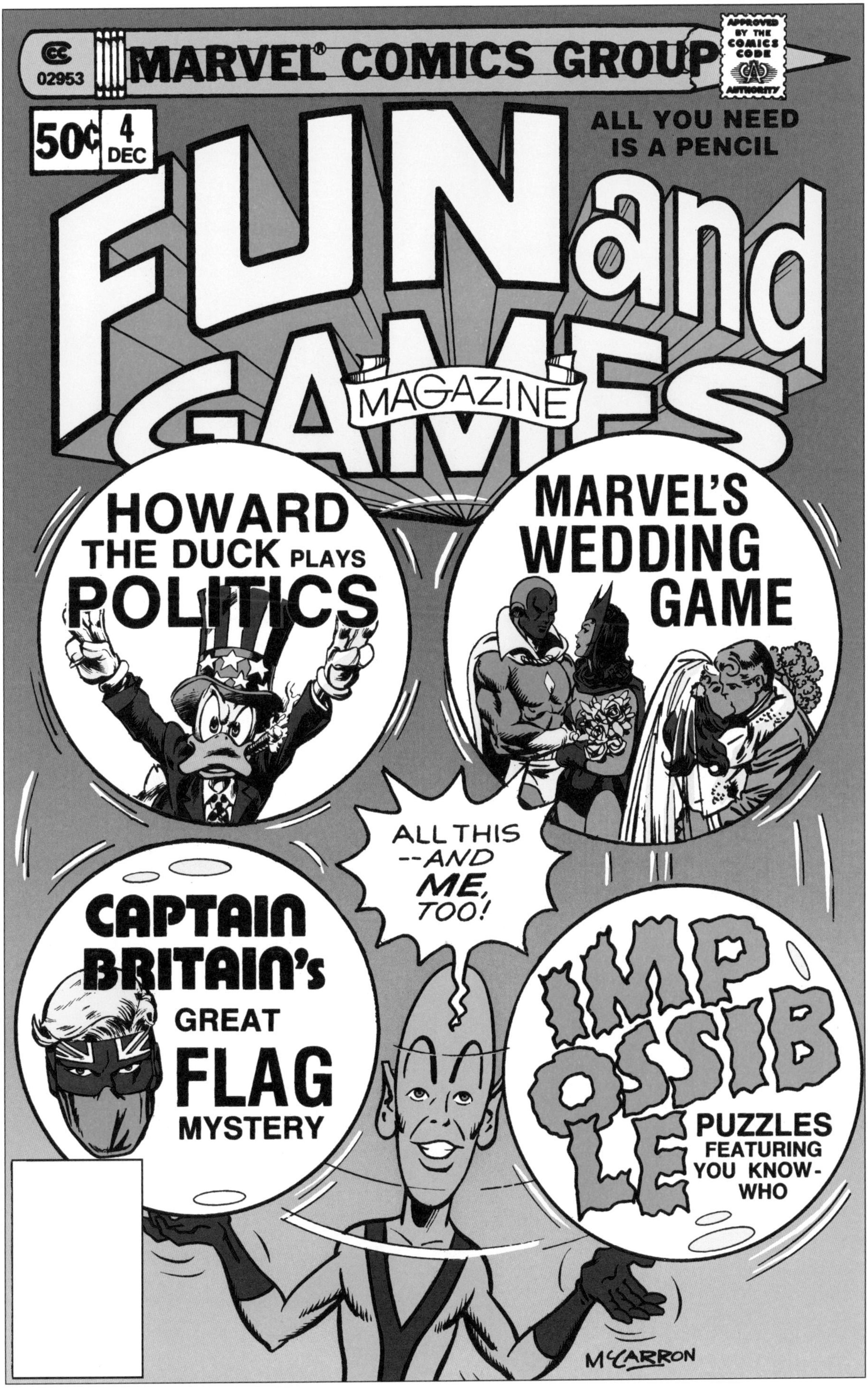
CC
02953
MARVEL® COMICS GROUP
APPROVED BY THE COMICS CODE AUTHORITY
50¢ 4 DEC
ALL YOU NEED IS A PENCIL
FUN and GAMES MAGAZINE
HOWARD THE DUCK PLAYS POLITICS
MARVEL'S WEDDING GAME
ALL THIS --AND ME, TOO!
CAPTAIN BRITAIN's GREAT FLAG MYSTERY
IMPOSSIBLE PUZZLES FEATURING YOU KNOW-WHO
McCARRON

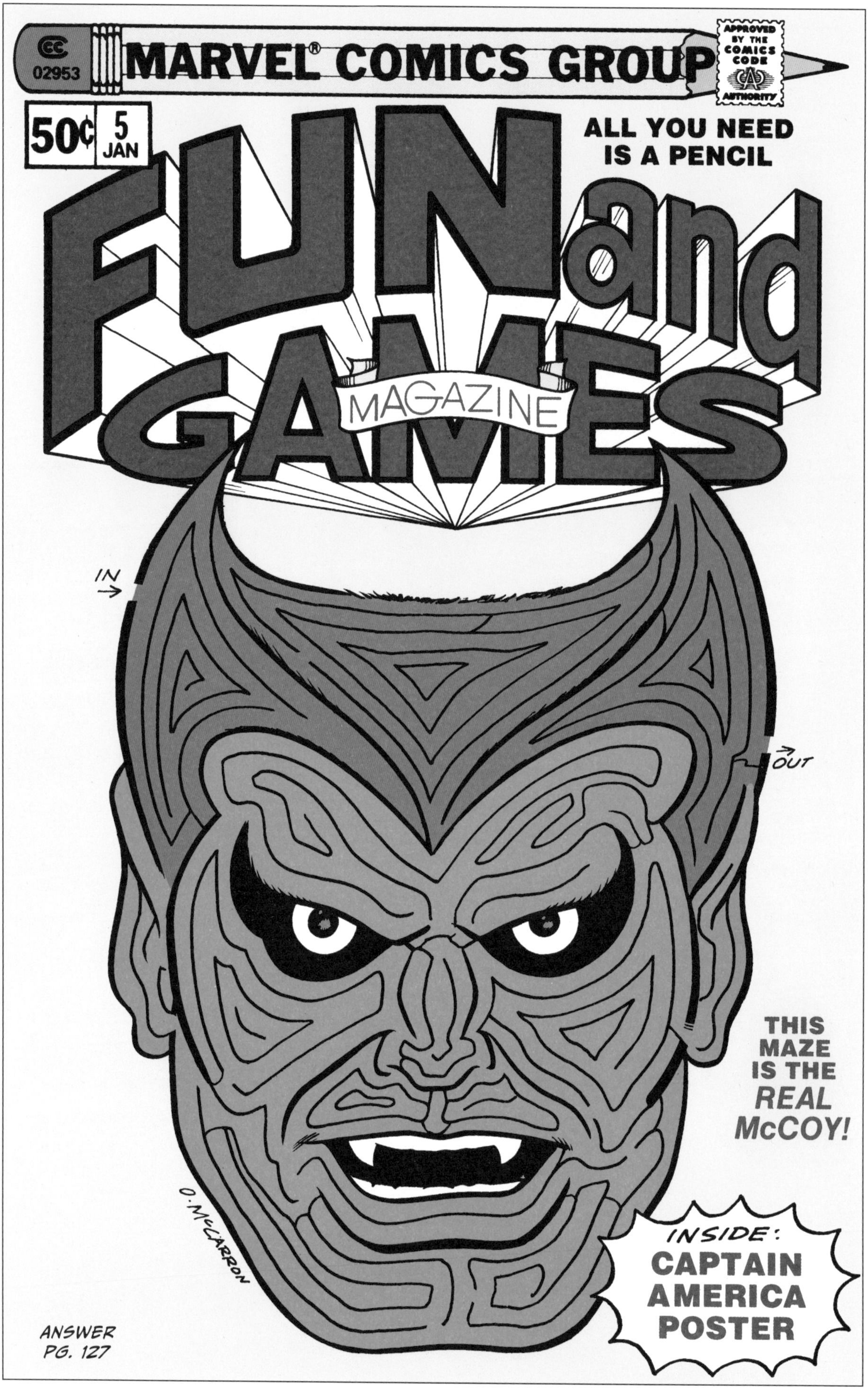
02953
MARVEL® COMICS GROUP
APPROVED BY THE COMICS CODE AUTHORITY
50¢
5
JAN
ALL YOU NEED IS A PENCIL
FUN and GAMES
MAGAZINE
IN
OUT
THIS MAZE IS THE REAL McCOY!
O. McCARRON
INSIDE:
CAPTAIN AMERICA POSTER
ANSWER PG. 127

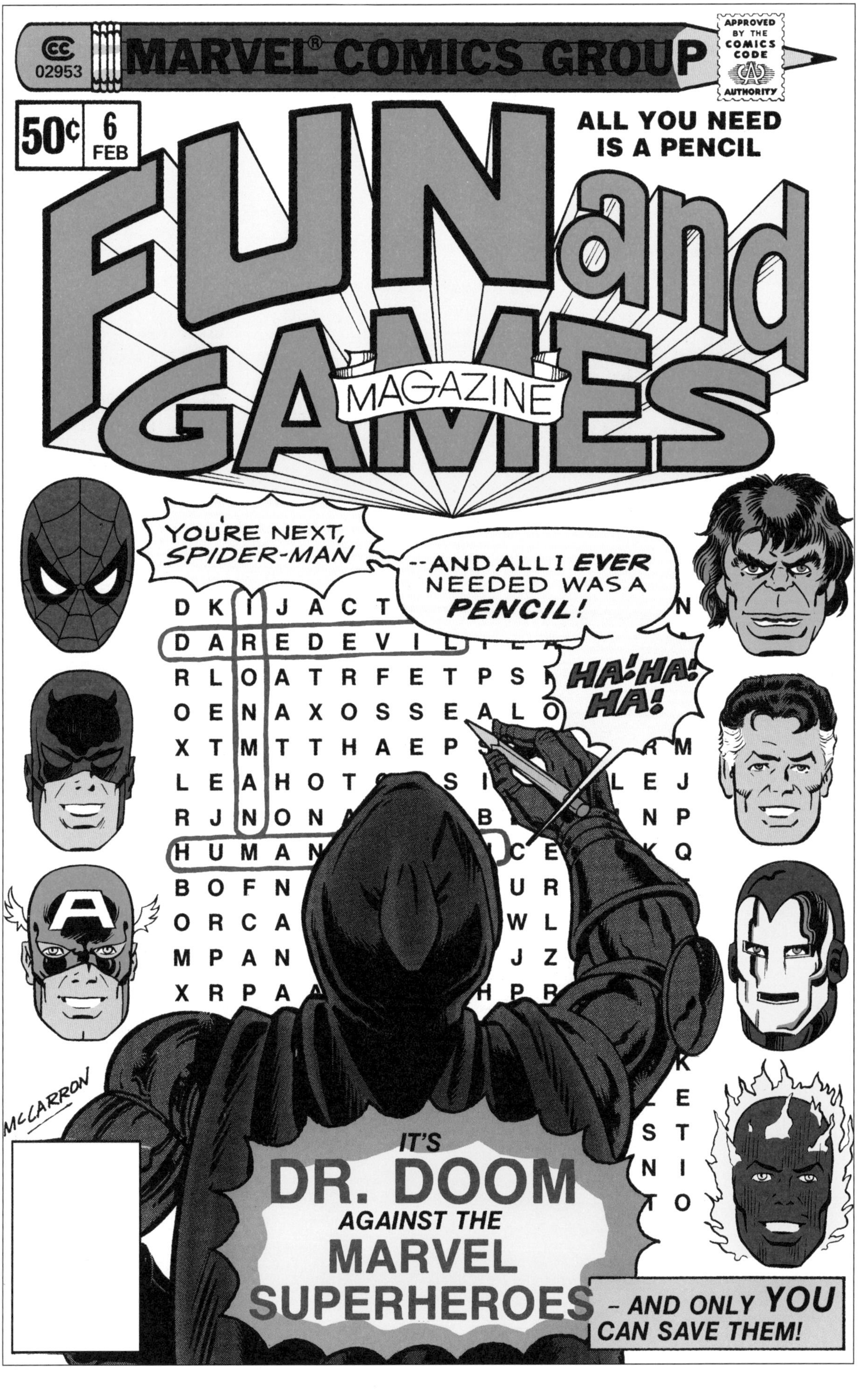
CC
02953
MARVEL® COMICS GROUP
APPROVED BY THE COMICS CODE AUTHORITY
50¢ 6 FEB
ALL YOU NEED IS A PENCIL
FUN and GAMES MAGAZINE
YOU'RE NEXT, SPIDER-MAN
--AND ALL I EVER NEEDED WAS A PENCIL!
HA! HA! HA!
McCARRON
IT'S DR. DOOM AGAINST THE MARVEL SUPERHEROES
- AND ONLY YOU CAN SAVE THEM!

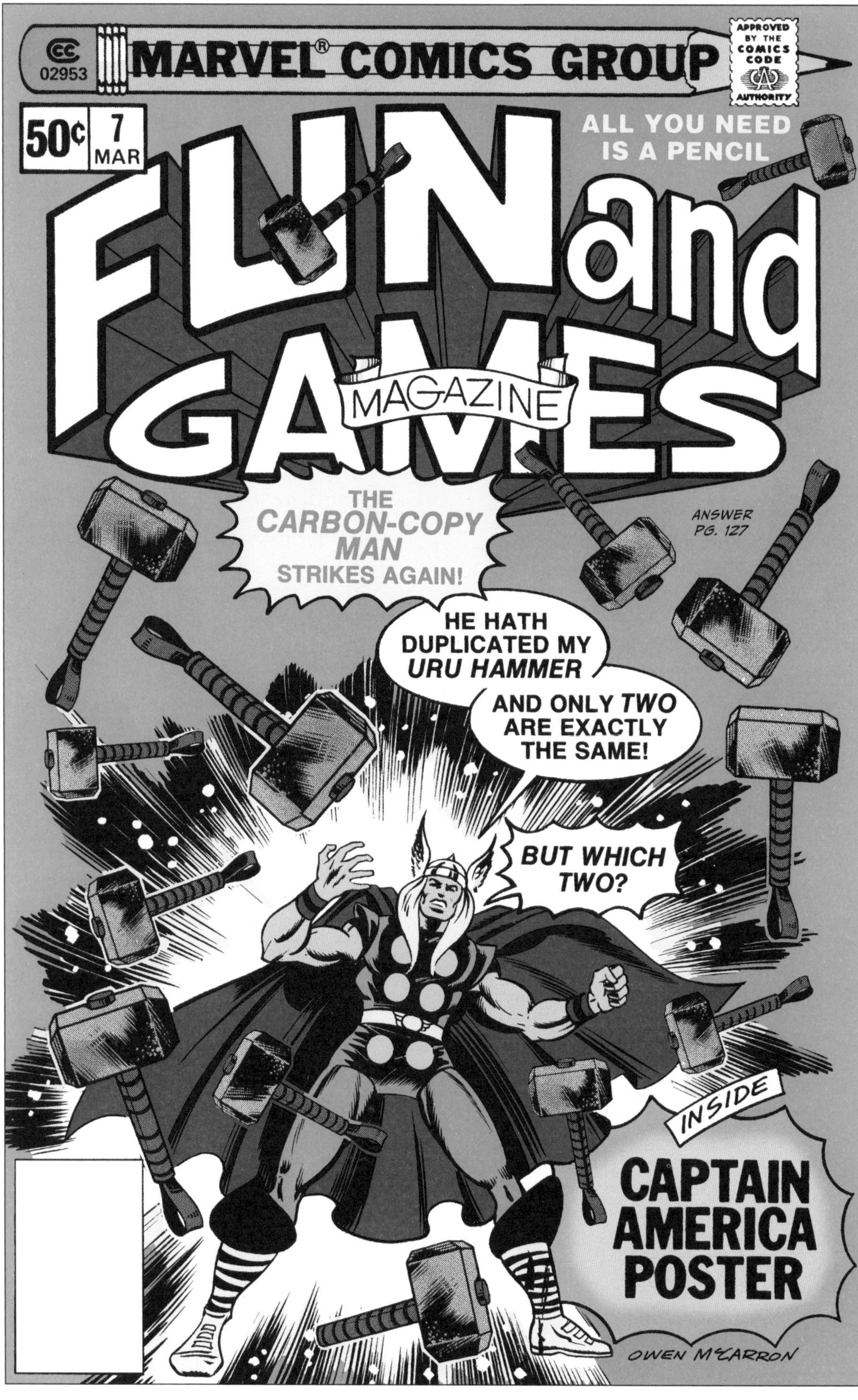
CC
02953
MARVEL® COMICS GROUP
APPROVED BY THE COMICS CODE AUTHORITY
50¢
7
MAR
ALL YOU NEED IS A PENCIL
FUN and GAMES
MAGAZINE
THE CARBON-COPY MAN STRIKES AGAIN!
ANSWER PG. 127
HE HATH DUPLICATED MY URU HAMMER
AND ONLY TWO ARE EXACTLY THE SAME!
BUT WHICH TWO?
INSIDE
CAPTAIN AMERICA POSTER
OWEN McCARRON

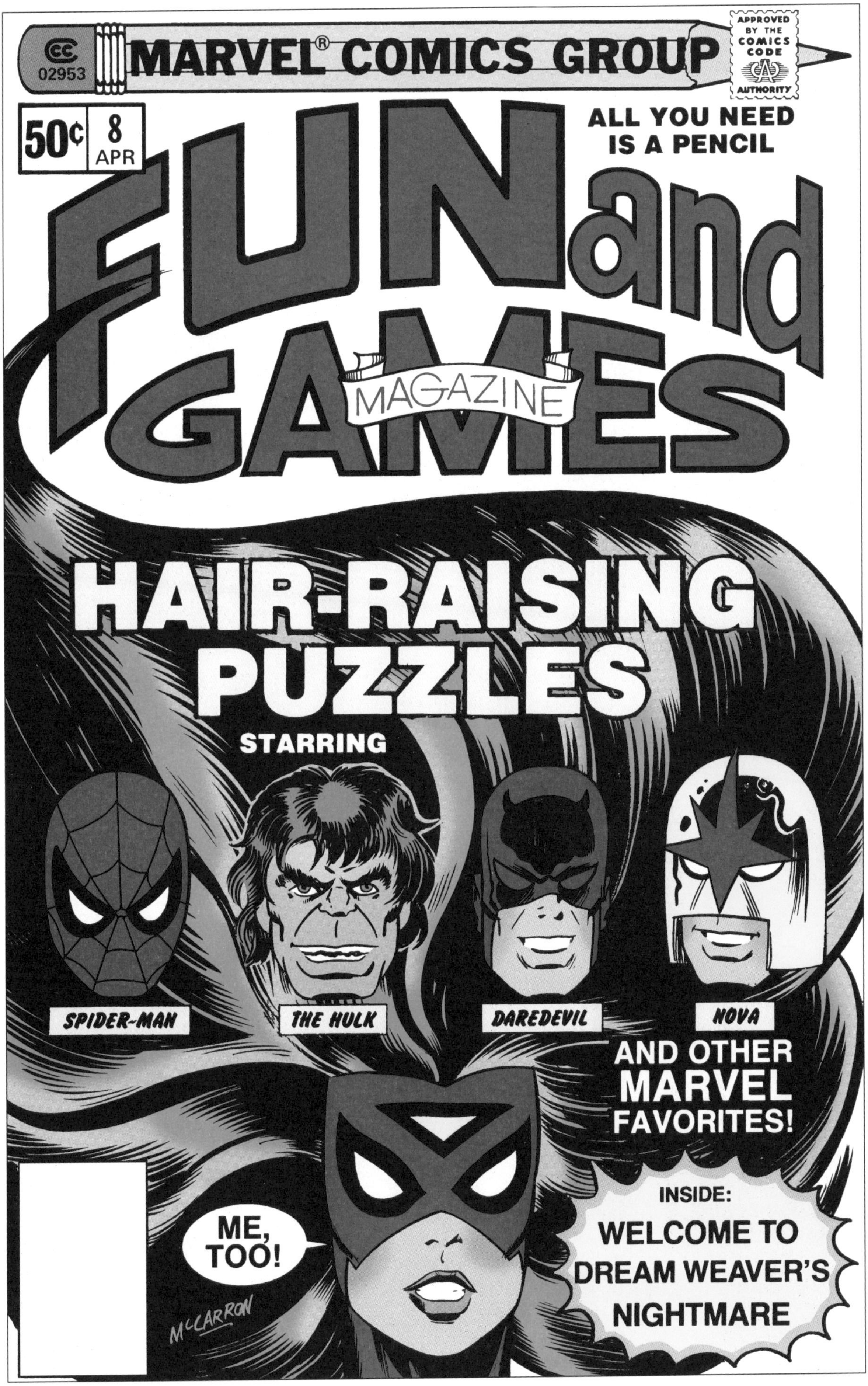

02953
MARVEL® COMICS GROUP
APPROVED BY THE COMICS CODE AUTHORITY
50¢
8
APR
ALL YOU NEED IS A PENCIL
FUN and GAMES
MAGAZINE
HAIR-RAISING PUZZLES
STARRING
SPIDER-MAN
THE HULK
DAREDEVIL
NOVA
AND OTHER MARVEL FAVORITES!
ME, TOO!
McCARRON
INSIDE:
WELCOME TO DREAM WEAVER'S NIGHTMARE

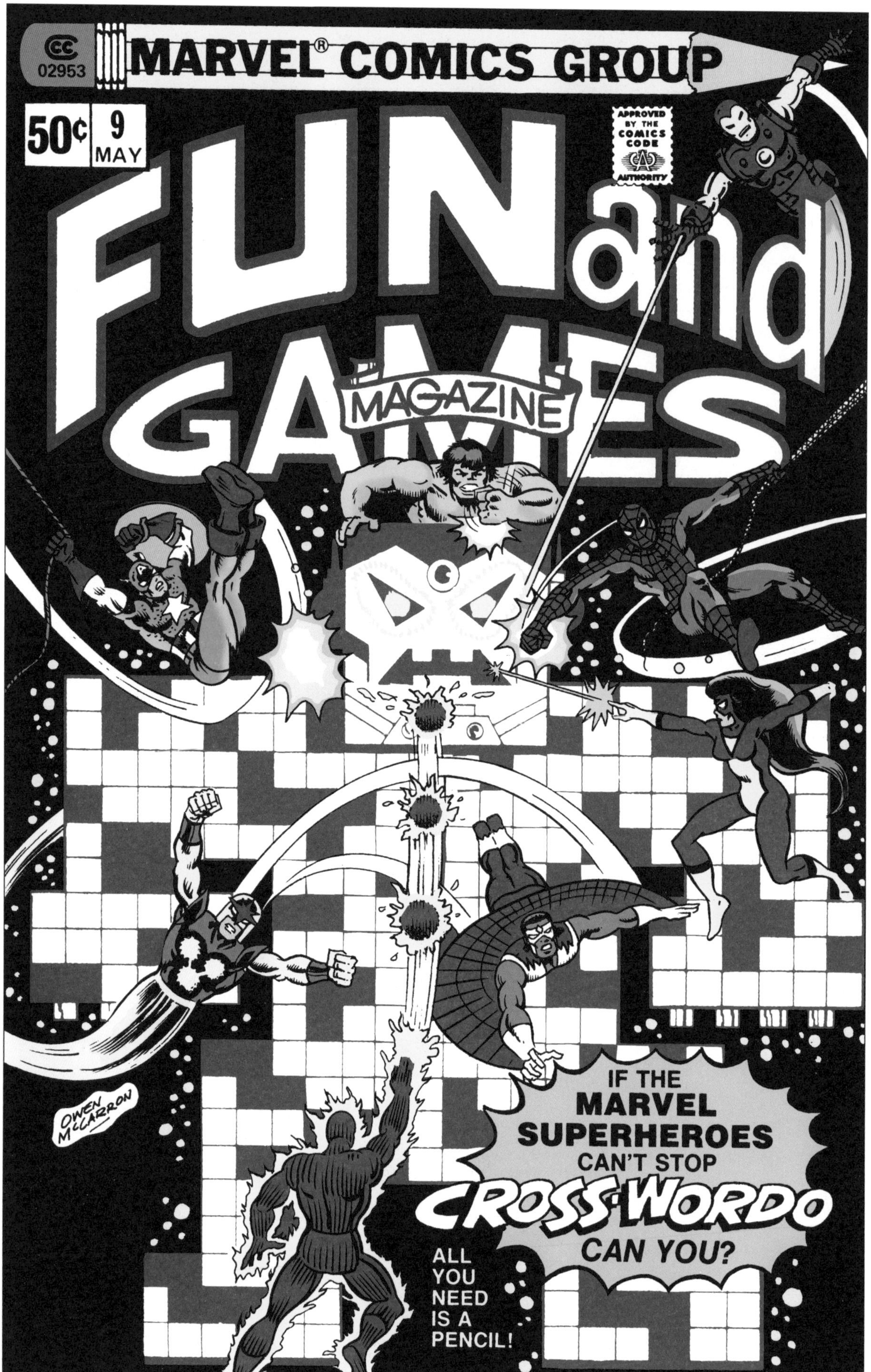
CC
02953
MARVEL® COMICS GROUP
50¢
9
MAY
APPROVED BY THE COMICS CODE AUTHORITY
FUN and GAMES
MAGAZINE
OWEN McCARRON
IF THE MARVEL SUPERHEROES CAN'T STOP CROSS-WORDO CAN YOU?
ALL YOU NEED IS A PENCIL!

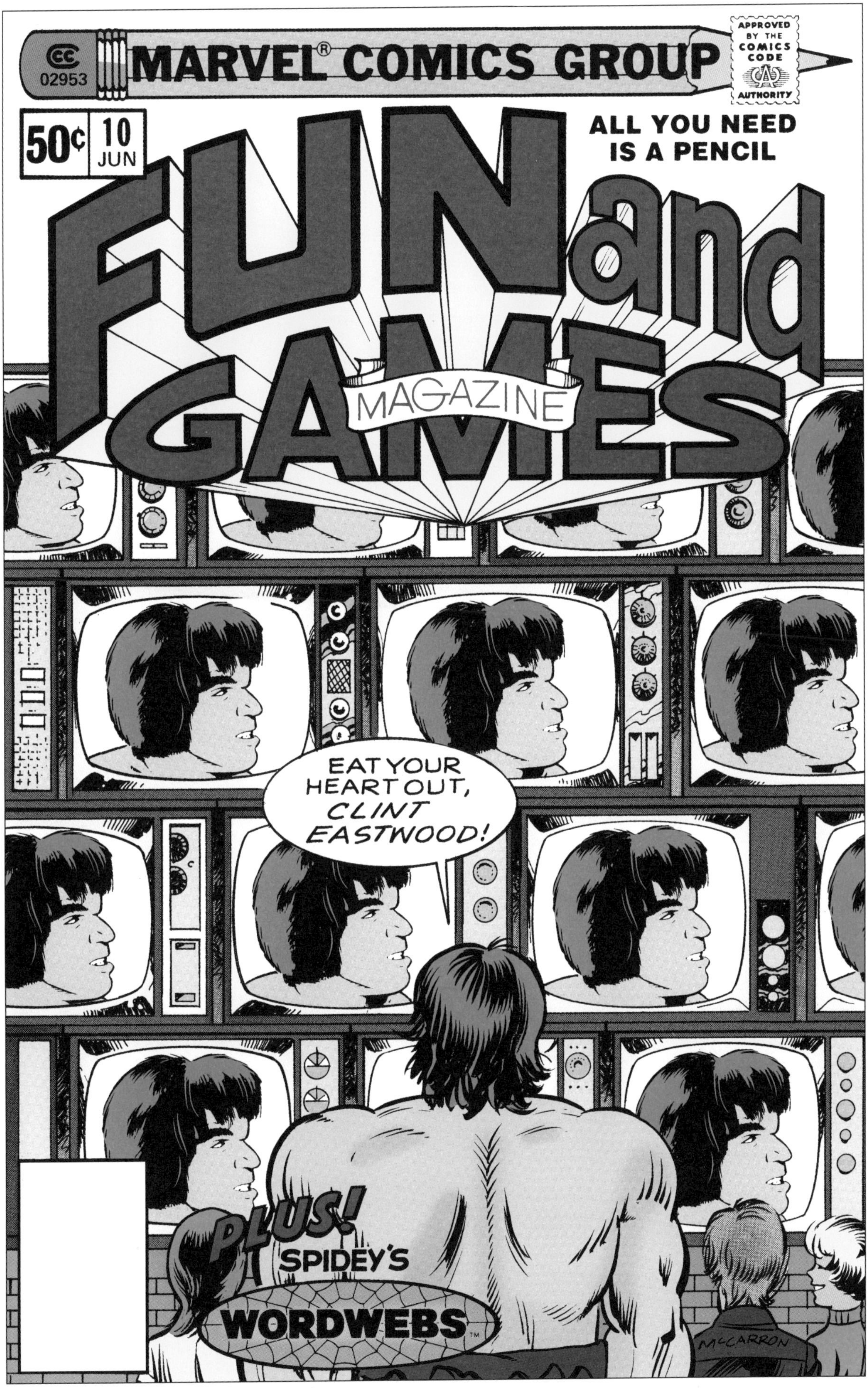

02953
MARVEL® COMICS GROUP
APPROVED BY THE COMICS CODE AUTHORITY
50¢
10 JUN
ALL YOU NEED IS A PENCIL
FUN and GAMES MAGAZINE
EAT YOUR HEART OUT, CLINT EASTWOOD!
PLUS! SPIDEY'S WORDWEBS™
McCARRON

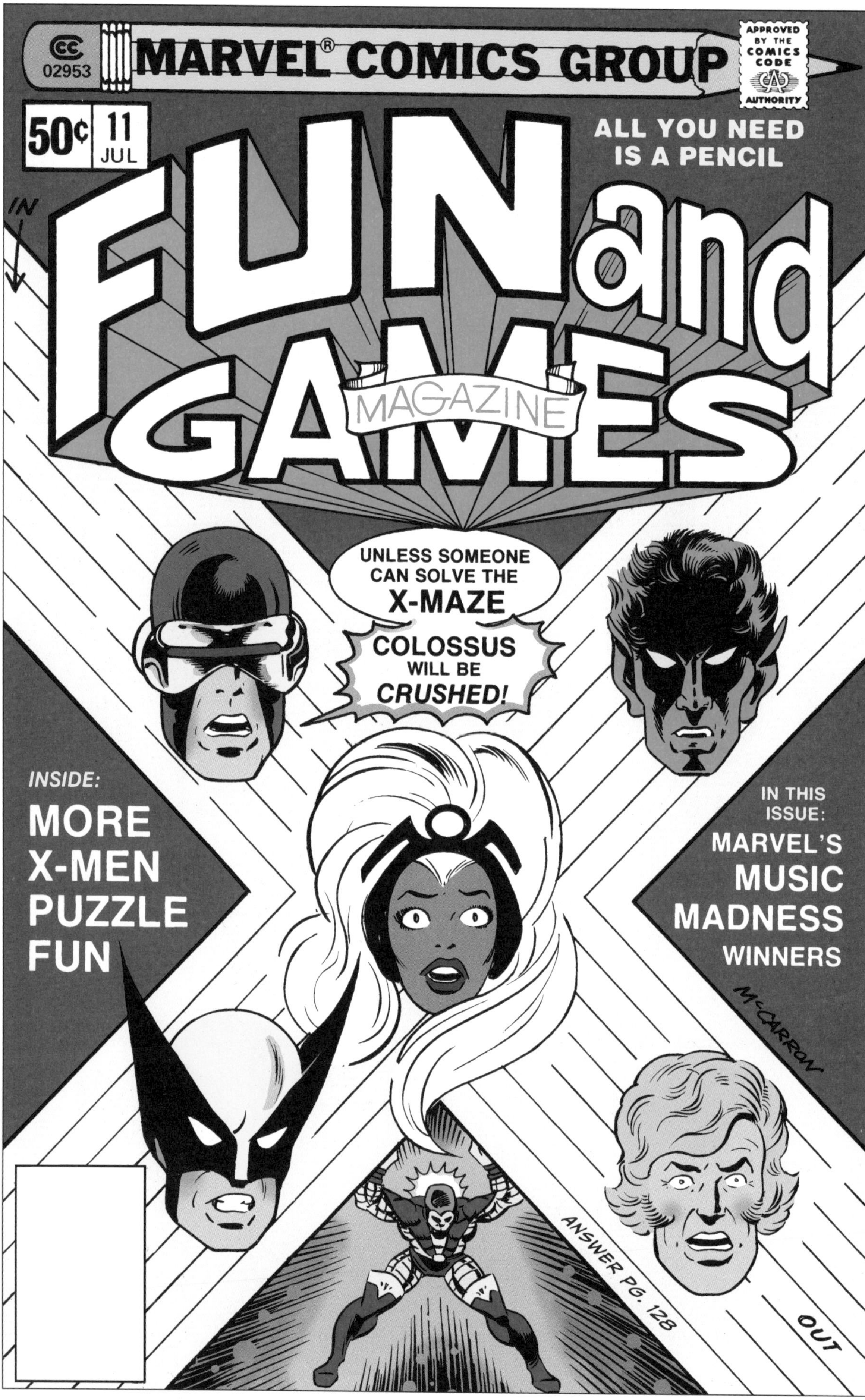

02953
MARVEL® COMICS GROUP
APPROVED BY THE COMICS CODE AUTHORITY
50¢ 11 JUL
ALL YOU NEED IS A PENCIL
IN
FUN and GAMES
MAGAZINE
UNLESS SOMEONE CAN SOLVE THE X-MAZE
COLOSSUS WILL BE CRUSHED!
INSIDE: MORE X-MEN PUZZLE FUN
IN THIS ISSUE: MARVEL'S MUSIC MADNESS WINNERS
McCARRON
ANSWER PG. 128
OUT

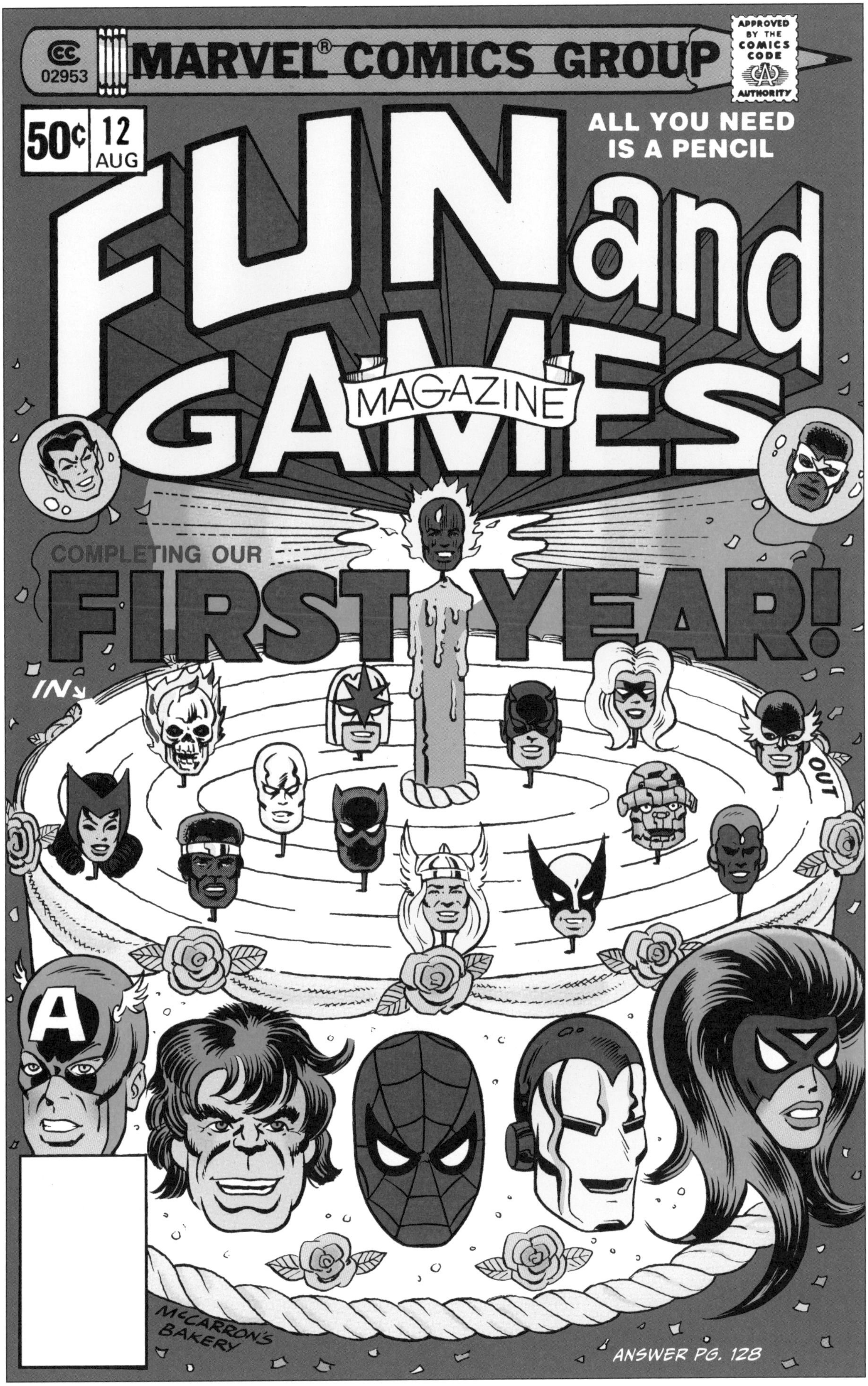
CC
02953
MARVEL® COMICS GROUP
APPROVED BY THE COMICS CODE AUTHORITY
50¢ 12 AUG
ALL YOU NEED IS A PENCIL
FUN and GAMES
MAGAZINE
COMPLETING OUR
FIRST YEAR!
IN
OUT
A
McCARRON'S BAKERY
ANSWER PG. 128

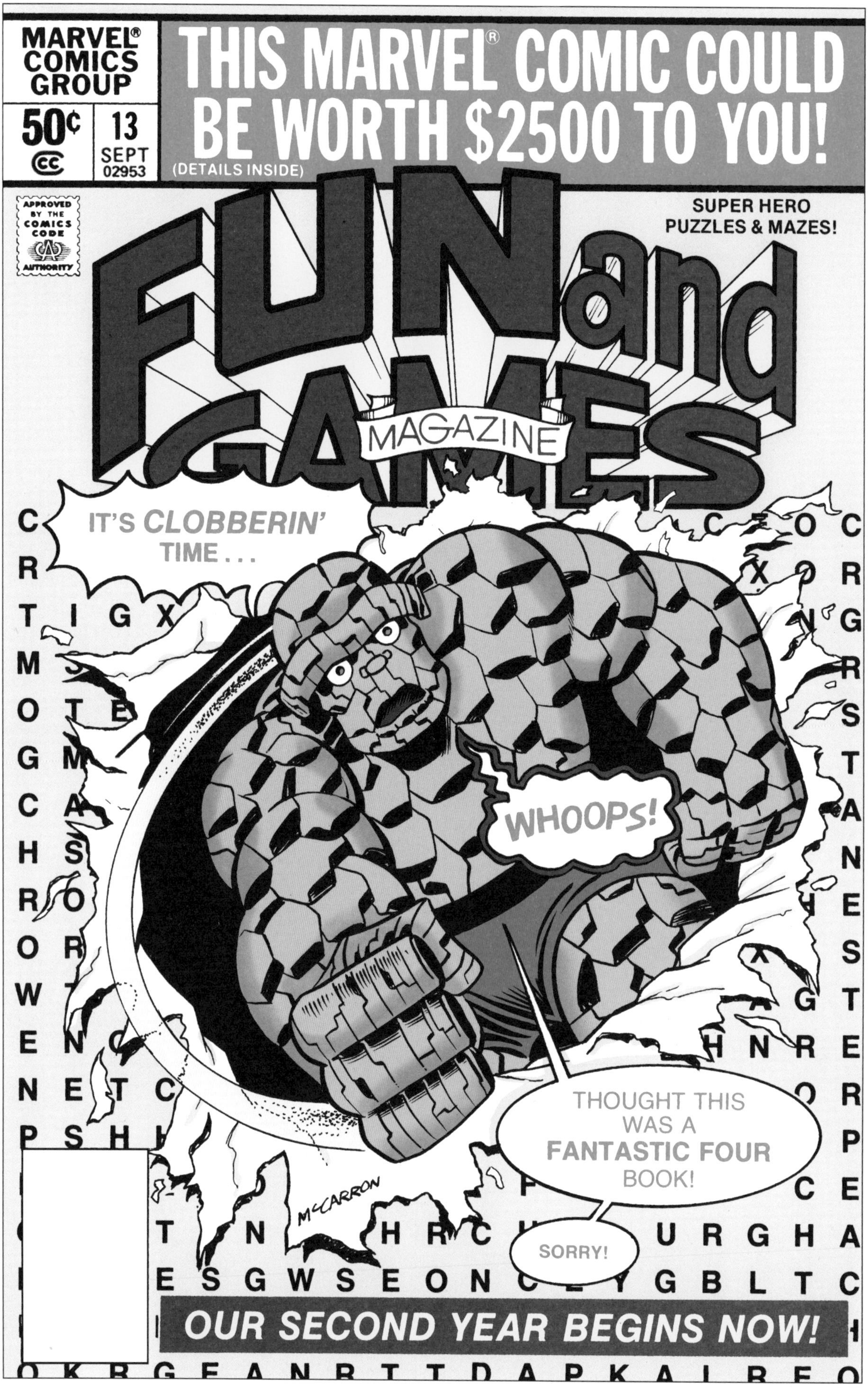

MARVEL® COMICS GROUP
50¢
13 SEPT 02953
THIS MARVEL® COMIC COULD BE WORTH $2500 TO YOU!
(DETAILS INSIDE)
APPROVED BY THE COMICS CODE AUTHORITY
SUPER HERO PUZZLES & MAZES!
FUN and GAMES
MAGAZINE
IT'S CLOBBERIN' TIME . . .
WHOOPS!
THOUGHT THIS WAS A FANTASTIC FOUR BOOK!
SORRY!
McCARRON
OUR SECOND YEAR BEGINS NOW!

## ARE YOU BRAVE ENOUGH, HERO?

**Gather your strength and wits
(and maybe a sidekick or parent)
to vanquish the challenges
in the pages ahead!**

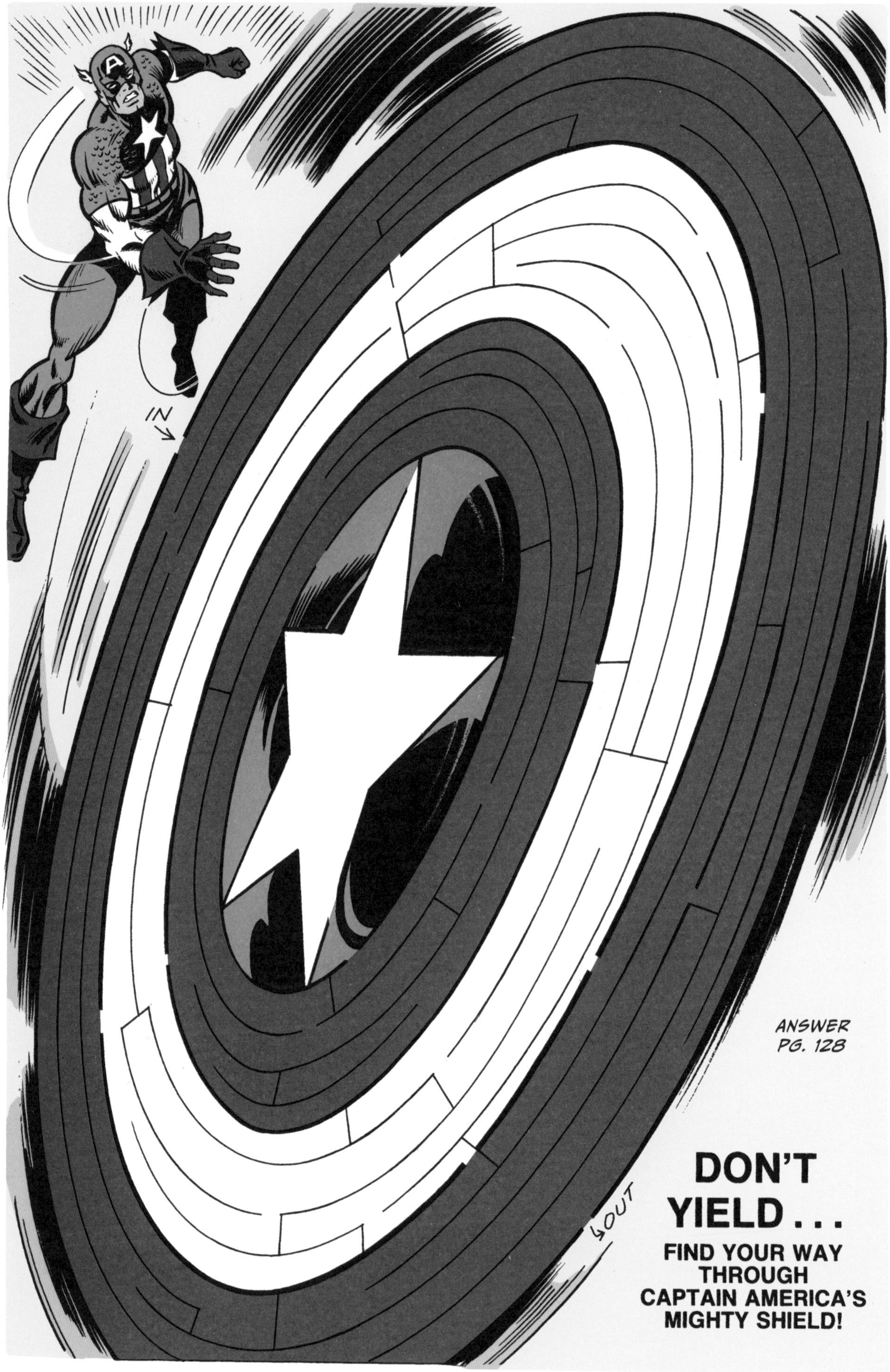
IN
OUT

ANSWER
PG. 128

## DON'T YIELD . . .

**FIND YOUR WAY THROUGH CAPTAIN AMERICA'S MIGHTY SHIELD!**

# SPIDEY ON TELEVISION

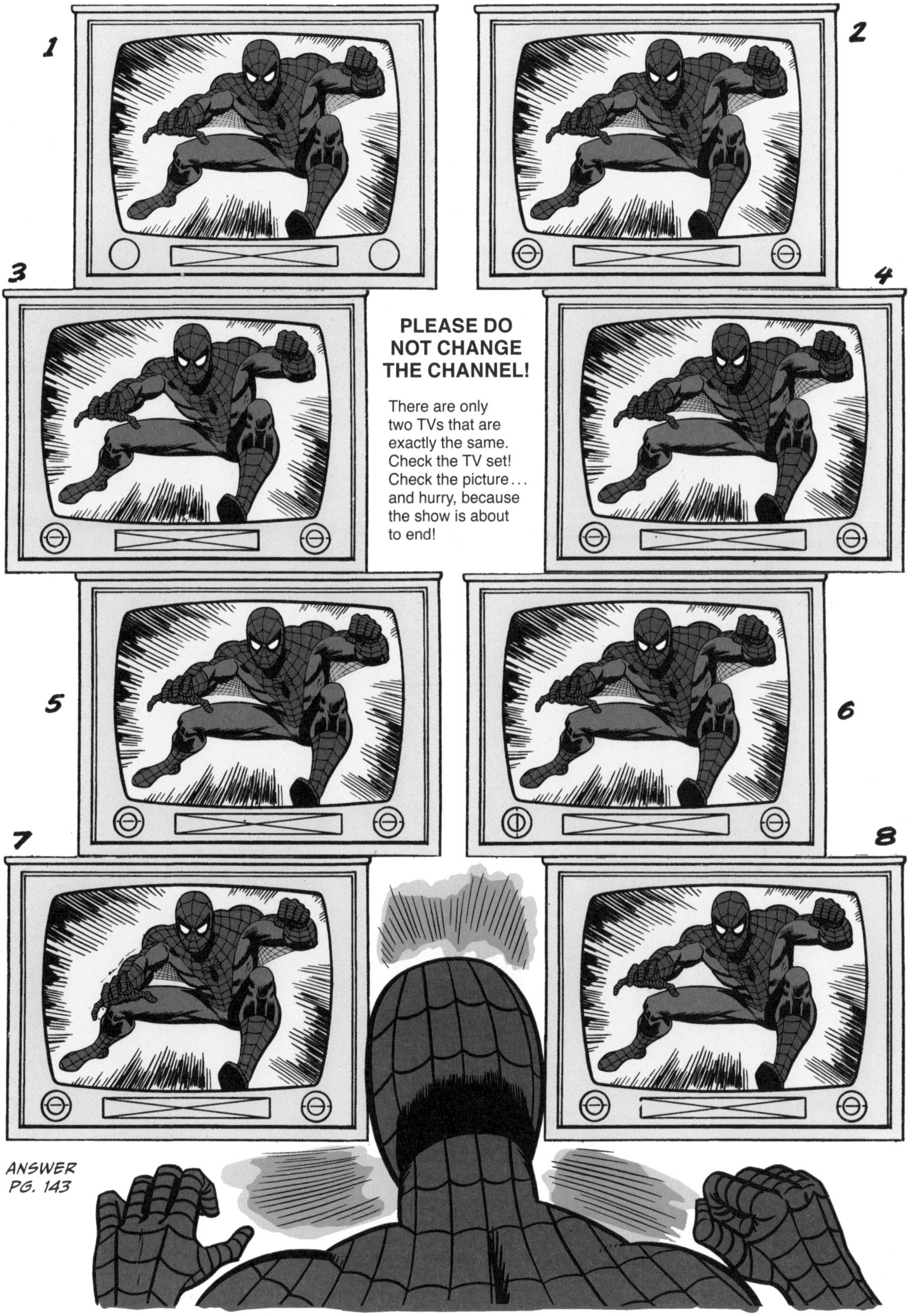
1
2
3
4
5
6
7
8

**PLEASE DO NOT CHANGE THE CHANNEL!**

There are only two TVs that are exactly the same. Check the TV set! Check the picture... and hurry, because the show is about to end!

ANSWER PG. 143

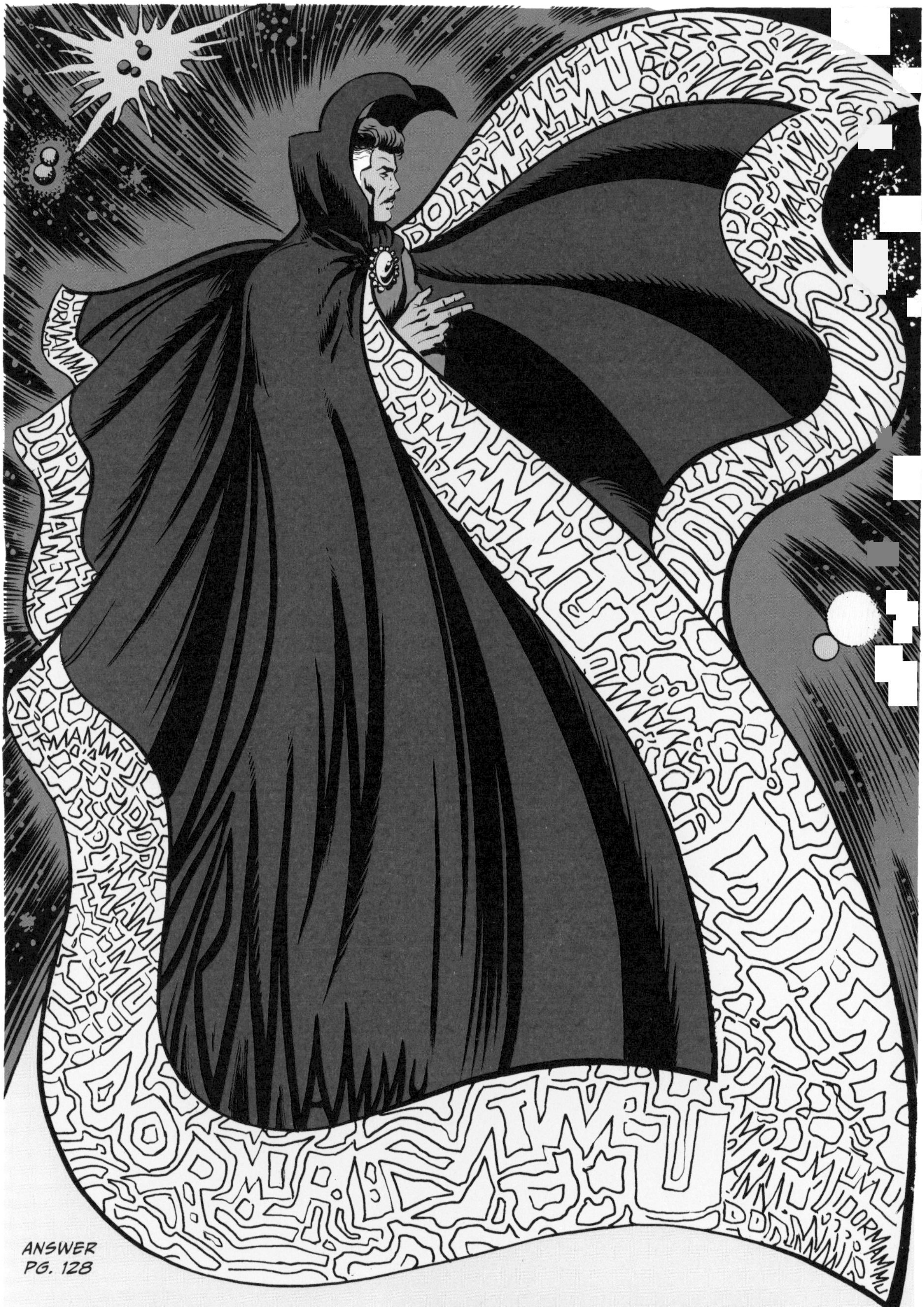

ANSWER
PG. 128

## HOW MANY TIMES CAN YOU FIND "DORMAMMU" IN DOCTOR STRANGE'S CLOAK?

If you're a Doctor Strange fan (and who isn't?), you have undoubtedly noticed the artists hiding names in the decoration of the Doc's cloak.

# HOW MANY MARVEL SUPER HEROES CAN YOU FIND . . . AND WHO ARE THEY?

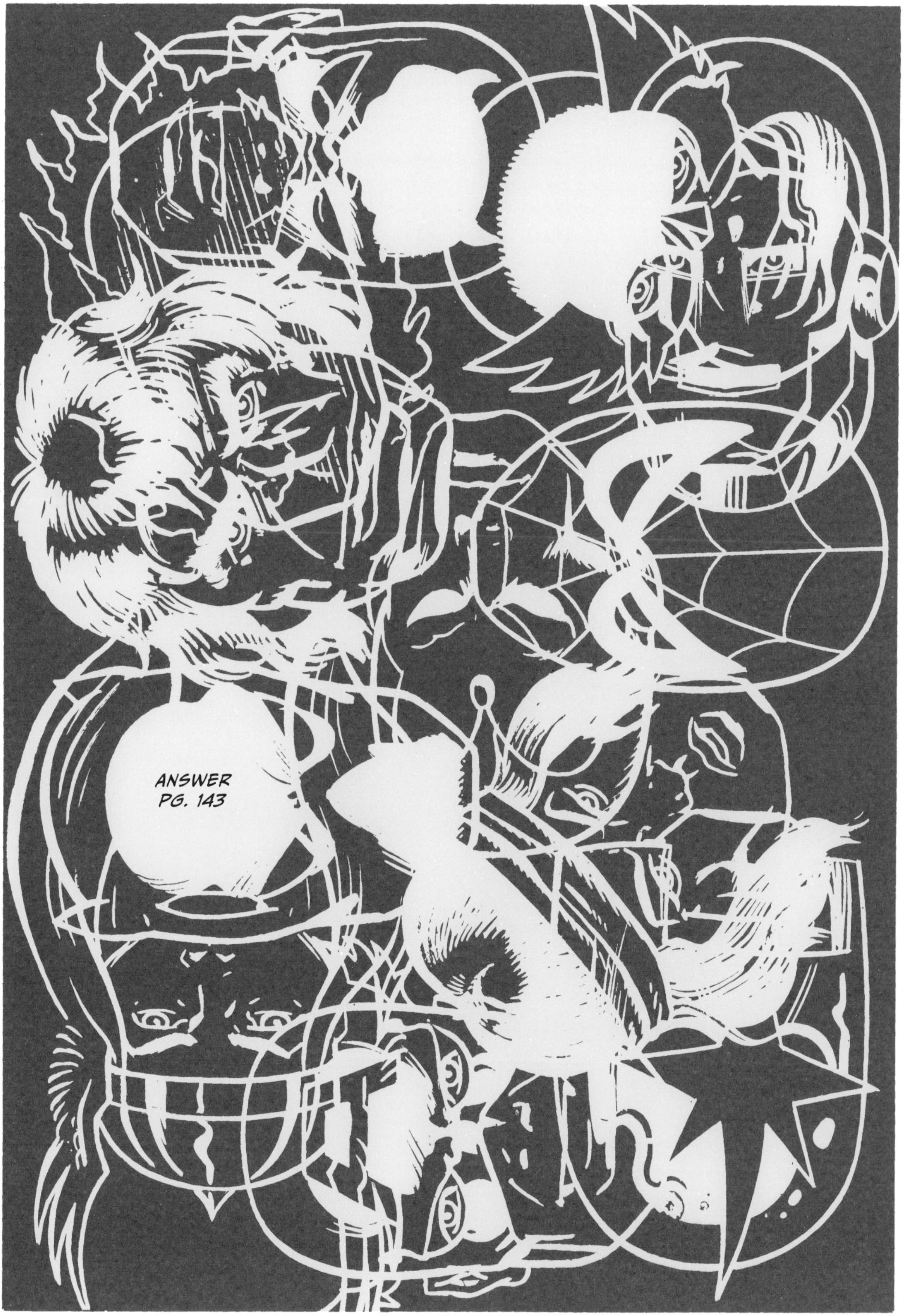
ANSWER PG. 143

# MINI-MARVELS

While they're small in size, they're big in downright trickery. All you have to do is find the name of the Super Hero (pictured) as many times as you can in each of their own puzzles. Find them horizontal, vertical, diagonal, and backward in a straight line without skipping letters.

ANSWER ON PG. 129

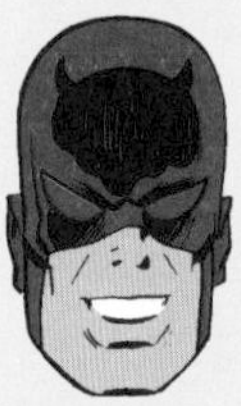

| | | | | | | | | | | |
|---|---|---|---|---|---|---|---|---|---|---|
| D | D | E | I | D | R | V | D | E | E | D |
| A | E | A | R | V | E | A | R | A | D | A |
| D | A | R | E | D | I | V | E | L | V | R |
| E | V | D | E | A | A | V | E | L | I | E |
| V | E | R | D | L | I | D | A | R | D | D |
| I | A | D | D | | | | I | V | L | E |
| D | R | E | V | | | | E | L | D | L |
| I | A | D | A | | | | L | E | I | I |
| L | A | R | V | | | | D | V | E | L |
| R | L | D | E | E | E | D | E | E | D | V |
| L | V | E | D | R | A | D | A | D | L | I |
| E | E | L | A | R | E | R | D | E | V | D |
| D | A | D | I | R | V | D | E | R | E | A |
| R | D | E | A | R | D | E | V | A | L | R |
| A | V | D | E | A | D | R | E | D | V | D |

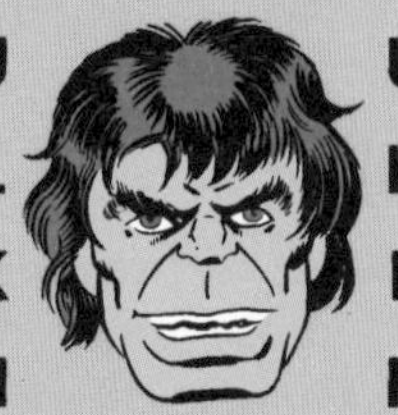

| | | | | | | | | | | |
|---|---|---|---|---|---|---|---|---|---|---|
| H | H | U | L | K | L | U | H | U | L | K |
| K | H | U | L | K | H | K | L | U | K | K |
| L | L | U | K | K | L | U | H | H | L | L |
| U | H | U | L | U | H | U | K | U | K | K |
| H | K | U | H | U | L | K | H | U | L | K |
| L | H | L | U | | | | U | H | U | K |
| U | H | K | L | | | | K | U | H | K |
| H | U | L | K | | | | L | H | L | K |
| U | L | H | H | | | | H | U | L | K |
| K | L | U | H | U | L | K | H | L | H | L |
| H | U | L | K | K | L | K | K | K | L | K |
| K | H | K | U | U | L | K | L | U | H | K |
| K | L | U | H | U | L | K | U | H | K | L |
| L | H | U | H | U | H | U | H | L | U | U |
| K | L | U | H | U | L | K | K | L | U | H |

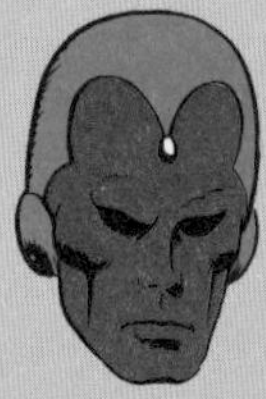

| | | | | | | | | | | |
|---|---|---|---|---|---|---|---|---|---|---|
| N | O | I | S | I | V | I | S | I | O | N |
| I | V | N | O | I | O | N | O | S | N | O |
| N | I | O | S | V | S | I | N | I | N | V |
| S | V | I | S | I | O | N | O | V | I | S |
| V | O | S | N | V | I | S | I | O | N | V |
| N | S | I | V | | | | S | O | S | I |
| O | I | V | I | | | | I | N | N | N |
| N | S | O | O | | | | V | S | O | S |
| I | V | N | S | | | | O | I | I | N |
| N | V | S | N | I | V | S | S | V | S | I |
| O | I | N | O | I | S | I | V | O | I | V |
| I | O | V | I | O | V | S | S | I | V | N |
| N | S | N | S | N | S | N | O | I | S | O |
| S | V | I | I | S | O | V | N | N | O | V |
| I | N | N | V | O | I | N | U | I | I | N |

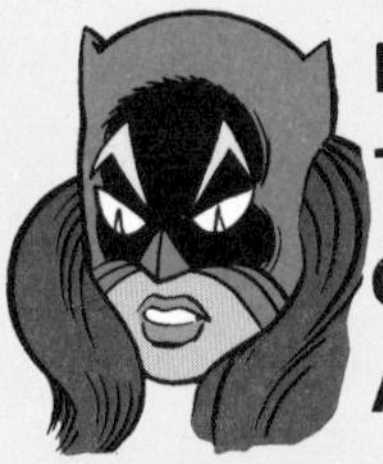

| | | | | | | | | | | |
|---|---|---|---|---|---|---|---|---|---|---|
| T | H | T | C | T | A | T | H | A | C | T |
| A | T | E | A | L | A | E | H | L | L | A |
| C | A | L | L | C | H | E | L | E | T | C |
| A | C | E | C | L | L | C | L | E | L | L |
| T | L | L | H | L | L | L | C | H | E | L |
| E | E | T | C | | | | E | A | C | A |
| H | H | A | A | | | | T | H | E | H |
| C | T | T | C | | | | C | T | T | E |
| H | T | E | L | | | | A | T | A | E |
| L | L | A | C | L | C | C | H | E | H | L |
| C | E | A | C | T | L | A | H | L | L | C |
| A | T | H | T | L | H | L | T | L | L | T |
| T | H | C | E | H | L | L | A | C | E | A |
| E | L | H | A | E | T | E | C | A | C | H |
| L | L | C | A | L | H | E | H | H | L | E |

# LEARN TO DRAW MARVEL CHARACTERS* | SCARLET WITCH

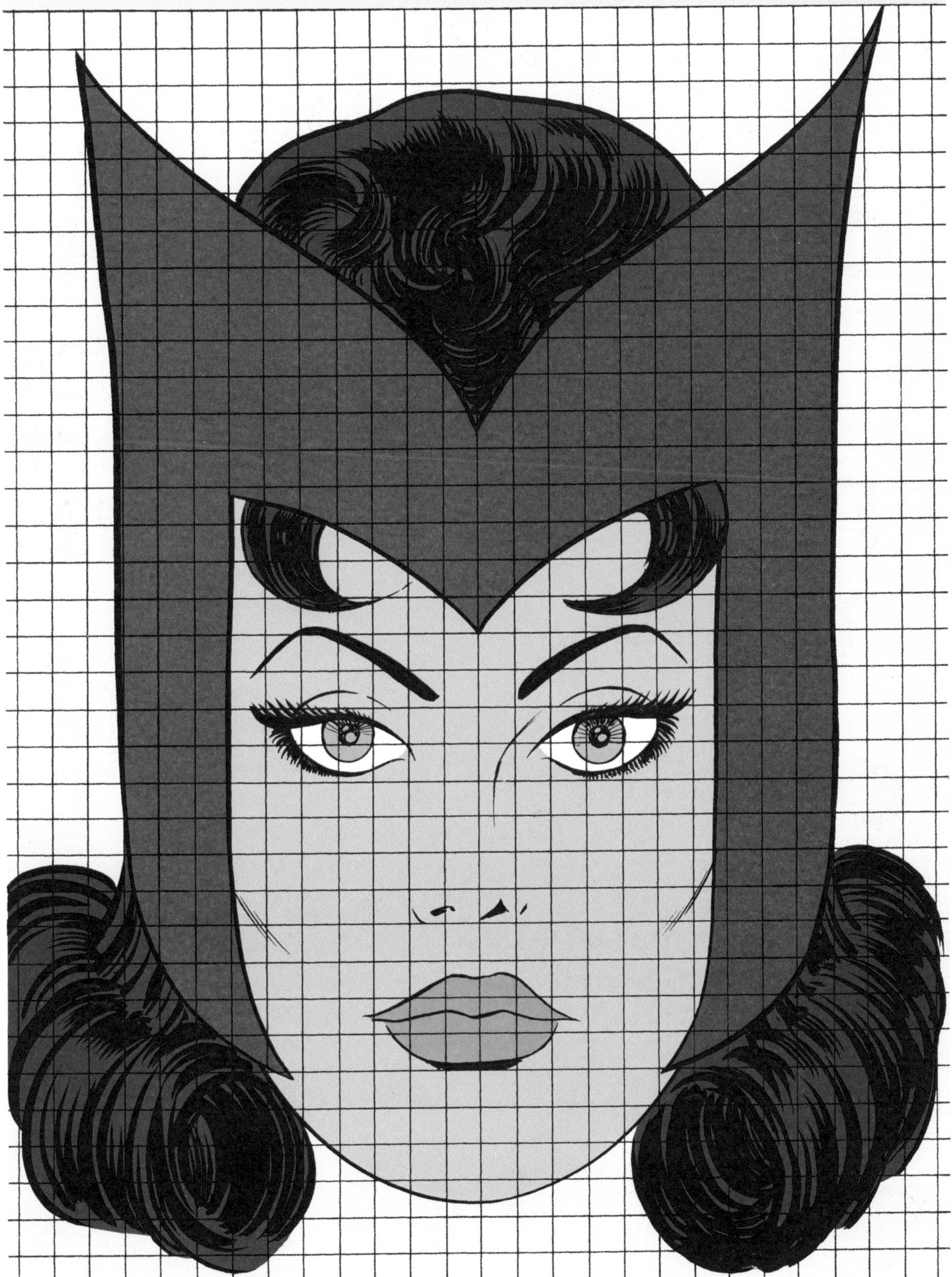

*GRAB SOME GRAPH PAPER TO DRAW LIKE THE PROS!

# MARVEL SUPER HEROES

| A | B |
|---|---|
|  |  |

## SECRET CODE BREAKER

Crack codes with your very own MARVEL SUPER HEROES SECRET CODE BREAKER. Each letter of the alphabet will be represented by the face of the Super Hero shown beneath it. Keep this around . . . you'll be needing it!

| C | D | E | F | G | H |
|---|---|---|---|---|---|
|  |  |  |  |  |  |

| I | J | K | L | M | N |
|---|---|---|---|---|---|
|  |  |  |  |  |  |

| O | P | Q | R | S | T |
|---|---|---|---|---|---|
|  |  |  |  |  |  |

| U | V | W | X | Y | Z |
|---|---|---|---|---|---|
|  |  |  |  |  | |

# UNSCRAMBLE

## THE MARVEL SUPER HEROES
### with your Secret Code Breaker!

1.

2.

3.

4.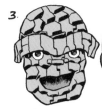

5.

6.

ANSWER PG. 143

25

# WHAT'S IN A NAME?

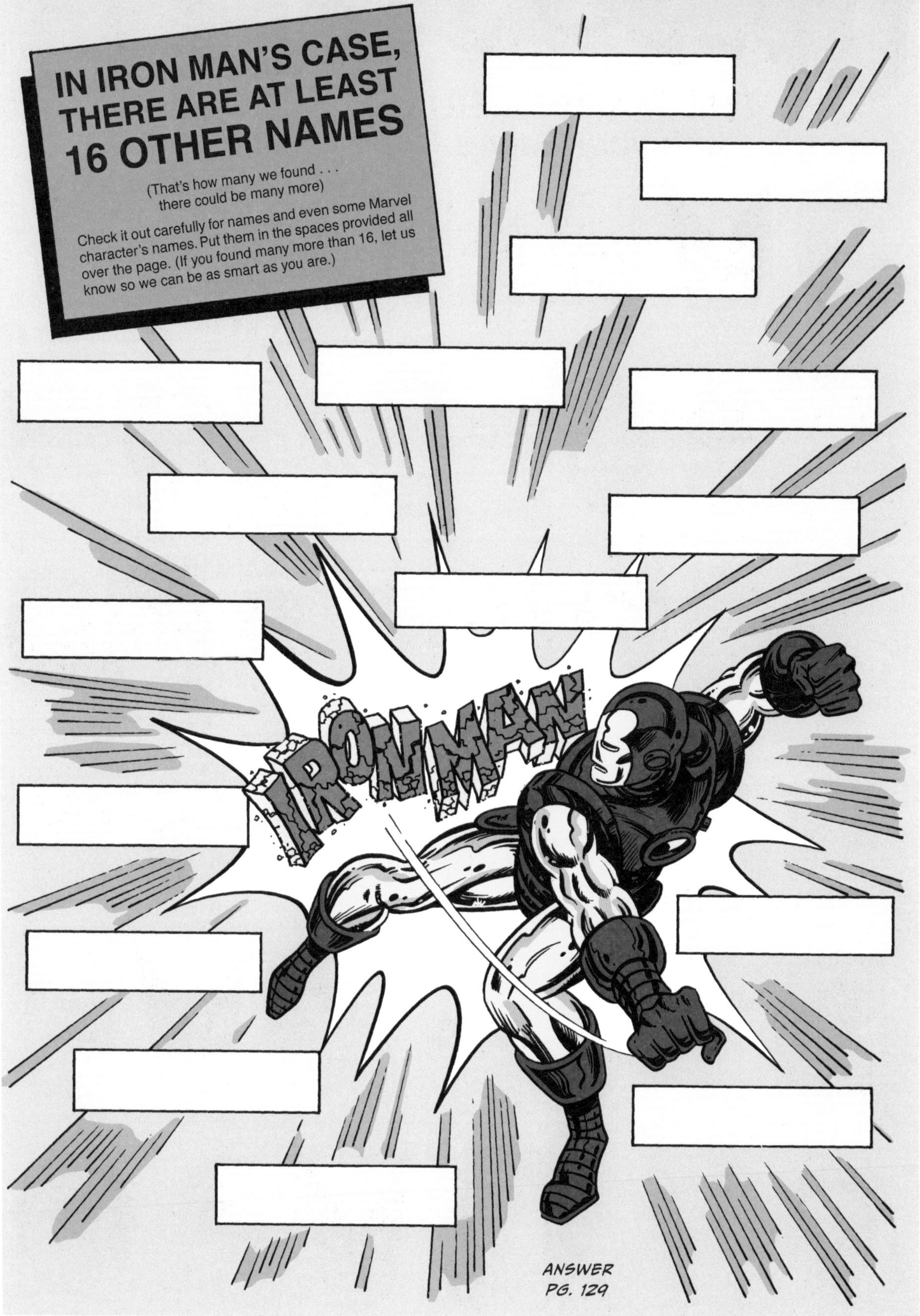
IN IRON MAN'S CASE, THERE ARE AT LEAST 16 OTHER NAMES
(That's how many we found . . . there could be many more)
Check it out carefully for names and even some Marvel character's names. Put them in the spaces provided all over the page. (If you found many more than 16, let us know so we can be as smart as you are.)
IRONMAN
ANSWER PG. 129

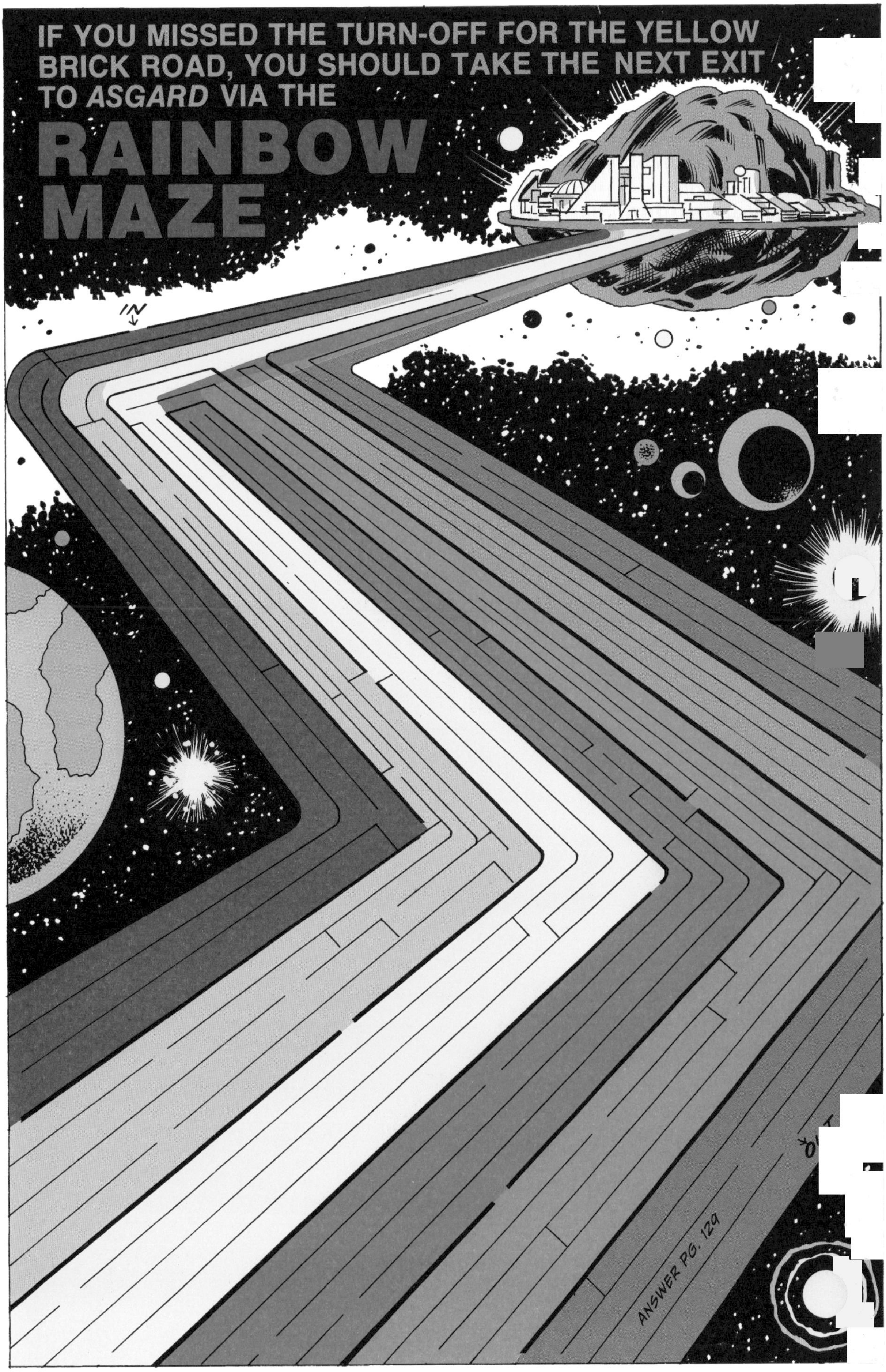
IF YOU MISSED THE TURN-OFF FOR THE YELLOW BRICK ROAD, YOU SHOULD TAKE THE NEXT EXIT TO *ASGARD* VIA THE
RAINBOW MAZE
IN
ANSWER PG. 129

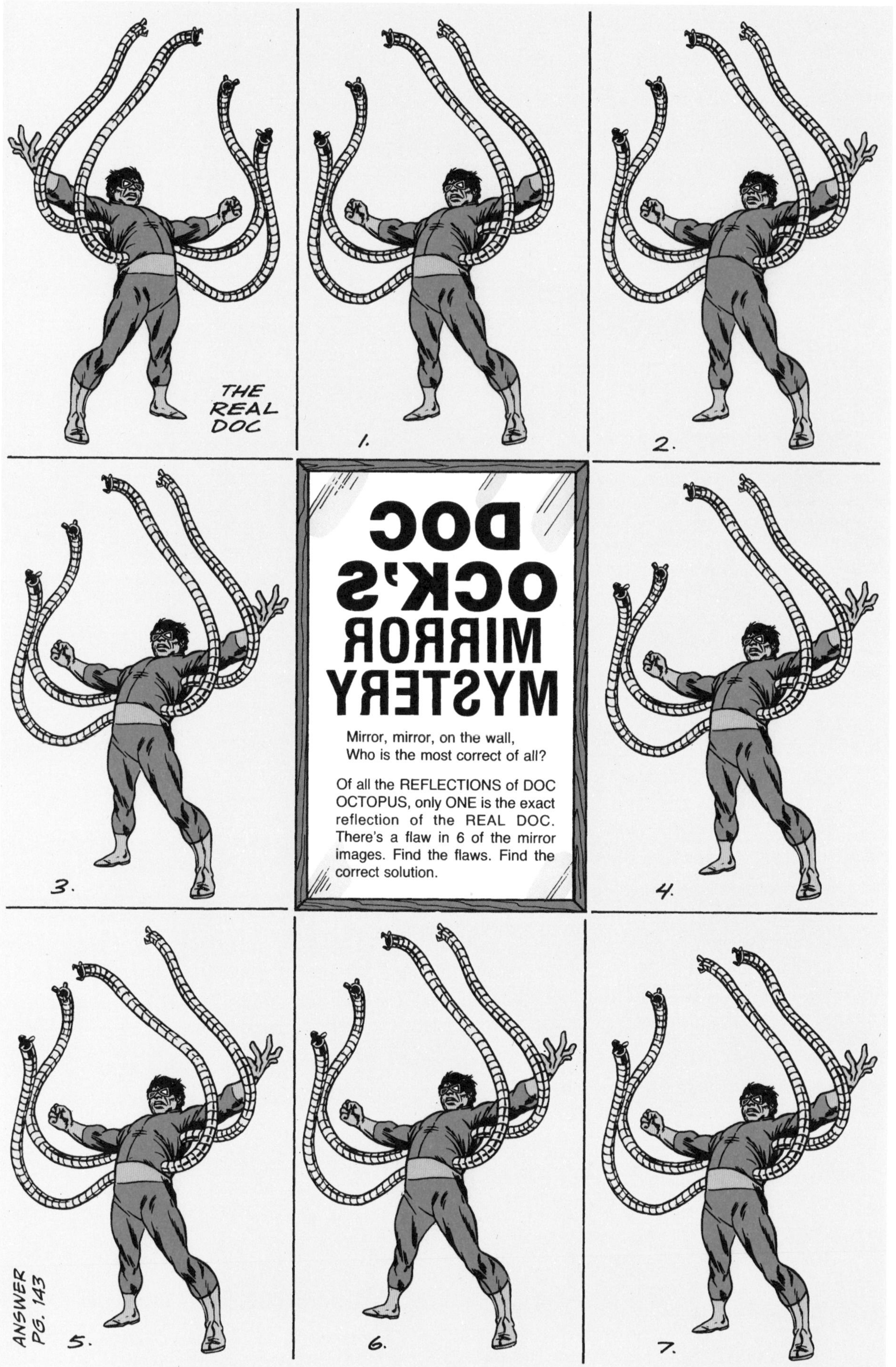
THE REAL DOC
1.
2.
3.
4.
5.
6.
7.
ANSWER PG. 143

# DOC OCK'S MIRROR MYSTERY

Mirror, mirror, on the wall,
Who is the most correct of all?

Of all the REFLECTIONS of DOC OCTOPUS, only ONE is the exact reflection of the REAL DOC. There's a flaw in 6 of the mirror images. Find the flaws. Find the correct solution.

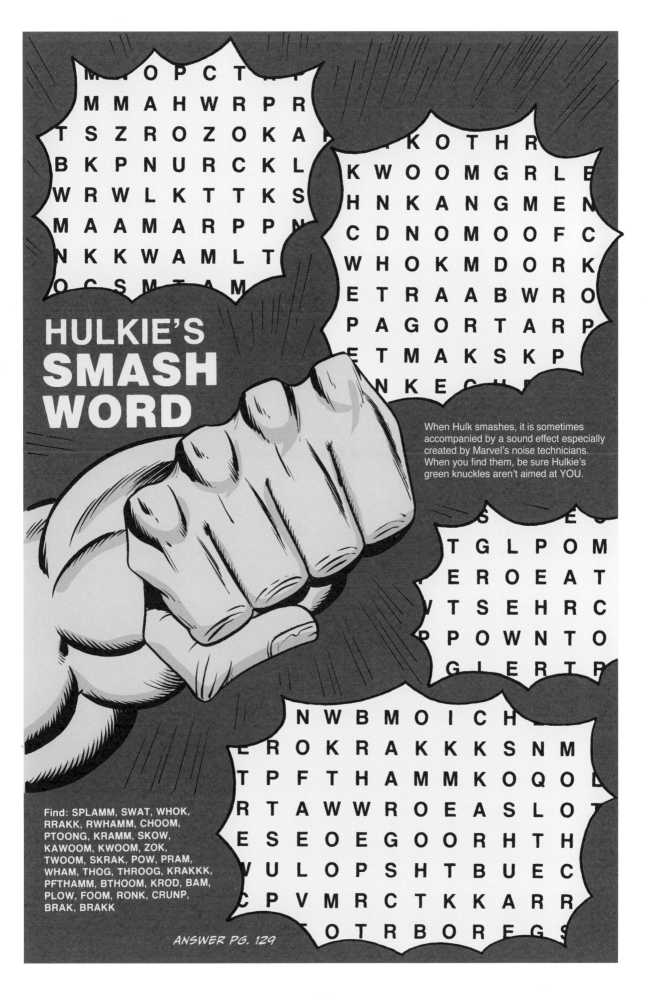

# HULKIE'S SMASH WORD

O P C T
M M A H W R P R
T S Z R O Z O K A
B K P N U R C K L
W R W L K T T K S
M A A M A R P P
N K K W A M L T

K O T H R
K W O O M G R L
H N K A N G M E
C D N O M O O F C
W H O K M D O R K
E T R A A B W R O
P A G O R T A R P
T M A K S K P
N K E

When Hulk smashes, it is sometimes accompanied by a sound effect especially created by Marvel's noise technicians. When you find them, be sure Hulkie's green knuckles aren't aimed at YOU.

T G L P O M
E R O E A T
T S E H R C
P P O W N T O
E R

N W B M O I C H
R O K R A K K K S N M
T P F T H A M M K O Q O
R T A W W R O E A S L O
E S E O E G O O R H T H
U L O P S H T B U E C
P V M R C T K K A R R
O T R B O R

**Find:** SPLAMM, SWAT, WHOK, RRAKK, RWHAMM, CHOOM, PTOONG, KRAMM, SKOW, KAWOOM, KWOOM, ZOK, TWOOM, SKRAK, POW, PRAM, WHAM, THOG, THROOG, KRAKKK, PFTHAMM, BTHOOM, KROD, BAM, PLOW, FOOM, RONK, CRUNP, BRAK, BRAKK

ANSWER PG. 129

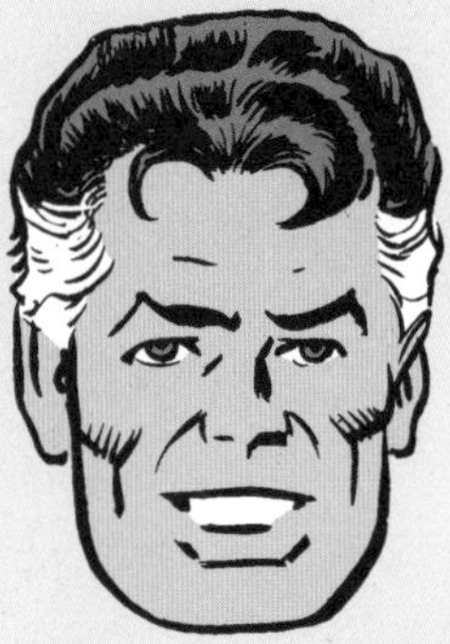

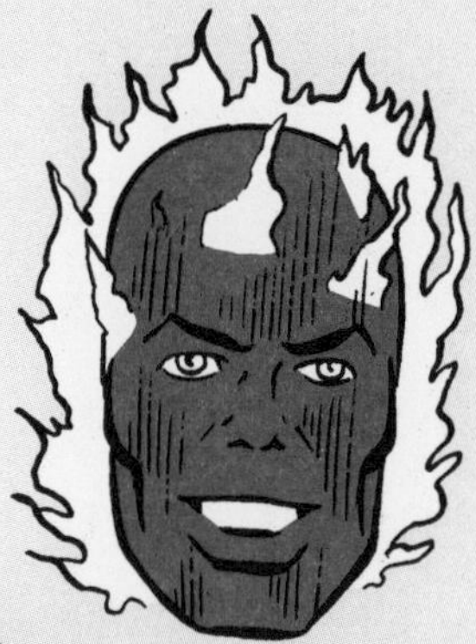

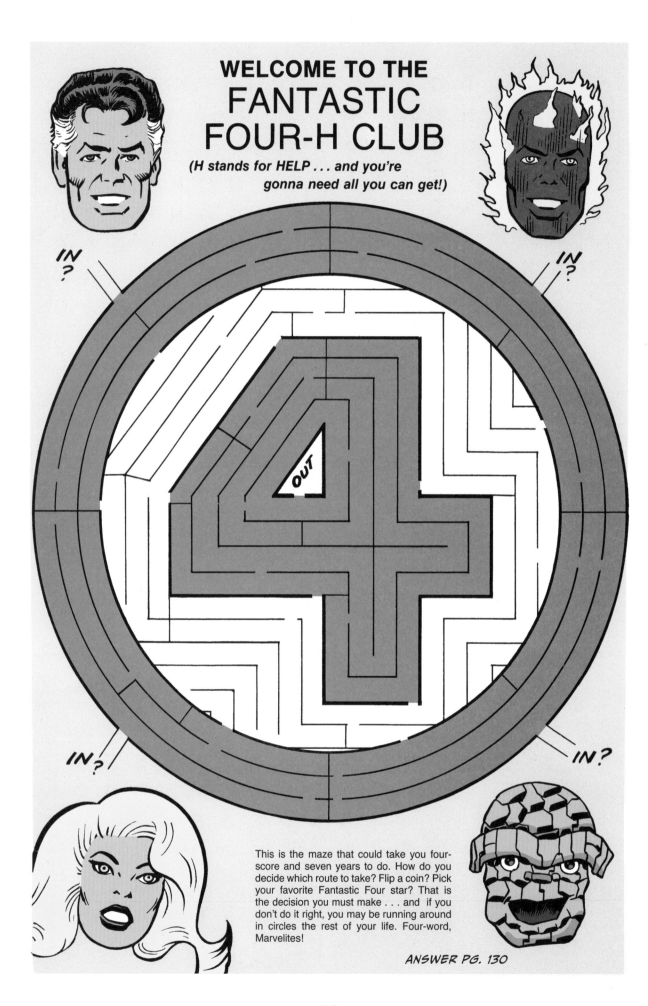

# WELCOME TO THE FANTASTIC FOUR-H CLUB

***(H stands for HELP . . . and you're gonna need all you can get!)***

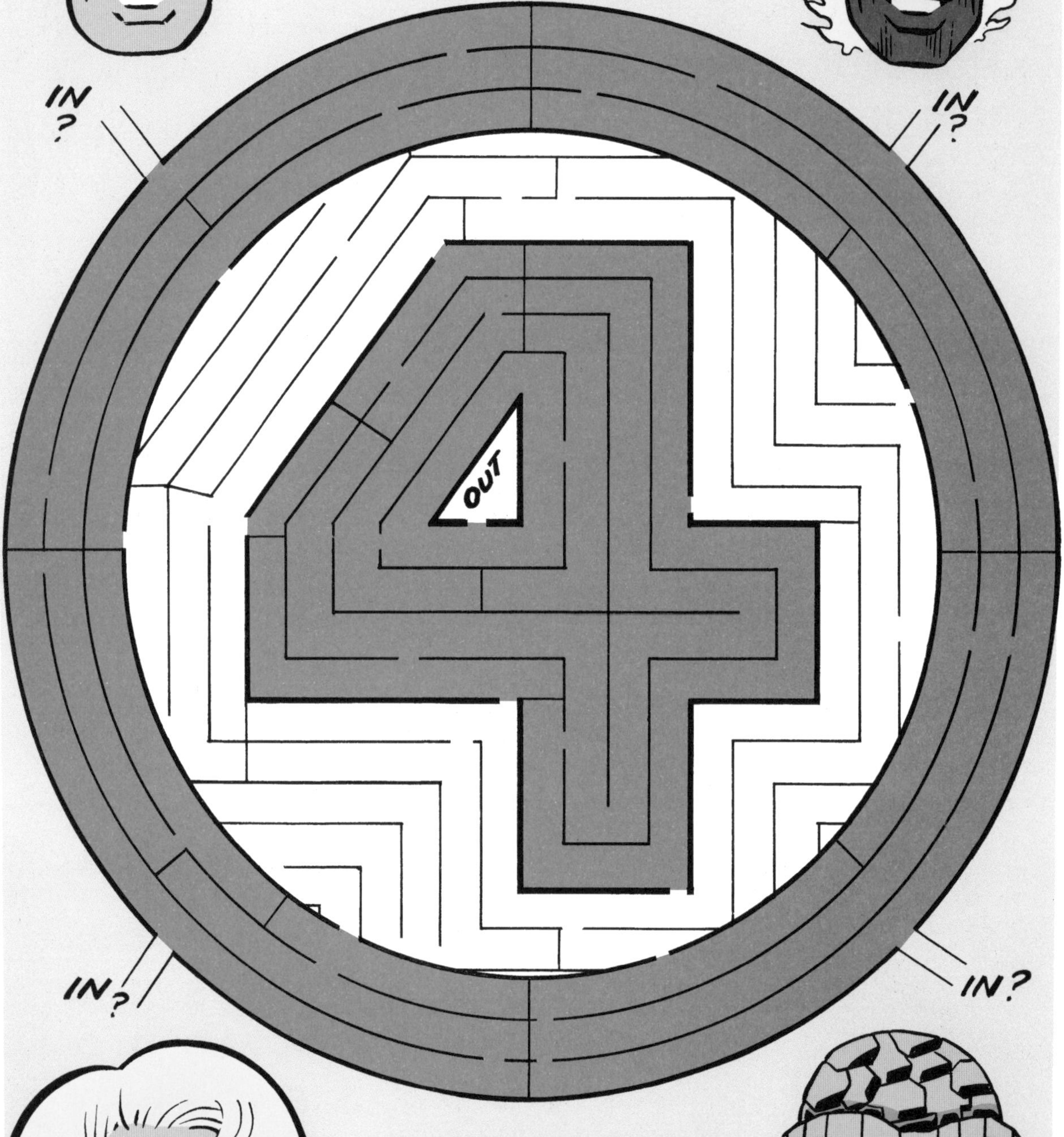
IN?
IN?
OUT
IN?
IN?

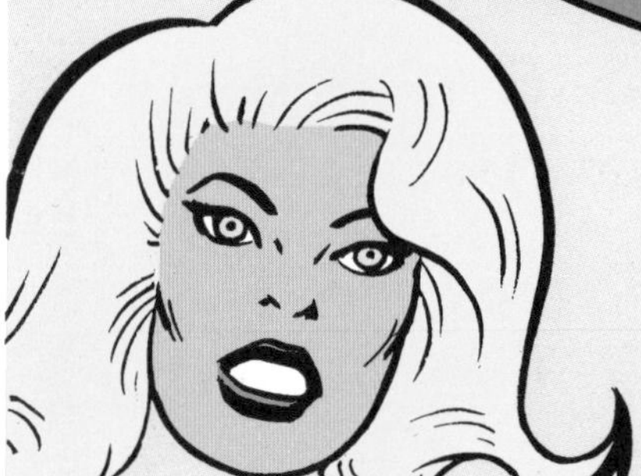

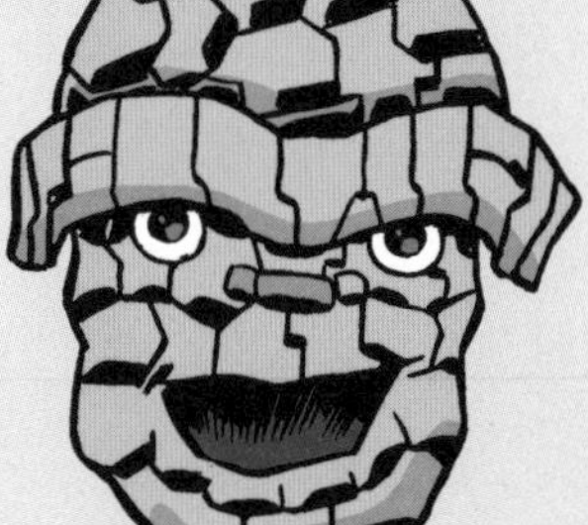

This is the maze that could take you four-score and seven years to do. How do you decide which route to take? Flip a coin? Pick your favorite Fantastic Four star? That is the decision you must make . . . and if you don't do it right, you may be running around in circles the rest of your life. Four-word, Marvelites!

ANSWER PG. 130

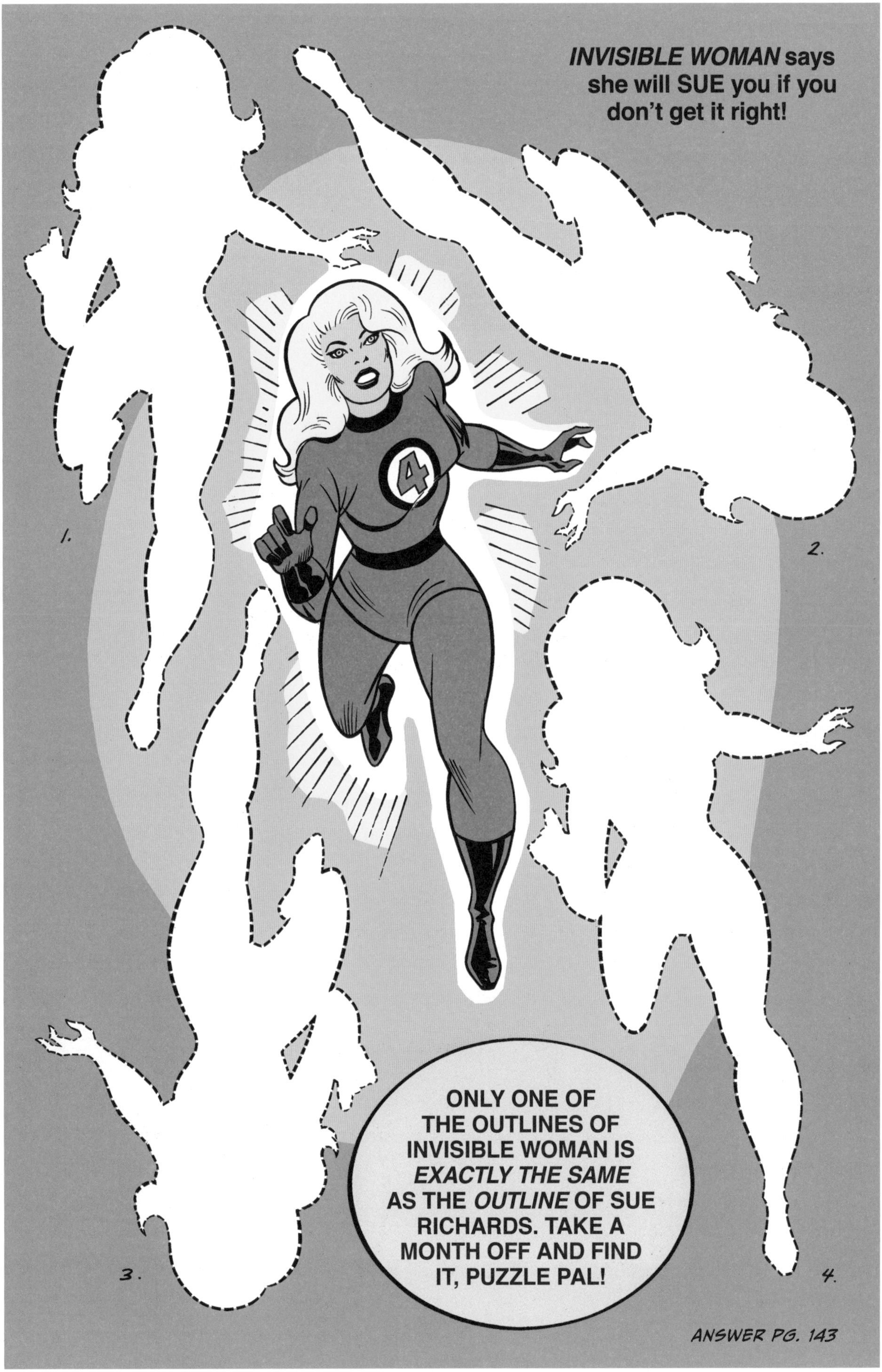
*INVISIBLE WOMAN* says
she will SUE you if you
don't get it right!
1.
2.
3.
4.
ONLY ONE OF
THE OUTLINES OF
INVISIBLE WOMAN IS
*EXACTLY THE SAME*
AS THE *OUTLINE* OF SUE
RICHARDS. TAKE A
MONTH OFF AND FIND
IT, PUZZLE PAL!
ANSWER PG. 143

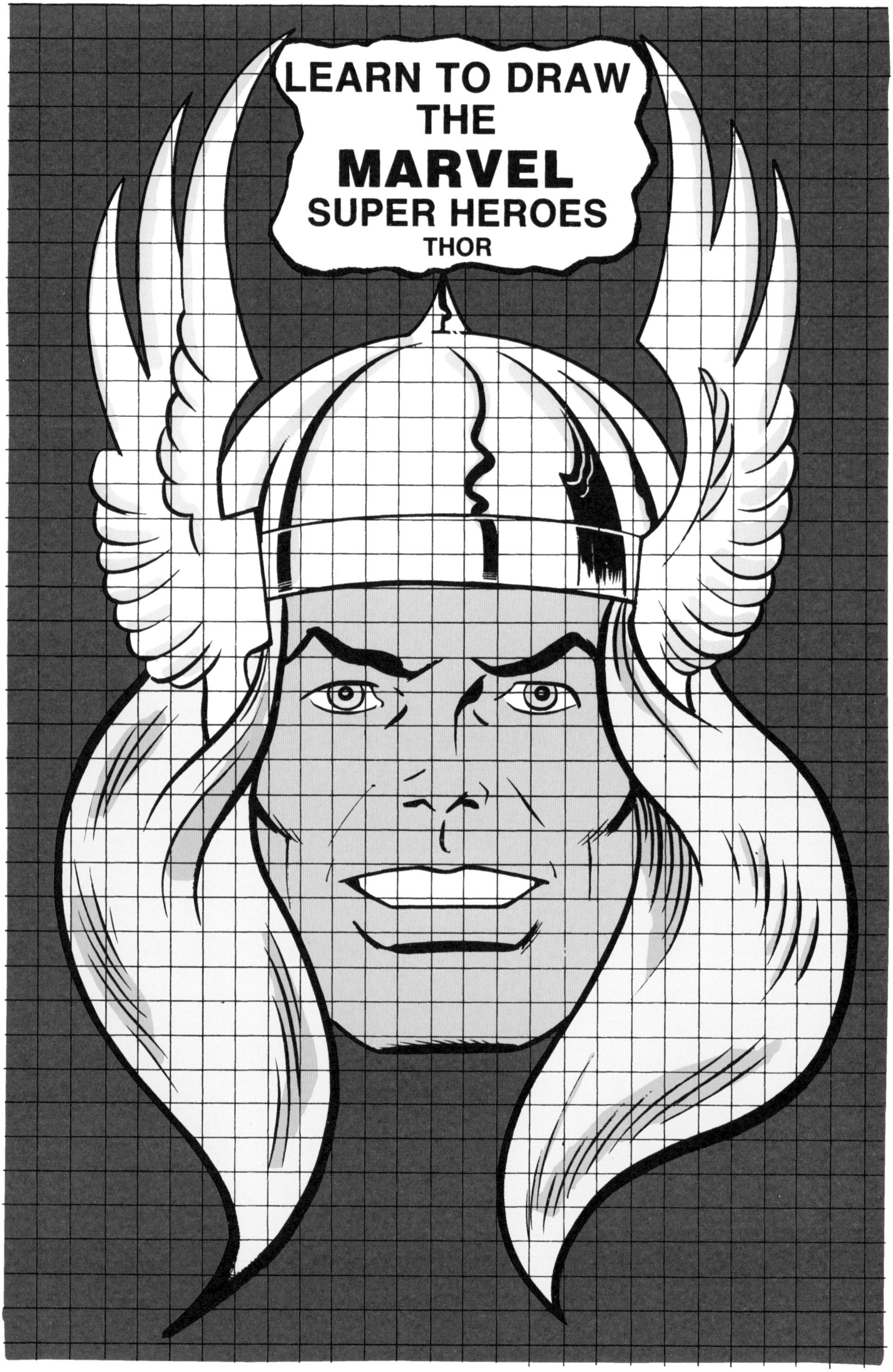
LEARN TO DRAW
THE
MARVEL
SUPER HEROES
THOR

# WHY IS SPIDEY ATTACKING A BOWL OF ALPHABET SOUP?

He's not, really. That baddie, ALPHA, bet (Alphabet?) Spidey he couldn't solve this 6-in-1 scramble, and he may be right. There are 6 villains involved here (Spidey's had a go at all of 'em at one time or another), and all you have to do is tell us which ones. Hope you got a weekend to spare to sort this one out.

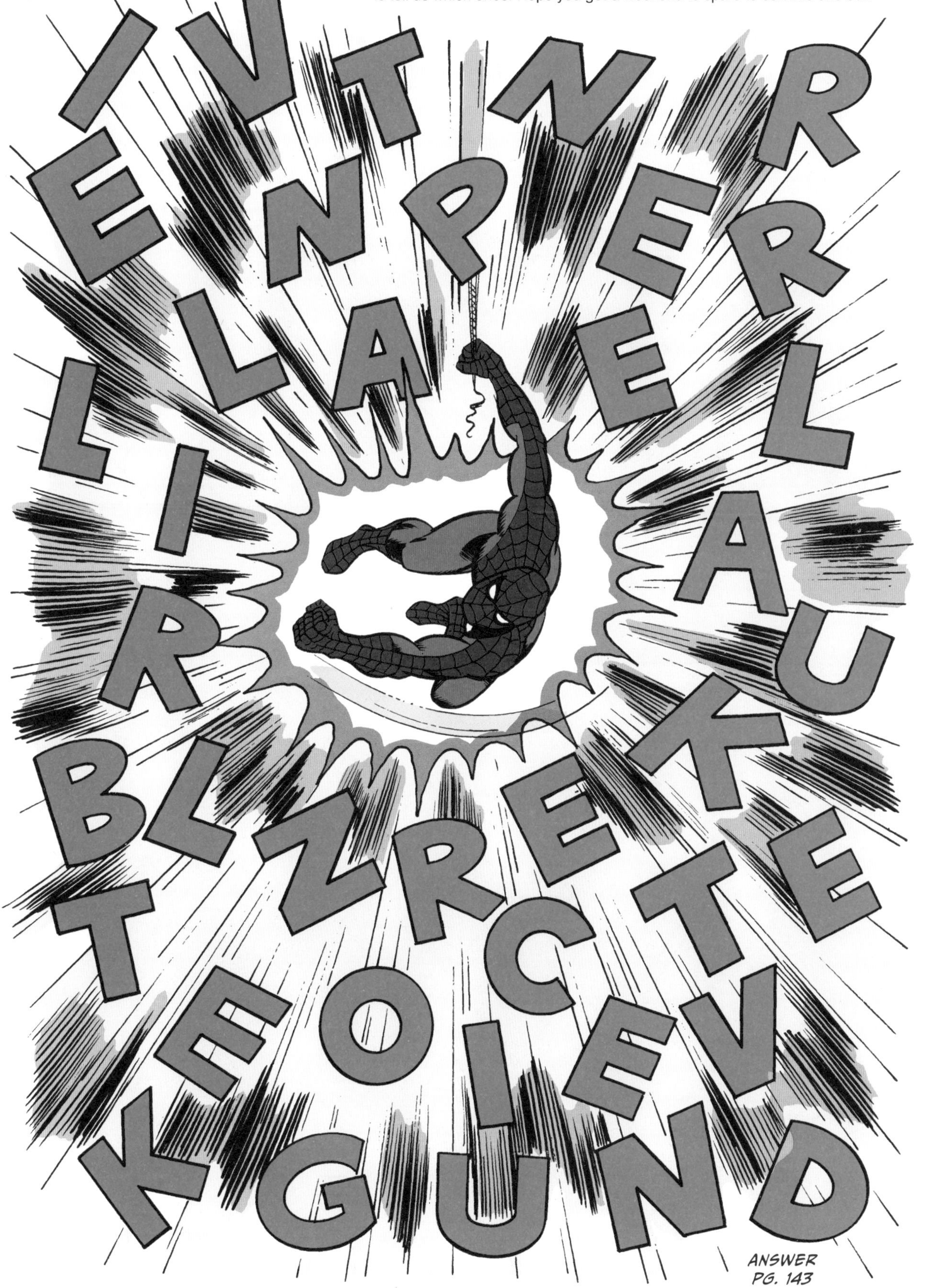
I V T N R
E N P E R
L A E R
L E L
I A
R U
B L Z R E K
T R C T E
E O C E V
K G I U N D

ANSWER PG. 143

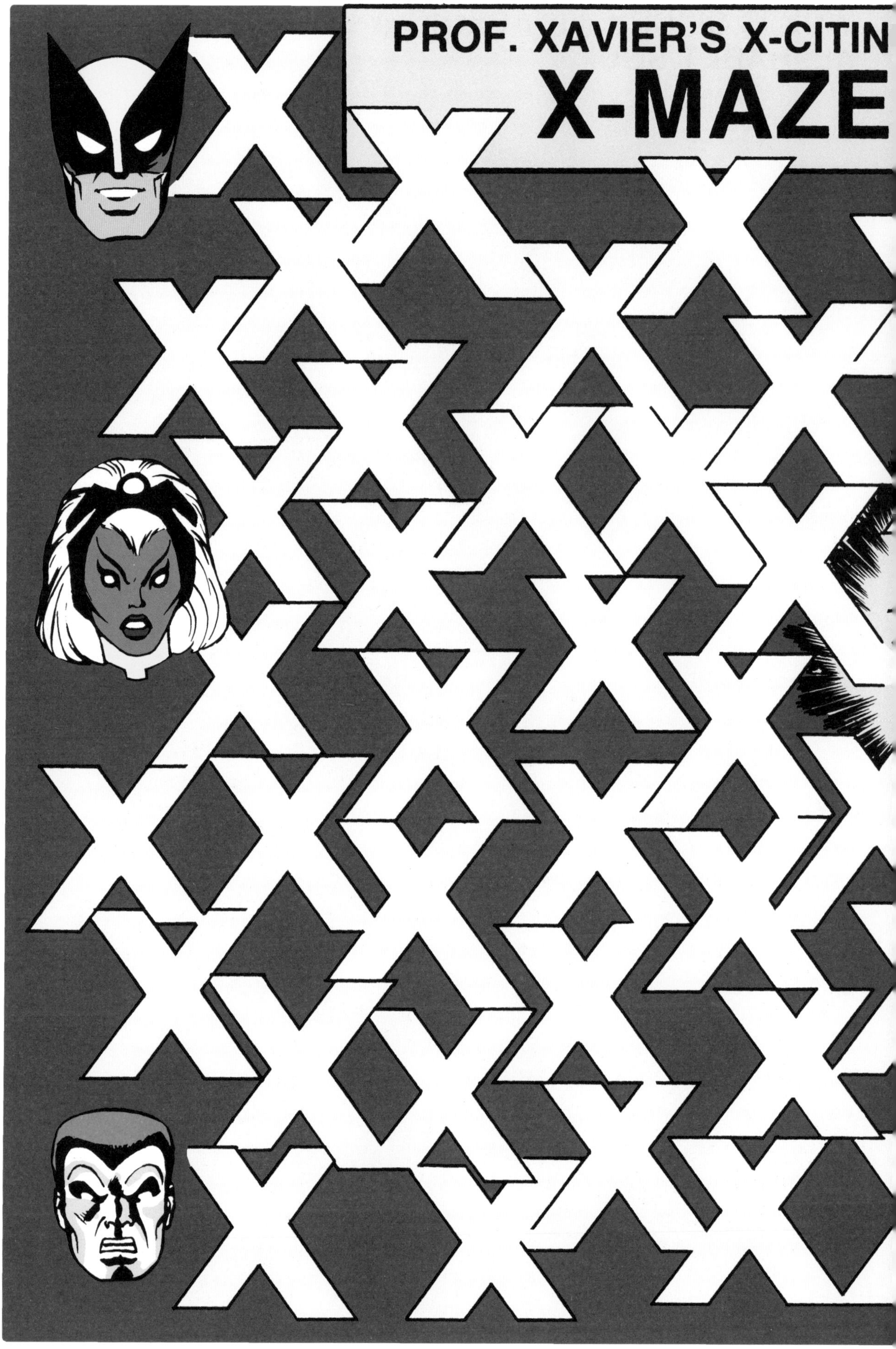
PROF. XAVIER'S X-CITIN
X-MAZE

## -ACTING

Prof is sending out X-waves and only one of the
ıp is receiving them. Which one can successfully
:h him by travelling the yellow X-maze?

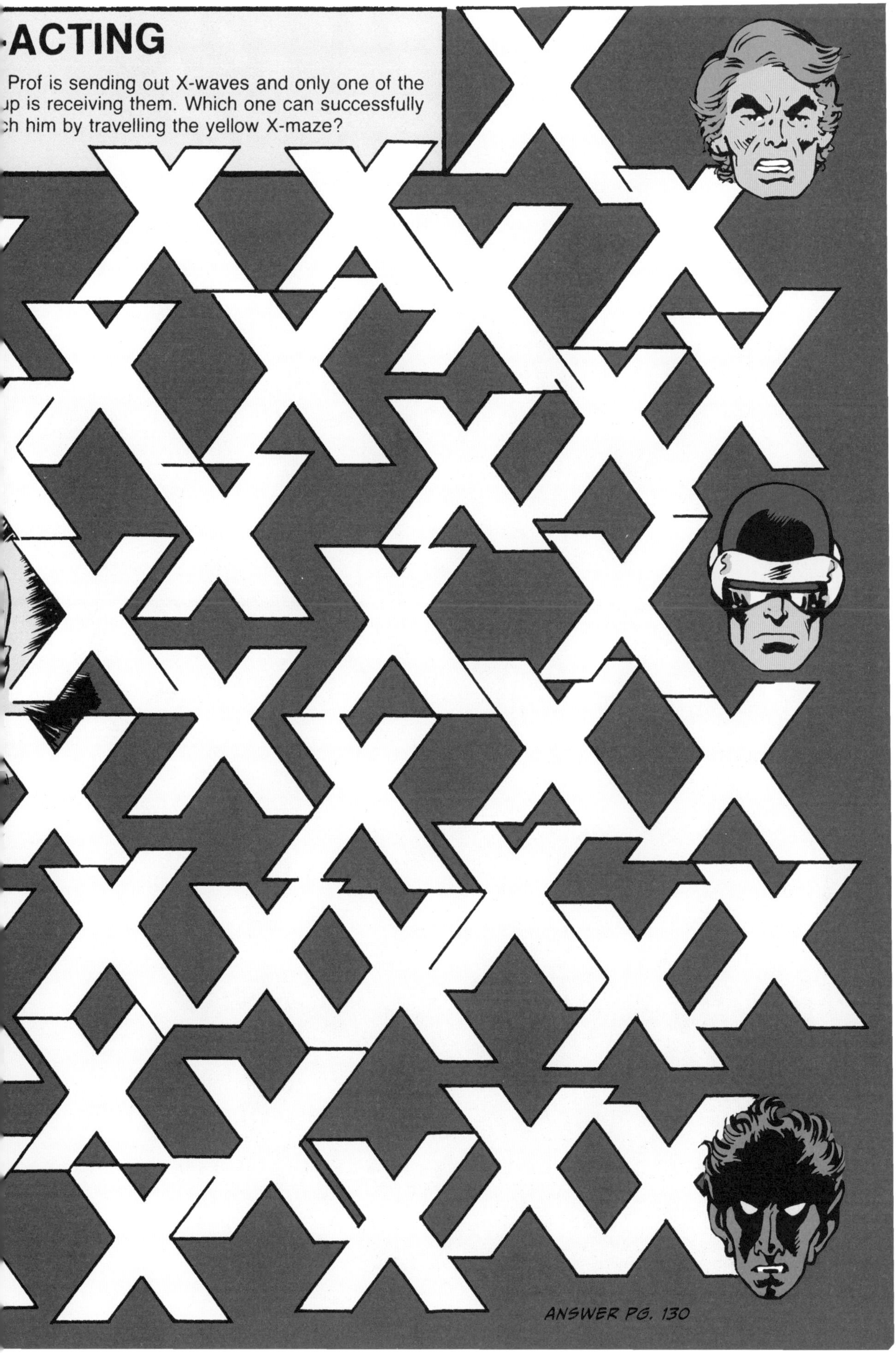

ANSWER PG. 130

# DOCTOR DOOM'S MIRROR MENACE

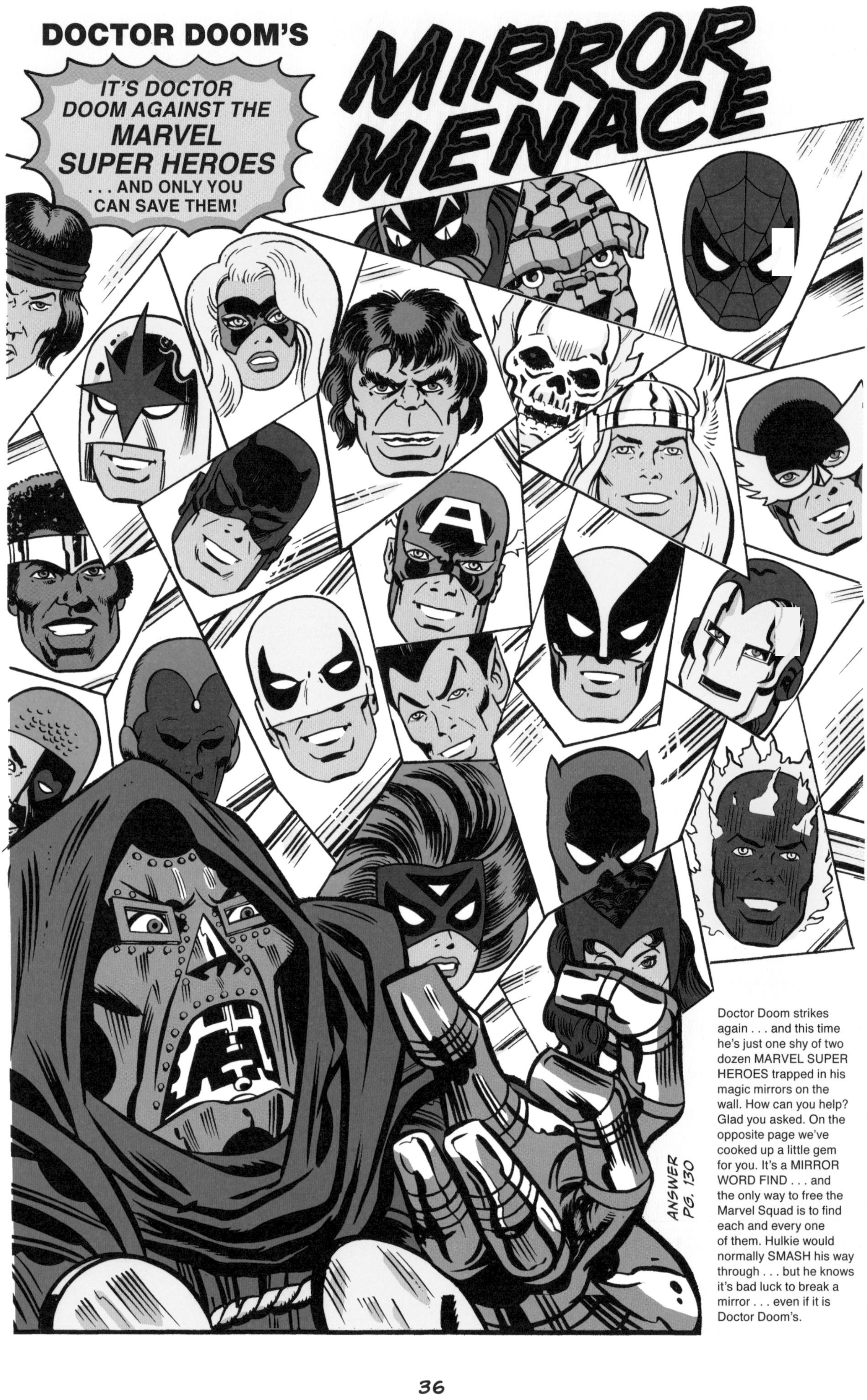
IT'S DOCTOR DOOM AGAINST THE MARVEL SUPER HEROES . . . AND ONLY YOU CAN SAVE THEM!
ANSWER PG. 130

Doctor Doom strikes again . . . and this time he's just one shy of two dozen MARVEL SUPER HEROES trapped in his magic mirrors on the wall. How can you help? Glad you asked. On the opposite page we've cooked up a little gem for you. It's a MIRROR WORD FIND . . . and the only way to free the Marvel Squad is to find each and every one of them. Hulkie would normally SMASH his way through . . . but he knows it's bad luck to break a mirror . . . even if it is Doctor Doom's.

B C E T S E C A P T I A P O S O S T A S
H A P R H A T H C T I W T E L R A C S P
R O L N P I S E T F S H A G I H C R G I
E T N C I R O N F I S T E H N F R T L D
R S E E K O E T R L A R H A H S R E S E
T P O B E N G S O I G K E I T L S O E R
M O O L L M Z N E V E L U A N E U R I W
E R T W C A R T N E S L E L T G T K C O
L H C T E N C S O D T H U L K O L X O M
E N E S A M E K V E F R O T N U A U C A
G A A O T C A H P R S K W A H T H G I N
T M E M R E L N E A H C A T T R N A W I
E R T H S T R L C D N A H T P I N E H G
T E R E T T T S E E R T I P S A M A C H
A W S C R E I A O H L U H D W R C H T A
L O G A A H C L N M W R T E L I U E N W
O P H L E N I R E V L O W S R L D A L K
R N O E H C E A C V O H O E H N E H C G
C G S C F N T W M N R T M F N E A I O S
U H T R O E O R O C H A U H O S C R P T
E R R T K H T S R E N R M E I T R T H S
A H I R C G E T S I T E O N S N T M C N
O E D E A R S I A E L W R O I W G H R A
F C E N J X D T H H S C N A V A E W O P
V T R S E F P I W C C T P E T C T I T O
R O T O S A T O P Z G H T S E I R P N R
E R A P C U L R A S O N R O I S N R A C
V E A N N V A A S U B M A R I N E R M C
N O T R E E M N D G E R T H N T F T U H
L T N A V O N A M R E D I P S O S N H E

# EXPLORE THE CONSTELLATIONS with STAR-LORD

Put these in their proper places:

Polaris, Ursa Minor, Ursa Major, Lepus, Scorpio, Lupus, Perseus, Aquila, Sagittarius, Taurus, Pollux, Serpens, Hercules, Pegasus, Andromeda, Cepheus, Cassiopeia, Capella, Bellatrix

These, too:

Leo, Ophiuchus, Centaurus, Columba, Sirius, Aries

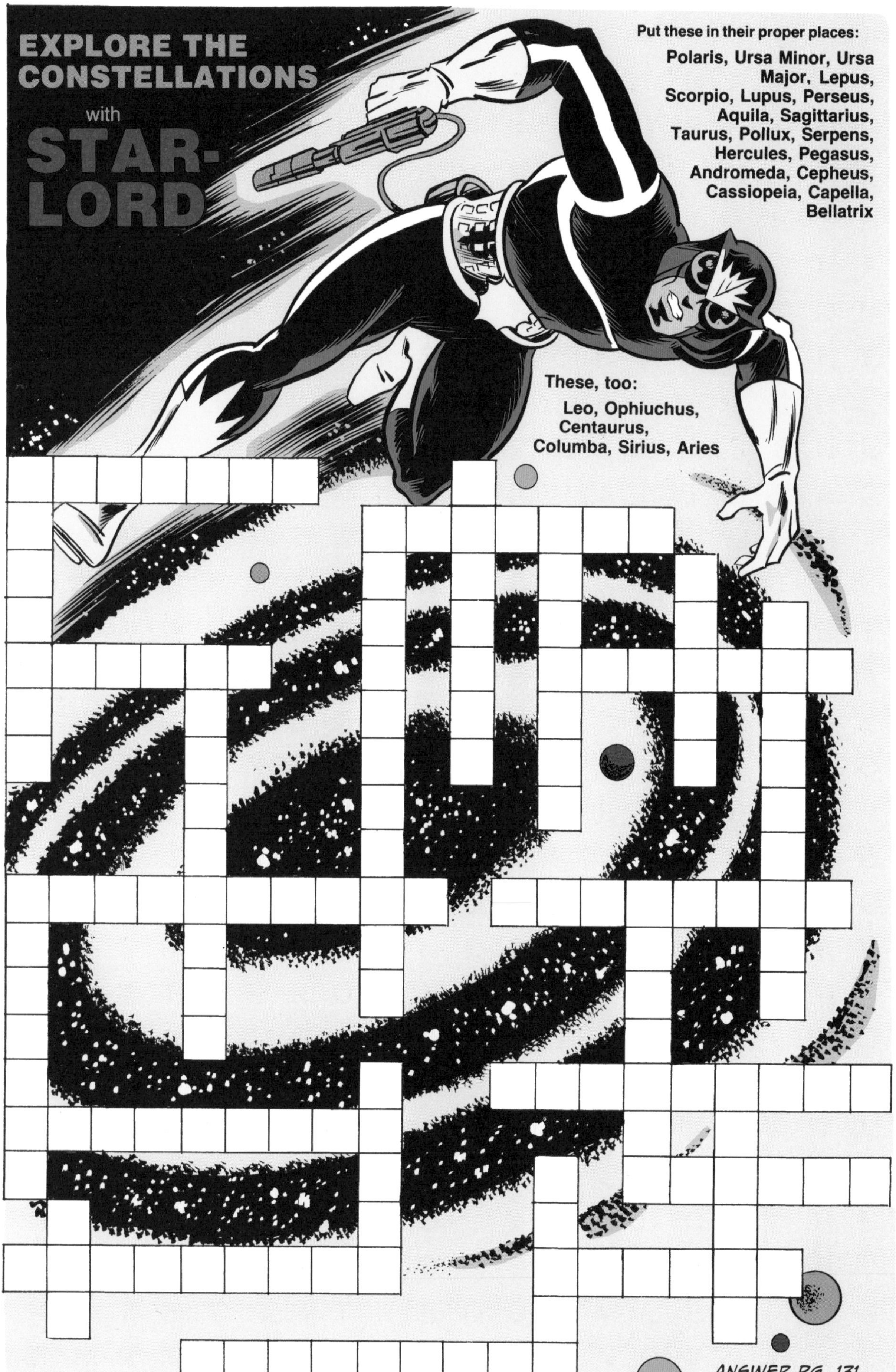

ANSWER PG. 131

# GROOTESQUE HUMOR

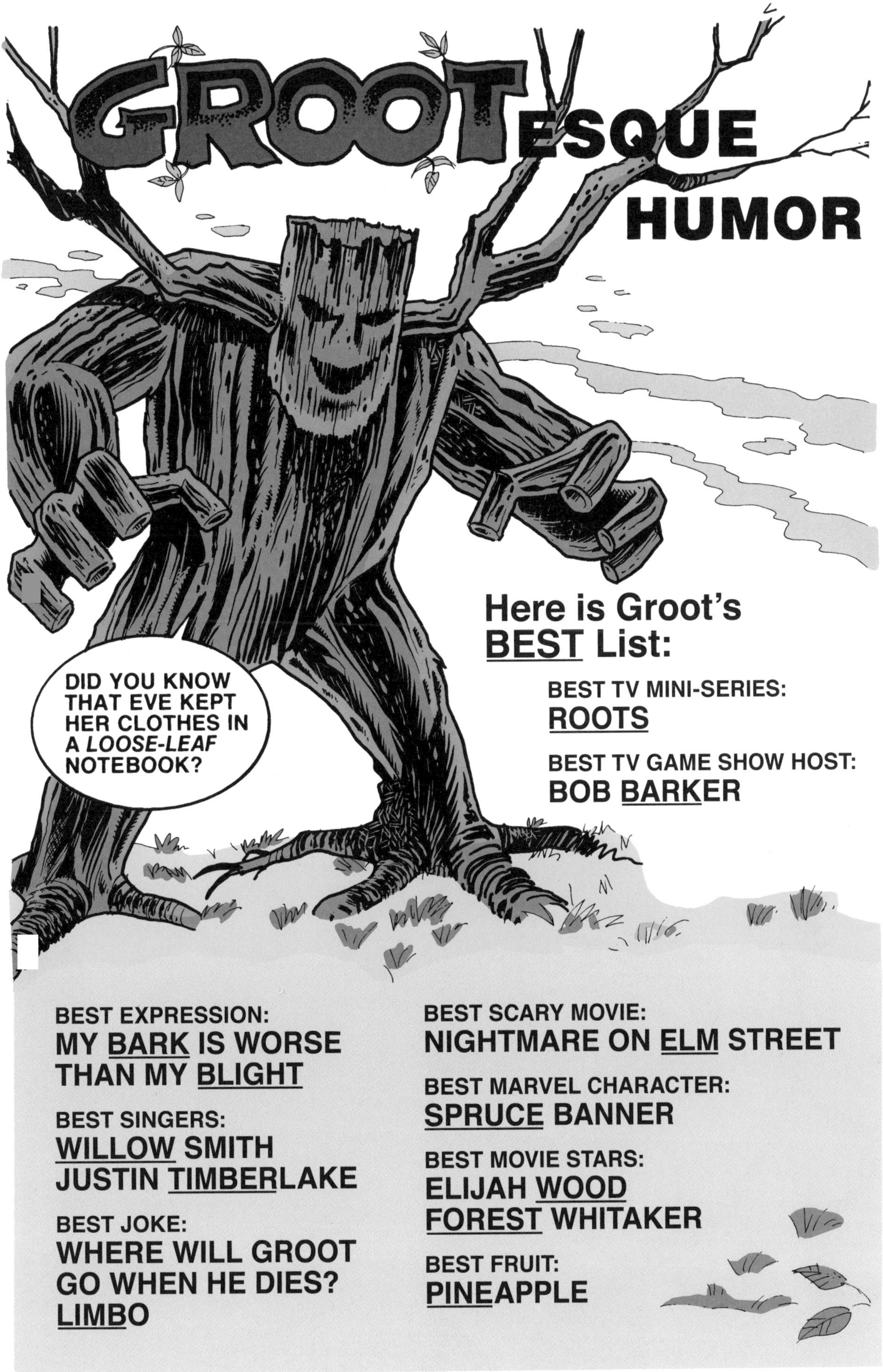
DID YOU KNOW THAT EVE KEPT HER CLOTHES IN A *LOOSE-LEAF* NOTEBOOK?

## Here is Groot's BEST List:

**BEST TV MINI-SERIES:**
**ROOTS**

**BEST TV GAME SHOW HOST:**
**BOB BARKER**

**BEST EXPRESSION:**
**MY BARK IS WORSE THAN MY BLIGHT**

**BEST SINGERS:**
**WILLOW SMITH**
**JUSTIN TIMBERLAKE**

**BEST JOKE:**
**WHERE WILL GROOT GO WHEN HE DIES?**
**LIMBO**

**BEST SCARY MOVIE:**
**NIGHTMARE ON ELM STREET**

**BEST MARVEL CHARACTER:**
**SPRUCE BANNER**

**BEST MOVIE STARS:**
**ELIJAH WOOD**
**FOREST WHITAKER**

**BEST FRUIT:**
**PINEAPPLE**

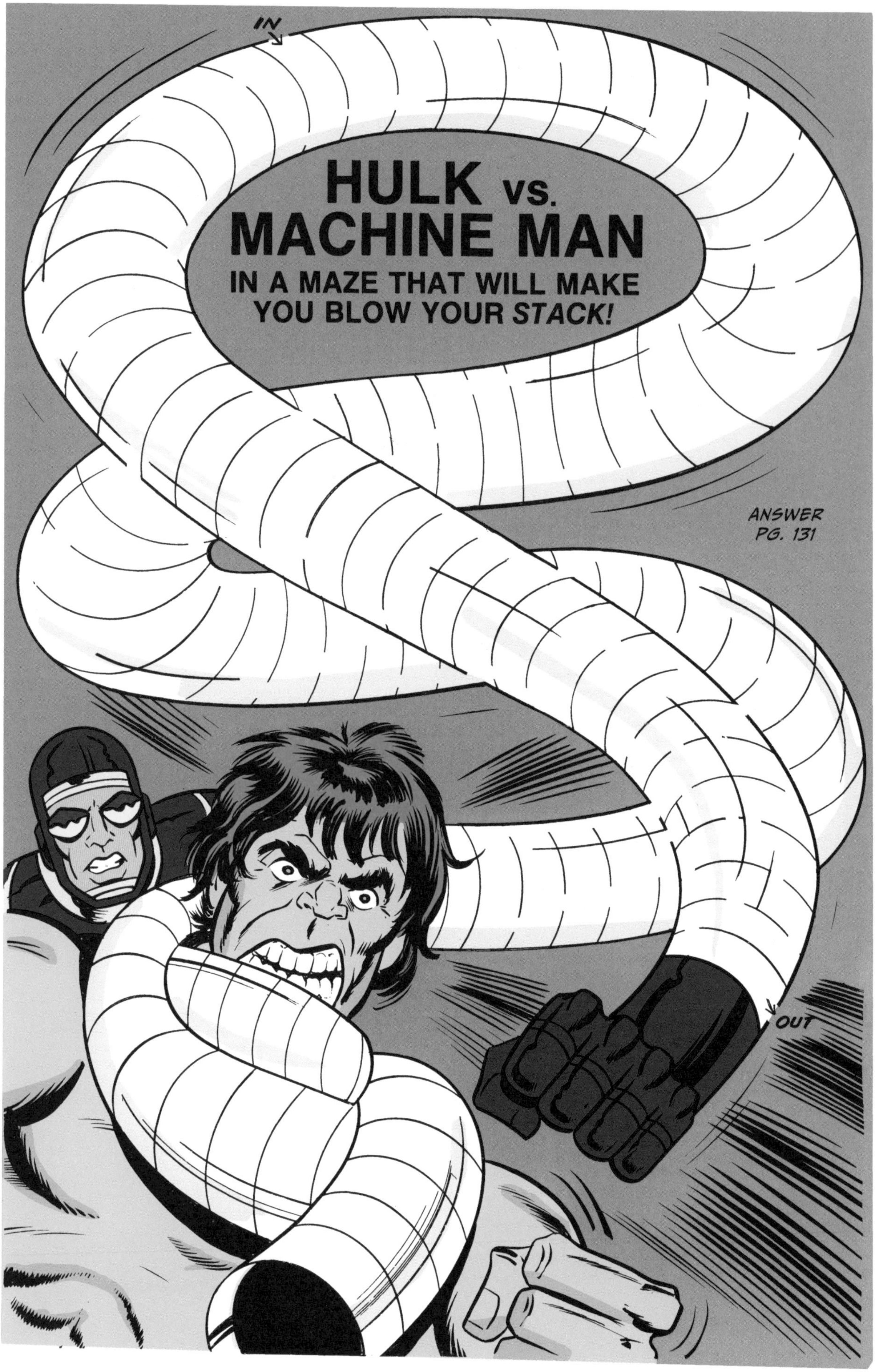
IN
HULK vs. MACHINE MAN
IN A MAZE THAT WILL MAKE YOU BLOW YOUR STACK!
ANSWER PG. 131
OUT

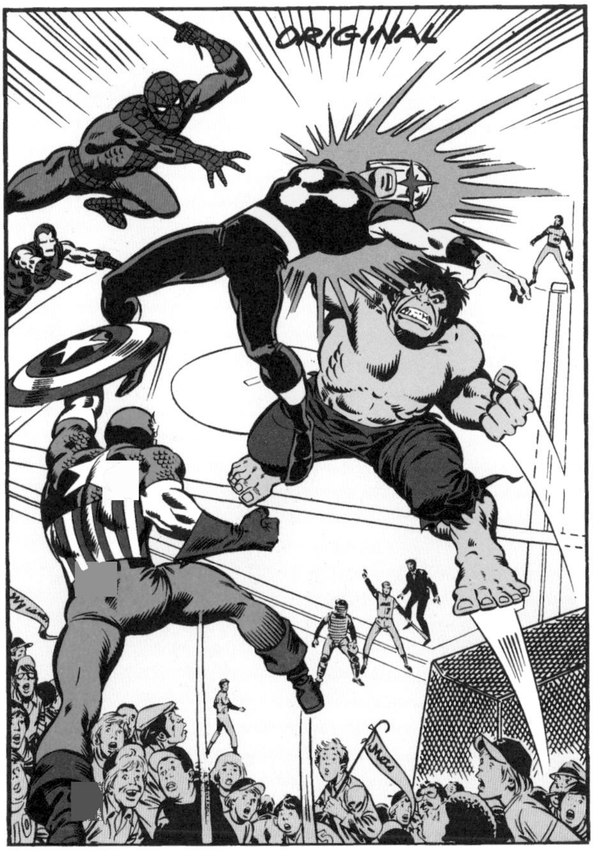
ORIGINAL

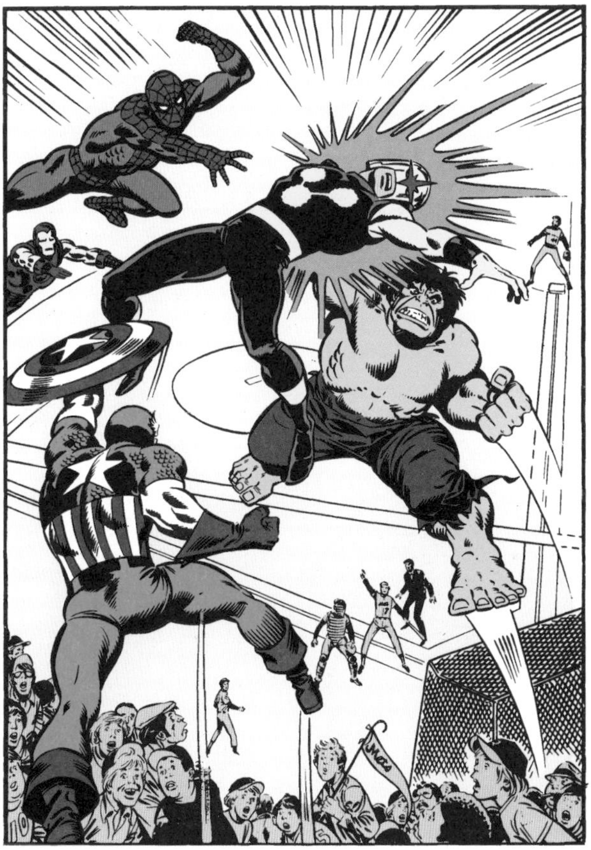

ANSWER PG. 131

# WHAT'S MISSING?

Captain America won't tell. Neither will Spider-Man, Nova, Hulk, or Iron Man. You're on your own, o searcher of missing things. Check the panels against the original and see for yourself. You can't find your pencil? OK, everyone, help this puzzle pal find their pencil. Now we've become a lost and found department. Sheesh!

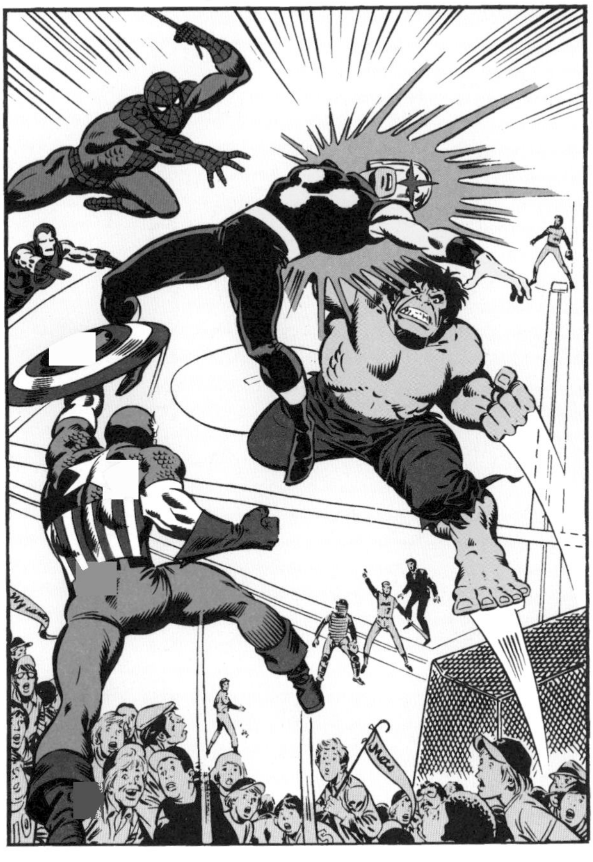

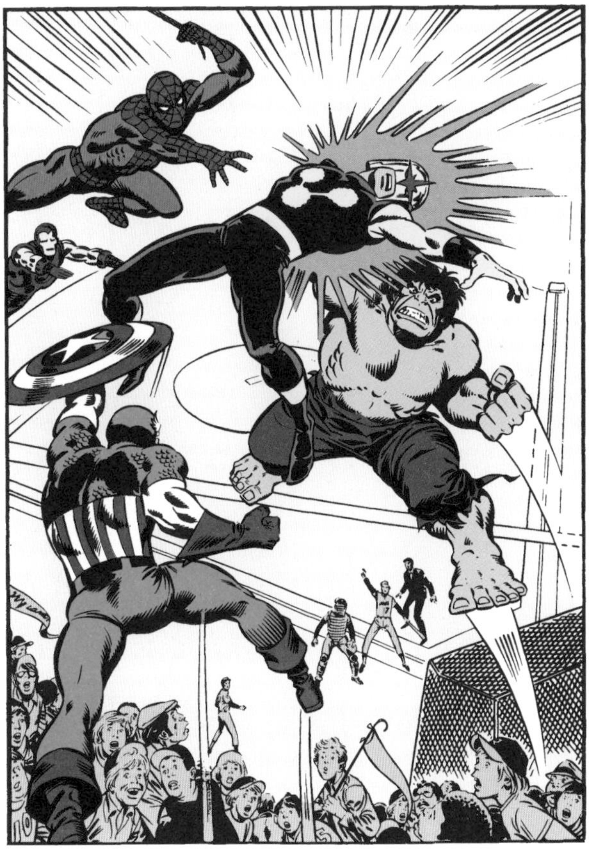

# STORM-ORORO X-WORD

You must find only STORM and ORORO in this uniquely Marvel Word Find. We've given you one freebie below to show you how it's done. And don't check the weather for clues because even the forecaster is having trouble spotting these storms!

```
S T R O O T S O S M O T S O S O S M
S T O R O R M T R R S R M T R M R R
R M O T R S O S O M O R O R R O T S
O R R R M R T R T R O R R R T S R T
O R O R M R O O O O M M O S O M O O
T R O R T R S R R S R R T O T O R M
R T O R O R O M O O R O R M T O R S
S T T R O R O T T M R T R T R O R T
S O O T O S M S S M S O O O S M O M
O M R R O R R T M T T R R O R R O R
M S O S O M O M T S O T R O M M R T
S R O T T R S R M R S R T S R O S R
O T S O M R O S O R T S M T O O T M
```

ANSWER PG. 131

42

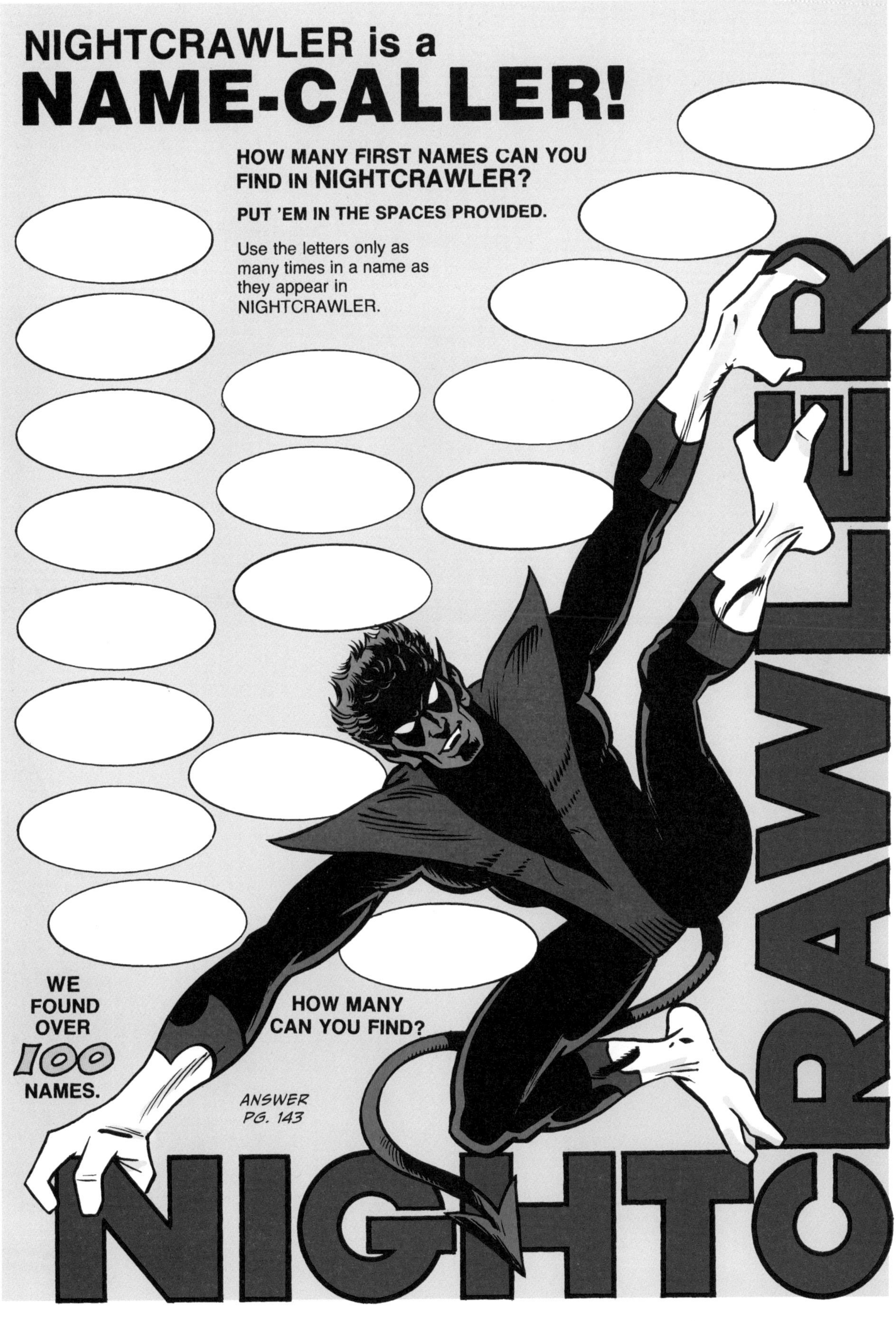
NIGHTCRAWLER is a
NAME-CALLER!
HOW MANY FIRST NAMES CAN YOU FIND IN NIGHTCRAWLER?
PUT 'EM IN THE SPACES PROVIDED.
Use the letters only as many times in a name as they appear in NIGHTCRAWLER.
WE FOUND OVER 100 NAMES.
HOW MANY CAN YOU FIND?
ANSWER PG. 143
NIGHTCRAWLER

*WRITTEN, DRAWN, AND EDITED BY OWEN McCARRON*

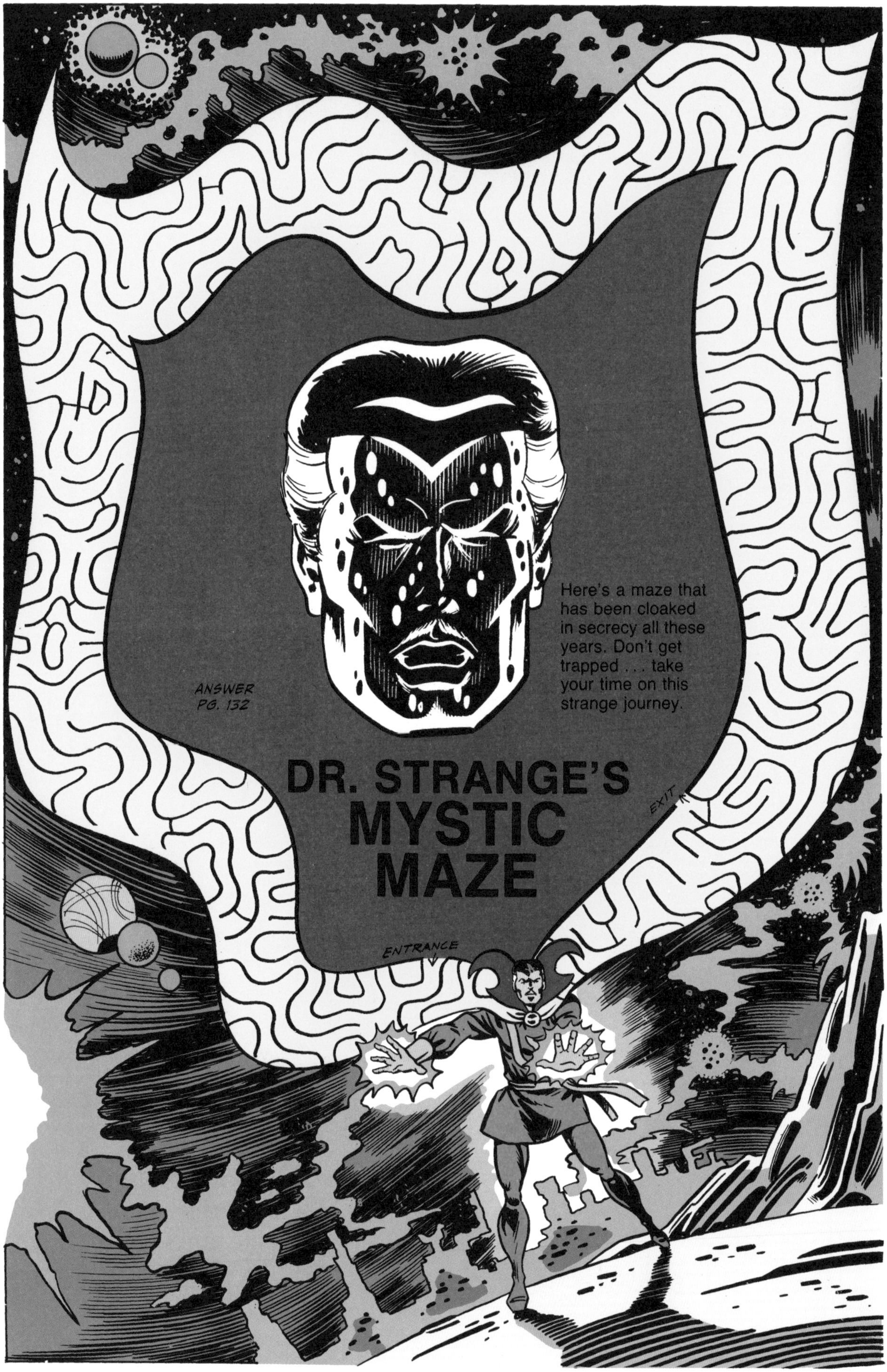
Here's a maze that has been cloaked in secrecy all these years. Don't get trapped . . . take your time on this strange journey.
ANSWER PG. 132
DR. STRANGE'S MYSTIC MAZE
EXIT
ENTRANCE

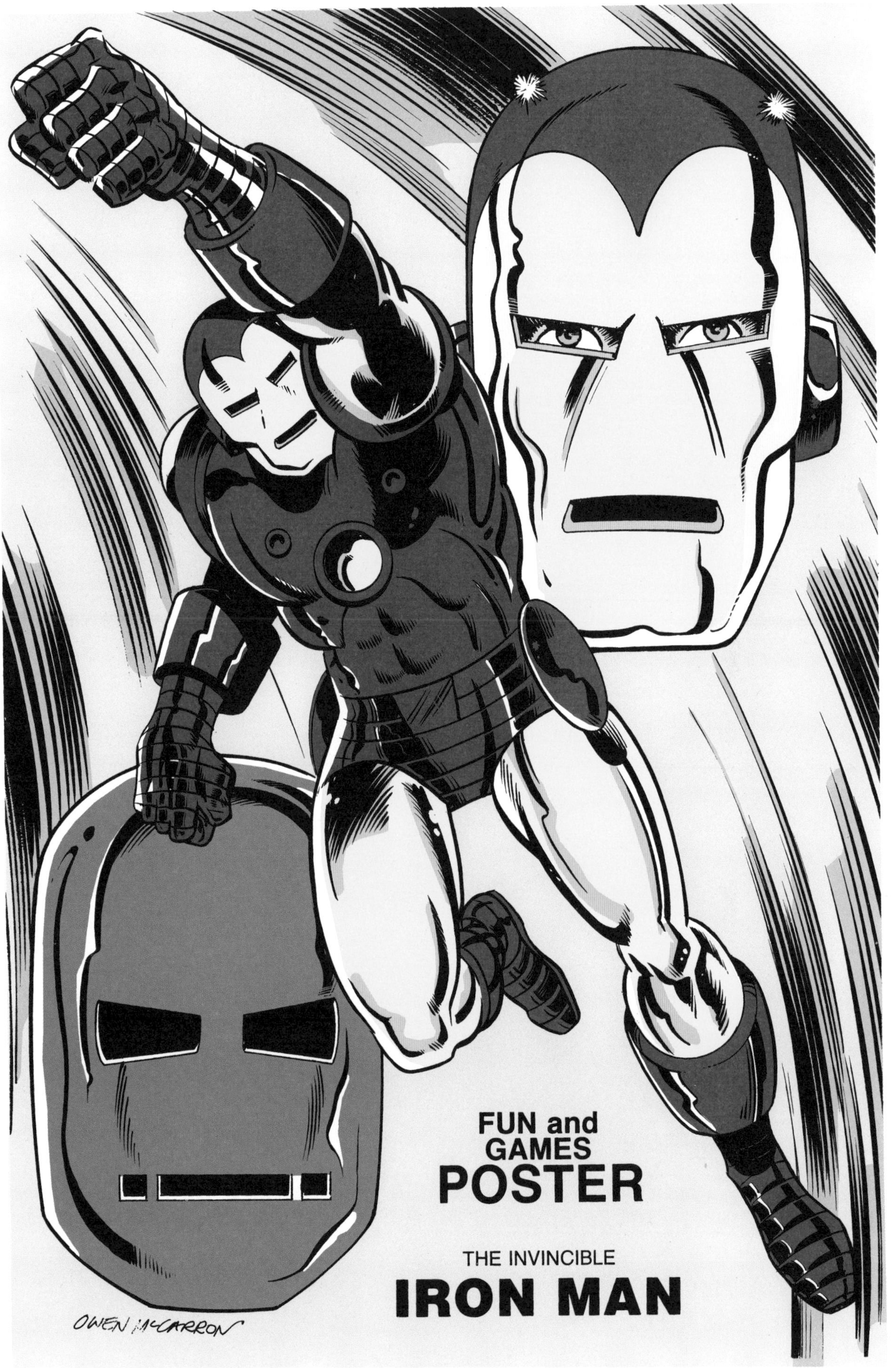
FUN and GAMES POSTER
THE INVINCIBLE
IRON MAN
OWEN McCARRON

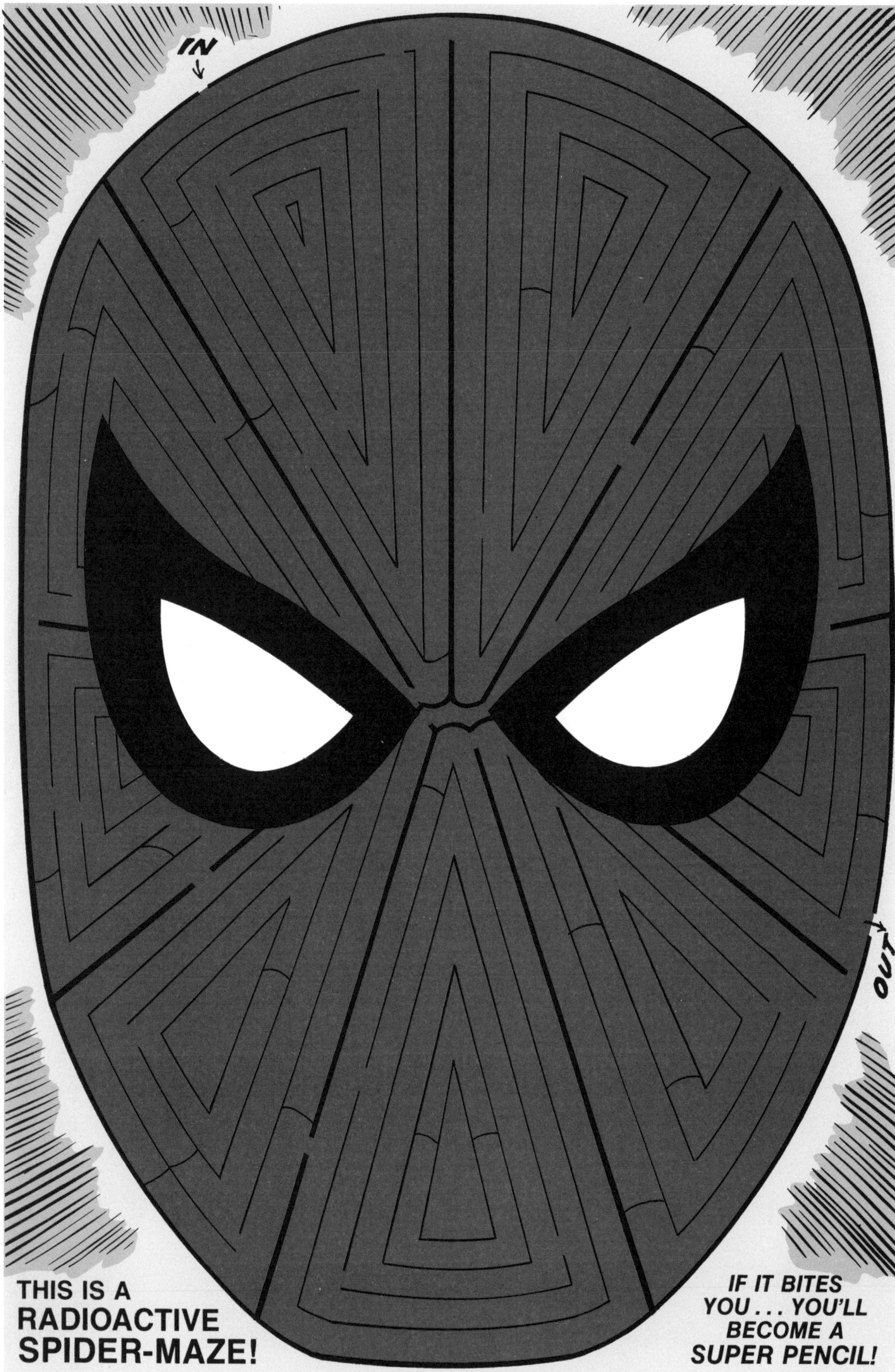
IN
OUT
THIS IS A RADIOACTIVE SPIDER-MAZE!
IF IT BITES YOU . . . YOU'LL BECOME A SUPER PENCIL!

ANSWER PG. 132

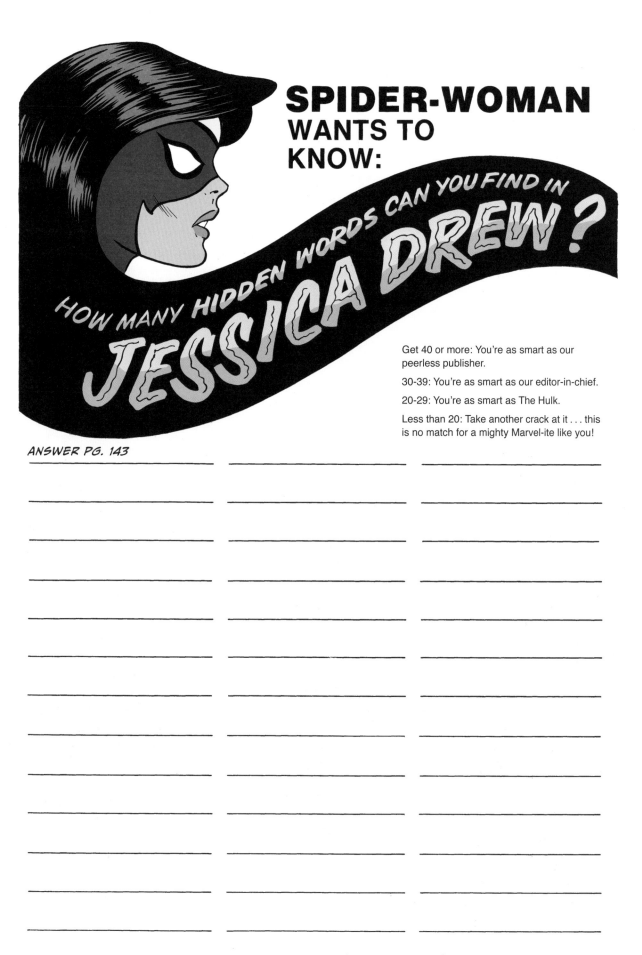

# SPIDER-WOMAN
## WANTS TO
## KNOW:

HOW MANY HIDDEN WORDS CAN YOU FIND IN JESSICA DREW?

Get 40 or more: You're as smart as our peerless publisher.

30-39: You're as smart as our editor-in-chief.

20-29: You're as smart as The Hulk.

Less than 20: Take another crack at it . . . this is no match for a mighty Marvel-ite like you!

ANSWER PG. 143

**WRITTEN, DRAWN, EDITED BY OWEN McCARRON**

# REFLECTIONS OF A MARVEL SUPER VILLAIN

These Marvel villains have been admiring themselves in the mirror. Your task: Find the exact reflection of each one. Draw a line from the villain to your choice. **(Color is not a consideration.)**

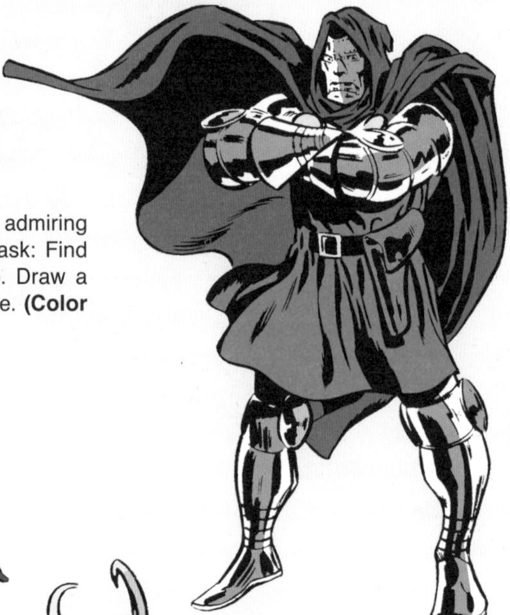

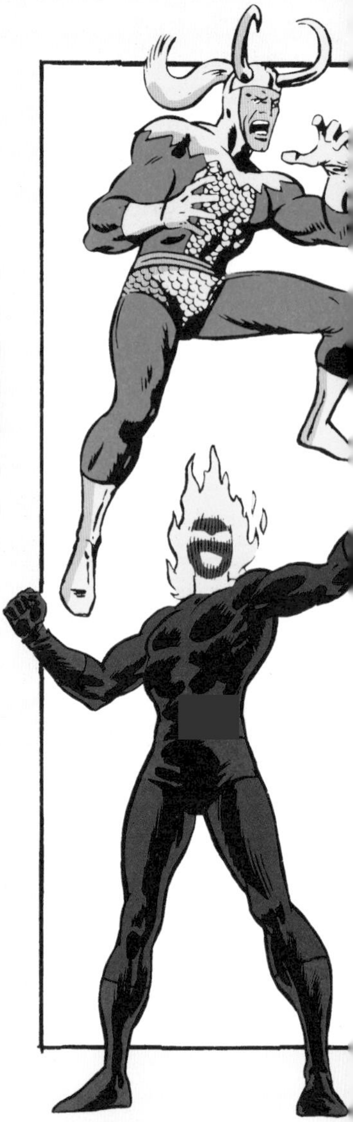

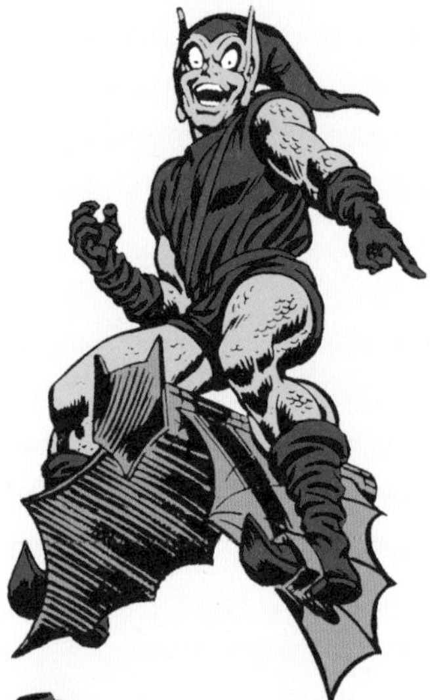

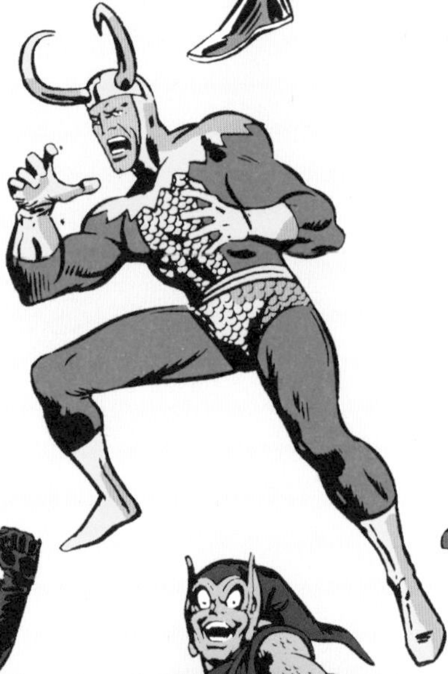

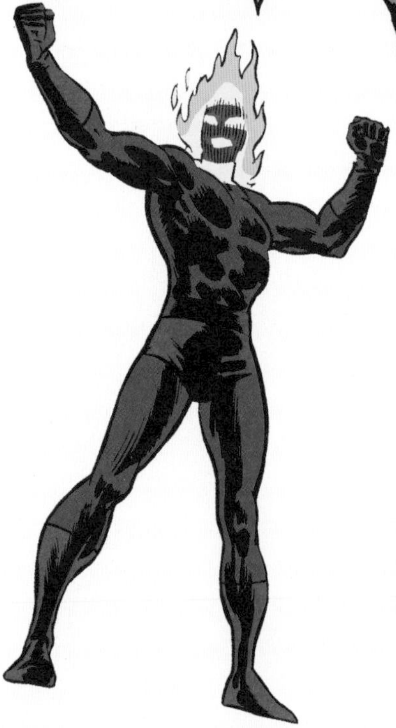

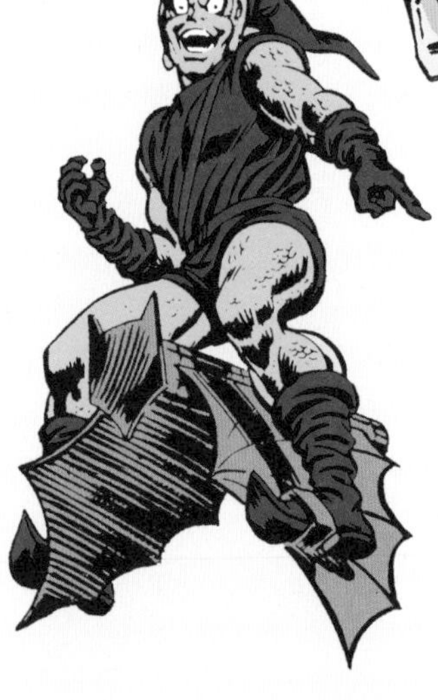

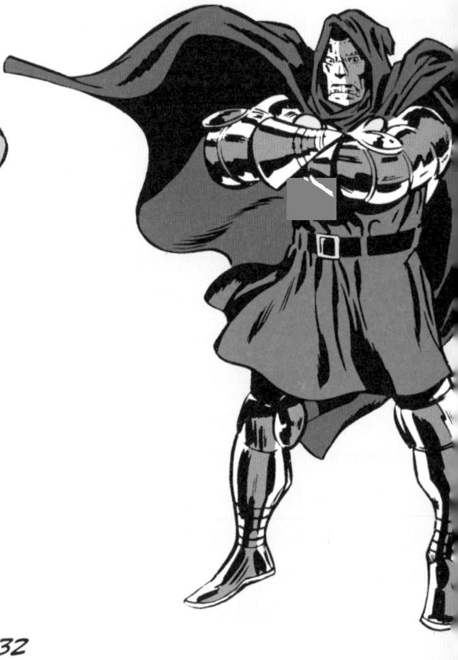

ANSWER PG. 132

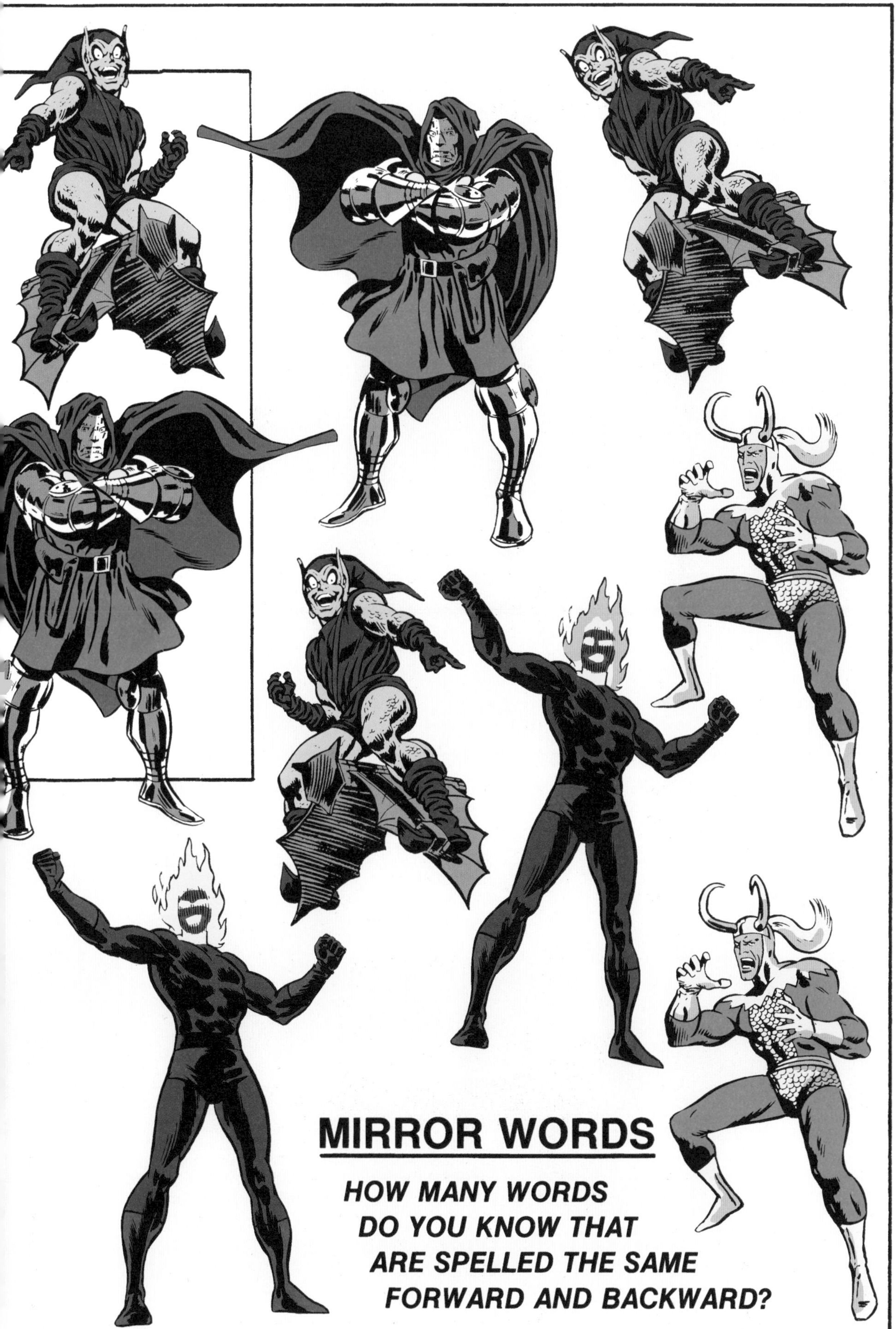

## MIRROR WORDS

***HOW MANY WORDS DO YOU KNOW THAT ARE SPELLED THE SAME FORWARD AND BACKWARD?***

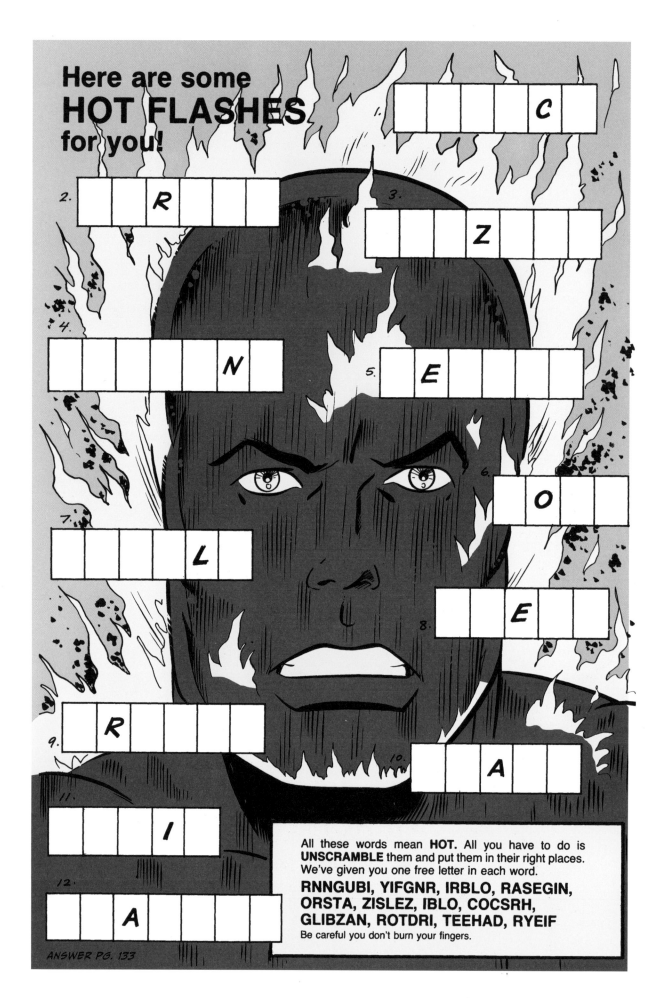

# Here are some HOT FLASHES for you!

1. ☐ ☐ ☐ ☐ C ☐ ☐

2. ☐ ☐ R ☐ ☐ ☐

3. ☐ ☐ ☐ Z ☐ ☐ ☐

4. ☐ ☐ ☐ ☐ N ☐ ☐

5. ☐ ☐ E ☐ ☐ ☐

6. ☐ ☐ O ☐ ☐

7. ☐ ☐ ☐ ☐ L ☐

8. ☐ ☐ ☐ E ☐ ☐

9. ☐ R ☐ ☐ ☐ ☐

10. ☐ ☐ A ☐ ☐

11. ☐ ☐ ☐ I ☐

12. ☐ ☐ A ☐ ☐ ☐ ☐

All these words mean **HOT**. All you have to do is **UNSCRAMBLE** them and put them in their right places. We've given you one free letter in each word.

**RNNGUBI, YIFGNR, IRBLO, RASEGIN, ORSTA, ZISLEZ, IBLO, COCSRH, GLIBZAN, ROTDRI, TEEHAD, RYEIF**

Be careful you don't burn your fingers.

ANSWER PG. 133

50

# LEARN TO DRAW MARVEL CHARACTERS*

# THE THING

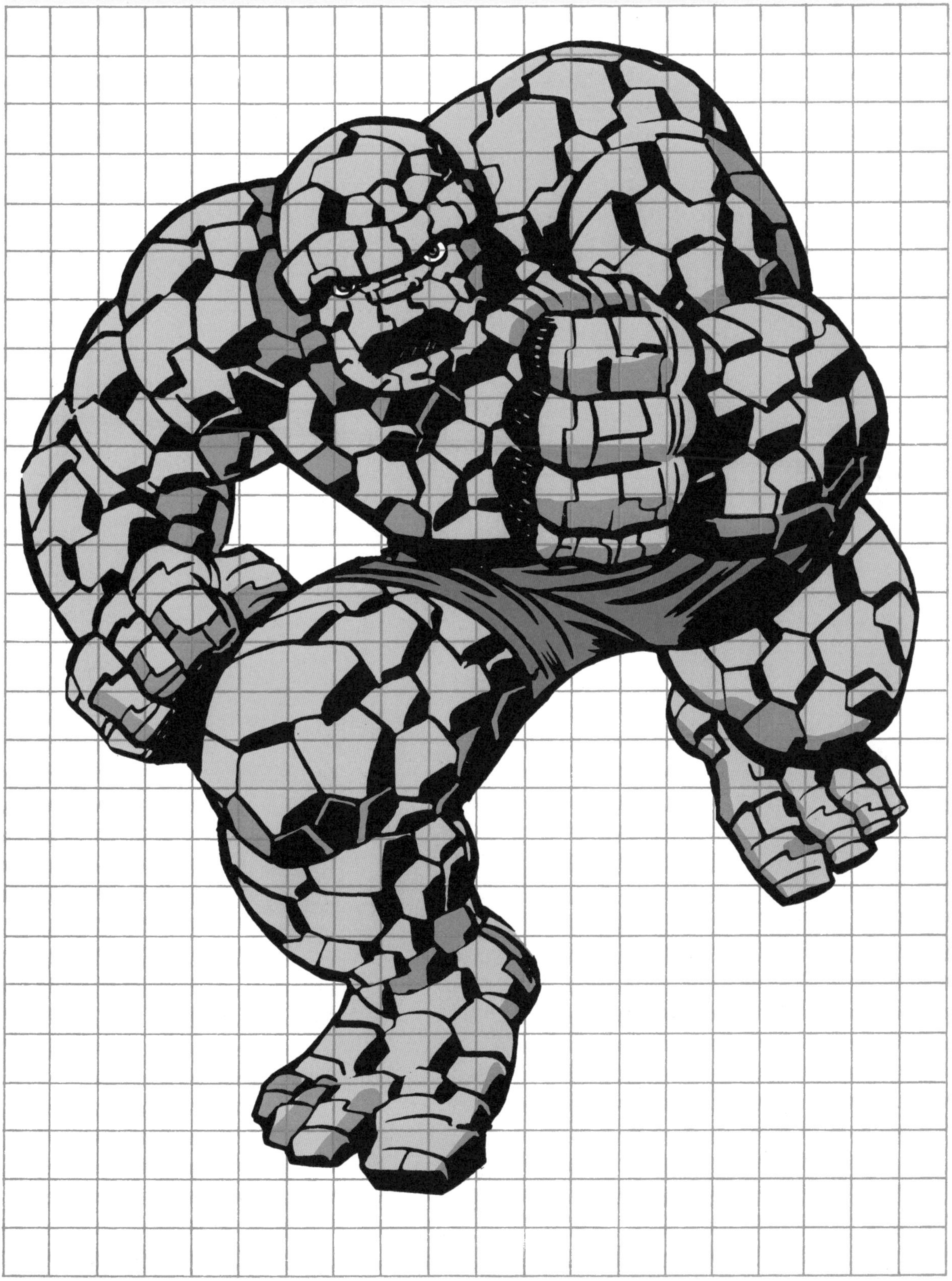

*GRAB SOME GRAPH PAPER TO DRAW LIKE THE PROS!

# THE MARVEL ALPHABET →

Bet you didn't even think we knew the alphabet. Fooled you again. All you have to do to show us how smart you are is to find all 26 Marvel characters in the letter litter below.

**AVENGERS**
**BLACK WIDOW**

**CLEA**
**DORMAMMU**
**ELECTRO**
**FALCON**
**GALACTUS**
**HELLCAT**

**ICEMAN**
**JANUS**
**KA-ZAR**
**LOCKJAW**
**MAGNETO**
**NITRO**

**OWL**
**PROWLER**
**QUICKSILVER**
**RINGMASTER**
**STEGRON**
**THOR**

**UNUS**
**VULTURE**
**WIZARD**
**XAVIER**
**YELLOWJACKET**
**ZEUS**

Horizontal, vertical, backward, diagonal, always in a straight line, and no skipping letters.

```
V A M H A G L T A W C O R T E L E T J H
L Z U E S R E L W O R P H E G B E H A N
U I Z L W L A K L D J E A U T L O W N O
T O V L O W O C L I O T G A L A C T U S
U M I C E M A N E W S R H Z J L E F S R
R D A A M E S T H K A C M K E R K Y R E
E R U T L U V M H C J A L A G U L E K D
M A A R N M U L G A A V M Z M T S L A N
A Z Q U I C K S I L V E R A R M O L Z E
N I D E R N T G L B L N O R R E U O A F
G W C O L E G H W I C G E L A S R W A E
E L C M G L R M O N A E L O Z T C J R D
T E L R A R F C A R T R P K C O H A F C
O J O C I N A H T S H S Y E L L O C J K
F N C R T R L W U R T C L T H U L K R H
L A K O T R C O N T S E P M A G N E T O
A R J N W I O X A V I E R T Q U I T O C
C T A O F E N R J T S D Q I A S Z P A T
O N W R I N N S G E T R O N O N C L N E
```

*ANSWER PG. 133*

USE YOUR **SECRET CODE BREAKER** FOR THIS ONE *unless you don't need it!*

## PLUS! FIND THE HIDDEN GROUP *WITHOUT ANY HELP FROM US!*

# ◀TWO-IN-ONE PUZZLER

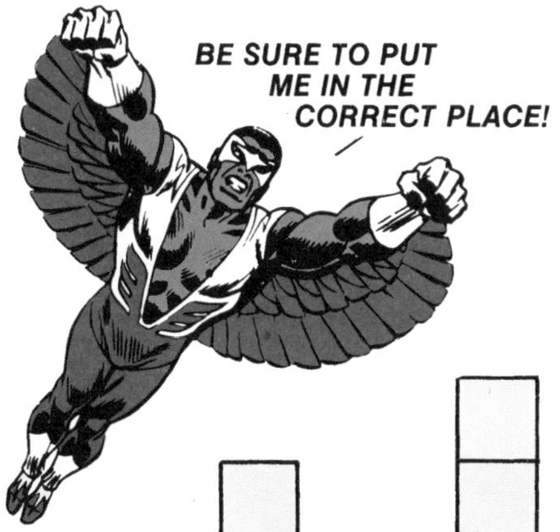
BE SURE TO PUT ME IN THE CORRECT PLACE!

Now that you have found all the characters on the opposite page, your next task is to put them in their proper places on this page. We have given you one free just to encourage you. Don't forget to include the guest group as well since we made a place for them.

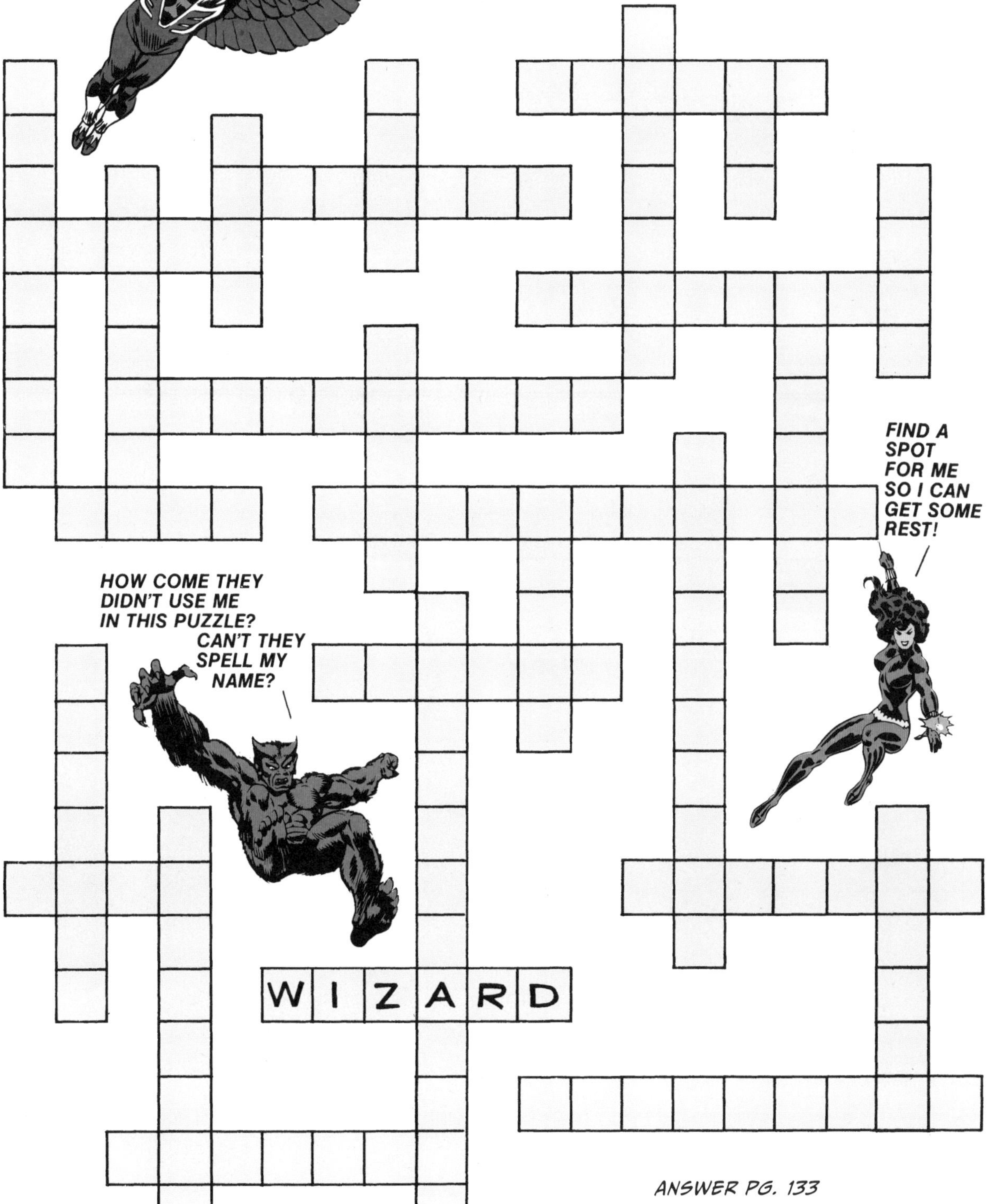
FIND A SPOT FOR ME SO I CAN GET SOME REST!
HOW COME THEY DIDN'T USE ME IN THIS PUZZLE? CAN'T THEY SPELL MY NAME?
WIZARD

ANSWER PG. 133

# HAVE YOU EVER BEEN ATTACKED BY AN ANT-WORD PUZZLE?

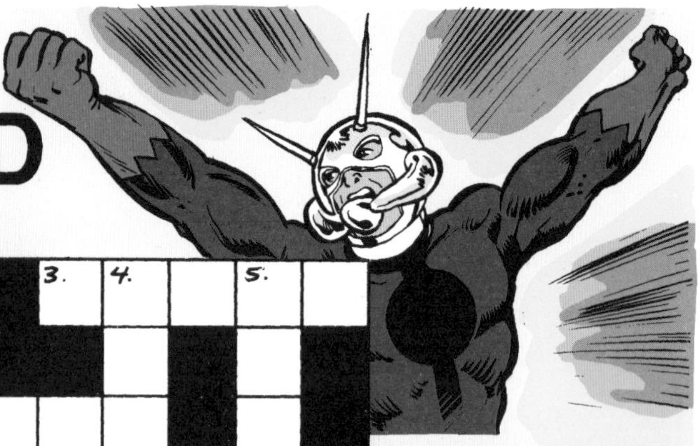

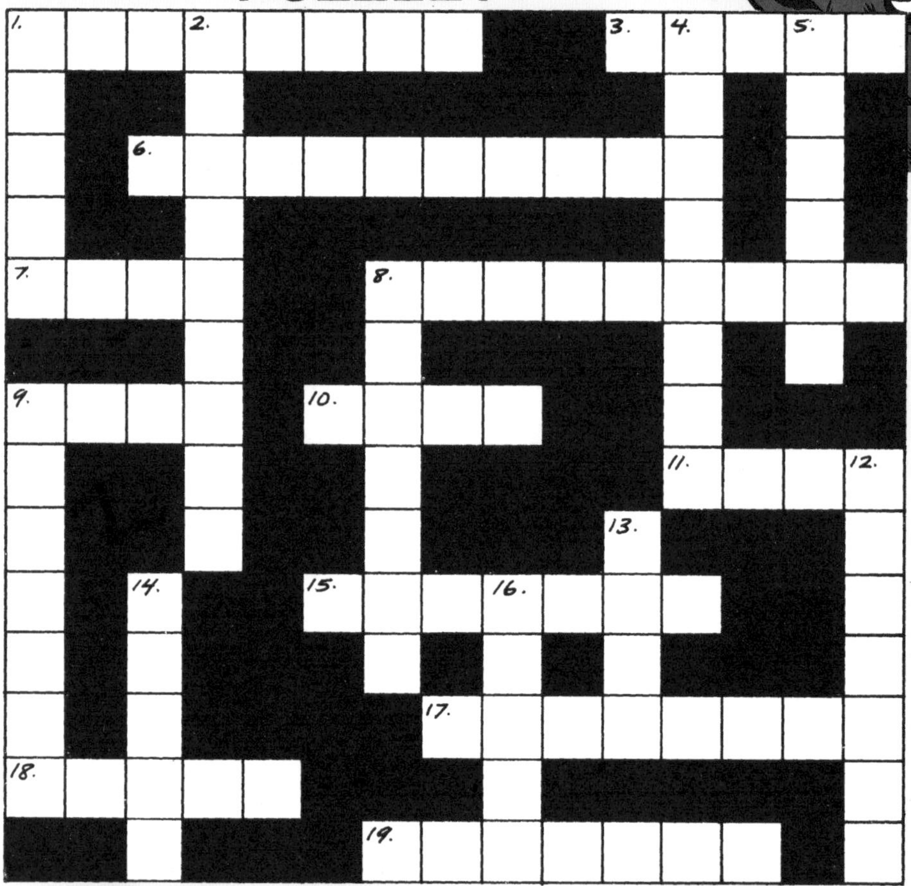
1. 2. 3. 4. 5. 6. 7. 8. 9. 10. 11. 12. 13. 14. 15. 16. 17. 18. 19.

The Ant-Man is angry . . . he woke up this morning with ants in his pants. You can help settle him down by getting 100% on this puzzle. Clue: Every answer to the definitions has the word "ANT" in it. What else would you expect?

## ACROSS

1. Our swamp creature
3. Hulk wears purple ones
6. Adversary
7. In architecture: a pillar on either side of a doorway into a Greek temple
8. Someone who celebrates
9. A prefix meaning against
10. What's crawling over Vision and Scarlet Witch?
11. A contraction
15. In Europe: agricultural worker
17. Animal with a long tongue
18. Italian poet, wrote "The Divine Comedy"
19. A realm explored by Ant-Man and the Wasp

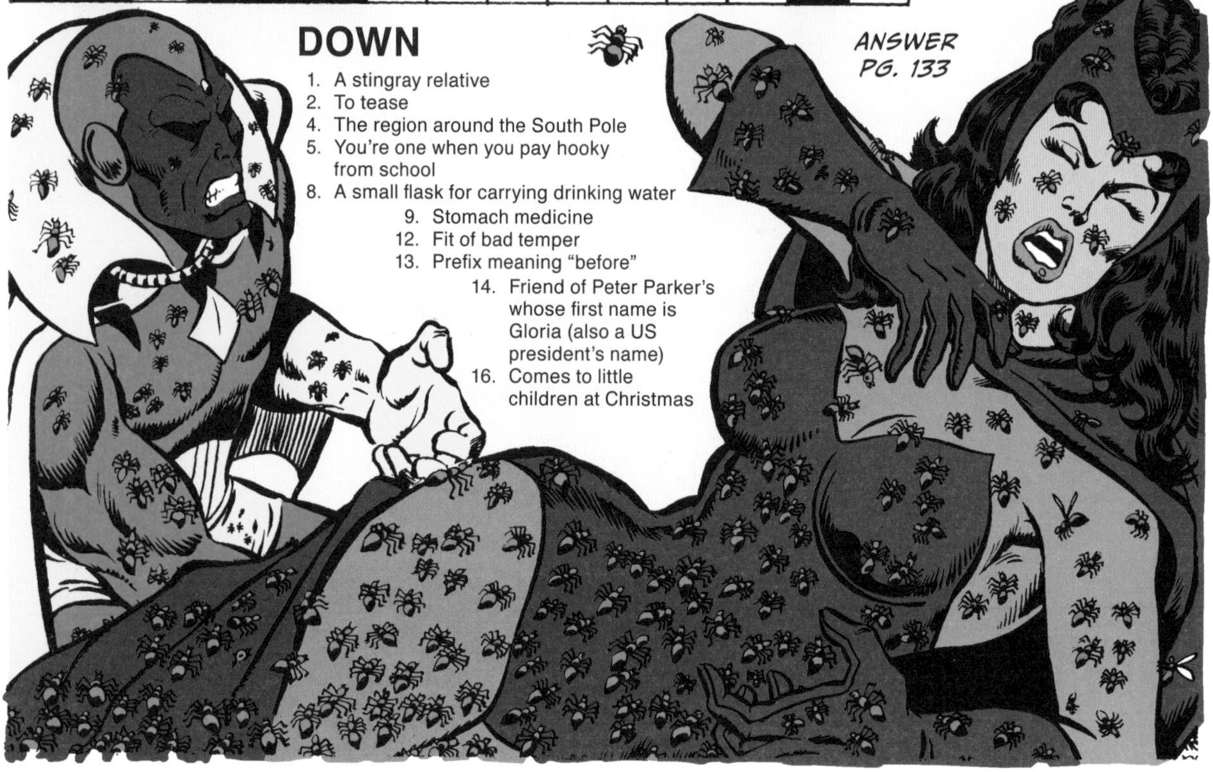

## DOWN

1. A stingray relative
2. To tease
4. The region around the South Pole
5. You're one when you pay hooky from school
8. A small flask for carrying drinking water
9. Stomach medicine
12. Fit of bad temper
13. Prefix meaning "before"
14. Friend of Peter Parker's whose first name is Gloria (also a US president's name)
16. Comes to little children at Christmas

ANSWER PG. 133

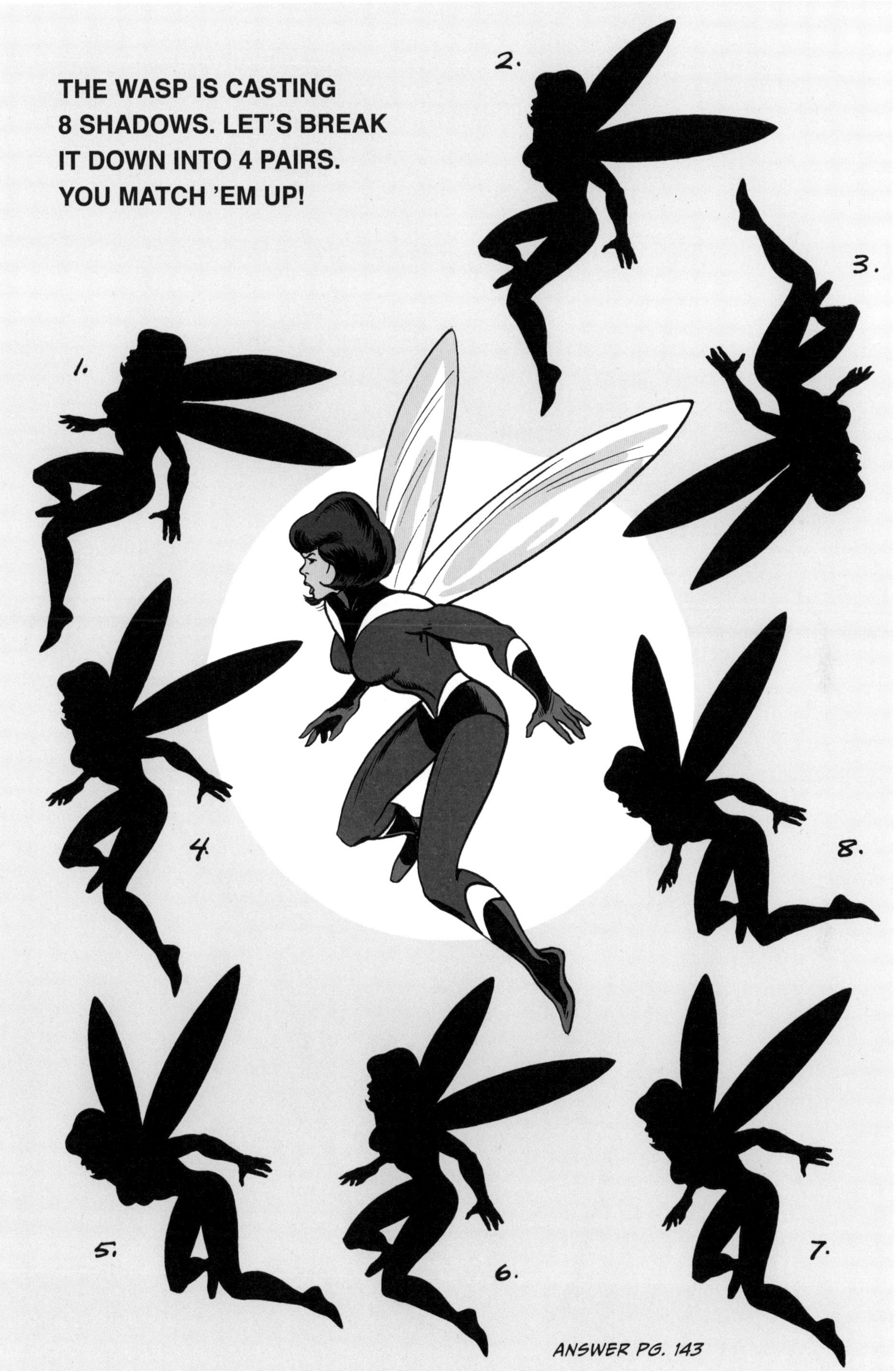
THE WASP IS CASTING
8 SHADOWS. LET'S BREAK
IT DOWN INTO 4 PAIRS.
YOU MATCH 'EM UP!
1.
2.
3.
4.
5.
6.
7.
8.
ANSWER PG. 143

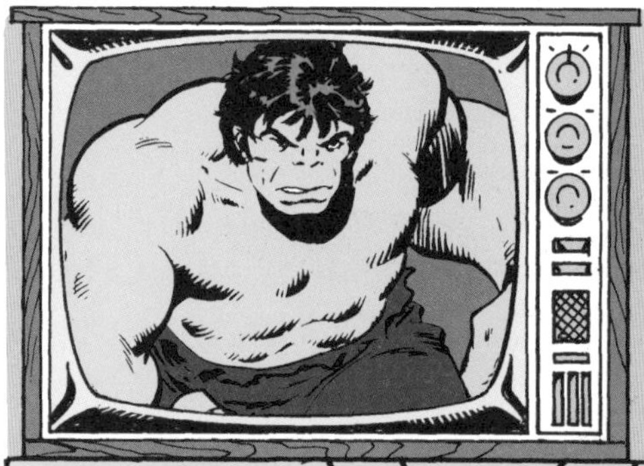

# HULK SMASHES THE SMALL SCREEN

Solve this maze before he gets angry . . . and hurry, before another commercial pops up!

ANSWER PG. 134

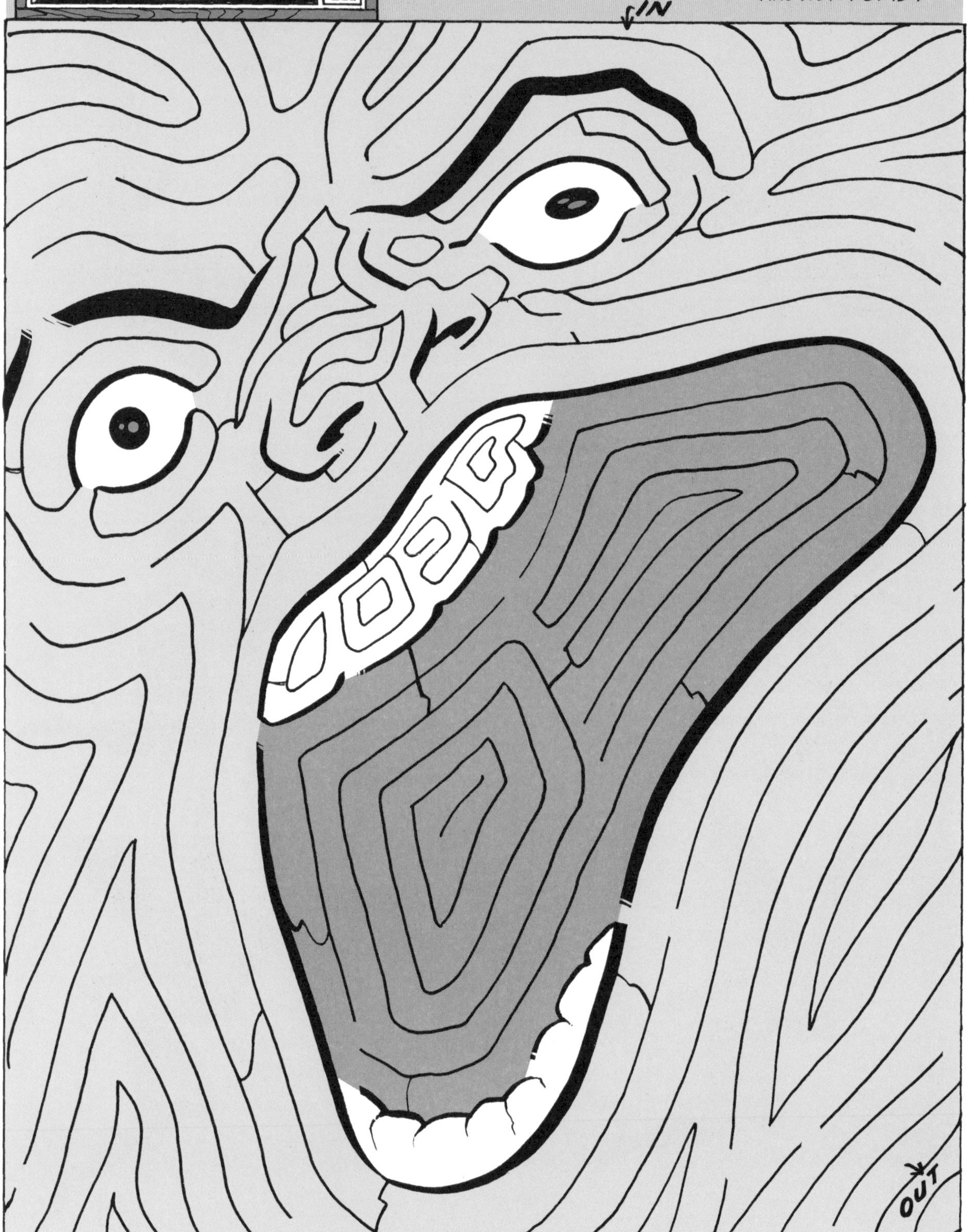
IN
OUT

# YOU FINISH DRAWING DAREDEVIL

## THE MAN WITHOUT FEAR

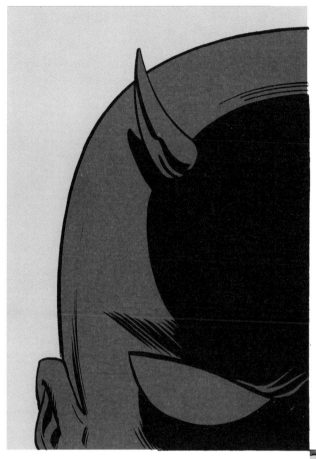

*. . . and color it, too!*

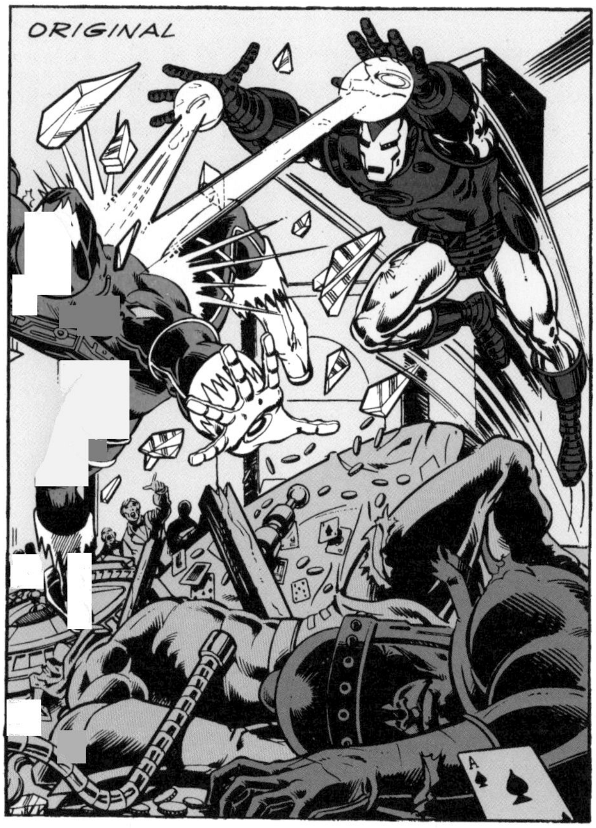
ORIGINAL

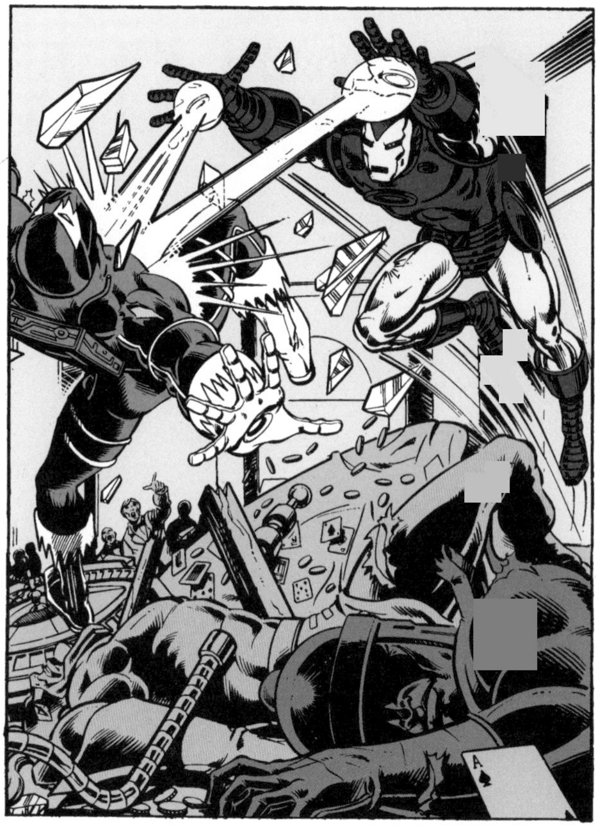

# WHAT'S MISSING

? ? ? ? ? ?

You're still working on WHAT'S MISSING on page 41? Either you've got your glasses on backward or you're using the wrong kind of private eye to help you. Why don't you call Jessica Jones . . . but be sure to ask her "how much" before she starts. After all, this could be the toughest case she ever tackled.

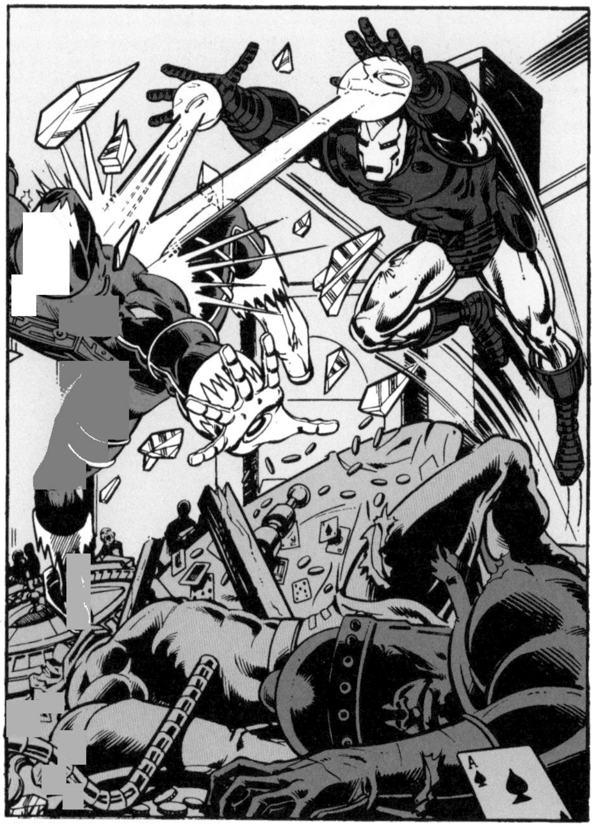

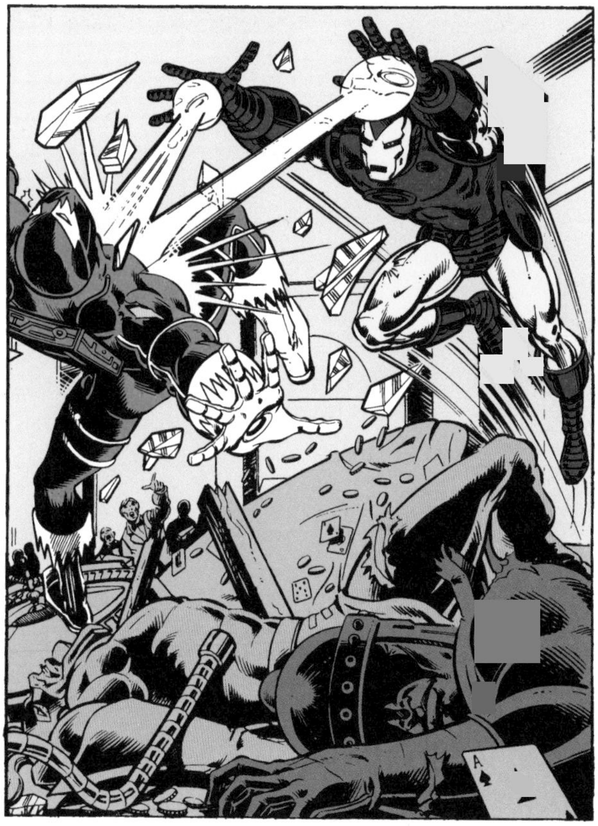

ANSWER PG. 134

# MINI-MARVELS

So. You're a Marvel Super Hero expert! OK, if you say so . . . but we wanna find out for sure. In each of these MINI-MARVELS, there are 10 villains carefully concealed who have met the Super Hero pictured in combat . . . usually the knuckle variety. Your job: Find them . . . before they find you. Lots of luck, expert. Ha!

```
T E S O L A R R N
N A A Y E T S A G
D S B T R A M R O
P R T N O T O T V
O G A S L N R P I
L N O I R A T E P
G L T O B C H S E D E S N
F S R Z O T C O R T A B E
E L E C S E O H T N I L C
N M L T M N G R I A L N O
O T R U O I R M O G R A G
T R E A K W U O N A V M U
S T C L B S A R G W E T M
N A E R S E D E T E P N I
O I O U S O R E S N N A S
O C R T R G S T R A E L S
M C P E T P E H A N I P U
```

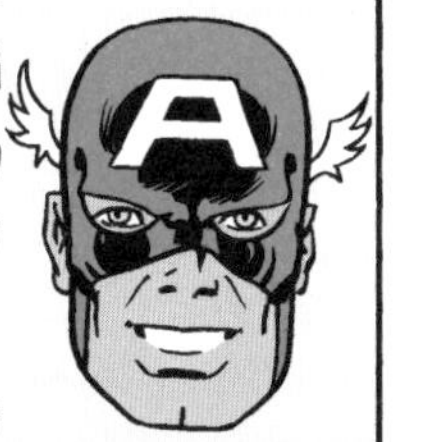

```
G T S P Y M A S T E R M R
M R P K E C D A E I G E M
A O A S O A R T N L T I O
N N X G E D D U P L O L S
B A S T A T O S E N O P O
U M O S A D I M T I Y T O
L T A I M M A D A M M F Y
L R M N A M S D R A U G K
T O G K           A C E D T
S F O A           D H O R U
E E R E           I O O N S
N T O R           M W I O S
T S E F           E C R C T
G X R S           O H O O E
O B L I Z Z A R D C H O N
E R G B T T N N E K A R K
P U T S Y P O N M T E N F
```

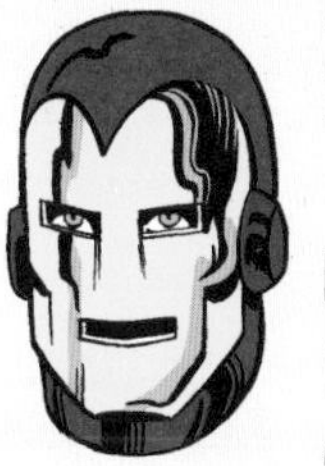

```
L R M O L T E N M A N T L
I O G E T G B O Z R A W S
Z N H L N I N I E O O P D
Z G O V T B L T T R N A C
A D L S U B O I P P R R G
R R L B A O T K Z F E A R
R A C O L N P R S A K Z E
D Z N A M D N A S Z C R E
S I U E J A C V B U O E N
T L R N O E L E M A H C G
R A E S M P L N R X S O O
        Y O R G L D C R B
        D N E I R S P O L
        E T A D Z A R D I
        S J A C K A L F N
        W O A N T S X O T
        C A M E L T R O N
```

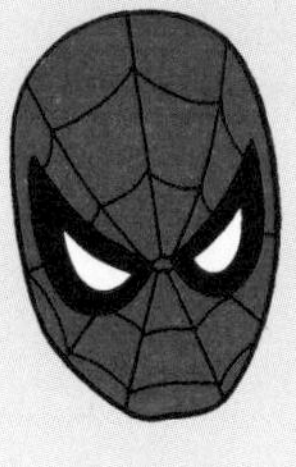

ANSWER PG. 134

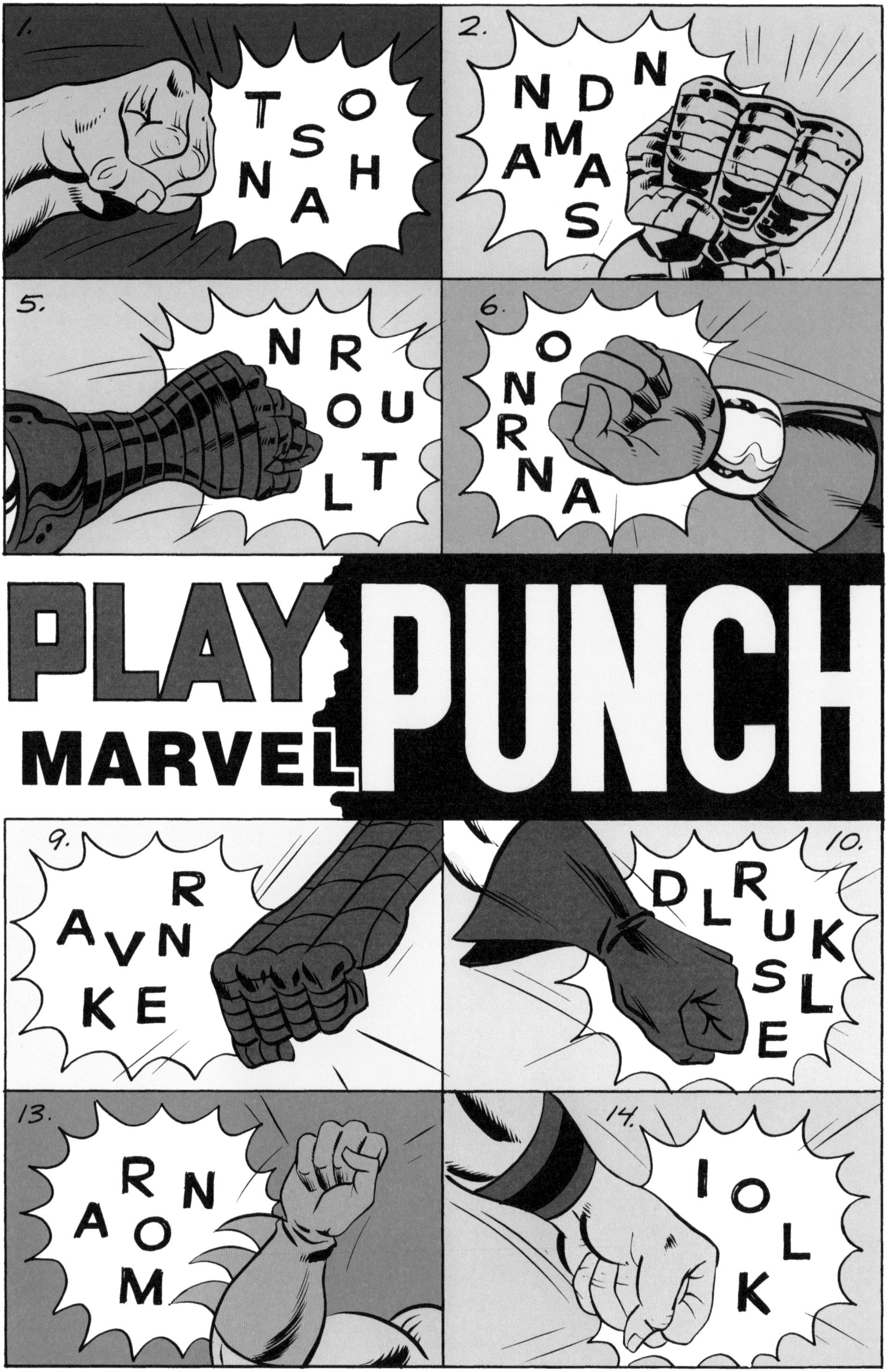
1.
T O S N H A
2.
N D N A M A S
5.
N R O U L T
6.
O N R N A
PLAY MARVEL PUNCH
9.
R A V N K E
10.
D L R U K S L E
13.
R N A O M
14.
I O L K

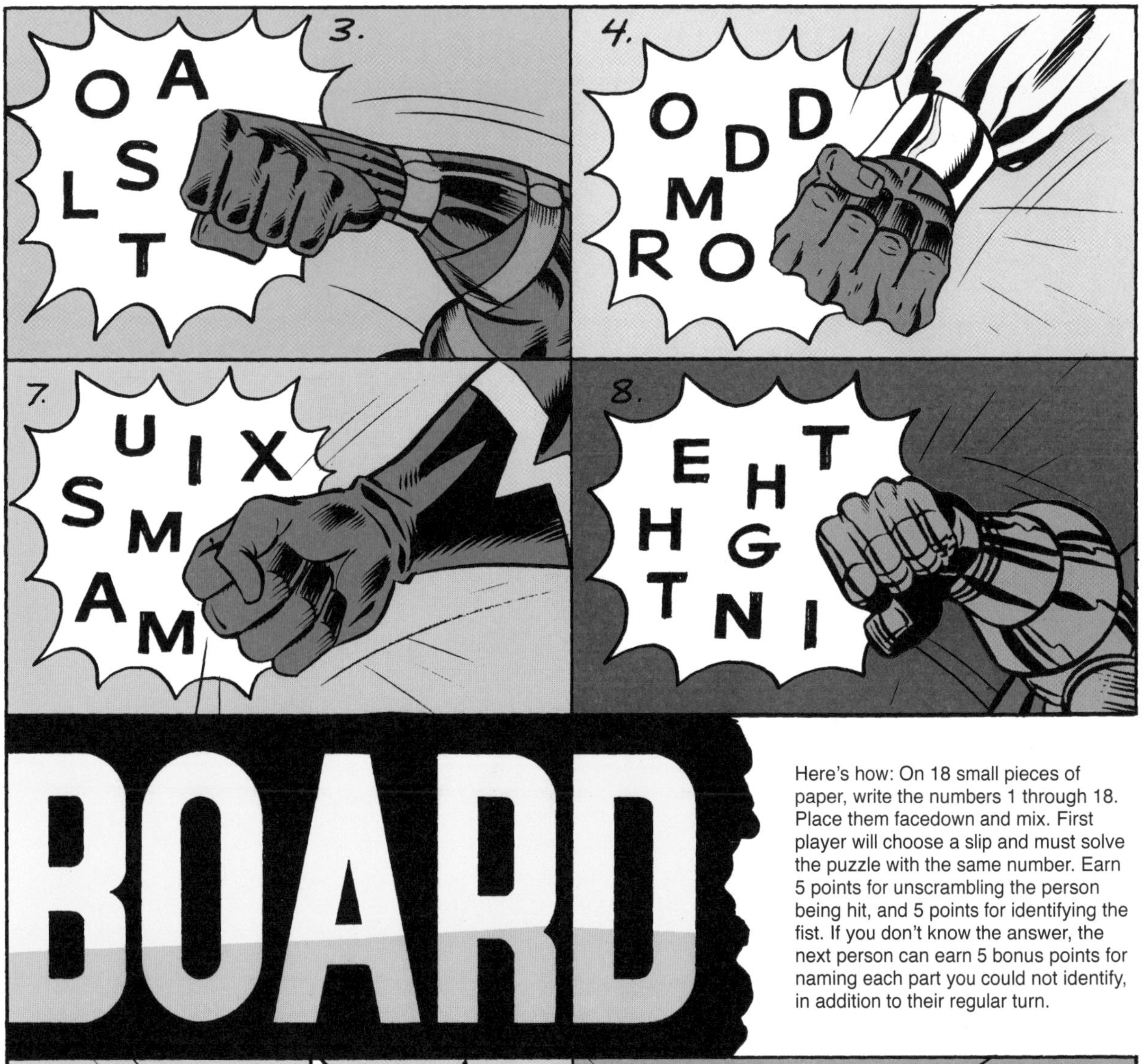

3.
O A S L T
4.
O D D D M R O
7.
U I X S M A M
8.
E T H H G T N I


# BOARD

Here's how: On 18 small pieces of paper, write the numbers 1 through 18. Place them facedown and mix. First player will choose a slip and must solve the puzzle with the same number. Earn 5 points for unscrambling the person being hit, and 5 points for identifying the fist. If you don't know the answer, the next person can earn 5 bonus points for naming each part you could not identify, in addition to their regular turn.

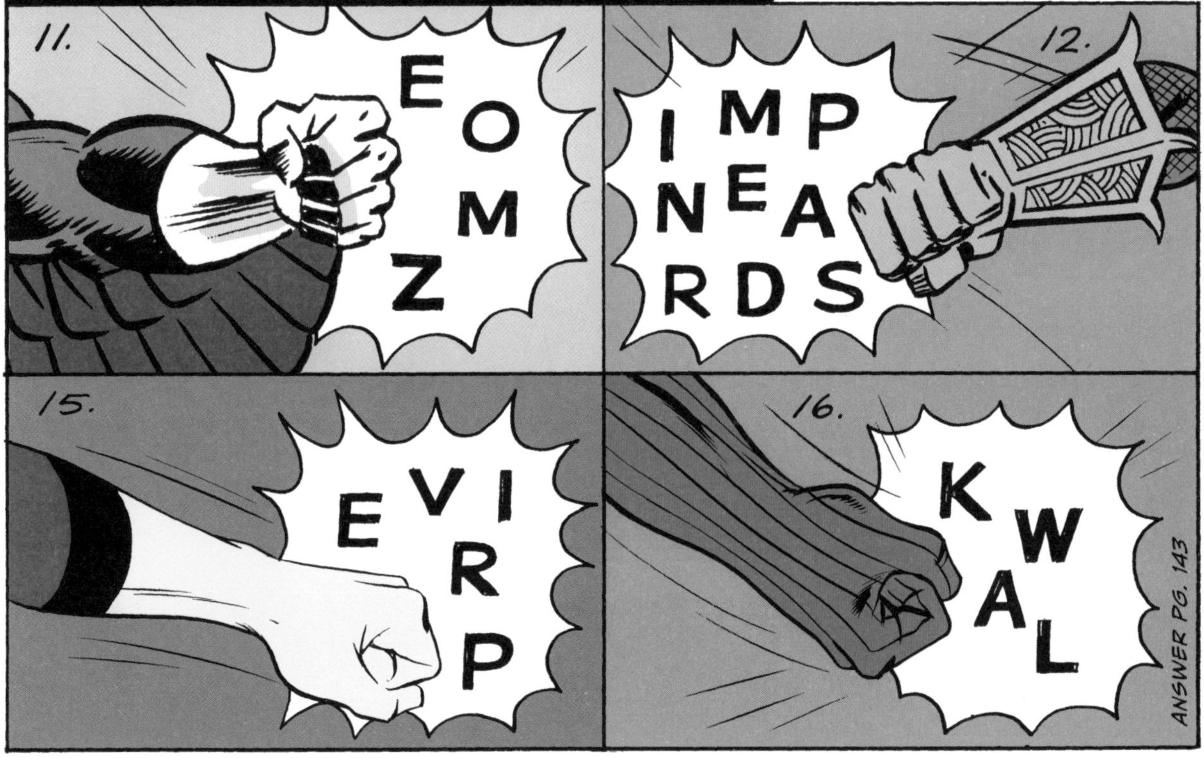

11.
E O M Z
12.
I M P N E A R D S
15.
E V I R P
16.
K W A L
ANSWER PG. 143

# AREN'T YOU THE LUCKY ONE! IT'S POETRY TIME!

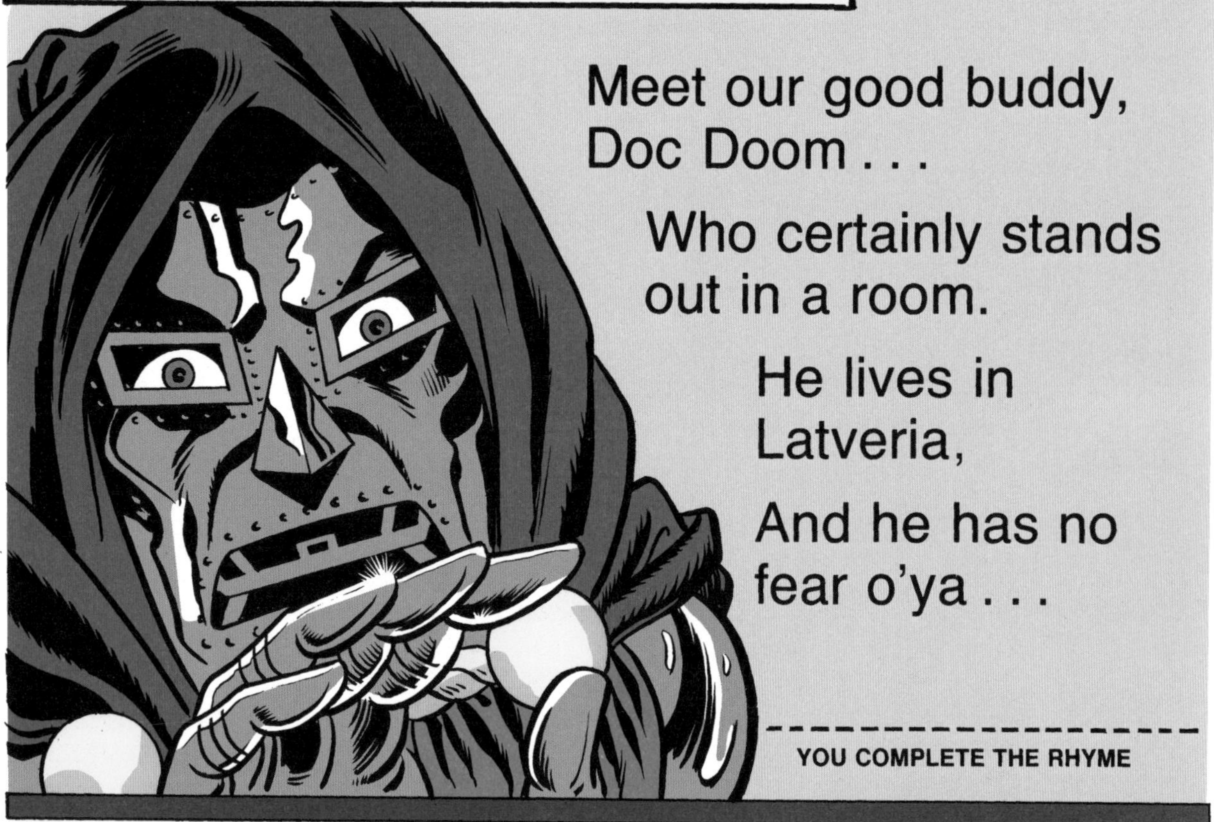
Meet our good buddy, Doc Doom . . .
Who certainly stands out in a room.
He lives in Latveria,
And he has no fear o'ya . . .
YOU COMPLETE THE RHYME

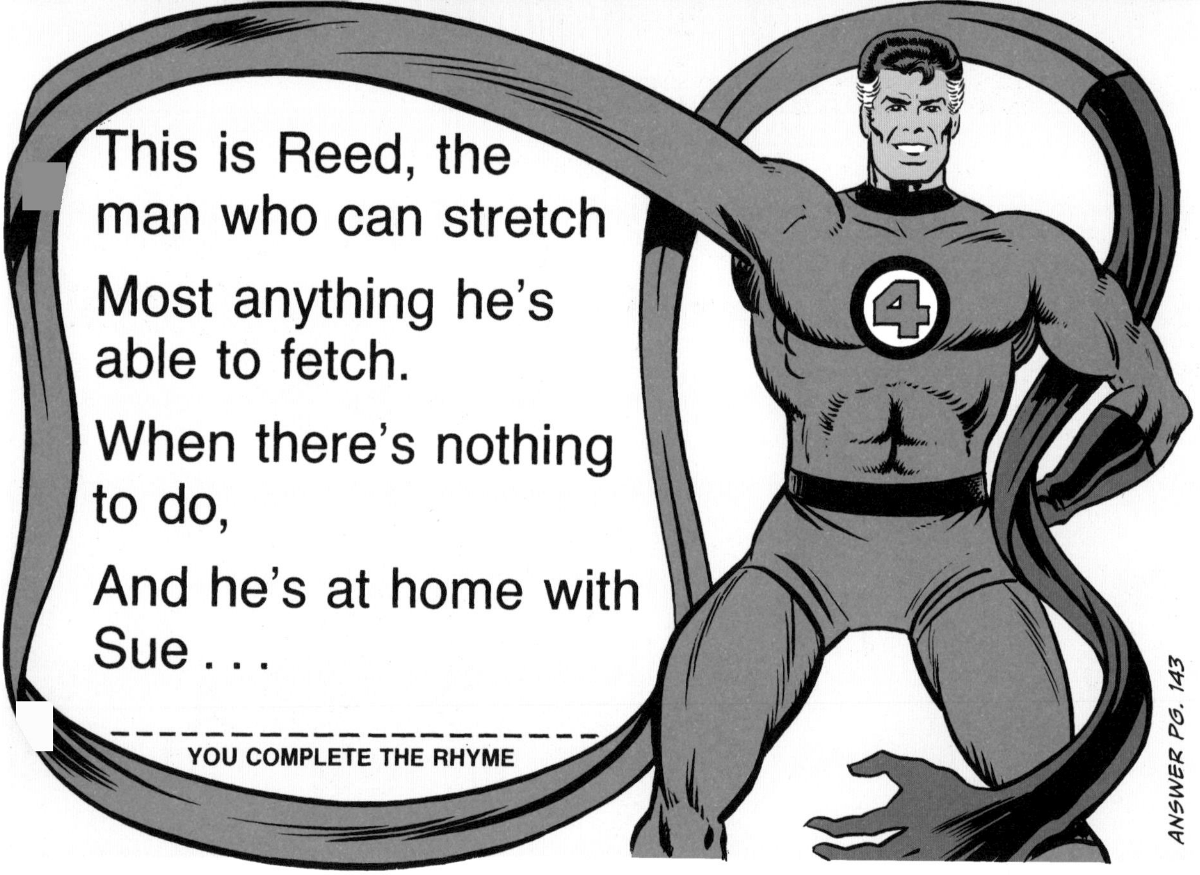
This is Reed, the man who can stretch
Most anything he's able to fetch.
When there's nothing to do,
And he's at home with Sue . . .
YOU COMPLETE THE RHYME

ANSWER PG. 143

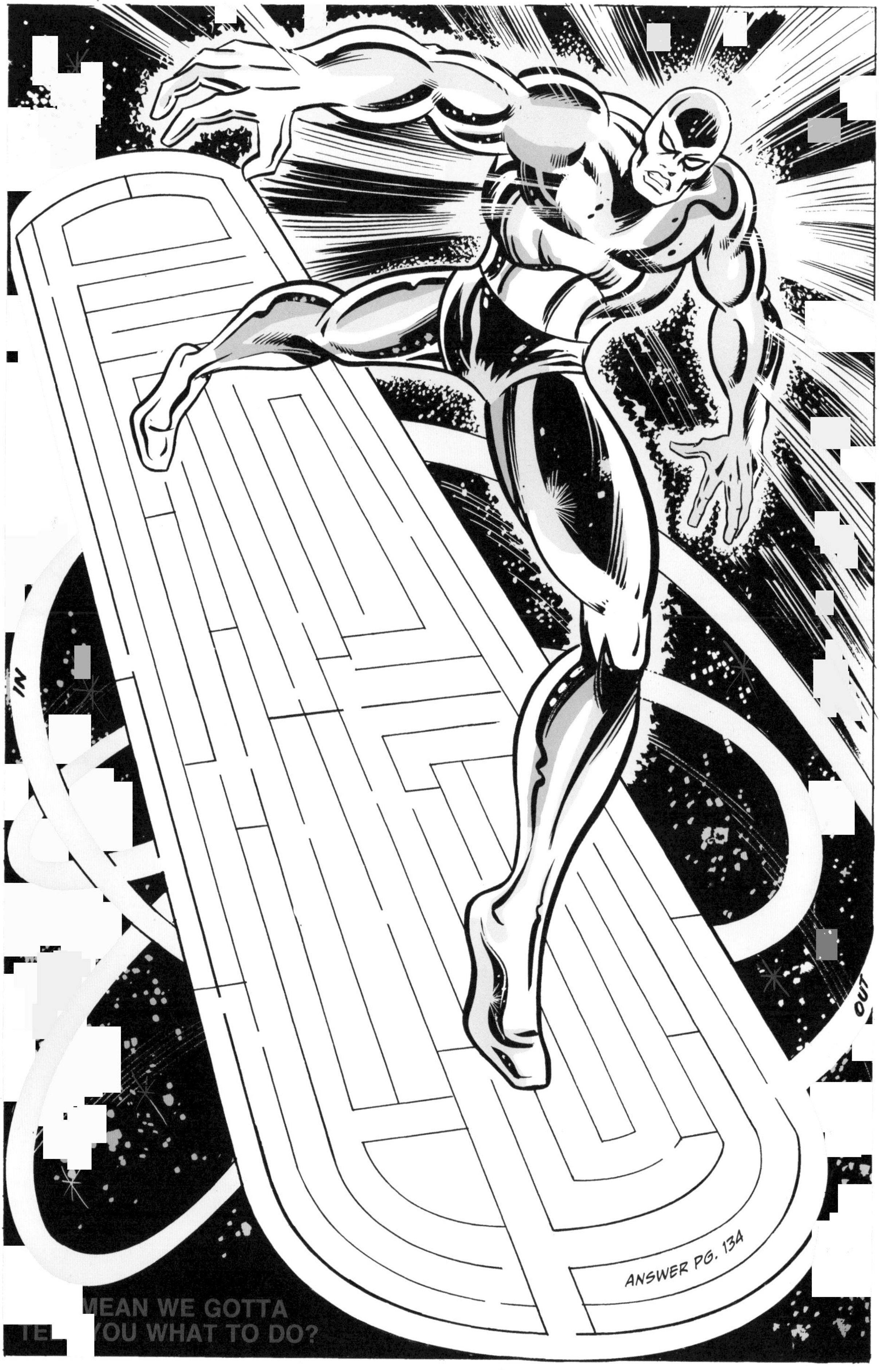
IN
OUT
ANSWER PG. 134
MEAN WE GOTTA
YOU WHAT TO DO?

# OPERATION: SUPER HERO

Only one thing worse than tramping on Benjamin Grimm's toes is getting NICK FURY angry. And he's angry now. Seems every time he sends one of his agents on a mission, the enemy knows the location within minutes. So he has come up with a foolproof idea. The name of each Super Hero below has the name of a place, outside North America, hidden in it. You find it and we know you won't tell anyone. Promise?

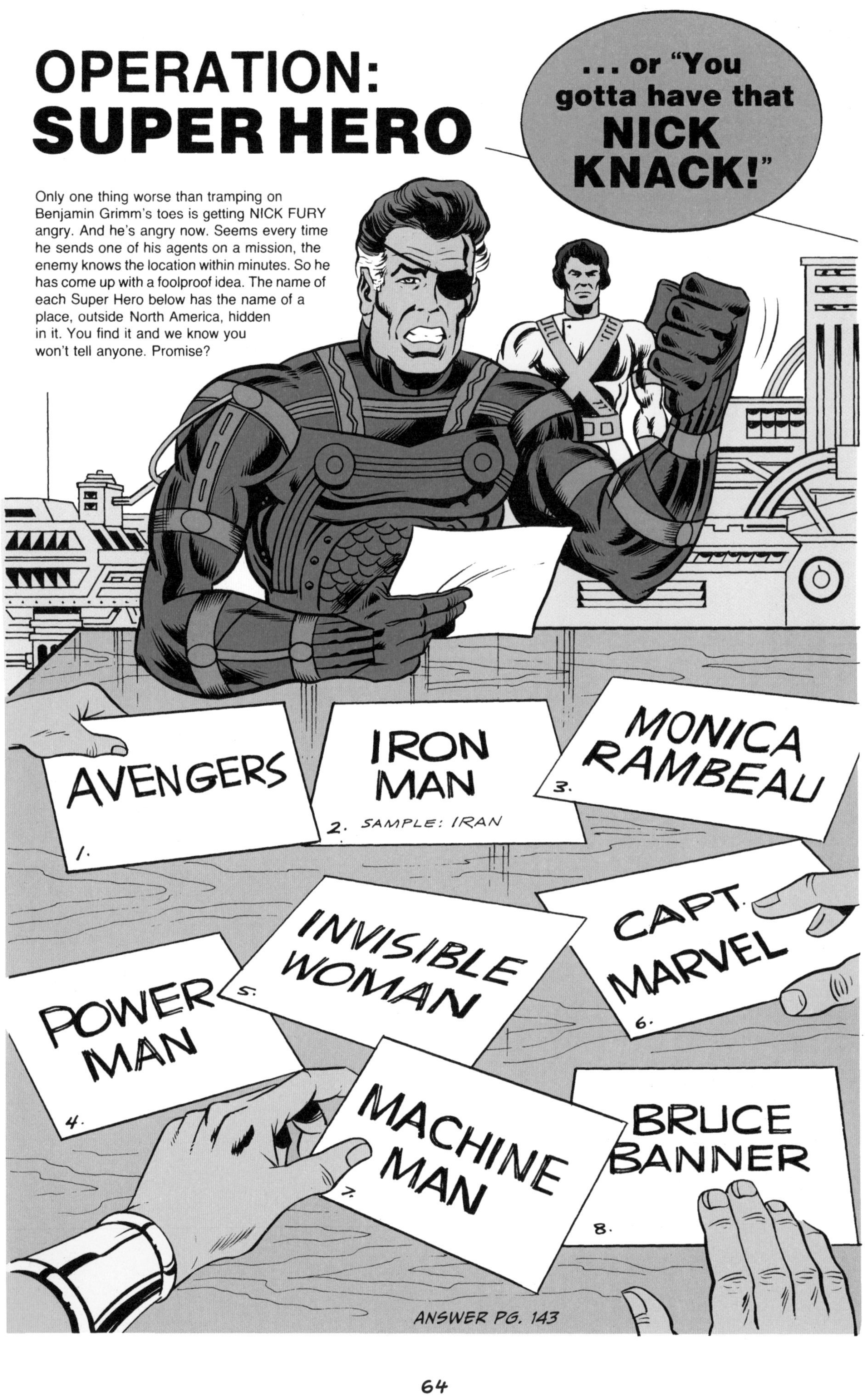
... or "You gotta have that NICK KNACK!"
AVENGERS 1.
IRON MAN 2. SAMPLE: IRAN
MONICA RAMBEAU 3.
POWER MAN 4.
INVISIBLE WOMAN 5.
CAPT. MARVEL 6.
MACHINE MAN 7.
BRUCE BANNER 8.

ANSWER PG. 143

# WHAT'S MISSING?

A total of 6 things are different between these drawings. Compare one against the other, and you should have no problems. The Hulk took only 5 days to find them all. That's how easy it is.

GREAT ACTION SHOTS LIKE THIS ON EVERY MARVEL COVER!

ANSWER PG. 135

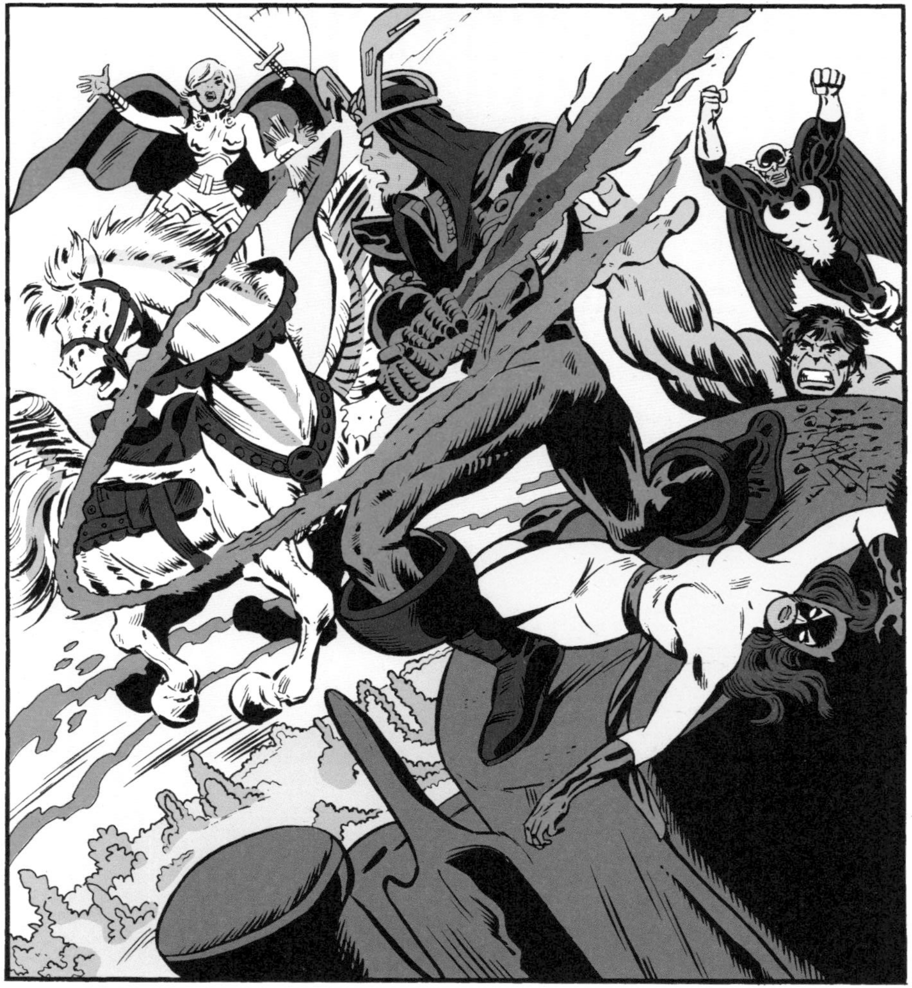

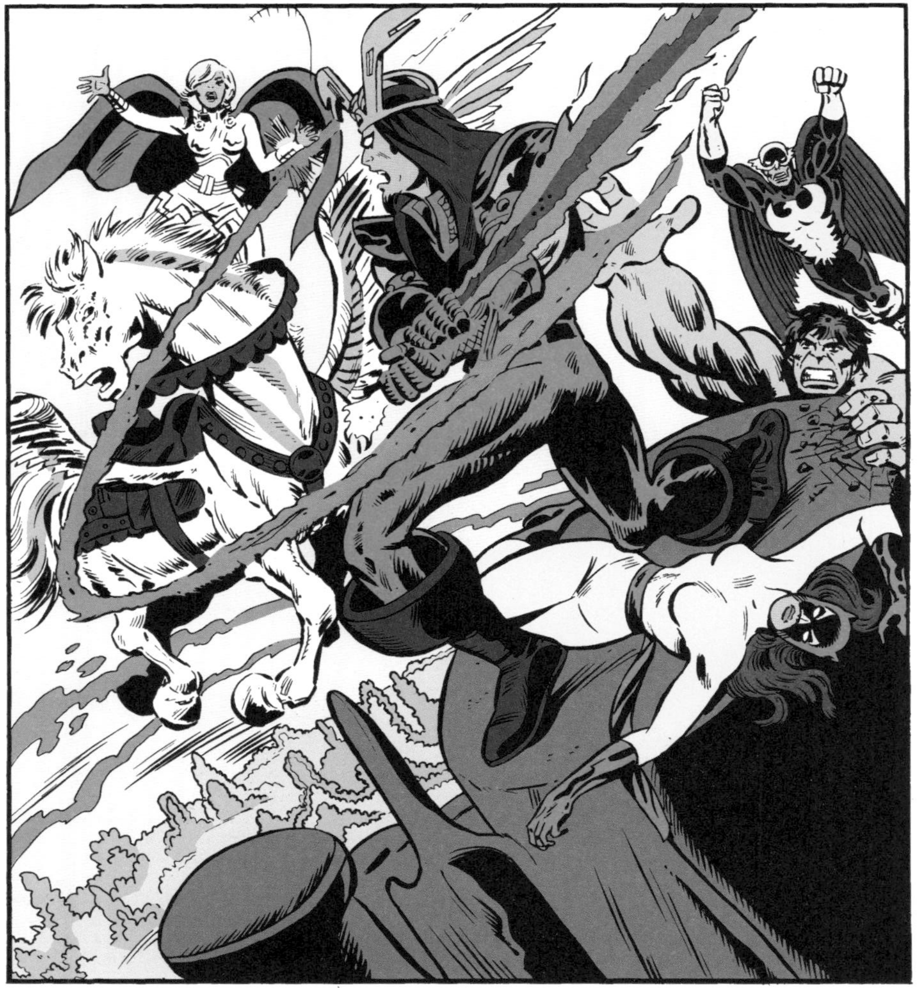

# THE EARLY BIRD GET

## . . . MINDWORM

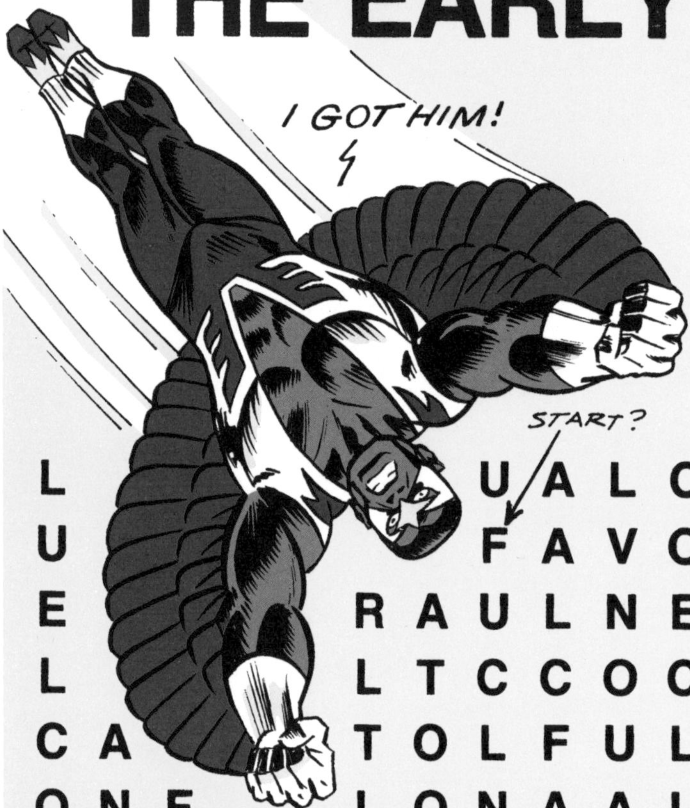
I GOT HIM!
START?

Here's a LETTER MAZE that
have you climbing up the side
your nest. Only ONE of these bi
folk can reach Mindworm . . .
*which one?* That's your problem .
all we have to do is dream up t
stuff. Spell FALCON or VULTU

### *LET'S G*

| | | | | | | | | | | | | | | | | | | |
|---|---|---|---|---|---|---|---|---|---|---|---|---|---|---|---|---|---|---|
| L | | | | | | | U | A | L | C | U | L | T | U | L | C | E | U |
| U | | | | | | | F | A | V | O | V | N | F | A | R | F | N | N |
| E | | | | | R | A | U | L | N | E | O | V | A | U | L | E | F | T |
| L | | | | | L | T | C | C | O | C | R | L | L | C | V | N | A | L |
| C | A | | | | T | O | L | F | U | L | T | U | C | T | O | E | L | U |
| O | N | F | | | L | O | N | A | A | L | F | N | O | U | R | C | V | C |
| L | A | F | E | V | O | C | L | N | C | A | V | U | L | A | L | U | O | L |
| C | A | V | L | A | U | N | T | F | A | E | L | C | V | F | U | N | L | T |
| O | N | C | F | N | F | L | L | U | R | A | T | L | O | N | A | L | U | F |
| T | U | F | O | L | U | A | C | F | L | U | F | N | V | U | V | E | A | E |
| L | A | N | R | E | V | T | O | C | O | A | V | C | N | L | C | L | R | U |
| V | C | U | A | F | L | N | U | L | N | F | E | U | T | O | C | O | L | A |
| O | T | L | L | O | U | F | R | O | A | L | R | O | N | L | O | F | N | |
| N | E | C | U | V | A | E | C | U | V | E | C | O | F | F | V | R | | |
| R | L | O | V | A | E | L | F | L | R | F | A | U | A | E | U | L | | |
| F | T | E | N | F | R | U | T | O | U | T | L | V | R | V | T | U | | |
| C | A | C | R | T | U | C | R | L | R | E | V | T | U | U | R | E | | |
| U | V | N | U | O | L | U | E | V | A | N | U | L | F | L | O | R | | |
| E | N | R | U | N | F | V | L | A | F | O | L | A | L | T | U | B | | |
| F | C | V | N | U | R | E | C | L | C | U | A | T | N | U | V | L | U | A |

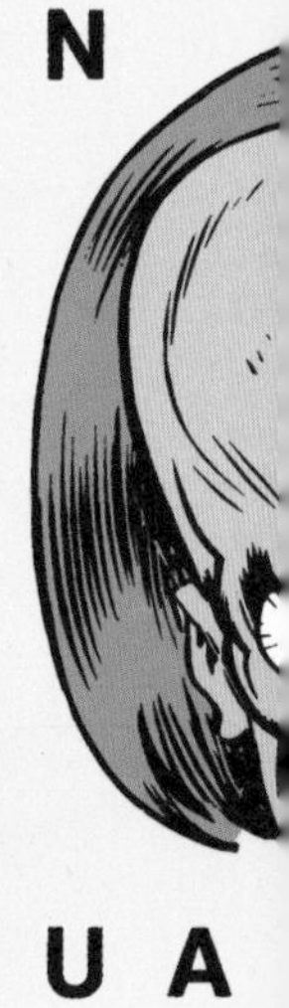

# THE WORM!

## HAT IS!!

ter by letter . . . over and over til you reach the target. You n go horizontal, vertical, back-rd, and diagonal, and you *n't* have to go in straight lines. t you don't get there first try.

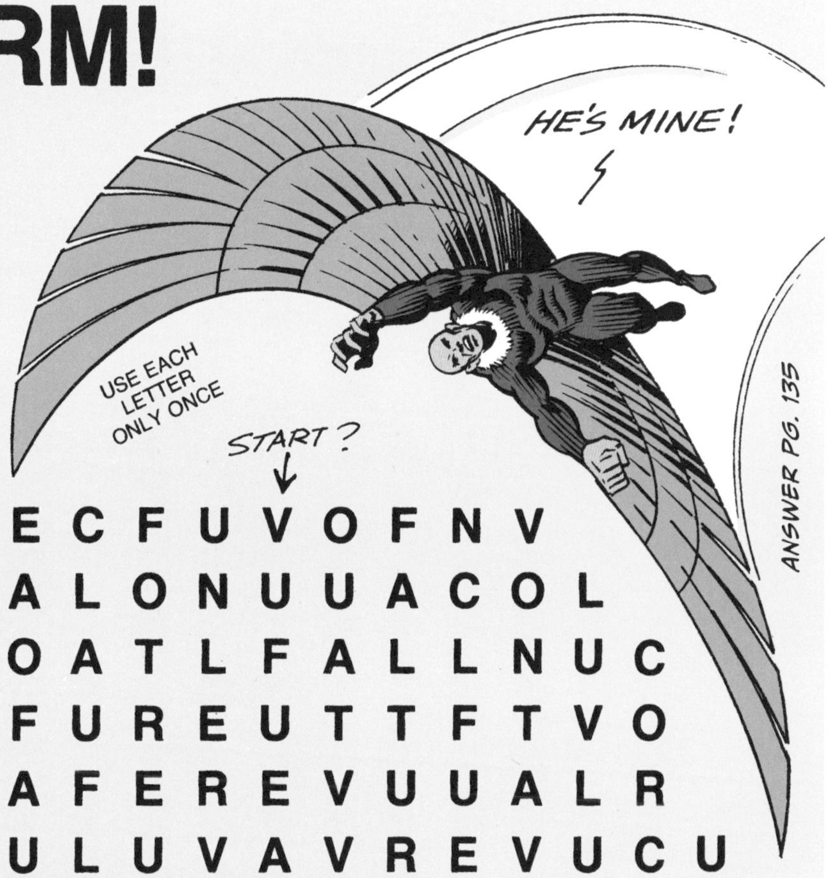

HE'S MINE!
USE EACH LETTER ONLY ONCE
START?


ANSWER PG. 135

## IRD LOVERS!

F U R E O N E C F U V O F N V

O A T C V F A L O N U U A C O L

C U L O U R O A T L F A L L N U C

F V C N L N F U R E U T T F T V O

E A E C O T A F E R E V U U A L R

L E U L U R U L U V A V R E V U C U

C T N T A E C T C F U E V U N O T V

A O A F L O L N O U L E U L T L F L

T U C C N F A F N F R T A R V U A U

C L N F E O L O A L A F E L E C R L

U F A N F C R C T C U V L U R E O V

L V C A L E N U O U C C T U V N R N

A E V V T V R U A F N L U T U A E

C F R F U V E L C F A L C L C V O

N U T L L U V O N T N O N U L F

O N O C T O C U E F E F L O N T

C F U L N U R L A R A E C T F E

L A L A F V E U T L V L R U A L

E U E A R U L R E E U N O E L R N

A L F V C F T R T U R U F L C R A O

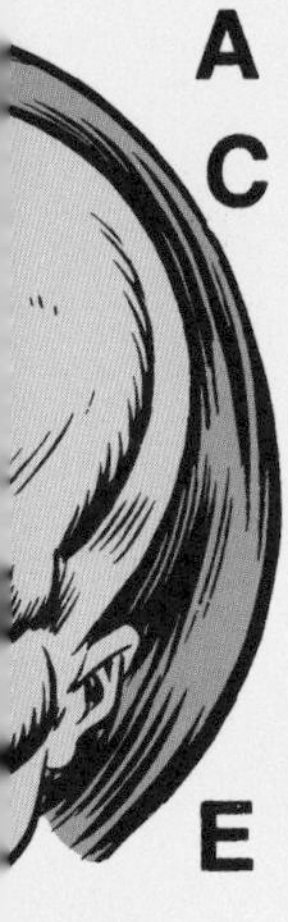

AS YOU ALL KNOW . . .

# THE CHAMELEON

CAN CHANGE HIS FACE TO WHOEVER HE DESIRES!

*Now . . . YOU get the chance to change it for him!*

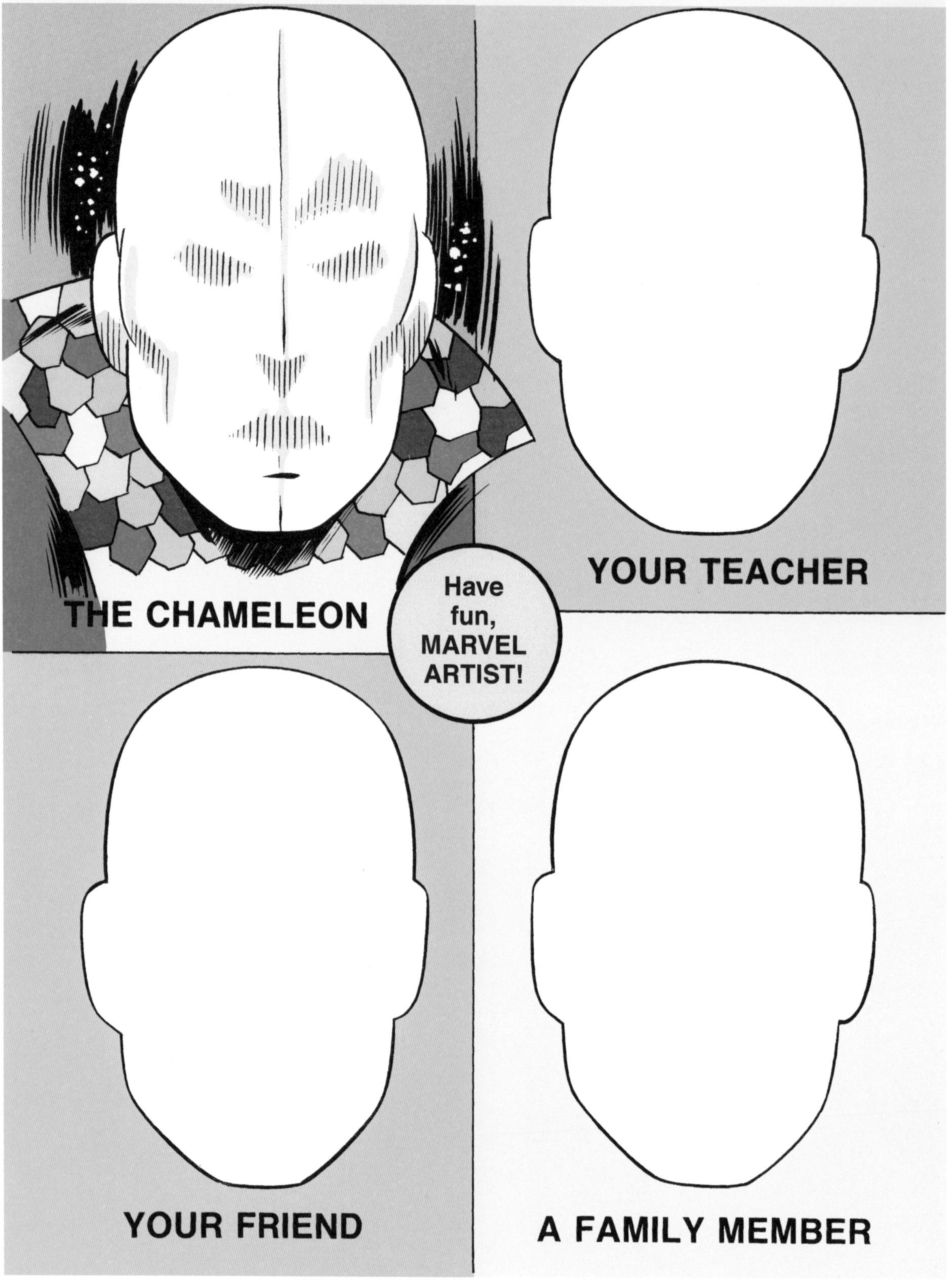
THE CHAMELEON
Have fun, MARVEL ARTIST!
YOUR TEACHER
YOUR FRIEND
A FAMILY MEMBER

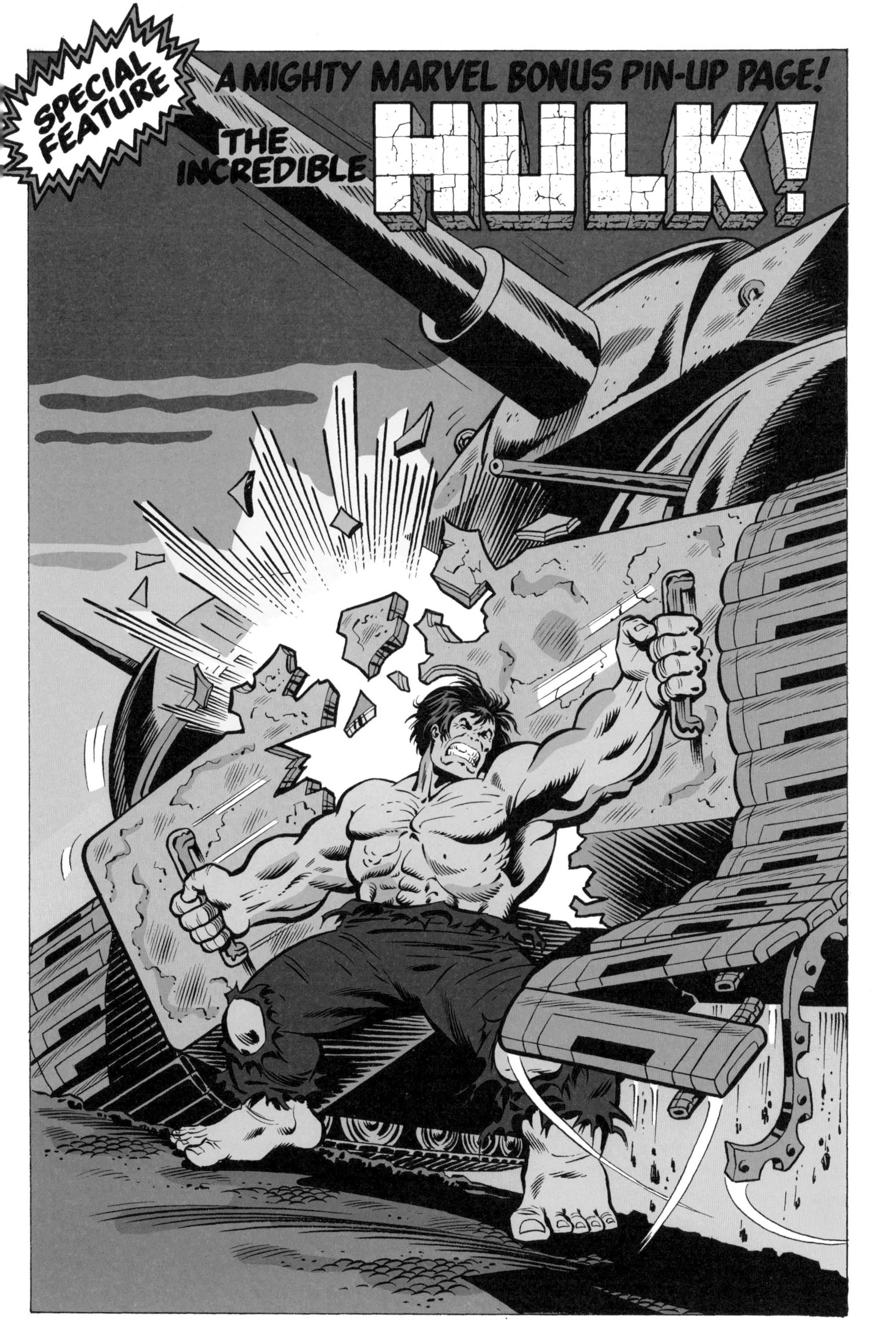
SPECIAL FEATURE
A MIGHTY MARVEL BONUS PIN-UP PAGE!
THE INCREDIBLE HULK!

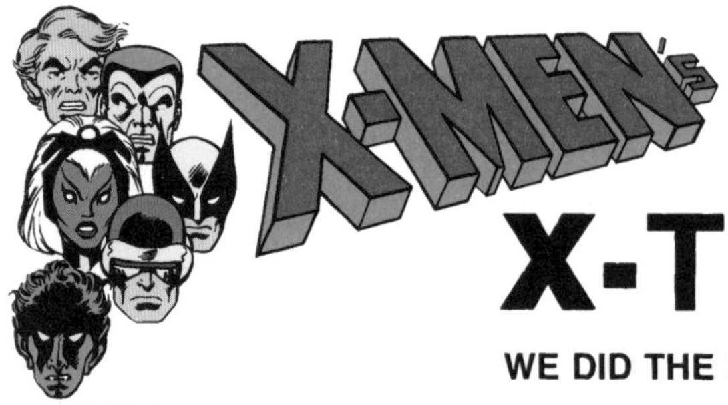
X-MEN'S

# X-WORD X-TRAVAGANZA

**WE DID THE HARDEST PART — PUTTING THE FREE X IN THE RIGHT PLACE. THE REST IS UP TO YOU, "X" X-PERT!**

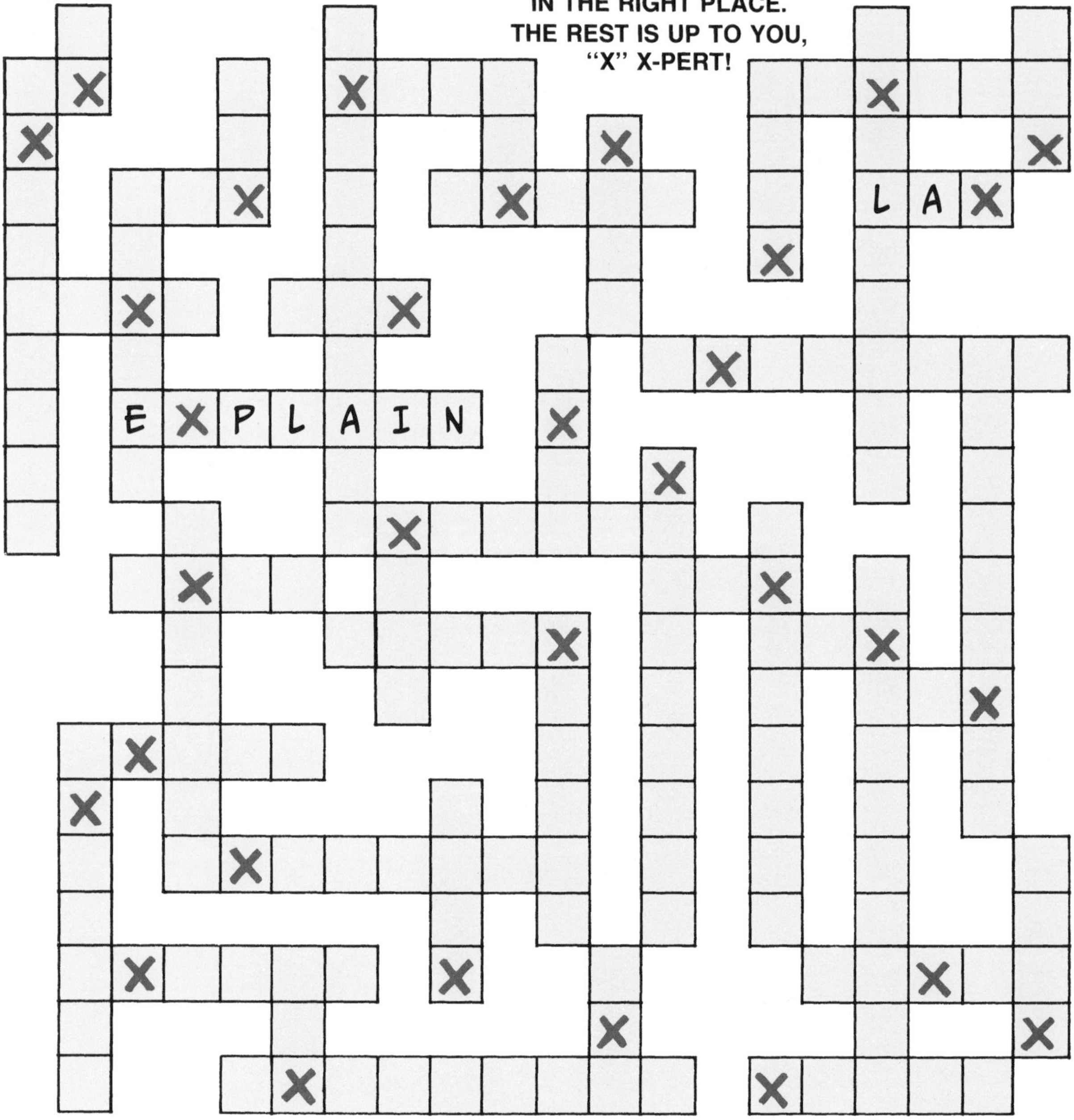
LAX
EXPLAIN

**PUT ALL THESE WORDS IN THEIR X-ACT PLACE, X-PERSON!**

2-LETTERS

RX
EX

3-LETTERS

TAX
REX
VEX
FOX
LAX
LOX
EXO-
HEX
SIX
POX
BOX

4-LETTERS

ALEX
KNOX
MARX
XMAS
NEXT
EXAM
X-MEN
EXIT
X-RAY

5-LETTERS

EXTRA
PIXIE
XENON
REMIX
EXUDE

6-LETTERS

EXPERT
MEXICO
BAXTER
XAVIER

7-LETTERS

EXCLUDE
EXPRESS
EXPLAIN
EXACTLY

8- TO 10-LETTERS

EXCHANGE
EXPOSURE
EXAMINER
XYLOPHONE
EXCLUSIVE
EXTENSION
EXPLOSION
EQUINOXES
EXHIBITION
EXAGGERATE

ANSWER PG. 135

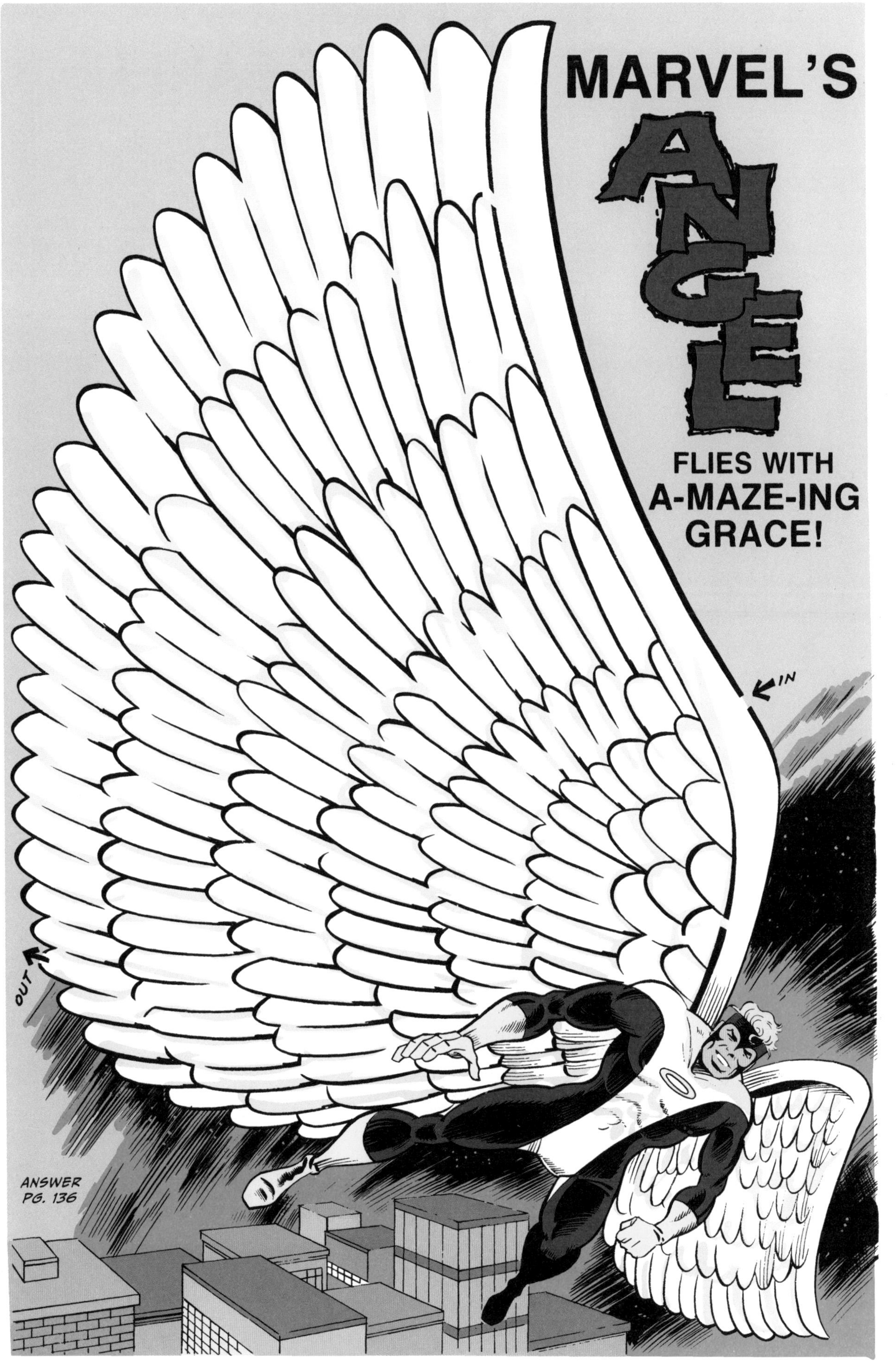
MARVEL'S
ANGEL
FLIES WITH
A-MAZE-ING
GRACE!
IN
OUT
ANSWER
PG. 136

**USE YOUR MARVEL**

# SECRET CODE BREAKER*

**TO DO THIS PUZZLE!**

## TRUE OR FALSE:

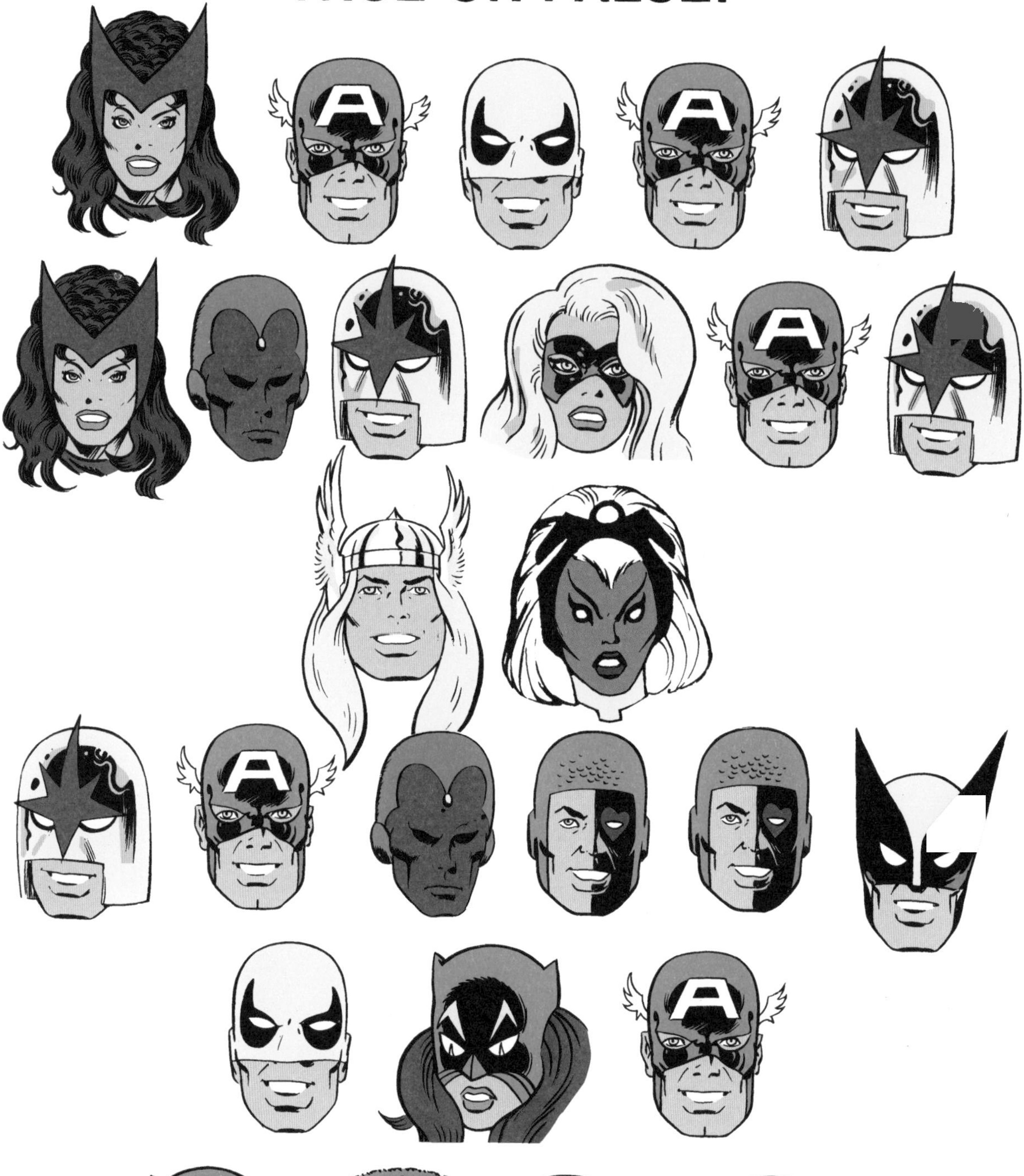

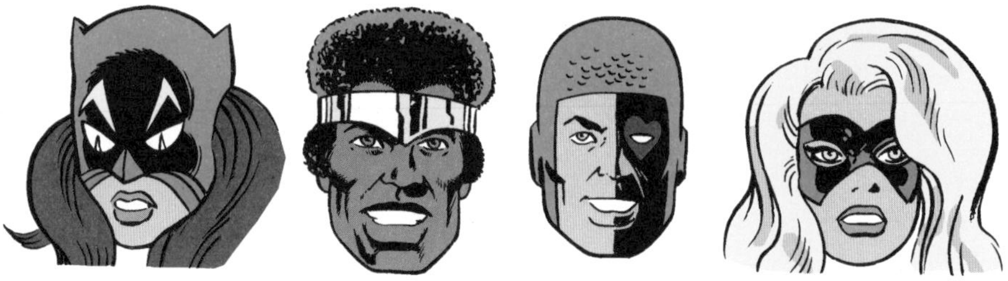

*CHECK PG. 24 TO CRACK THIS ONE!

ANSWER PG. 143

# HELLCAT'S CATNIP CATASTROPHE

Hellcat is trying to round up all her cat friends. Help her out, won't you?

LYNX
LION
JAGUAR
CHEETAH
OCELOT
LEOPARD
PANTHER
MANX
TABBY
SIAMESE
PERSIAN
BURMESE
CORNISH REX
DEVON REX
HAVANA
WILDCAT
ABYSSINIAN
KORAT
BOBTAIL
BALINESE
EGYPTIAN MAU
TONKINESE
BIRMAN
MARGAY
PUMA
TIGER

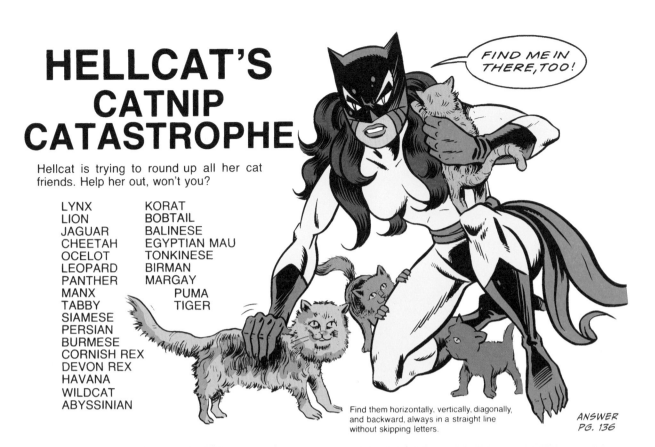

FIND ME IN THERE, TOO!

Find them horizontally, vertically, diagonally, and backward, always in a straight line without skipping letters.

ANSWER PG. 136

```
P A T H N E R E S T L V I S Y M B R J A
E O L M S B D X E R H S I N R O C K C G
R B O B T A I L M E U A T Z S M E H Z D
S M I A A T G C A X M A R G A Y E R Q R
I K O L B R W I I E F W L I H E R Y C B
A Q N I Y A H B S N U G X E T I G E U I
N N H N T O L E C O S N F A T X N G A R
A J N E A I N K L I Y J H W E P L Q M M
I S Y S S I P W I L D C A T A B B Y N A
N P A E K O R R A T C V T D X O E F A N
I I K N K R R E H T N A P C E A S T I U
S K O R A T A T U H N A T S R K E U T S
S T C H A B U O A S T R A X N A M U P A
Y R A D E P G V H K O B B V O I R C Y O
B L L E O P A R D T A K B N V A U Y G N
A B Y S I N J I A T I G E R E K B L E E
B U R M A S E T G I E R B I D M A N C A
```

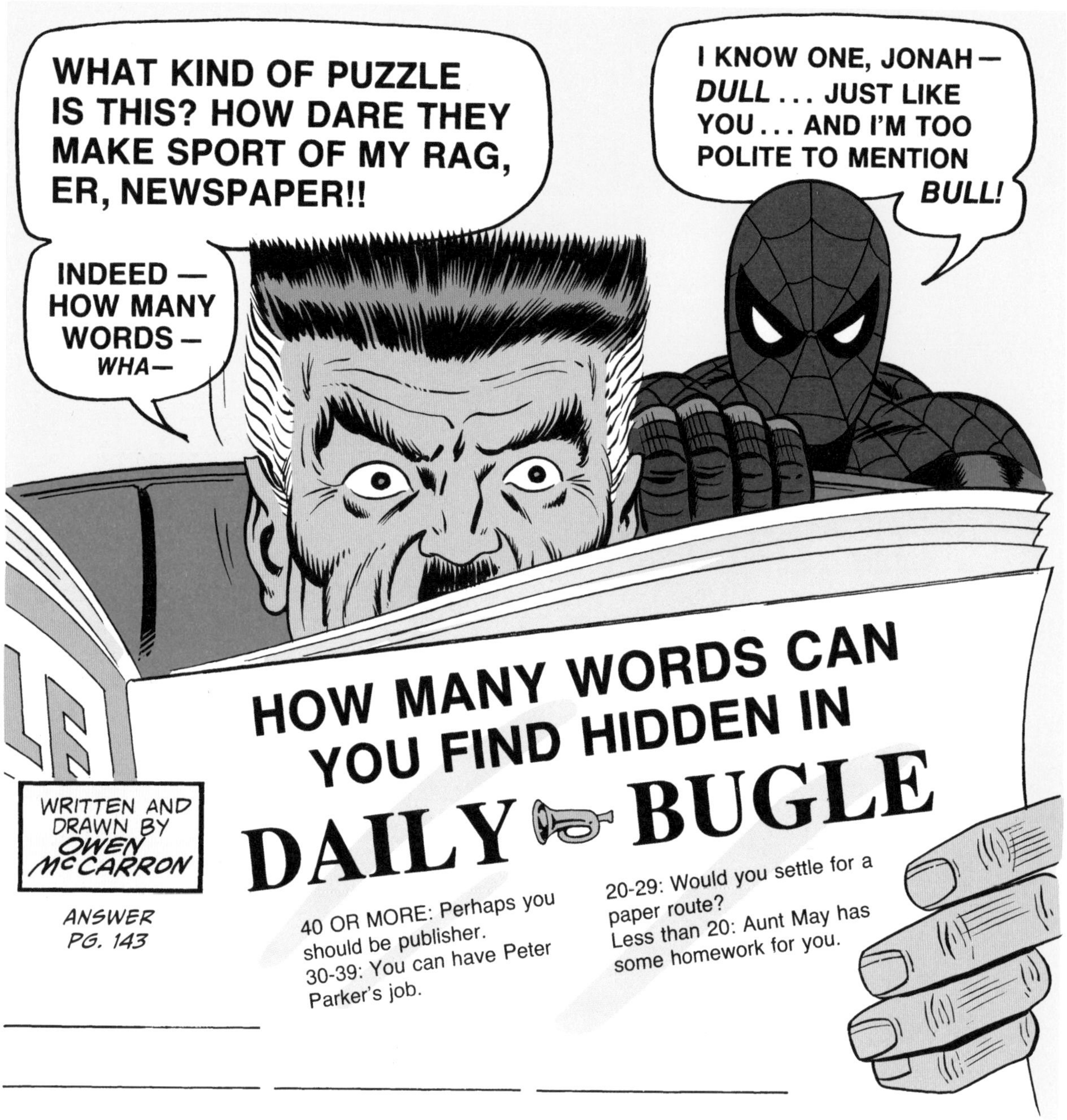
WHAT KIND OF PUZZLE IS THIS? HOW DARE THEY MAKE SPORT OF MY RAG, ER, NEWSPAPER!!
INDEED — HOW MANY WORDS — WHA—
I KNOW ONE, JONAH — DULL . . . JUST LIKE YOU . . . AND I'M TOO POLITE TO MENTION BULL!
HOW MANY WORDS CAN YOU FIND HIDDEN IN
DAILY BUGLE
40 OR MORE: Perhaps you should be publisher.
30-39: You can have Peter Parker's job.
20-29: Would you settle for a paper route?
Less than 20: Aunt May has some homework for you.
WRITTEN AND DRAWN BY OWEN McCARRON

ANSWER PG. 143

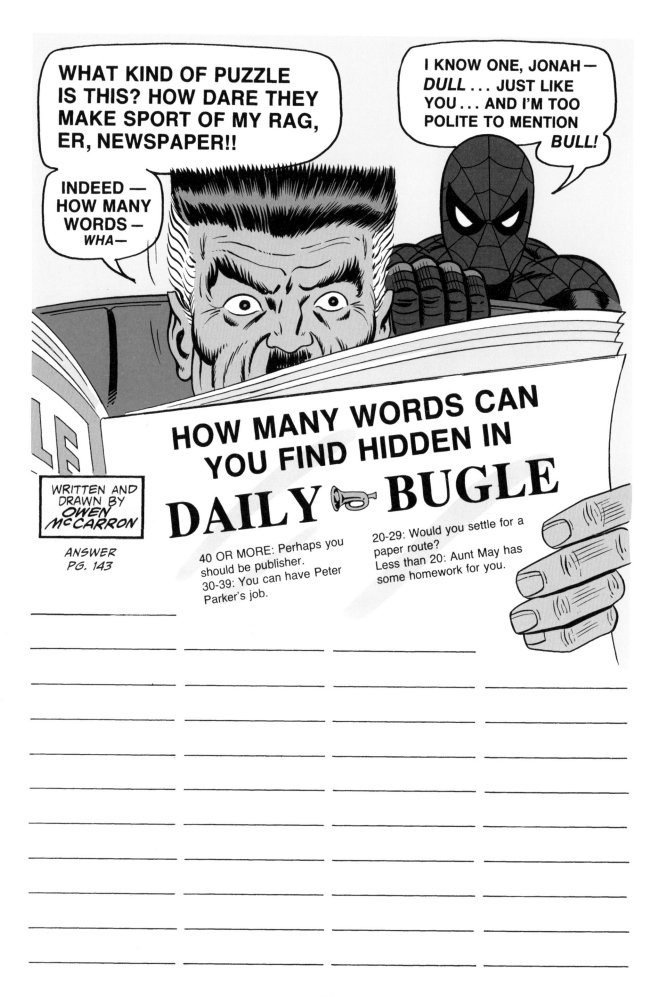

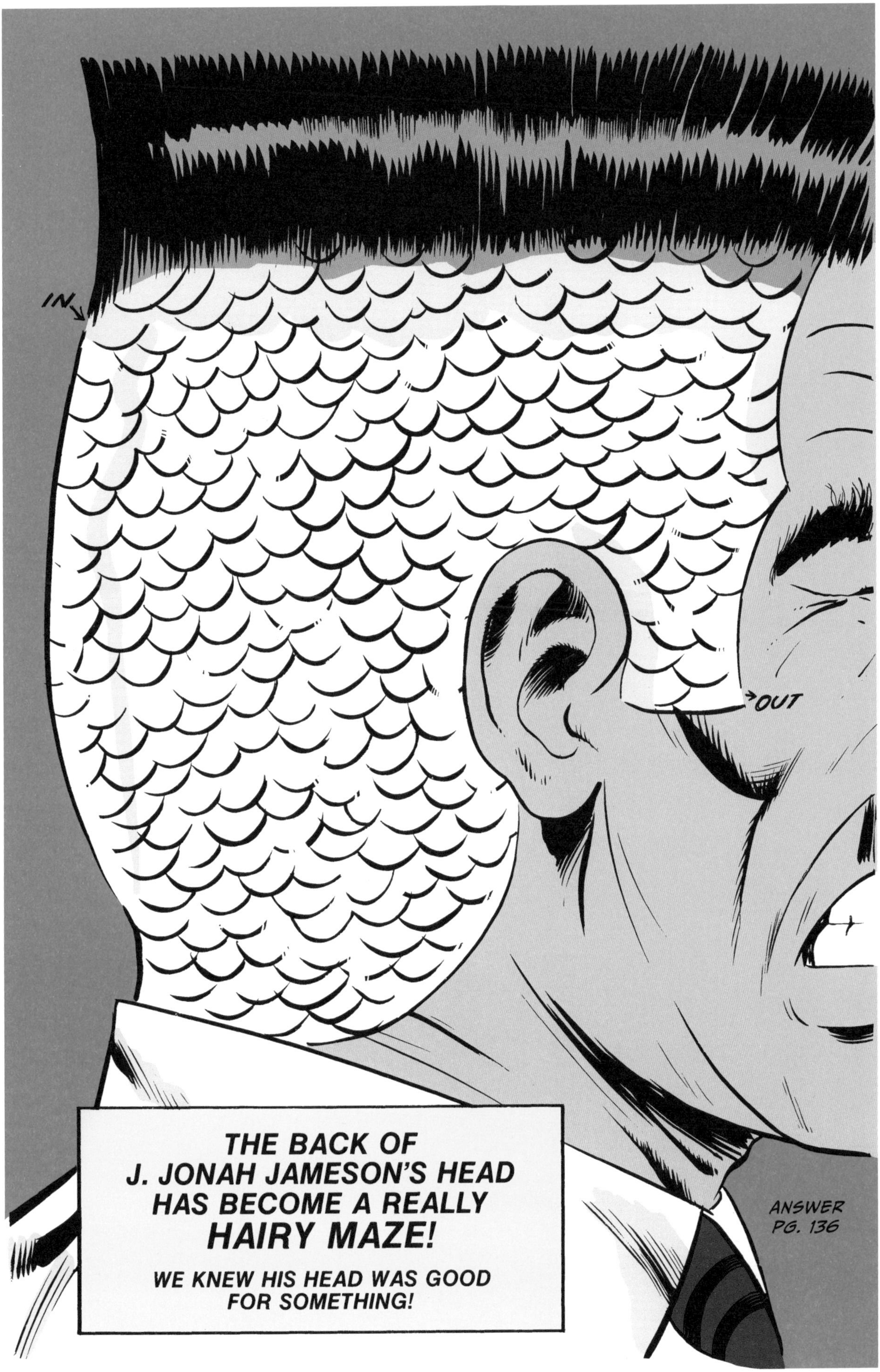
IN
OUT
THE BACK OF J. JONAH JAMESON'S HEAD HAS BECOME A REALLY HAIRY MAZE!
WE KNEW HIS HEAD WAS GOOD FOR SOMETHING!
ANSWER PG. 136

# HOW MANY WORDS CAN YOU FIND HIDDEN IN THE NAME
# SUB-MARINER?

We'll make it easy for you . . . all we want are 39 words.
Orca the Killer Whale could do that well.

*ANSWER PG. 143*

Names of people or places and plurals are not acceptable. That makes it a bit harder, doesn't it?

# IF YOU'VE ALWAYS WANTED TO BE A HAIRDRESSER . . . *THIS IS YOUR BIG OPPORTUNITY!*

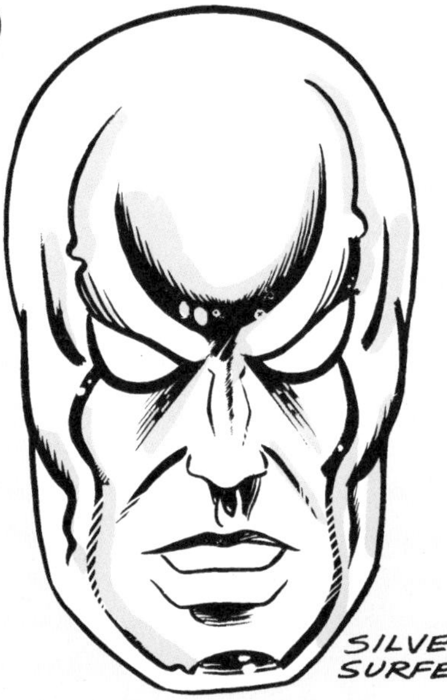

SILVER SURFER

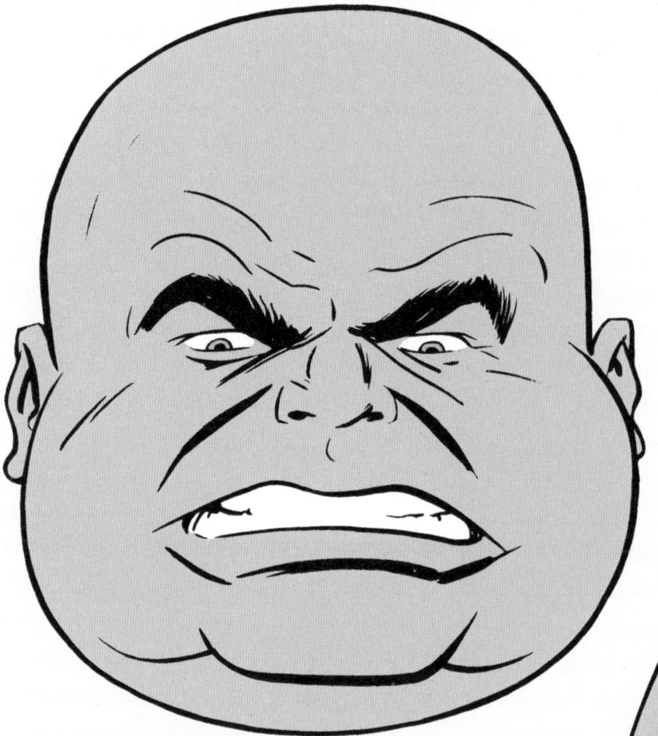

KINGPIN

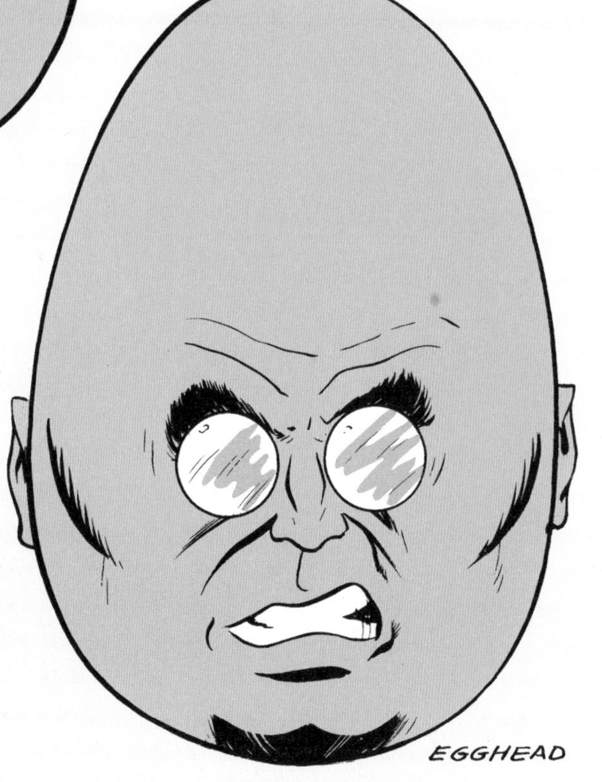

EGGHEAD

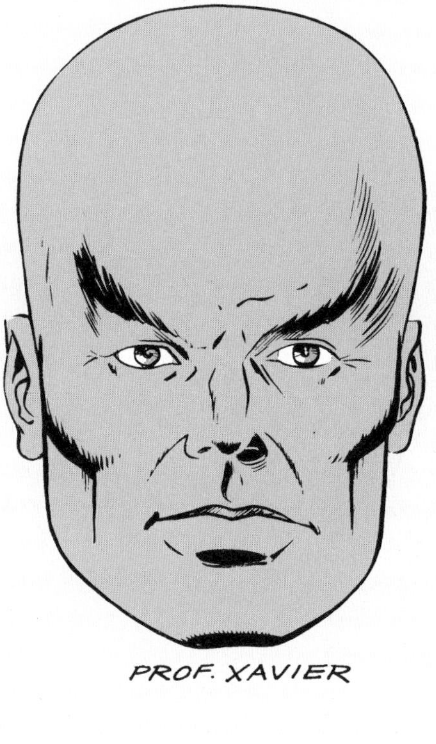

PROF. XAVIER

These four have had many hair-raising adventures over the years . . . without the hair. They have all decided to buy a hairpiece or have a hair transplant but want to give the hairstylist a design. That's your task. Draw (and color) a hairstyle you think would best reflect the personality of these fugitives from a barber shop.

# HOW MANY "THINGS" CAN YOU FIND?

**GET 'EM ALL . . . OR BIG BEN GRIMM MAY TRY TO FIND YOU!**

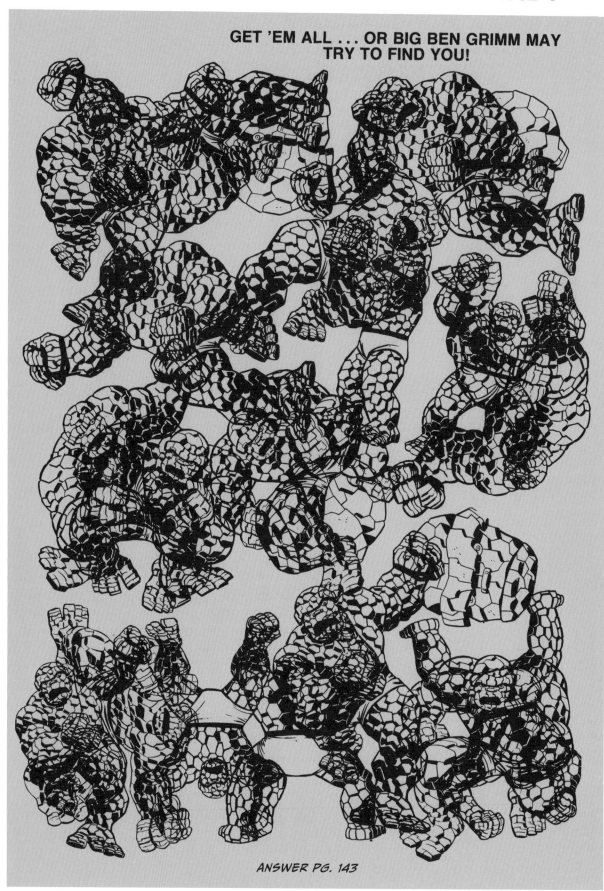

*ANSWER PG. 143*

# PLAY **CHARADES** WITH **BEN GRIMM**

***CLUE: IT'S AN EXPRESSION***

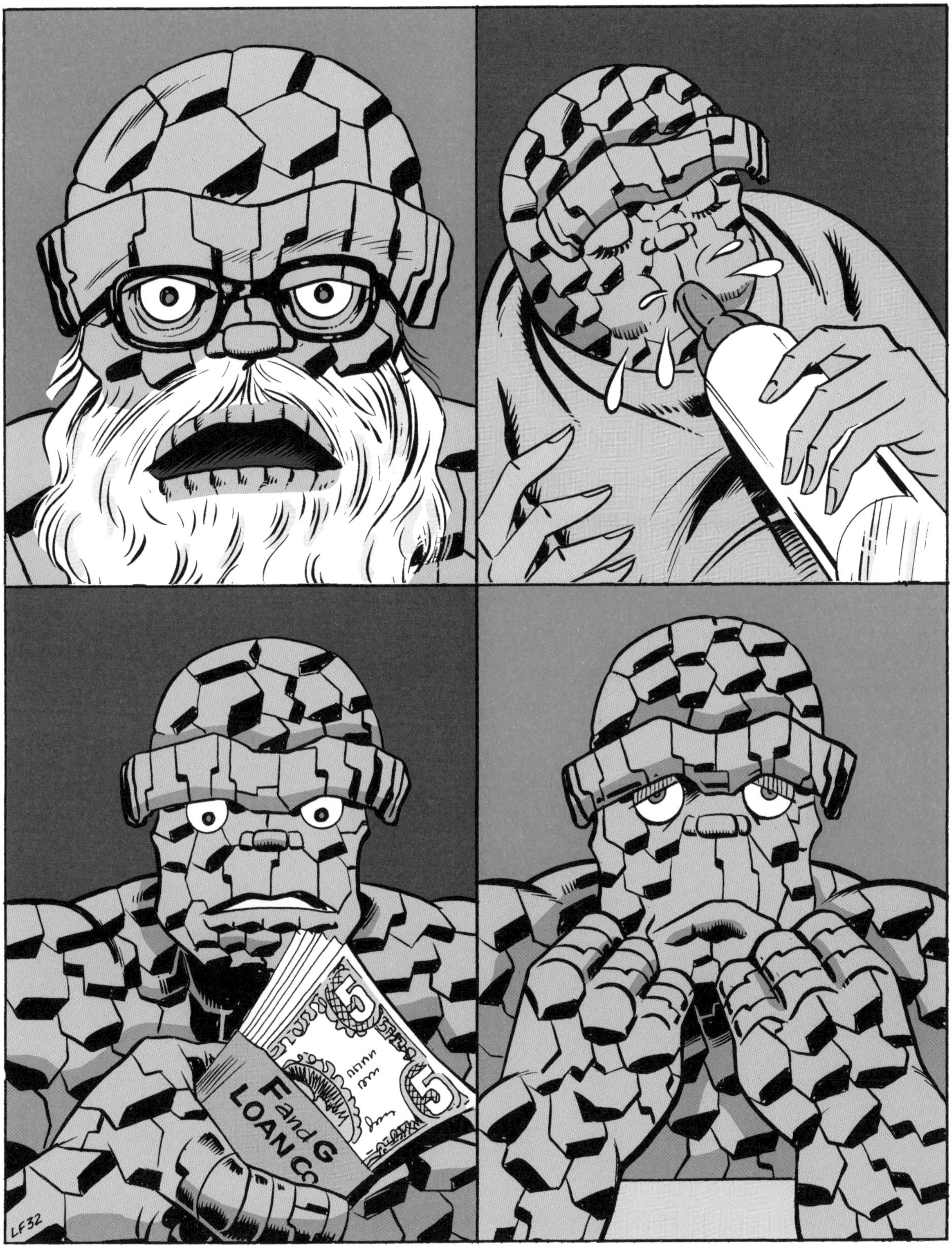
F and G
LOAN Co
LF32

*WRITTEN, DRAWN, AND EDITED BY* ***OWEN McCARRON***

*ANSWER PG. 143*

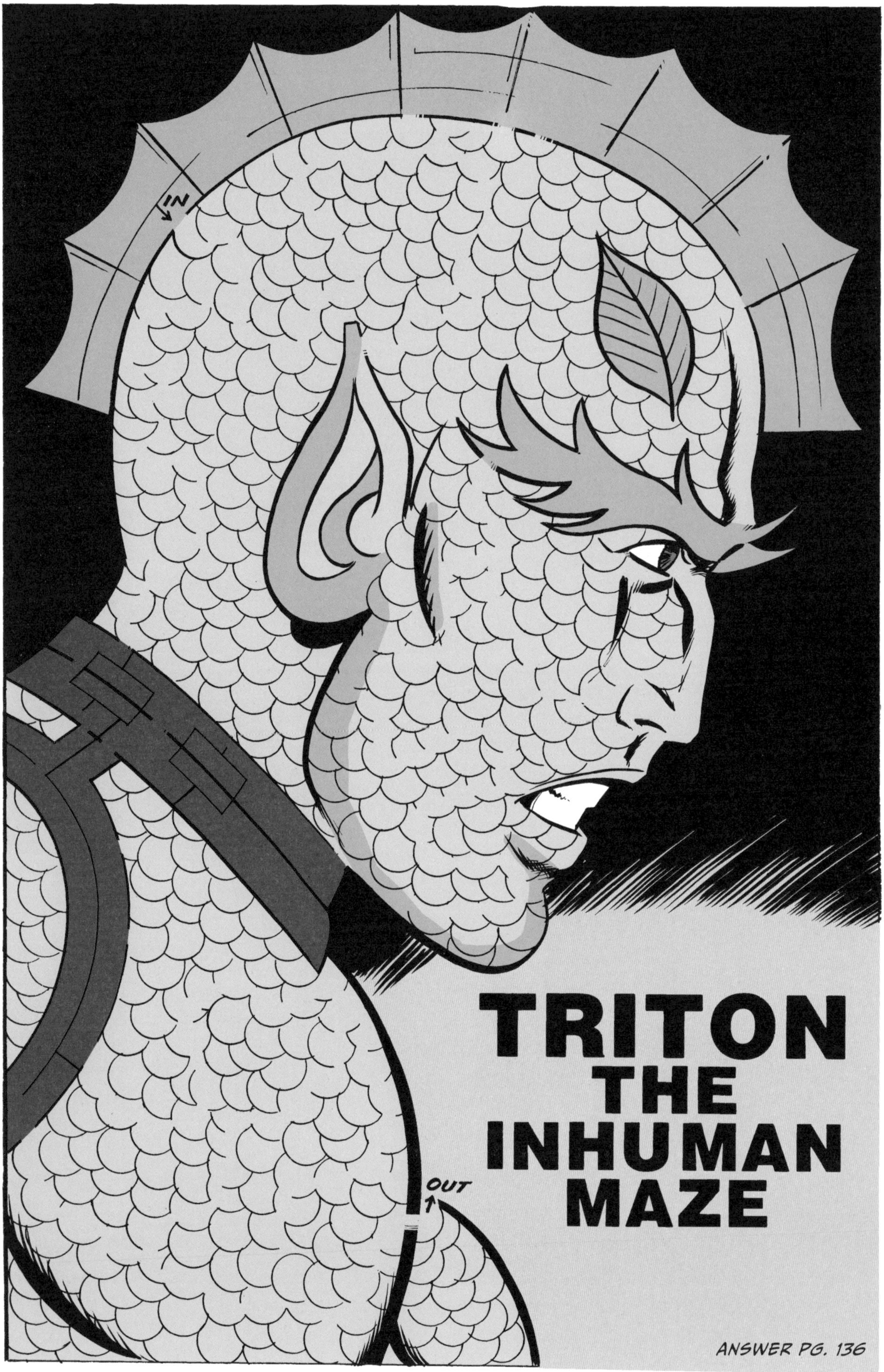
IN
OUT
TRITON THE INHUMAN MAZE
ANSWER PG. 136

# HAIR YE! HAIR YE!

What makes Medusa's hair so nice? Only her hairdresser knows for sure. And, you must realize her hair requires more-than-ordinary attention, especially when it has wrapped around some greasy gunman, a dusty demon, or a sooty super villain. Find all the words in this hair-raising puzzle.

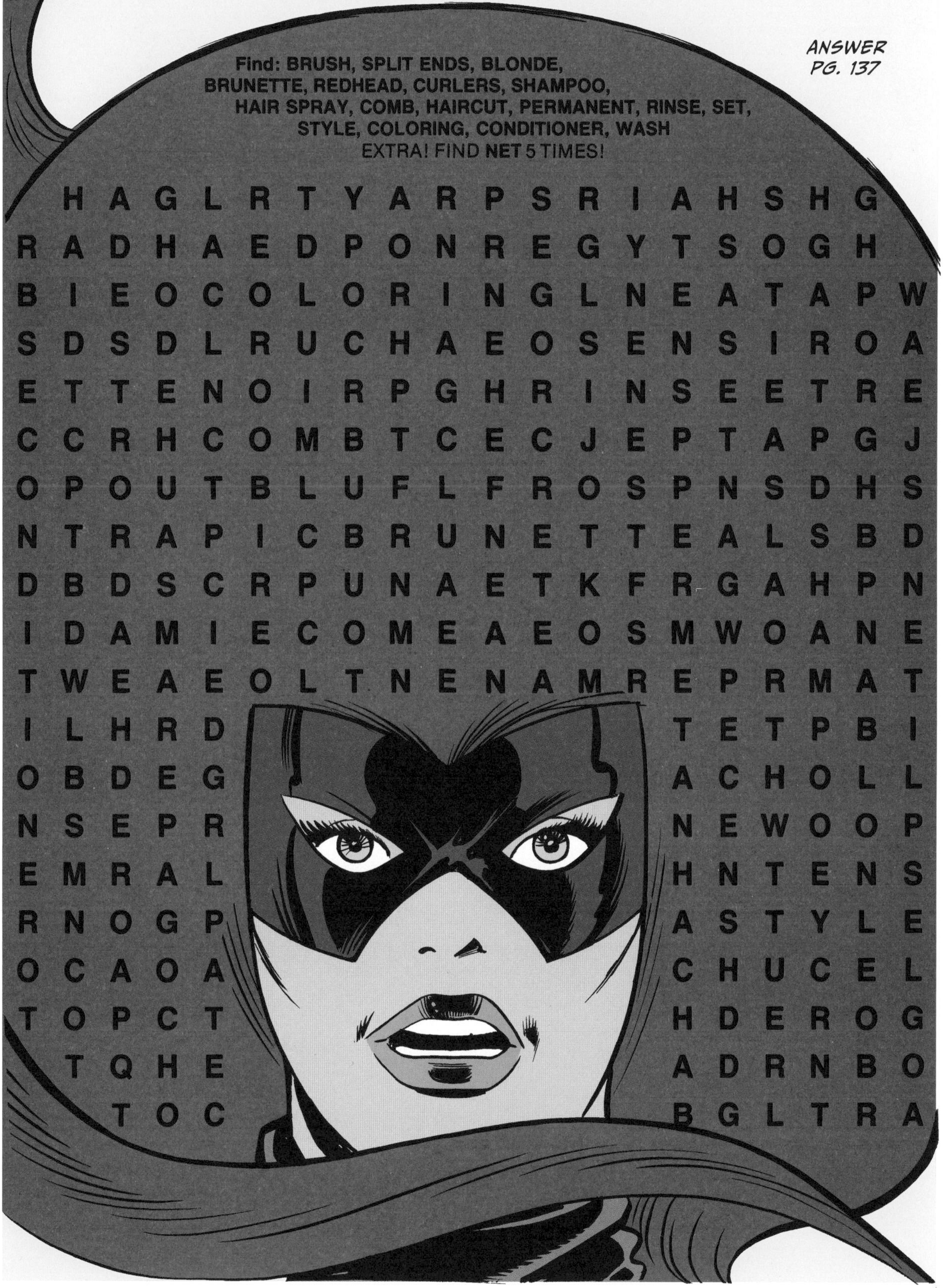

ANSWER PG. 137

Find: BRUSH, SPLIT ENDS, BLONDE, BRUNETTE, REDHEAD, CURLERS, SHAMPOO, HAIR SPRAY, COMB, HAIRCUT, PERMANENT, RINSE, SET, STYLE, COLORING, CONDITIONER, WASH

EXTRA! FIND **NET** 5 TIMES!

| | | | | | | | | | | | | | | | | | | | |
|---|---|---|---|---|---|---|---|---|---|---|---|---|---|---|---|---|---|---|---|
| | H | A | G | L | R | T | Y | A | R | P | S | R | I | A | H | S | H | G | |
| R | A | D | H | A | E | D | P | O | N | R | E | G | Y | T | S | O | G | H | |
| B | I | E | O | C | O | L | O | R | I | N | G | L | N | E | A | T | A | P | W |
| S | D | S | D | L | R | U | C | H | A | E | O | S | E | N | S | I | R | O | A |
| E | T | T | E | N | O | I | R | P | G | H | R | I | N | S | E | E | T | R | E |
| C | C | R | H | C | O | M | B | T | C | E | C | J | E | P | T | A | P | G | J |
| O | P | O | U | T | B | L | U | F | L | F | R | O | S | P | N | S | D | H | S |
| N | T | R | A | P | I | C | B | R | U | N | E | T | T | E | A | L | S | B | D |
| D | B | D | S | C | R | P | U | N | A | E | T | K | F | R | G | A | H | P | N |
| I | D | A | M | I | E | C | O | M | E | A | E | O | S | M | W | O | A | N | E |
| T | W | E | A | E | O | L | T | N | E | N | A | M | R | E | P | R | M | A | T |
| I | L | H | R | D | | | | | | | | | | T | E | T | P | B | I |
| O | B | D | E | G | | | | | | | | | | A | C | H | O | L | L |
| N | S | E | P | R | | | | | | | | | | N | E | W | O | O | P |
| E | M | R | A | L | | | | | | | | | | H | N | T | E | N | S |
| R | N | O | G | P | | | | | | | | | | A | S | T | Y | L | E |
| O | C | A | O | A | | | | | | | | | | C | H | U | C | E | L |
| T | O | P | C | T | | | | | | | | | | H | D | E | R | O | G |
| | T | Q | H | E | | | | | | | | | | A | D | R | N | B | O |
| | | T | O | C | | | | | | | | | | B | G | L | T | R | A |

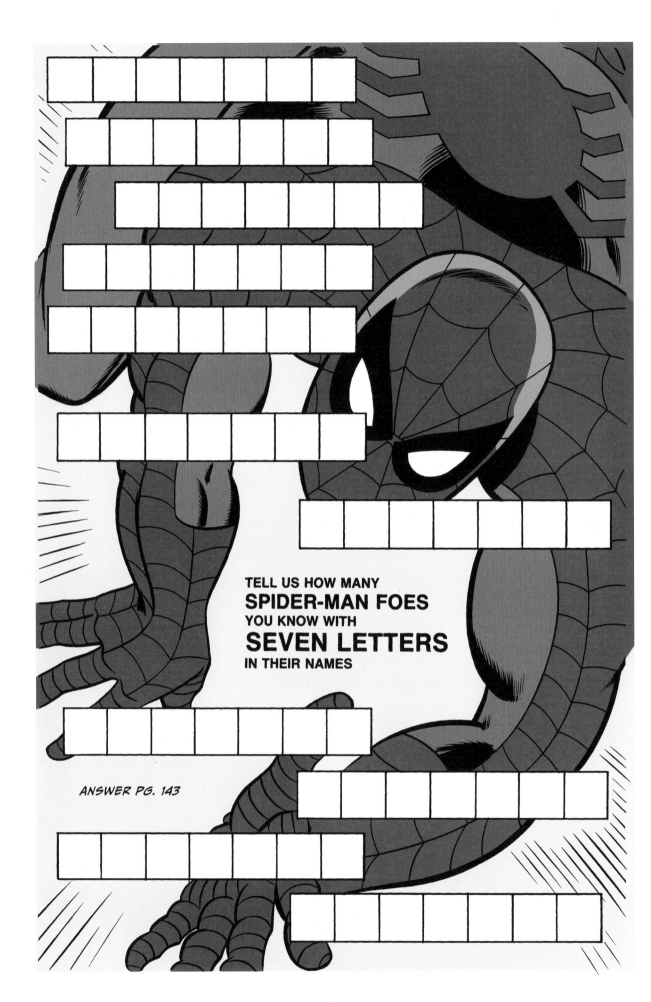

TELL US HOW MANY
**SPIDER-MAN FOES**
YOU KNOW WITH
**SEVEN LETTERS**
IN THEIR NAMES

*ANSWER PG. 143*

YOU
DRAW
THIS
HALF

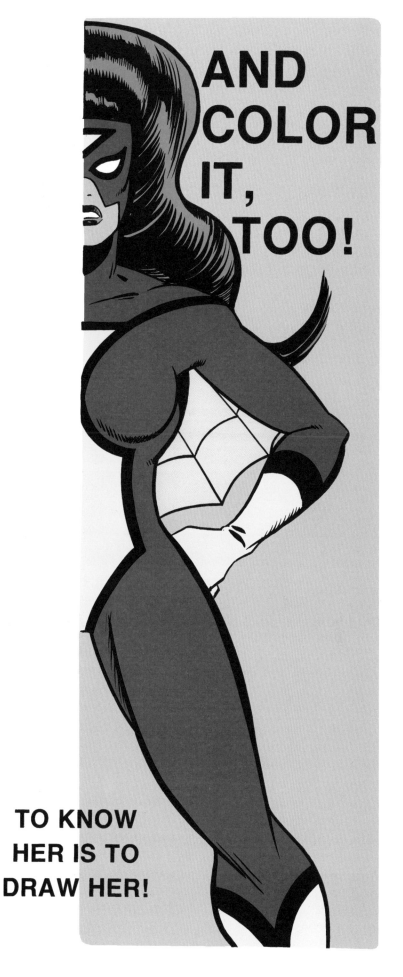

AND
COLOR
IT,
TOO!

TO KNOW
HER IS TO
DRAW HER!

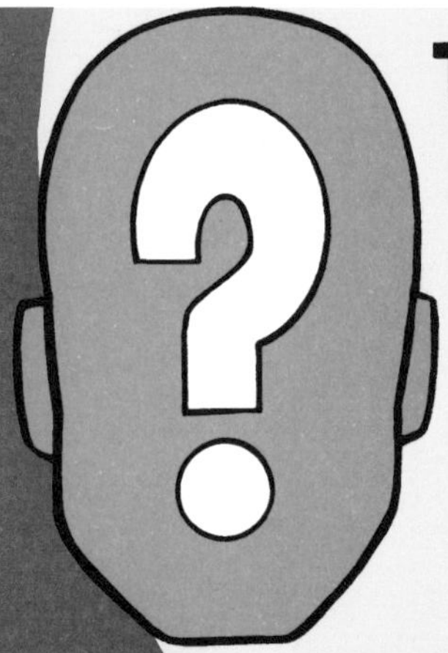

# THE GAME OF THE NAME IS THE NAME OF THE GAME!

All you have to do is to put the secret identities **(FIRST NAME ONLY)** of the mighty Marvel group below in the right places. We'll give you six free to help get you started.

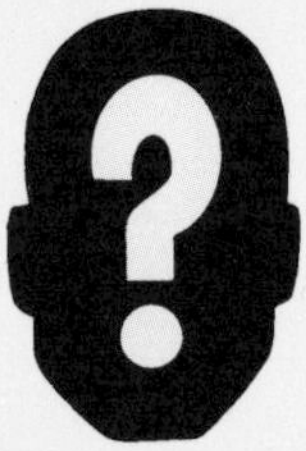

HUMAN TORCH
SPIDER-MAN
IRON MAN
~~ANGEL~~
HELLCAT
YELLOWJACKET
NIGHTHAWK
PHOENIX
WASP
MAN-WOLF
HAWKEYE
CAPTAIN AMERICA
MR. FANTASTIC
SPIDER-WOMAN
STORM
THE THING
~~NOVA~~
SUB-MARINER
SUNFIRE
MORBIUS
~~STINGRAY~~
FALCON
CAPTAIN MARVEL
THE COUNTESS
~~MADAME MASQUE~~
IRON FIST
~~GHOST RIDER~~
WINTER SOLDIER
CYCLOPS
DR. STRANGE
SCARLET WITCH
STAR-LORD
DR. DOOM
BLACK WIDOW
INVISIBLE WOMAN
~~MOCKINGBIRD~~
THE HULK
~~PROFESSOR X~~
THE BEAST
DAREDEVIL
STARLIGHT
~~WHIZZER~~
POWER MAN

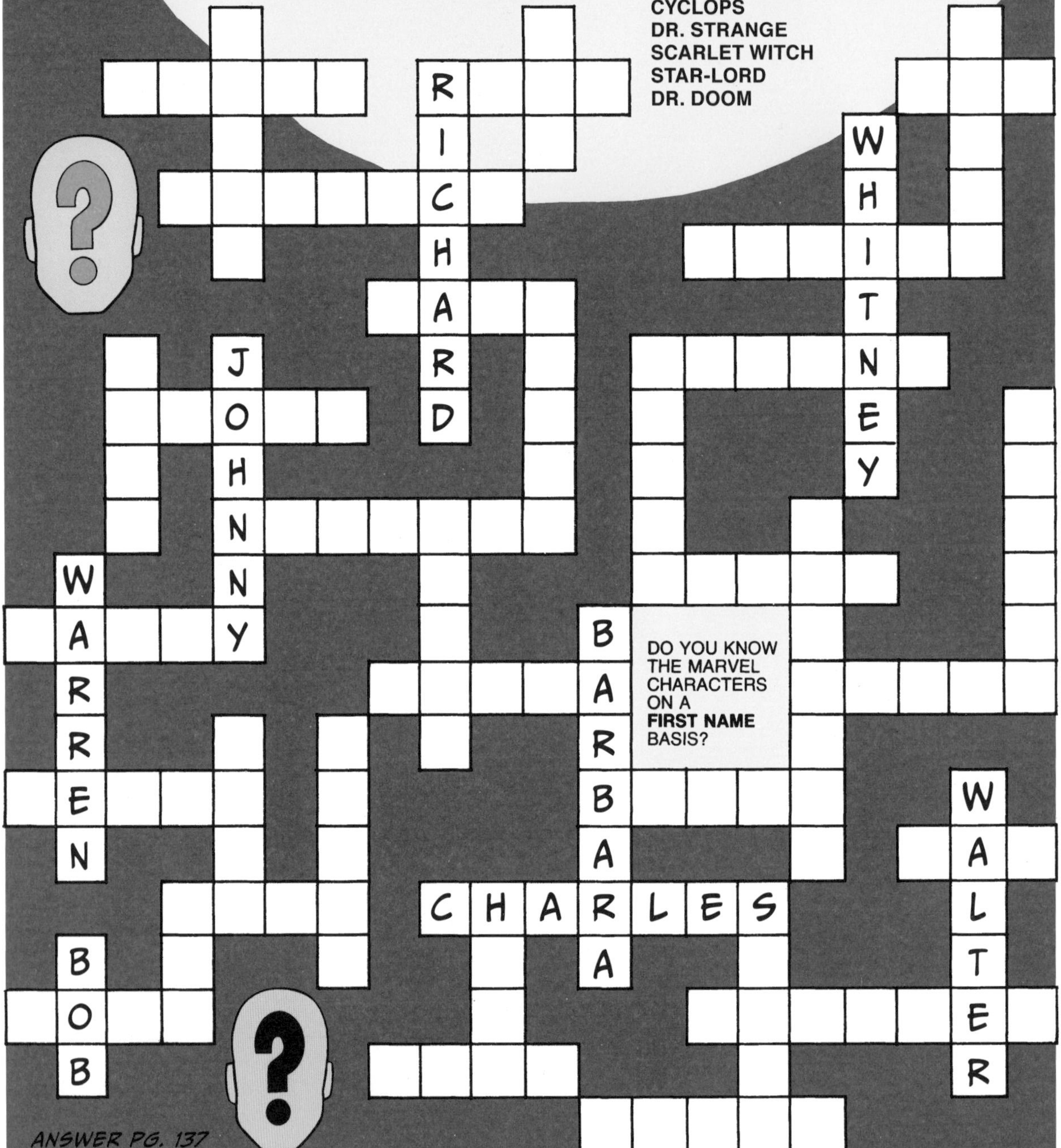

RICHARD
WHITNEY
JOHNNY
WARREN
BARBARA
CHARLES
WALTER
BOB


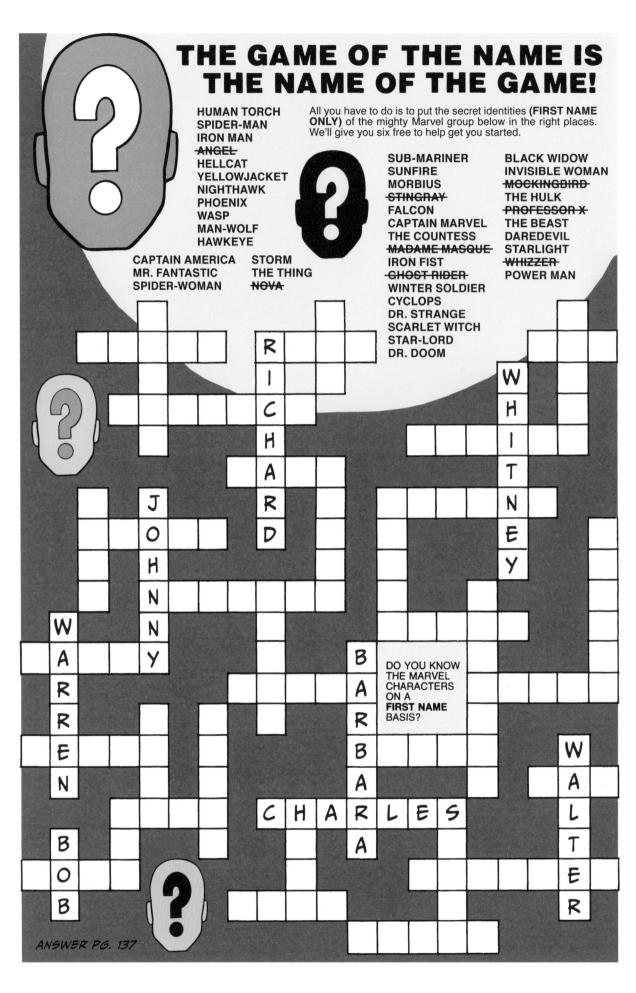

DO YOU KNOW THE MARVEL CHARACTERS ON A **FIRST NAME** BASIS?

ANSWER PG. 137

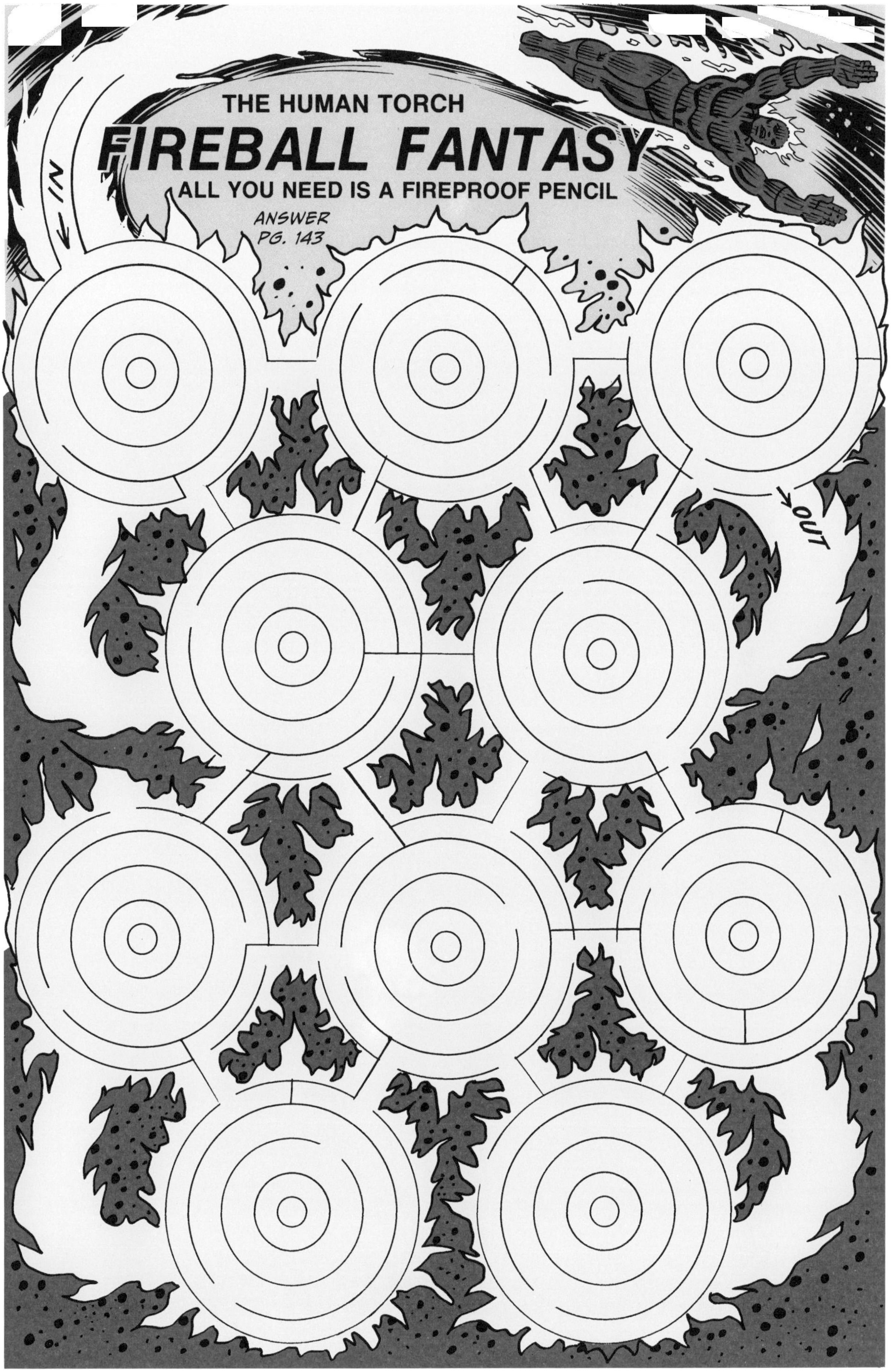
THE HUMAN TORCH
FIREBALL FANTASY
ALL YOU NEED IS A FIREPROOF PENCIL
ANSWER PG. 143
IN
OUT

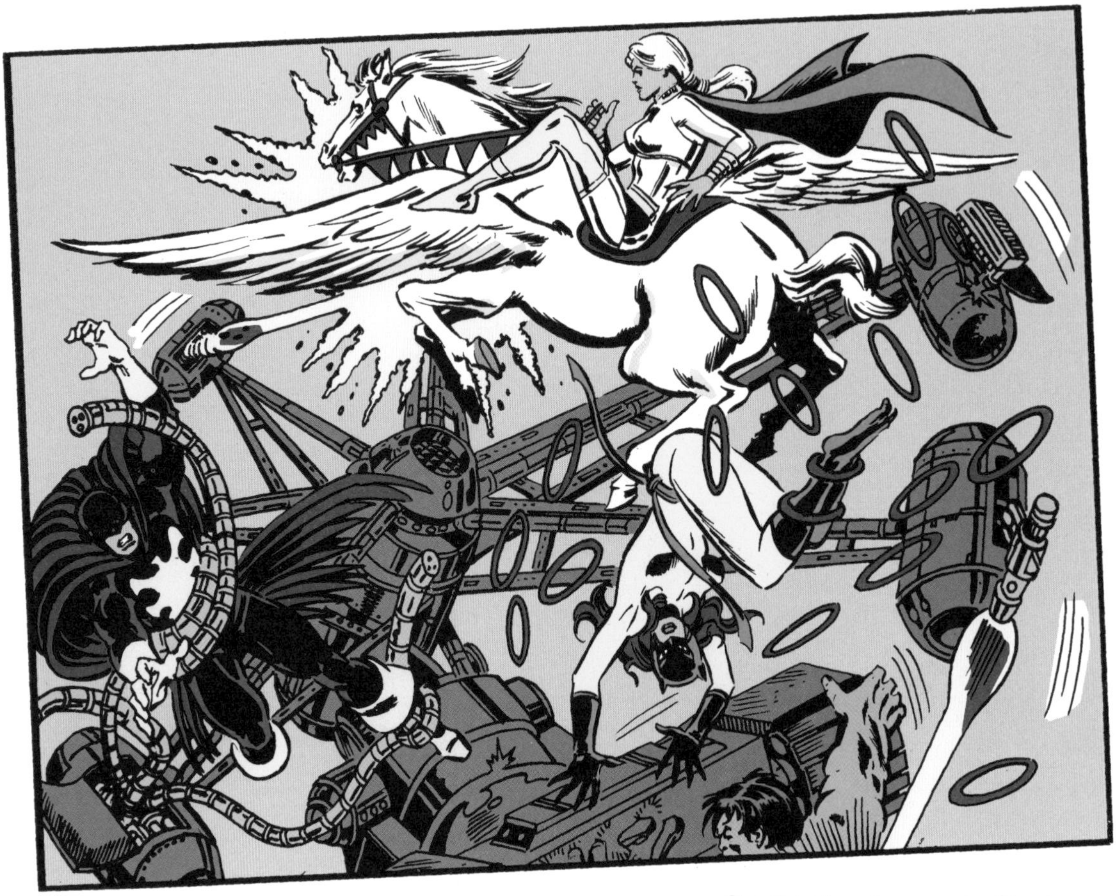

# WHAT'S MISSING?

Check both action panels. Check one against the other very carefully, because there are different things missing in each one.

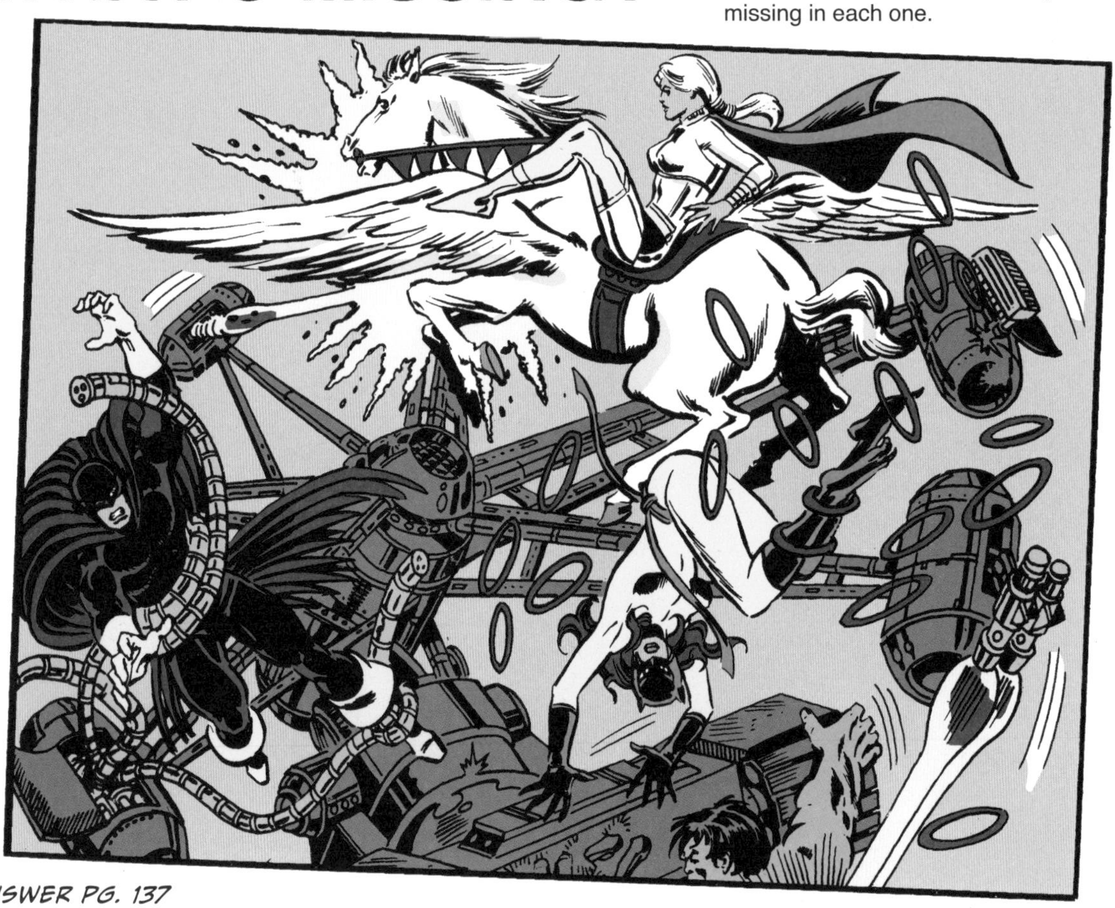

ANSWER PG. 137

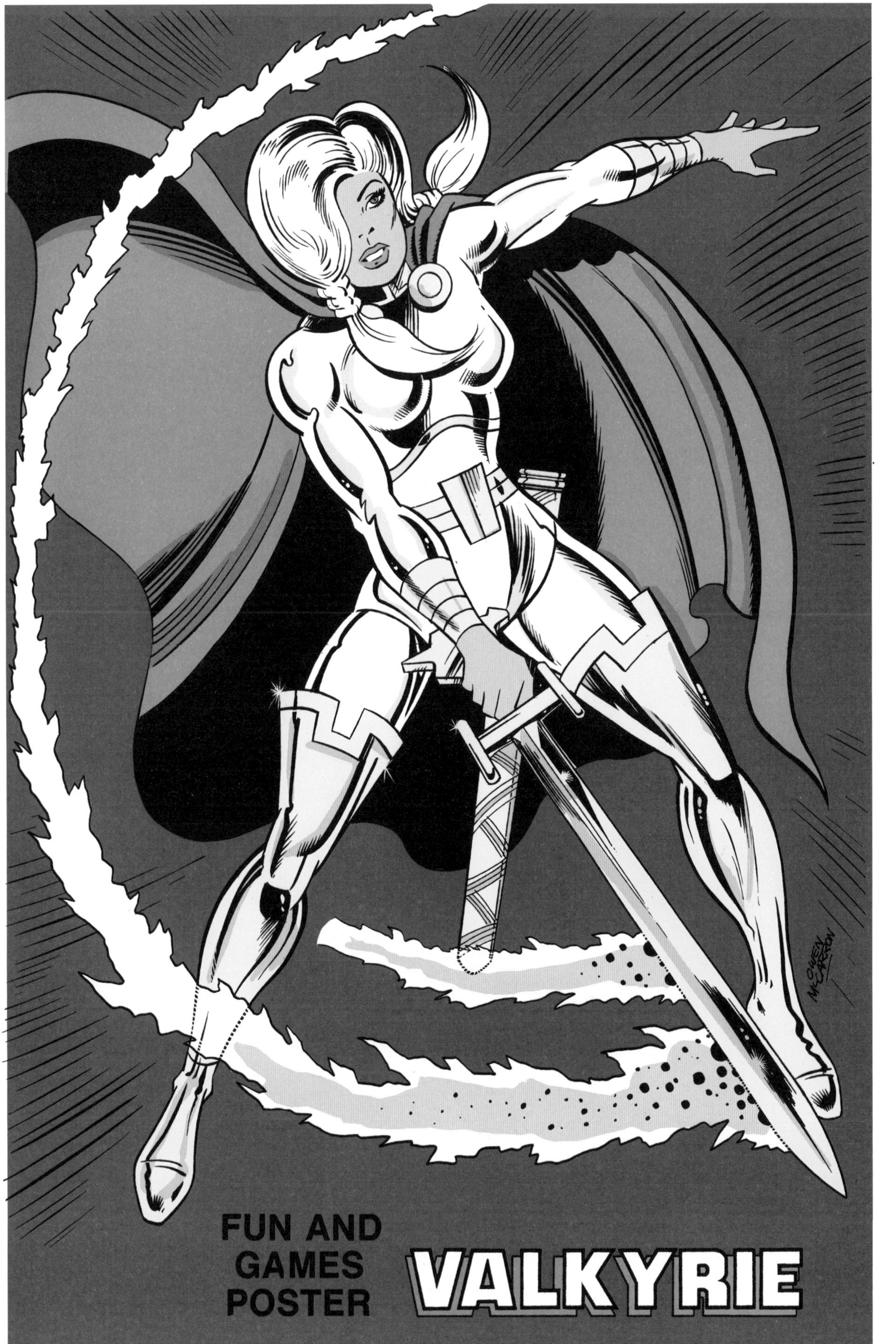
OWEN McCARRON
FUN AND GAMES POSTER
VALKYRIE

DAREDEVIL  NOVA  SPIDER-WOMAN  VISION  HULK  SPIDER-MAN  IRON MAN  THOR  HELLCAT

# FIND THESE FAMOUS SUPER HEROES IN MARVEL'S NEWEST NIGHTMARE!

PLUS!
• WOLVERINE
• FALCON • HAWKEYE
• MS. MARVEL • BEAST

# SKIP·A·LETTER

### THE FREE SAMPLE SAYS IT ALL!

ANSWER PG. 138

USUAL WORD FIND RULES APPLY EXCEPT THIS TIME YOU MUST *SKIP-A-LETTER!*

```
S I P S I R D O E D R N M E A R N V N S
S H C M E W R E A D K B P N I K T H A W
P H U D R O N H C E T L L C A P O E N R
D S I S L L M Y O W E F X G O C H A T O
I O T P O A O E A P O G S B C E P W S U
E P S M V A N H P S F P I R G L E N A L
D F A F N O I R P E T R L D A B A T S B
M A E A G N X E L E H A C N I L H H L V
E A C L M N S O M G A S R G V T E R L O
W L A V E S U A N E R T G A O C R O S E
R C L M A T I R F A T M O D A E M A B I
O O S E H O X M O R A I N I G R I V T R
W O L A N T V O S O N Y H N V P E S I C
N O N L S N E J I O A D N H E O I S Y I
O N E S R T S O T H N E T R U L D A O E
A R O E G R M R E C W G R R M R A G T N
M J H R P B E G H O L V U E W A L R E D
O D G A L R O E A D A E N V F I R L F E
A H R N A I S E M T S W H I D O Q U K S
P E T E R Y T E R K C W S A N H Y N O T
N S C P I R E D R W E M W O O N M A A N
```

# COMPLETE THE RHYMES

Here's your big opportunity to unleash those poetic tendencies and put it all on paper.
Examine the two limericks below. All you have to do is write a last line that completes the rhyme.

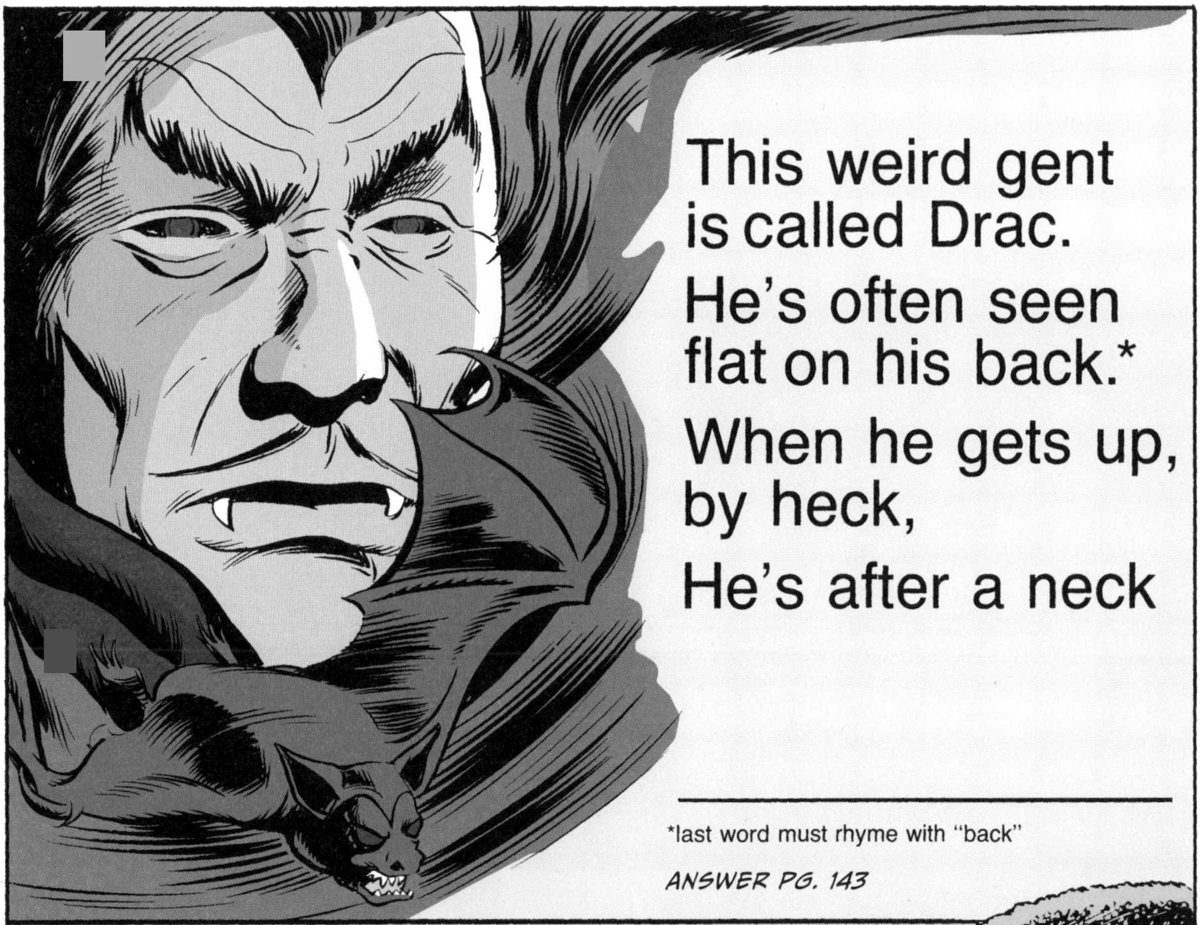

This weird gent is called Drac.
He's often seen flat on his back.*
When he gets up, by heck,
He's after a neck
*last word must rhyme with "back"


ANSWER PG. 143

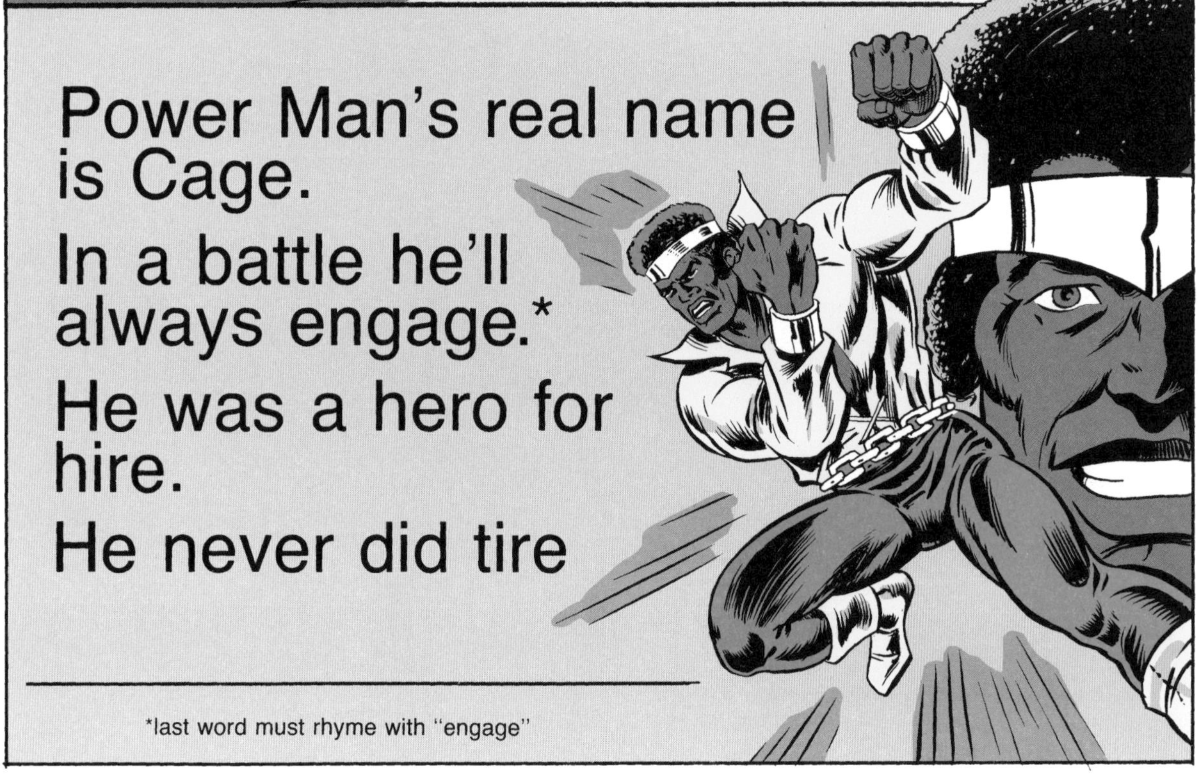

Power Man's real name is Cage.
In a battle he'll always engage.*
He was a hero for hire.
He never did tire
*last word must rhyme with "engage"

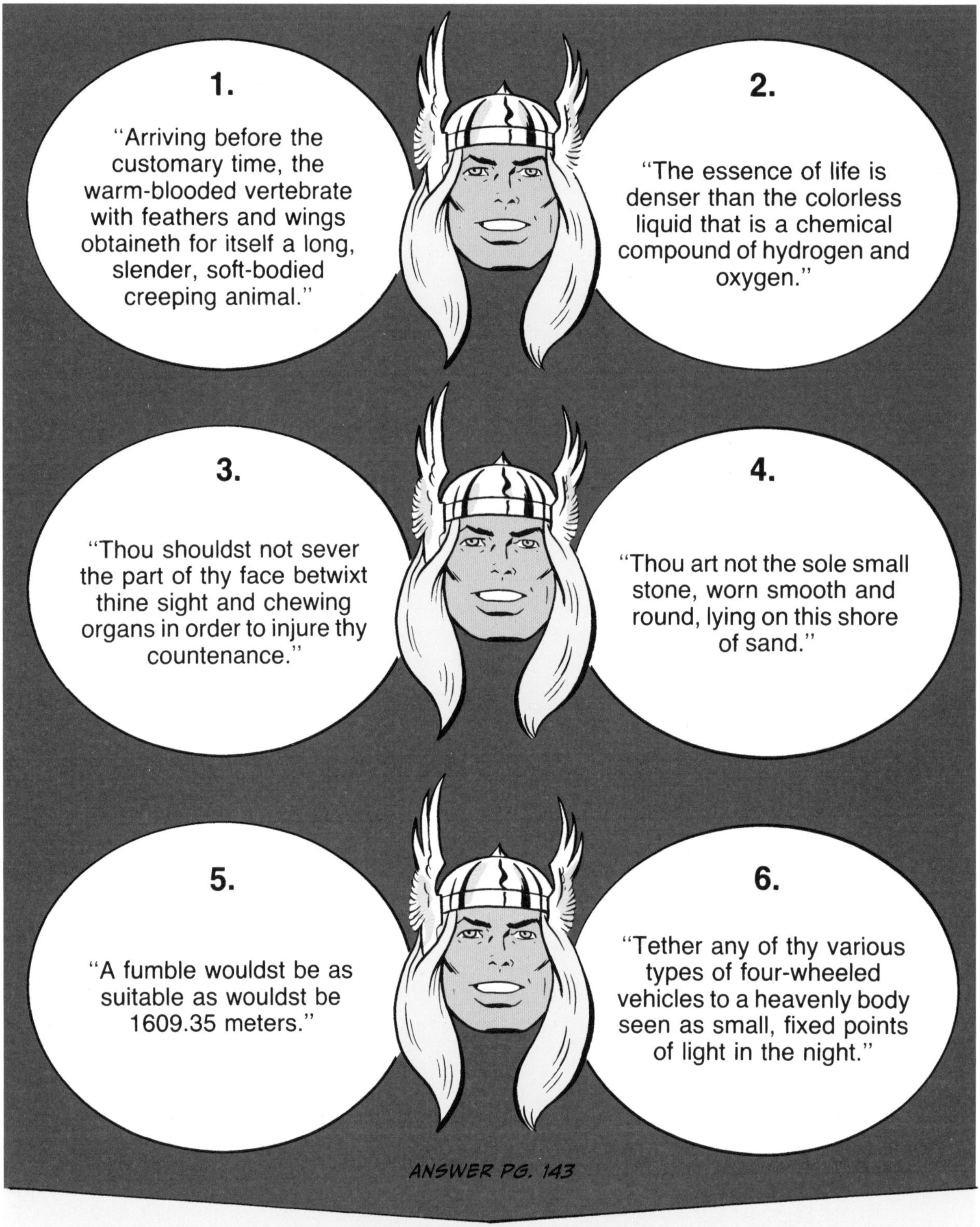
1.
"Arriving before the customary time, the warm-blooded vertebrate with feathers and wings obtaineth for itself a long, slender, soft-bodied creeping animal."
2.
"The essence of life is denser than the colorless liquid that is a chemical compound of hydrogen and oxygen."
3.
"Thou shouldst not sever the part of thy face betwixt thine sight and chewing organs in order to injure thy countenance."
4.
"Thou art not the sole small stone, worn smooth and round, lying on this shore of sand."
5.
"A fumble wouldst be as suitable as wouldst be 1609.35 meters."
6.
"Tether any of thy various types of four-wheeled vehicles to a heavenly body seen as small, fixed points of light in the night."
ANSWER PG. 143

# WHAT DID HE SAY?

What makes Thor such an interesting character is his sheer eloquence . . . whether he's doing a soliloquy or making a major speech, it's music to the ears. Wonder how many villains he's clobbered really knew what he was talking about. Which leads us to this question: What would Thor do with some of today's well-known expressions? We had to find out, so we asked Thor (he just happened to be passing by) to translate a number of familiar phrases into his very best Asgardian. Listen to what Thor says then tell us the phrases . . . which may never be the same. As the title says: "What did he say?"

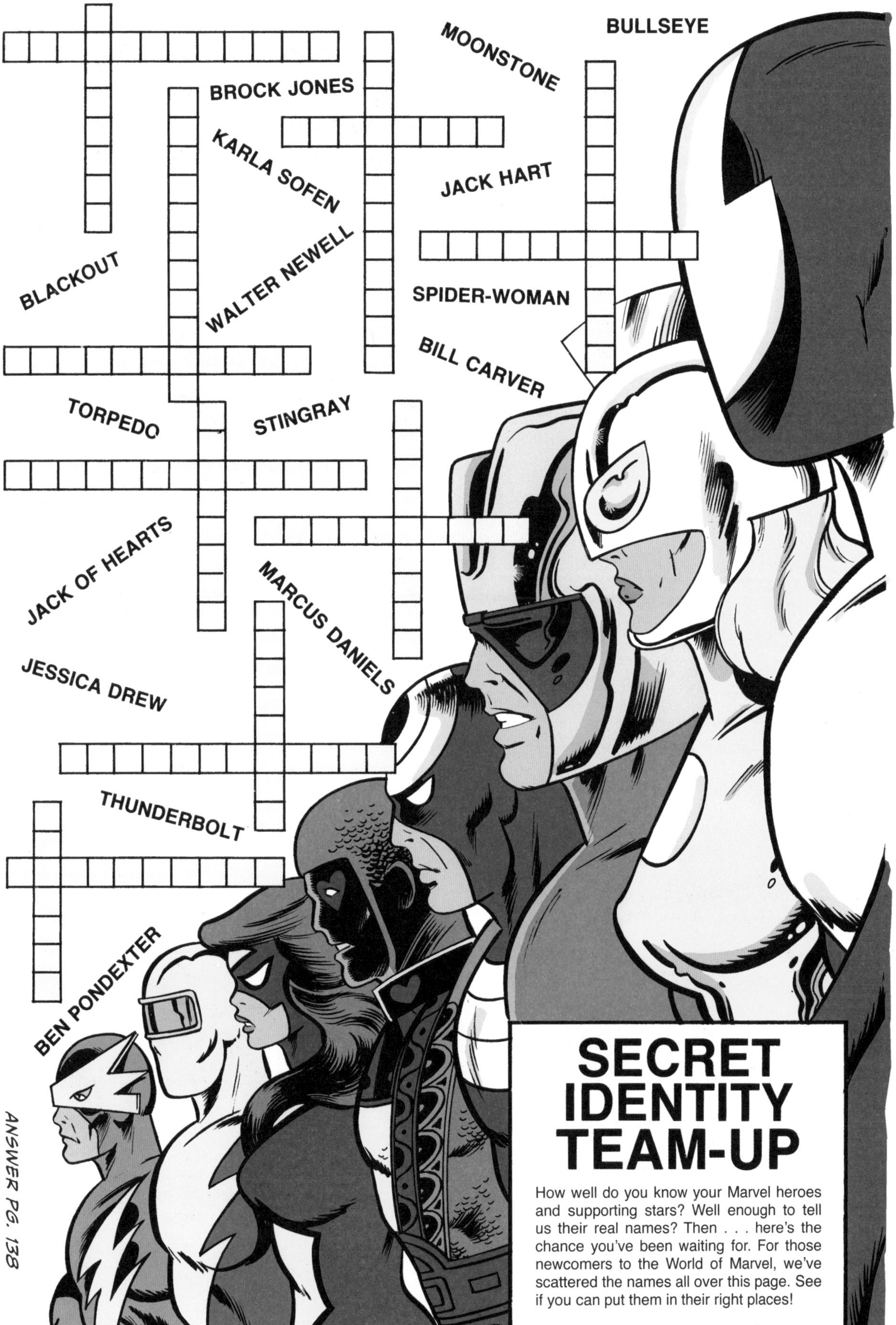

# SECRET IDENTITY TEAM-UP

How well do you know your Marvel heroes and supporting stars? Well enough to tell us their real names? Then . . . here's the chance you've been waiting for. For those newcomers to the World of Marvel, we've scattered the names all over this page. See if you can put them in their right places!

MOONSTONE
BULLSEYE
BROCK JONES
KARLA SOFEN
JACK HART
BLACKOUT
WALTER NEWELL
SPIDER-WOMAN
BILL CARVER
TORPEDO
STINGRAY
JACK OF HEARTS
MARCUS DANIELS
JESSICA DREW
THUNDERBOLT
BEN PONDEXTER

ANSWER PG. 138

# CIRCLE WORD

Don't be frightened away . . . it's really only a SCRAMBLE jazzed up a wee bit. But there's something we gotta tell ya . . . in our haste to put this one together, a letter has been left out of each one, so look it over carefully before jumping to it.

**P.S. TAKE THE LETTERS LEFT OUT OF THE CIRCLES, REARRANGE THEM AND SEE WHOSE NAME YOU COME UP WITH. AMAZING COINCIDENCE THAT THE MISSING LETTERS COULD FORM A NAME, ISN'T IT?**

1.

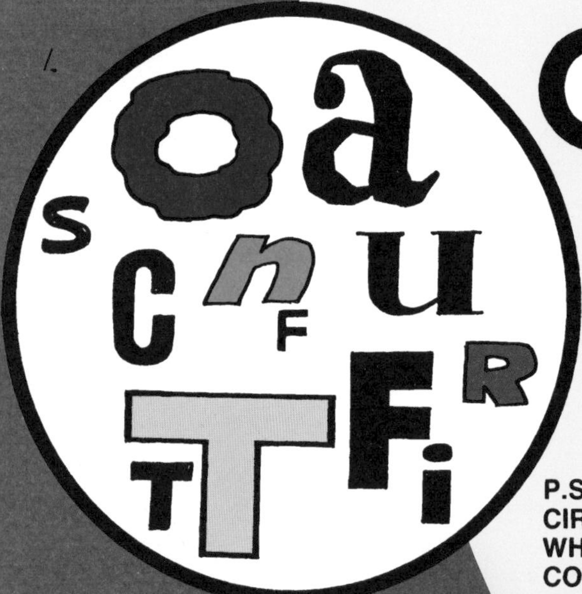
o a s C n u F R T T F i

2.

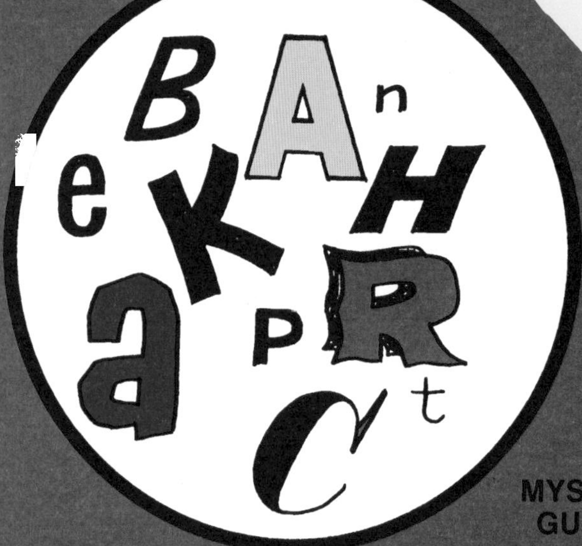
B A n e K H a P R C t

4.

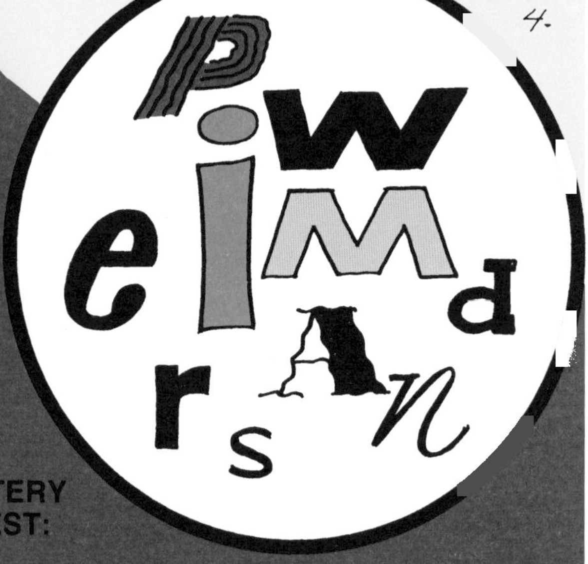
P w i e M d A r s n

**MYSTERY GUEST:**

____________

3.

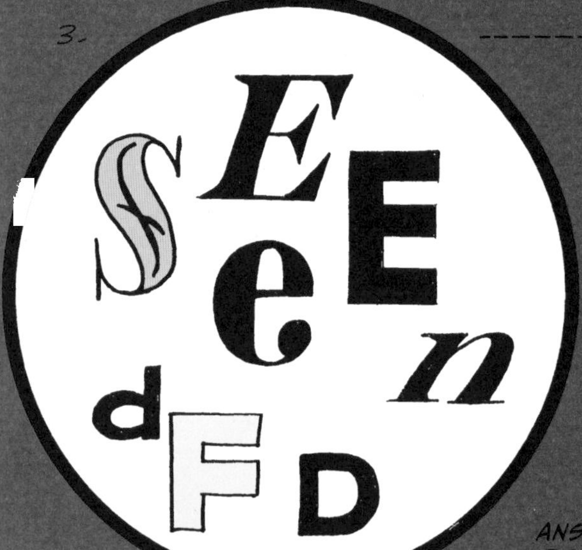
S E E e n d F D

5.

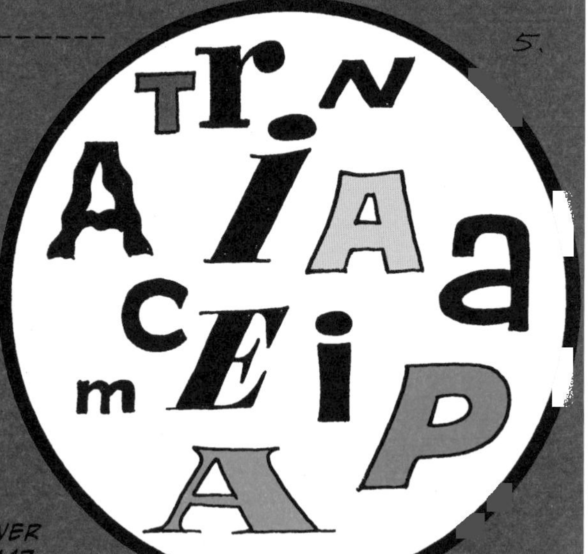
T r N A i A a c E i m P A

ANSWER PG. 143

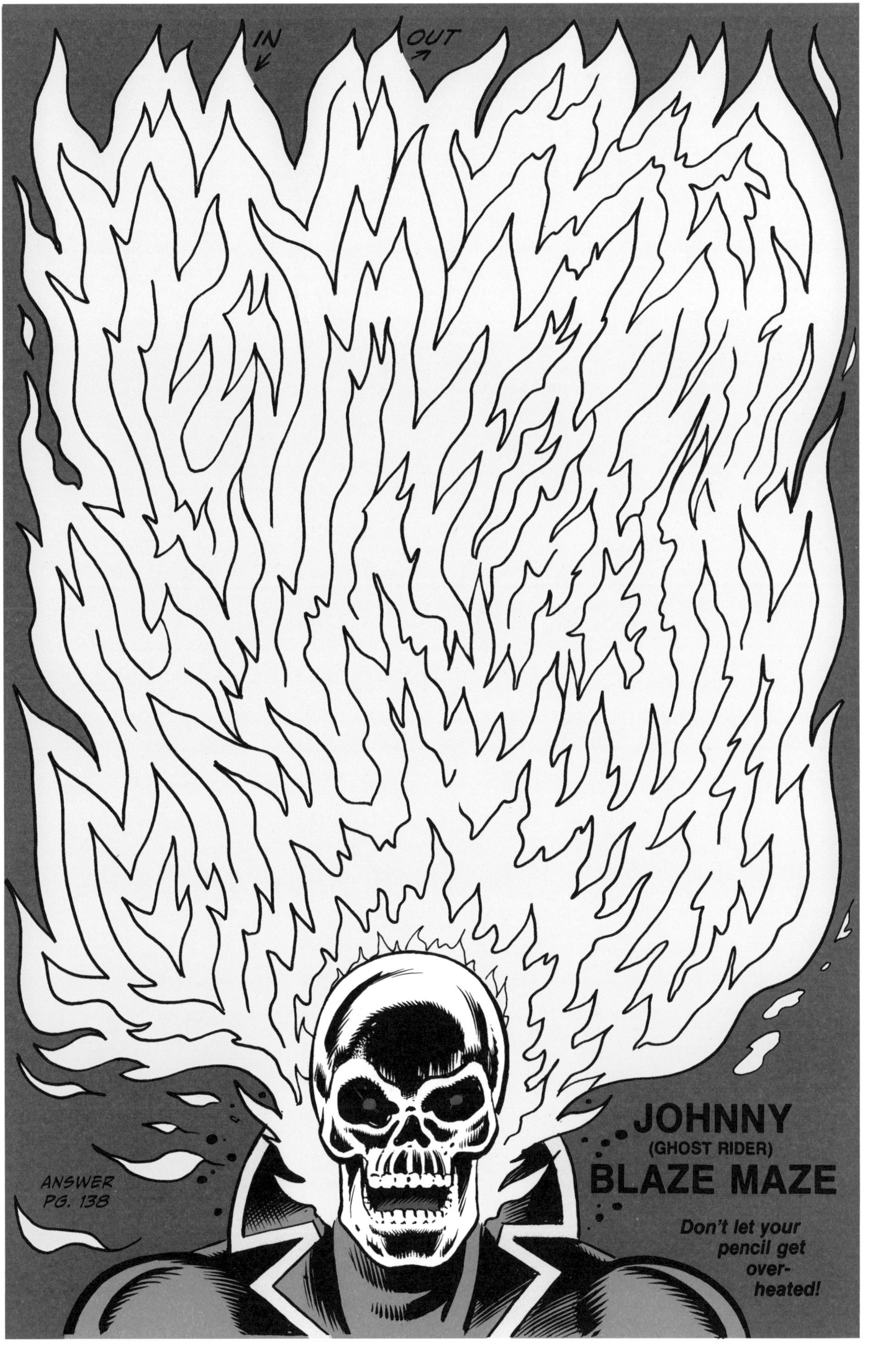
IN
OUT
JOHNNY
(GHOST RIDER)
BLAZE MAZE
Don't let your pencil get over-heated!
ANSWER PG. 138

COMPARE THEM AGAINST THIS ONE!

# WHAT'S MISSING IN THIS PULSE-POUNDING PANEL PUZZLE?

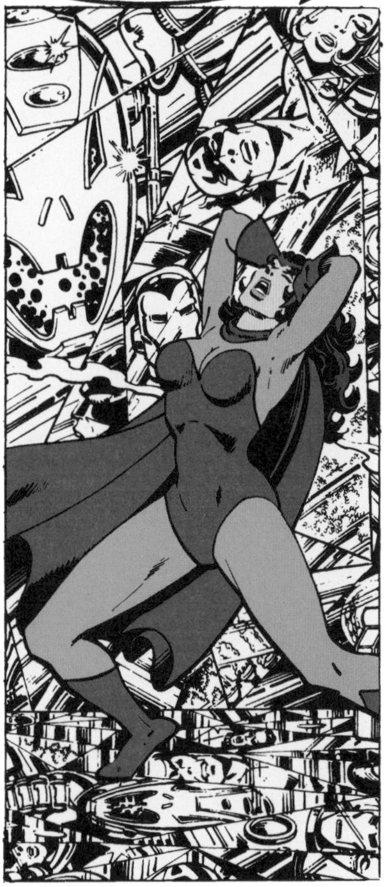

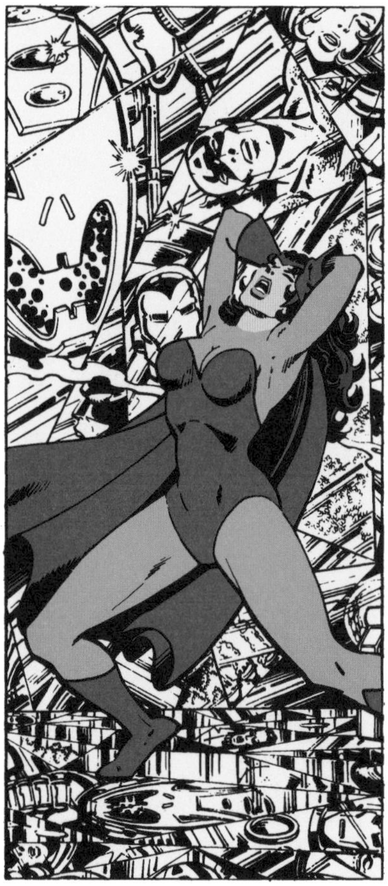

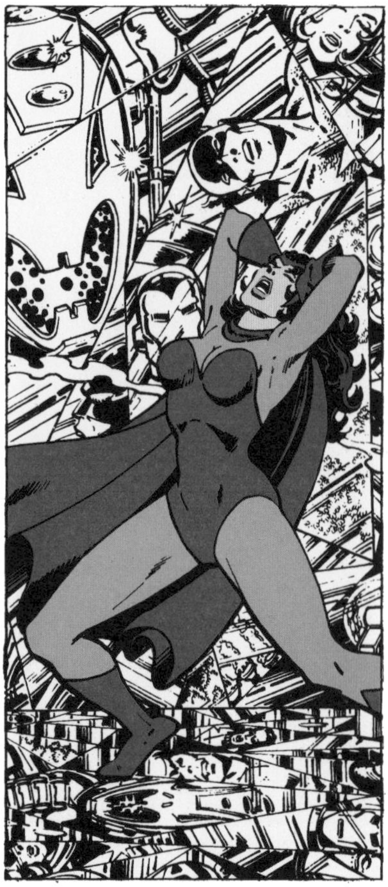

HINT: THERE ARE THREE THINGS MISSING IN EACH PANEL – GENEROUS OWEN

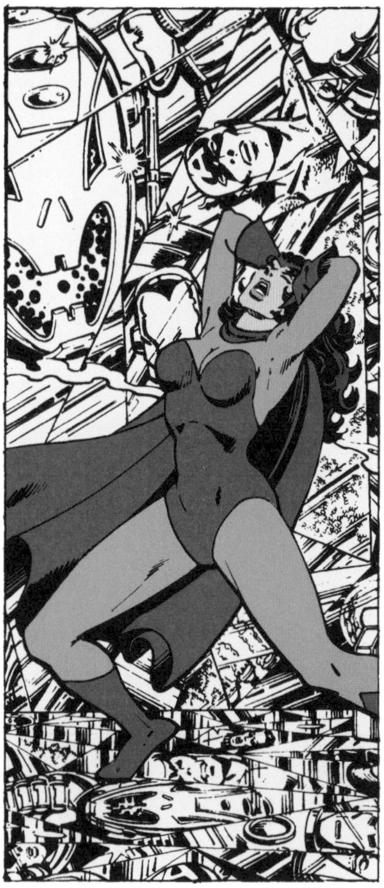

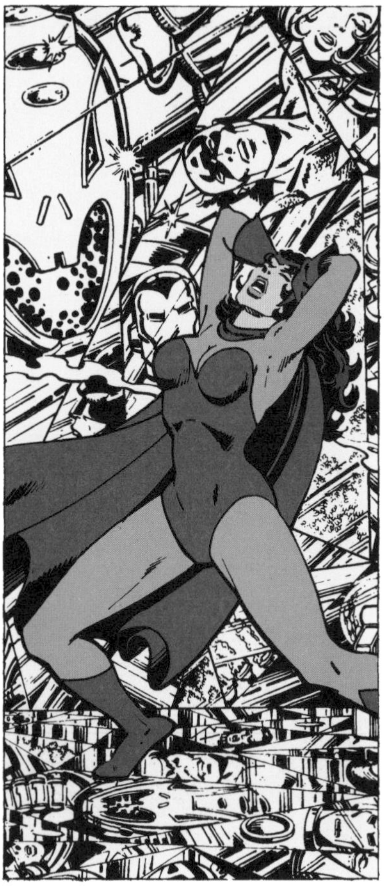

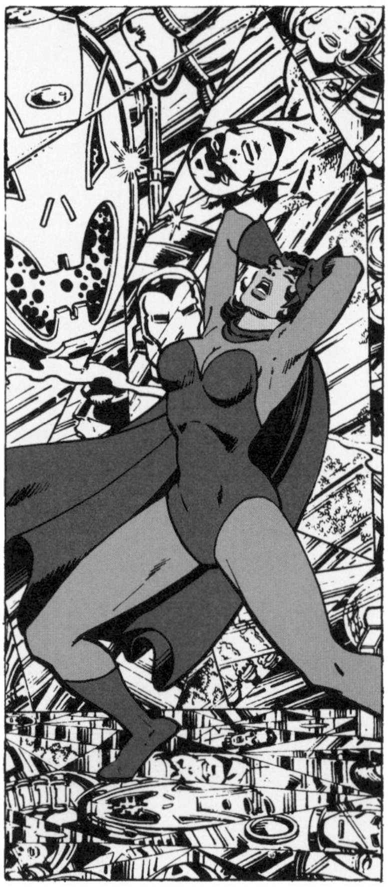

ANSWER PG. 143

# LEARN TO DRAW MARVEL CHARACTERS*

## THE VISION

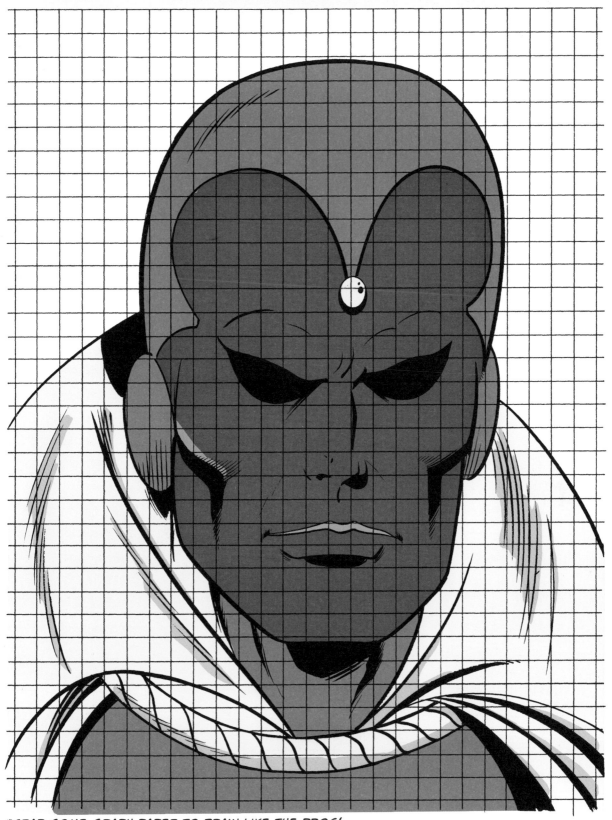

*GRAB SOME GRAPH PAPER TO DRAW LIKE THE PROS!

# WEB-HEAD'S WORDWEBS™

THREE FREEBIES ON EACH PAGE!

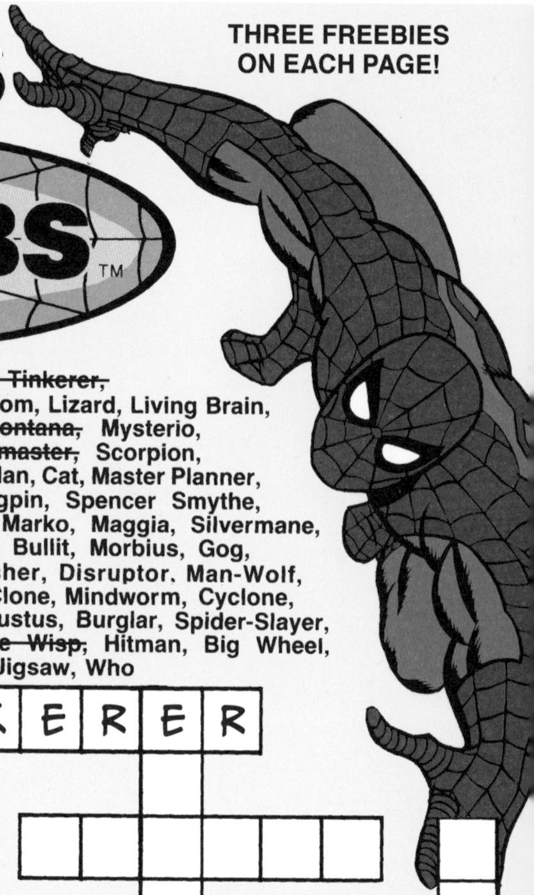

**LOCATE ALL THESE BADDIES WHO APPEARED IN THE FIRST 200 ISSUES of THE AMAZING SPIDER-MAN**

Chameleon, Vulture, ~~Terrible Tinkerer,~~ Dr. Octopus, Sandman, Dr. Doom, Lizard, Living Brain, Electro, Fancy Dan, Ox, ~~Montana,~~ Mysterio, Green Goblin, Kraven, ~~Ringmaster,~~ Scorpion, Beetle, Crime Master, Molten Man, Cat, Master Planner, Looter, Rhino, Shocker, Kingpin, Spencer Smythe, ~~Brainwasher,~~ Man Mountain Marko, Maggia, Silvermane, Prowler, Schemer, Kangaroo, Bullit, Morbius, Gog, Gibbon, Hammerhead, Smasher, Disruptor, Man-Wolf, Punisher, Jackal, Tarantula, Clone, Mindworm, Cyclone, Fearsome Fly, Mirage, Dr. Faustus, Burglar, Spider-Slayer, Stegron, Photon, ~~Will O' The Wisp,~~ Hitman, Big Wheel, Rocket Racer, ~~White Dragon,~~ Jigsaw, Who

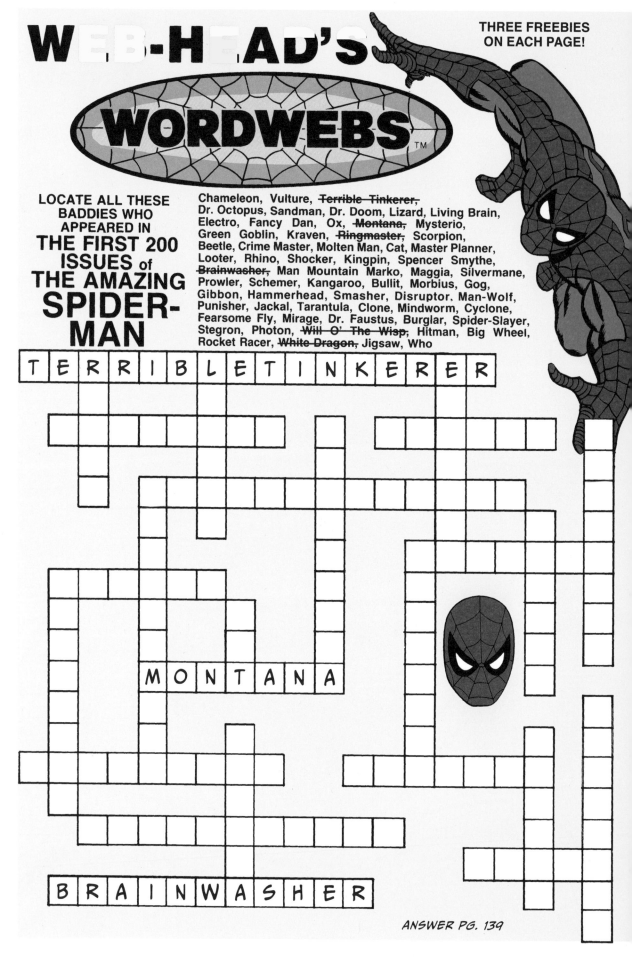

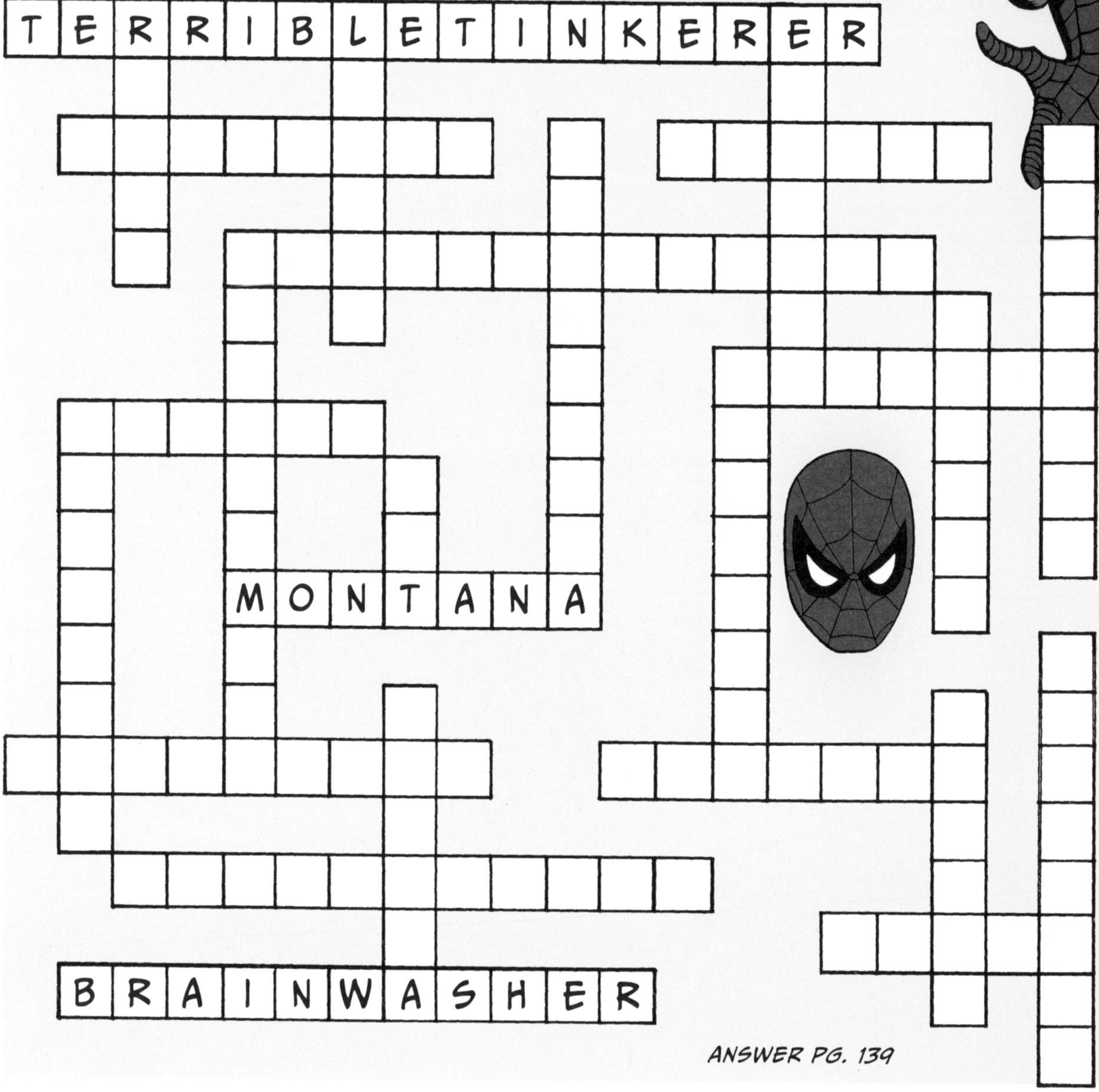
TERRIBLETINKERER
MONTANA
BRAINWASHER

ANSWER PG. 139

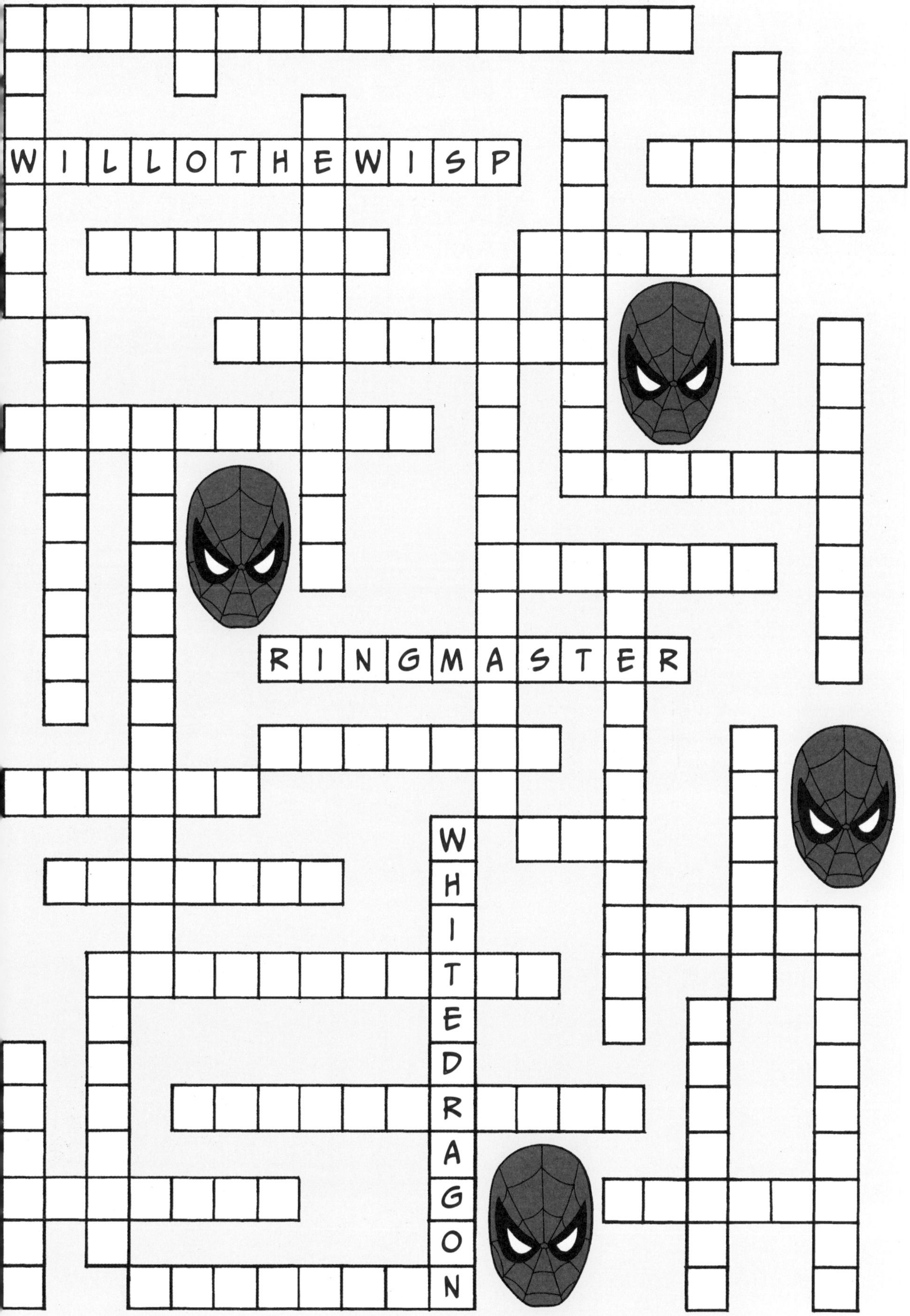
WILLOTHEWISP
RINGMASTER
WHITEDRAGON

***SHOW 'EM HOW TO DO IT, SPIDER-FAN!***

# SLIME-RHYME

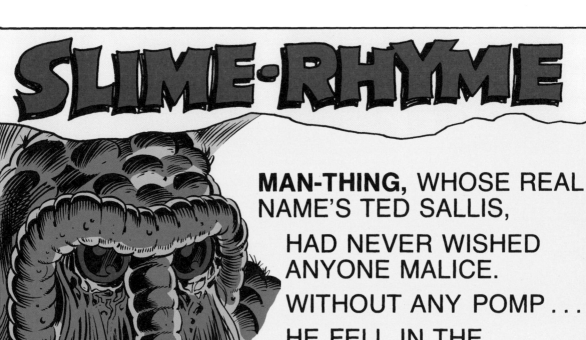

**MAN-THING,** WHOSE REAL NAME'S TED SALLIS,

HAD NEVER WISHED ANYONE MALICE.

WITHOUT ANY POMP . . .

HE FELL IN THE SWAMP

Chemist **Ted Sallis** was part of a top-secret experiment that backfired and made him part man, part monster. He is now **MAN-THING.**

**COMPLETE THE RHYME:** LAST WORD MUST RHYME WITH SALLIS.

# CRIME-RHYME

A VILLAINOUS GENT IS **MYSTERIO** . . .

CRIME SEEMS TO BE HIS FORTISSIMO.

HIS TRADEMARK'S A MIST —

HE'S A REAL MASOCHIST

**COMPLETE THE RHYME:** LAST WORD MUST RHYME WITH MYSTERIO.
*ANSWER PG. 143*

**MYSTERIO** pops up from time to time to do battle with everyone's favorite web-slinging wonder, the Amazing **SPIDER-MAN.**

NO . . . THIS ISN'T FOGGY OL' LONDON!
YOU'RE TRAPPED IN THE

# MISTY MAZE OF

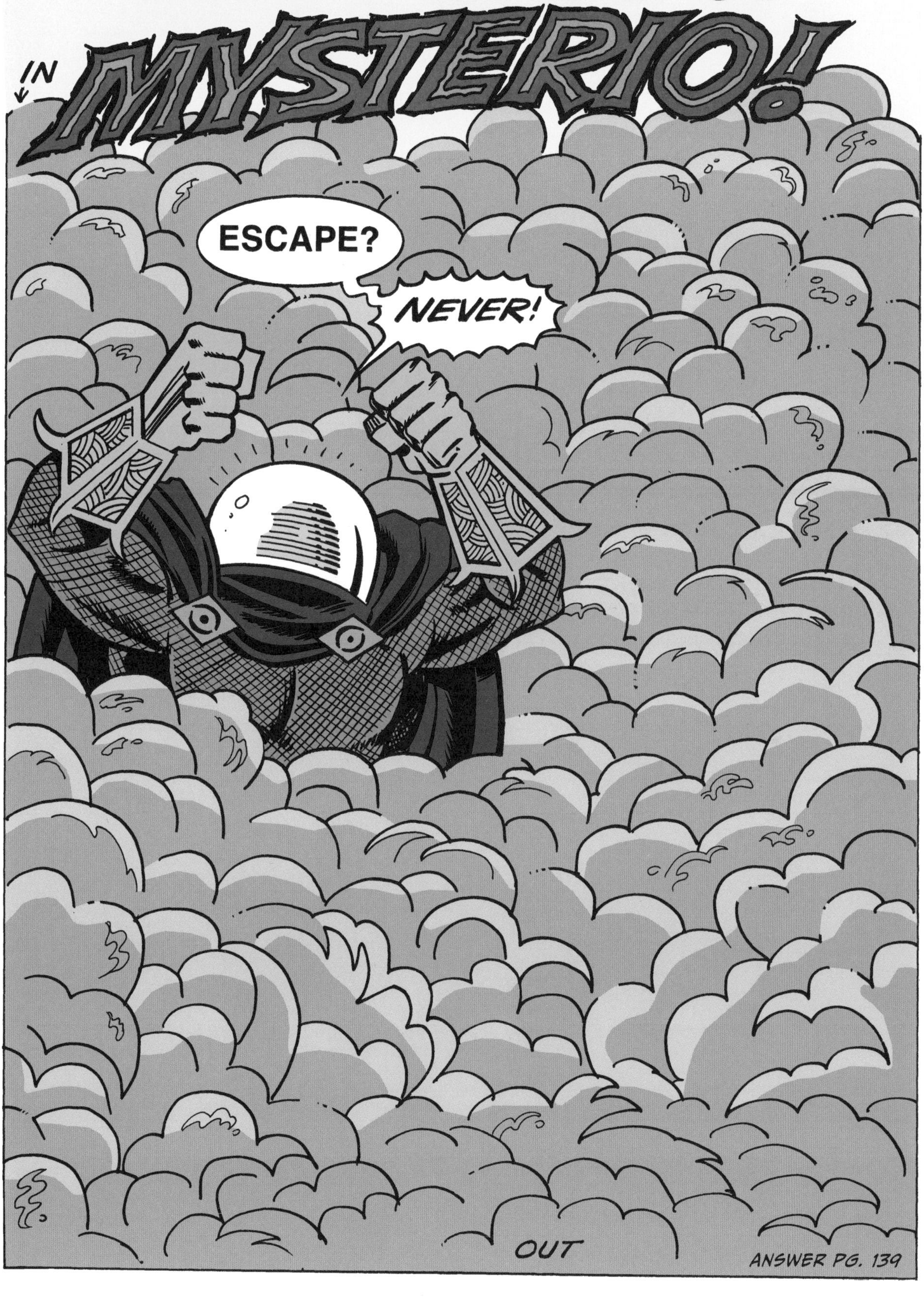
IN
MYSTERIO!
ESCAPE?
NEVER!
OUT
ANSWER PG. 139

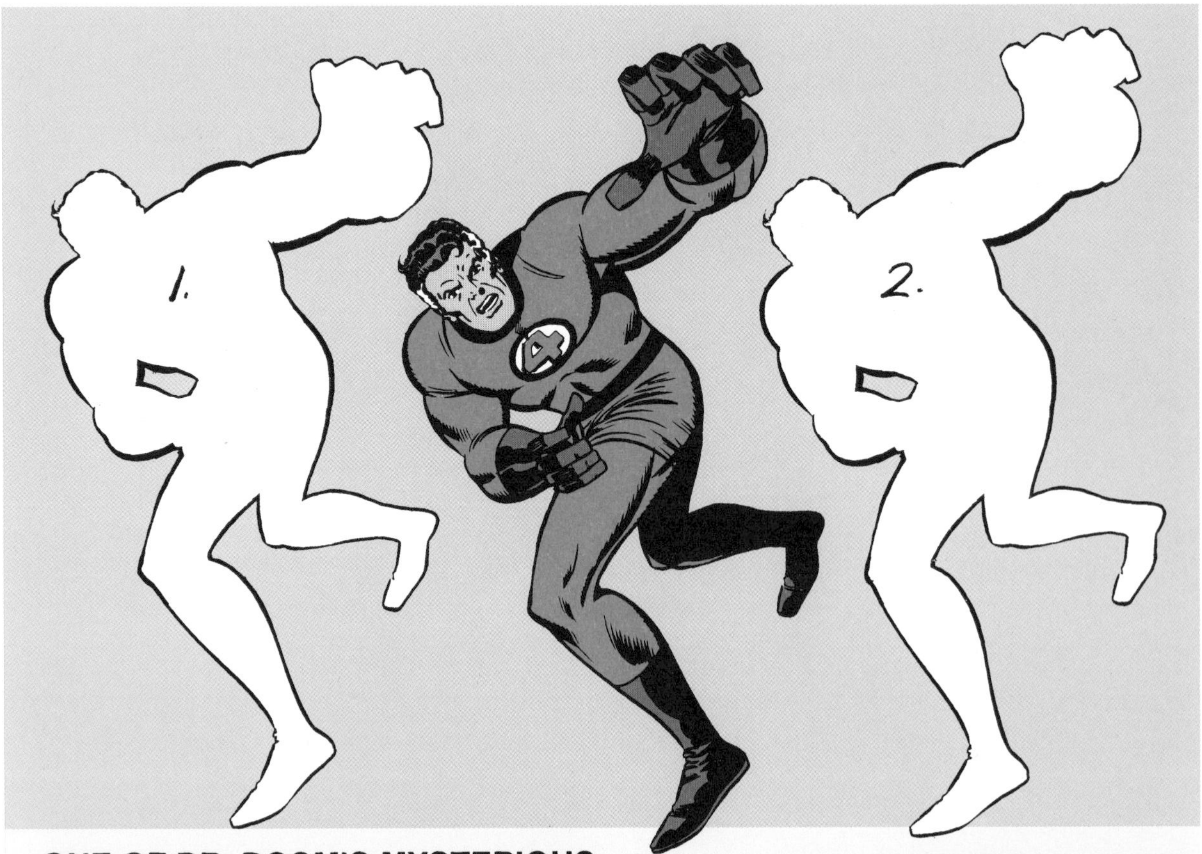
1.
2.

**ONE OF DR. DOOM'S MYSTERIOUS GIZMOS HAS JUST TURNED REED (MR. FANTASTIC) RICHARDS INTO AN OUTLINE. ONLY ONE IS EXACTLY THE VERY SAME AS THE F.F. LEADER'S PICTURE . . . BUT WHICH ONE? HURRY BEFORE OL' DOC DOOM DOES THE SAME THING TO YOU, PUZZLE PAL.**

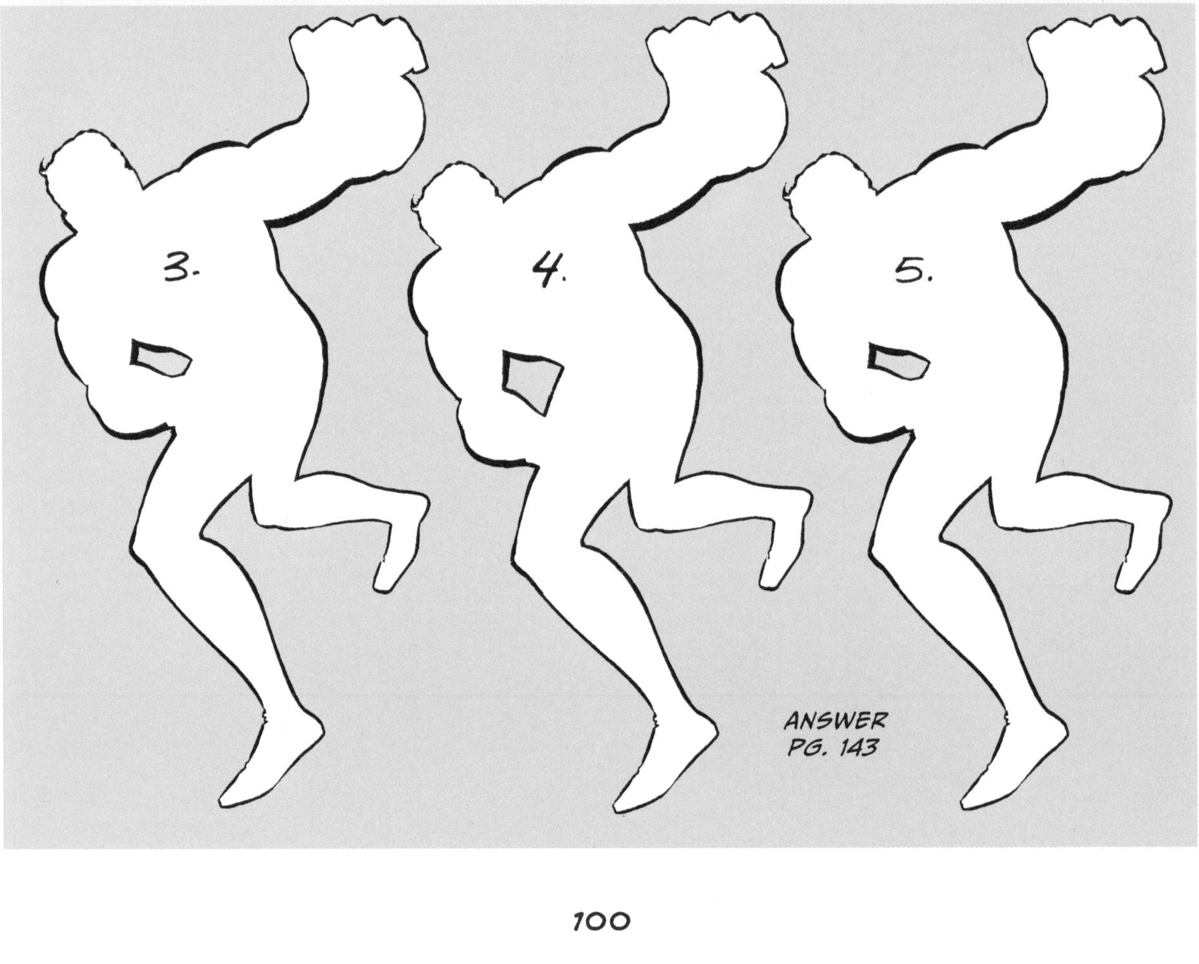
3.
4.
5.
ANSWER
PG. 143

# ANYONE FOR AN INVISIBLE PUZZLE?

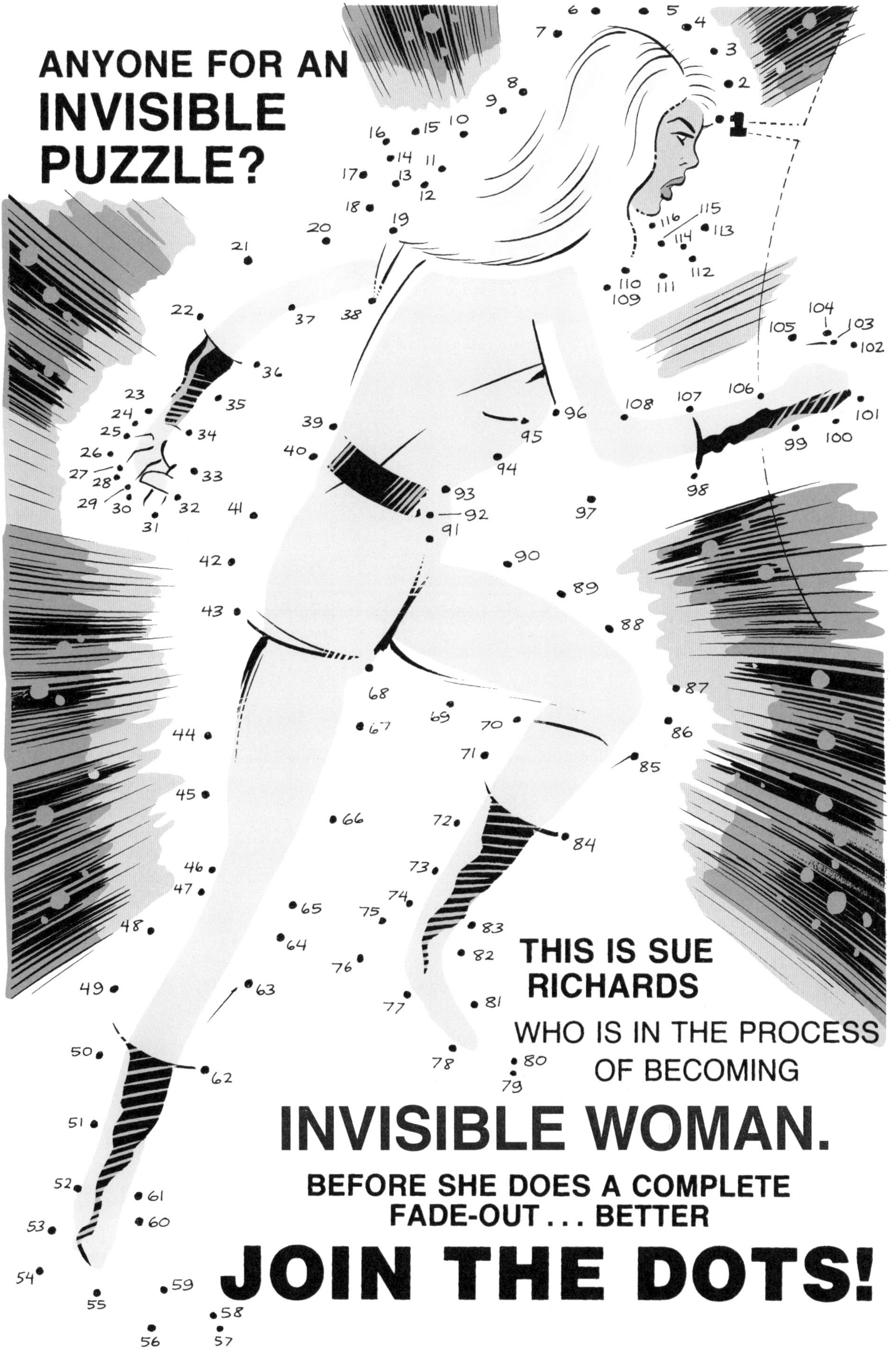

**THIS IS SUE RICHARDS**
WHO IS IN THE PROCESS OF BECOMING

# INVISIBLE WOMAN.

**BEFORE SHE DOES A COMPLETE FADE-OUT . . . BETTER**

# JOIN THE DOTS!

# MARVEL FUN AND GAMES'

# QUIZ-A-WHIZ

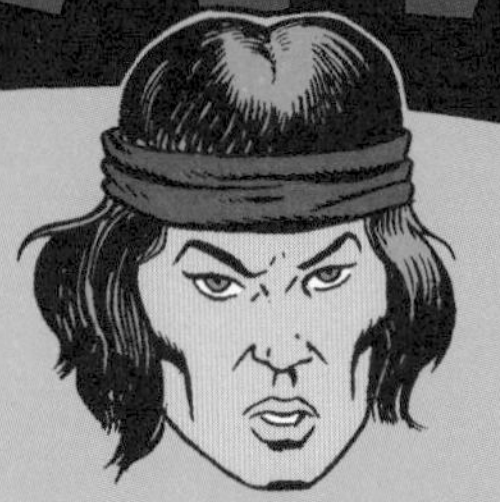

SHANG-CHI,
MASTER OF
KUNG FU

ANSWER PG. 143

1. WHO IS "THE MAN WITHOUT FEAR"?
   - ☐ DOCTOR DOOM
   - ☐ DAREDEVIL
   - ☐ GREEN GOBLIN

2. CAPTAIN AMERICA'S REAL NAME IS
   - ☐ KENNY ROGERS
   - ☐ BUCK ROGERS
   - ☐ STEVE ROGERS

3. WHO IS THE MASTER OF TIME?
   - ☐ ELECTRO
   - ☐ KRONUS
   - ☐ THE LIZARD

4. WANDA MAXIMOFF'S BROTHER IS
   - ☐ WHIZZER
   - ☐ QUICKSILVER
   - ☐ WONDER MAN

5. BLACK PANTHER'S REAL NAME IS
   - ☐ T'CHALLA
   - ☐ OKOYE
   - ☐ M'BAKU

6. HE WAS DOCTOR DOOM'S ROBOT
   - ☐ HUMAN TORCH
   - ☐ GROWING MAN
   - ☐ SEEKER

7. HE'S THE LIVING VAMPIRE
   - ☐ MORBIUS
   - ☐ WOLVERINE
   - ☐ SPIDER-MAN

8. S.H.I.E.L.D. TRAINING ROBOT
   - ☐ THE VISION
   - ☐ IMPACT
   - ☐ GROWING MAN

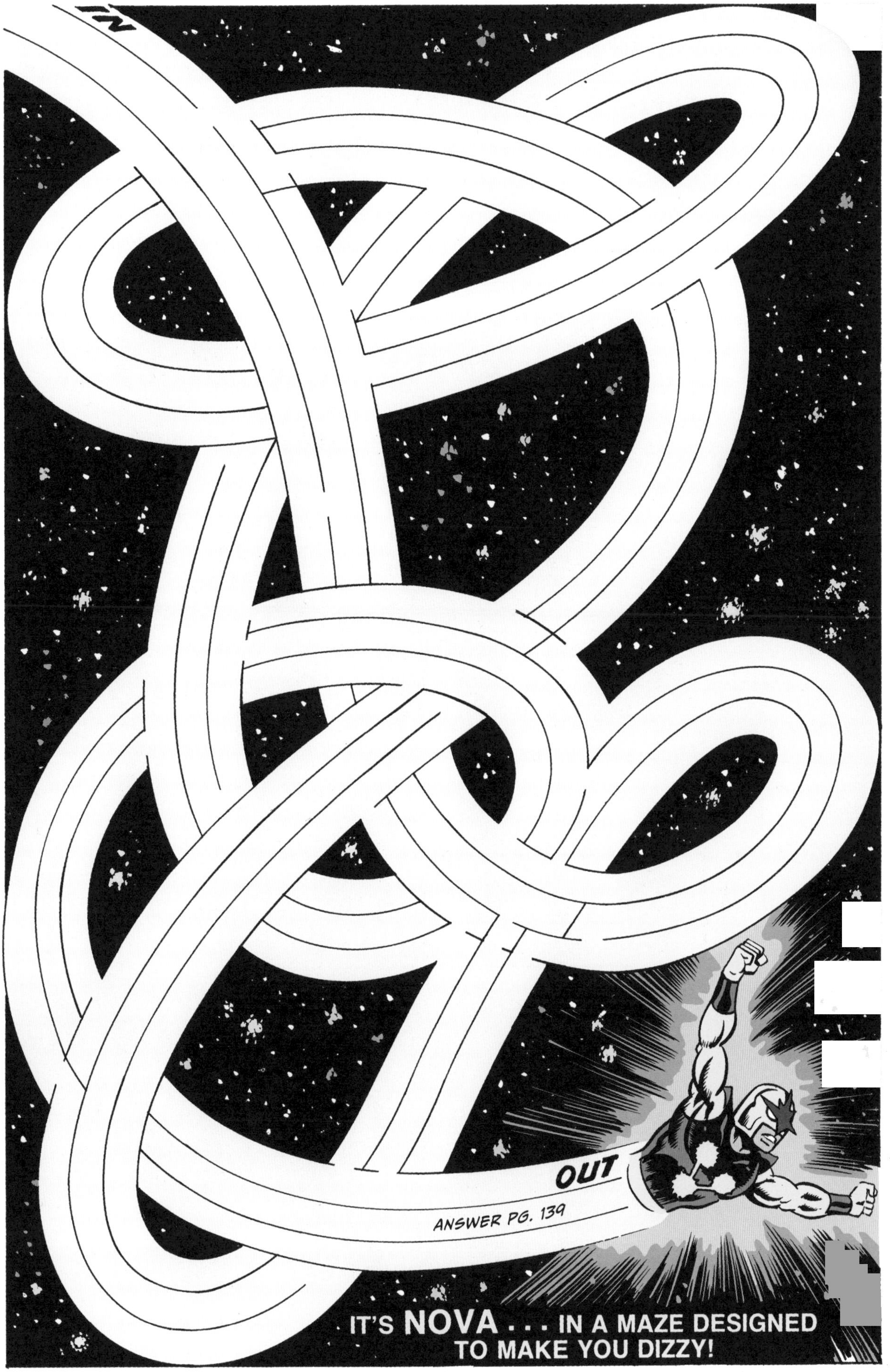
IN
OUT
ANSWER PG. 139
IT'S NOVA . . . IN A MAZE DESIGNED TO MAKE YOU DIZZY!

# USE YOUR SECRET CODE BREAKER*

## TO FIND THE MARVEL SUPER HEROES AND VILLAINS, TOO!

This one's a little different. We'll give you the actual name . . . use your Secret Code Breaker and come up with the answer in pictures. It's just like any word game, only it's visual. We'll give you a freebie just to help you out. Do it horizontal, vertical, diagonal, and backward, in a straight line, and no skipping.

**Find: Wasp, Beast, Iceman, Loki, Falcon, Cyclops, Eel, Storm, Hercules, Valkyrie, Angel, Wizard, Owl, Odin, Blob, Ox, Cobra, Ivan, Lizard, and Hela**

*ANSWER PG. 140*

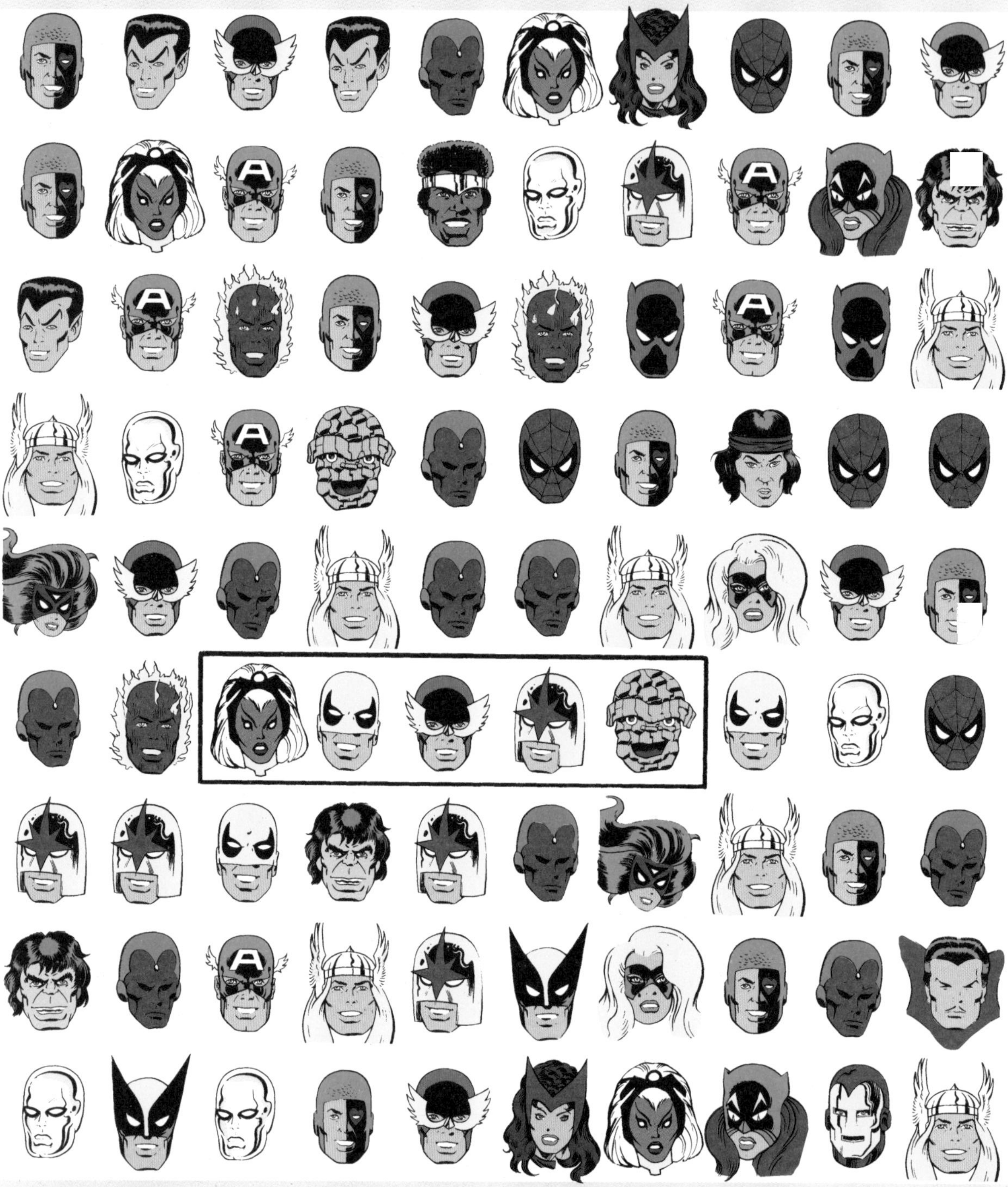

**BONUS!** There's a number of Marvel Super Heroes left over. Simply rearrange the letters they represent (using your secret Code Breaker) and you'll know who it is.

*CHECK PG. 24 TO CRACK THIS ONE!

# FAMILY REUNION TIME
## with SUB-MARINER

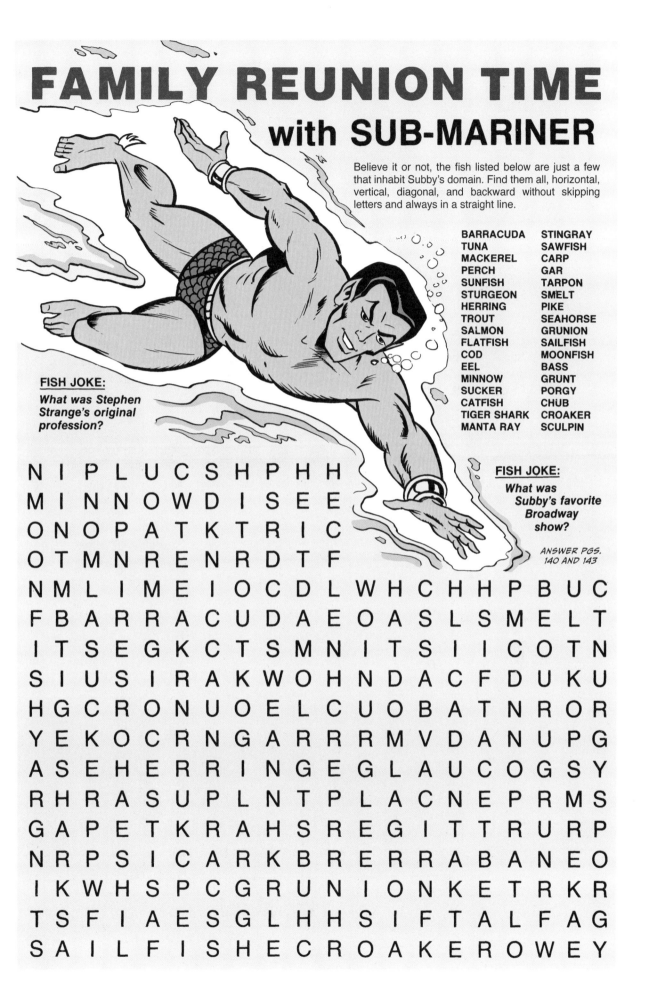

Believe it or not, the fish listed below are just a few that inhabit Subby's domain. Find them all, horizontal, vertical, diagonal, and backward without skipping letters and always in a straight line.

| | |
|---|---|
| BARRACUDA | STINGRAY |
| TUNA | SAWFISH |
| MACKEREL | CARP |
| PERCH | GAR |
| SUNFISH | TARPON |
| STURGEON | SMELT |
| HERRING | PIKE |
| TROUT | SEAHORSE |
| SALMON | GRUNION |
| FLATFISH | SAILFISH |
| COD | MOONFISH |
| EEL | BASS |
| MINNOW | GRUNT |
| SUCKER | PORGY |
| CATFISH | CHUB |
| TIGER SHARK | CROAKER |
| MANTA RAY | SCULPIN |

**FISH JOKE:**
*What was Stephen Strange's original profession?*

**FISH JOKE:**
*What was Subby's favorite Broadway show?*

*ANSWER PGS. 140 AND 143*

```
N I P L U C S H P H H
M I N N O W D I S E E
O N O P A T K T R I C
O T M N R E N R D T F
N M L I M E I O C D L W H C H H P B U C
F B A R R A C U D A E O A S L S M E L T
I T S E G K C T S M N I T S I I C O T N
S I U S I R A K W O H N D A C F D U K U
H G C R O N U O E L C U O B A T N R O R
Y E K O C R N G A R R R M V D A N U P G
A S E H E R R I N G E G L A U C O G S Y
R H R A S U P L N T P L A C N E P R M S
G A P E T K R A H S R E G I T T R U R P
N R P S I C A R K B R E R R A B A N E O
I K W H S P C G R U N I O N K E T R K R
T S F I A E S G L H H S I F T A L F A G
S A I L F I S H E C R O A K E R O W E Y
```

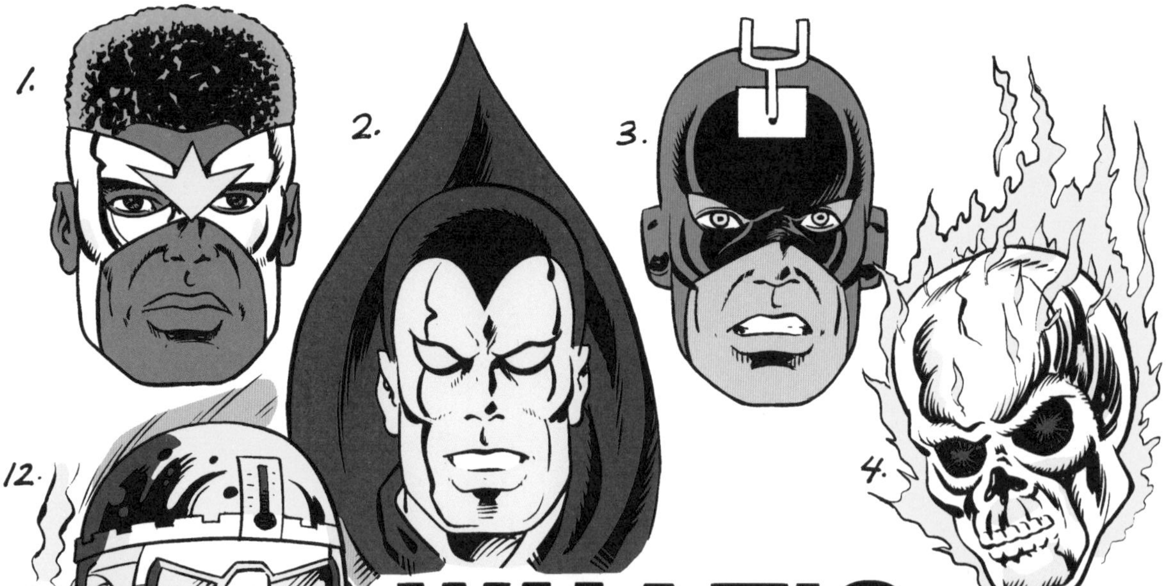

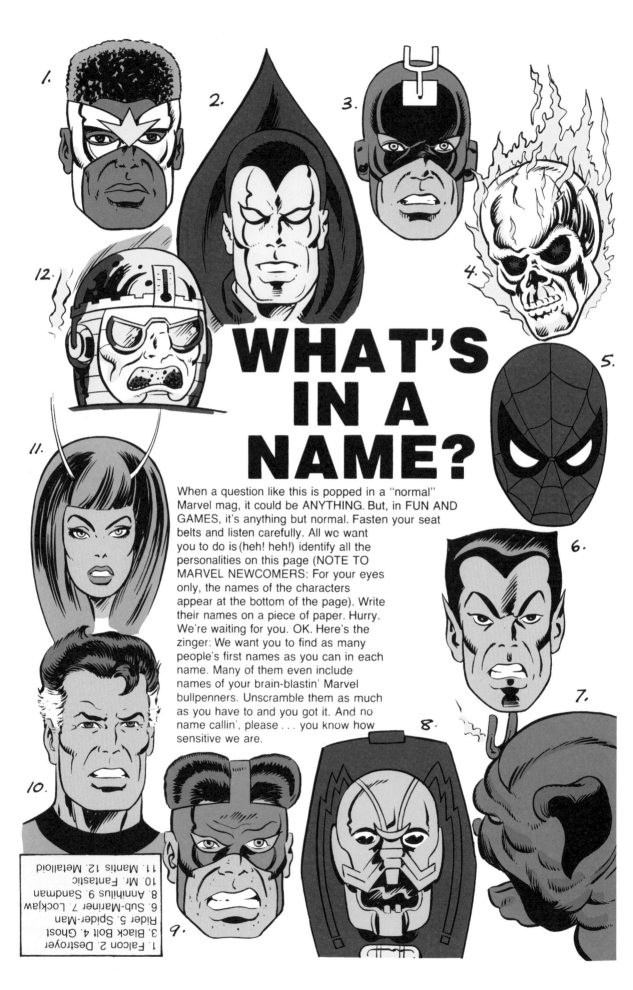

# WHAT'S IN A NAME?

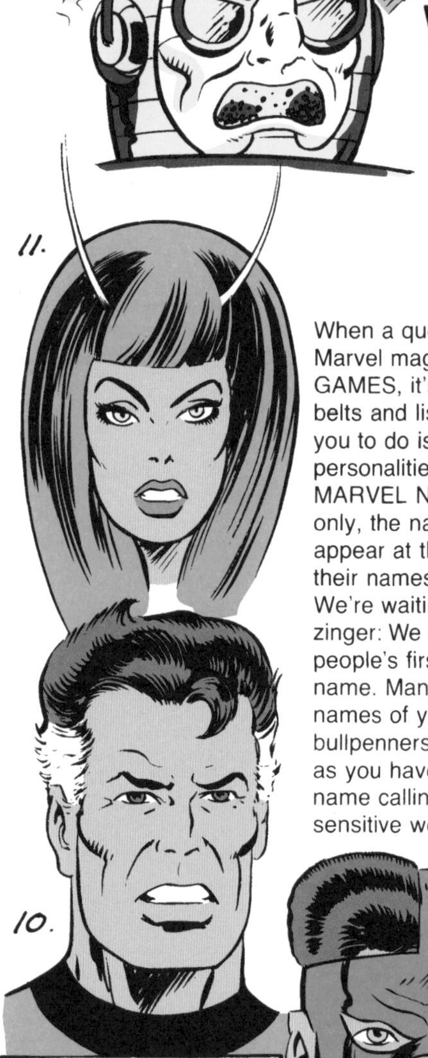

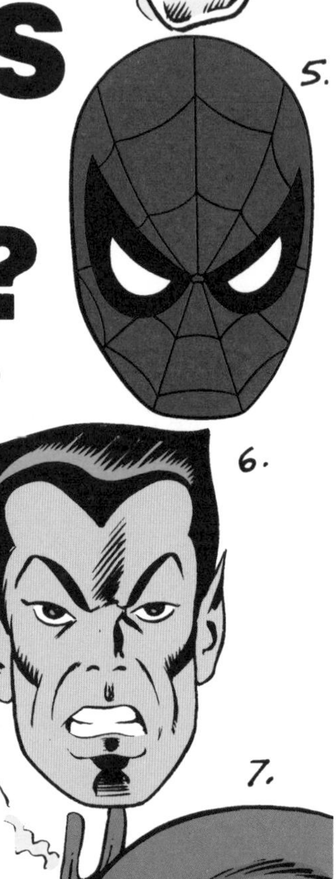

When a question like this is popped in a "normal" Marvel mag, it could be ANYTHING. But, in FUN AND GAMES, it's anything but normal. Fasten your seat belts and listen carefully. All we want you to do is (heh! heh!) identify all the personalities on this page (NOTE TO MARVEL NEWCOMERS: For your eyes only, the names of the characters appear at the bottom of the page). Write their names on a piece of paper. Hurry. We're waiting for you. OK. Here's the zinger: We want you to find as many people's first names as you can in each name. Many of them even include names of your brain-blastin' Marvel bullpenners. Unscramble them as much as you have to and you got it. And no name callin', please . . . you know how sensitive we are.

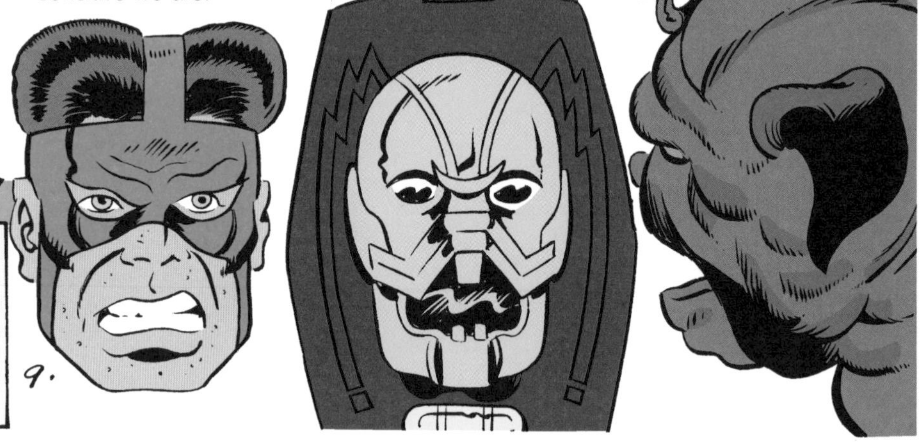

1. Falcon 2. Destroyer 3. Black Bolt 4. Ghost Rider 5. Spider-Man 6. Sub-Mariner 7. Lockjaw 8. Annihilus 9. Sandman 10. Mr. Fantastic 11. Mantis 12. Metalloid

# LEARN TO DRAW MARVEL CHARACTERS*

# HELLCAT

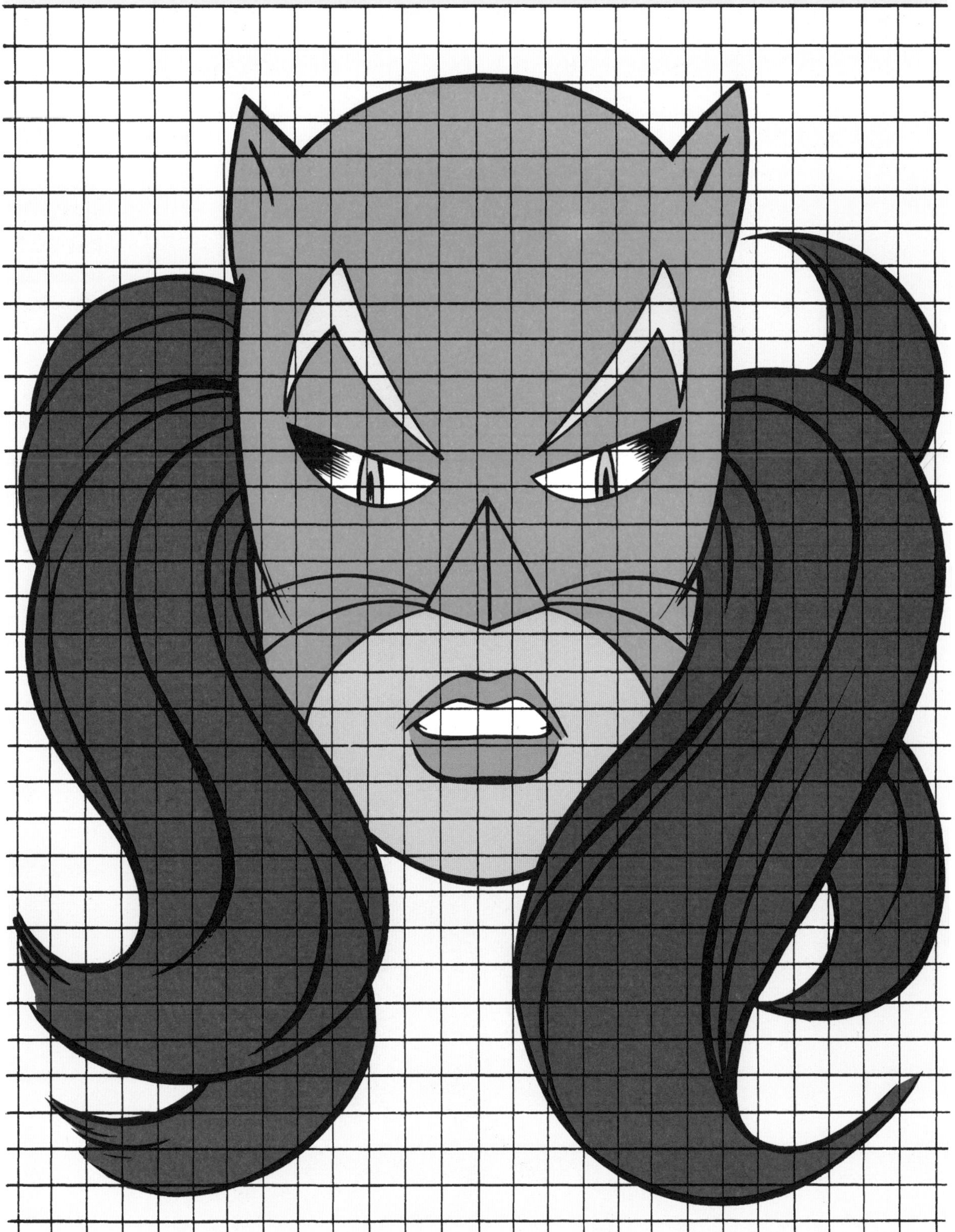

*GRAB SOME GRAPH PAPER TO DRAW LIKE THE PROS!

# WHAT'S MISSING?

There are 3 different things missing in each drawing. Compare them carefully against each other and you'll have no problem. We had special orders from Doctor Doom to go easy with this one . . . and when he speaks . . . guess who listens?

ANSWER PG. 140

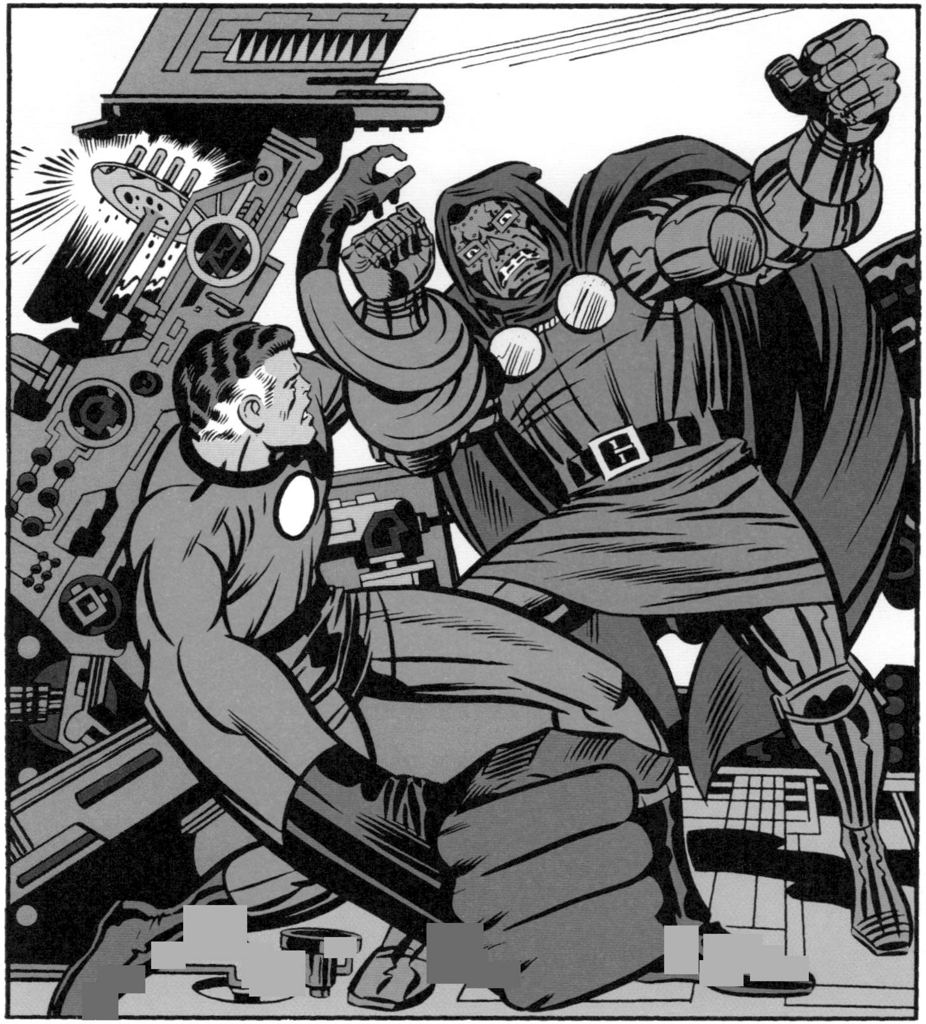

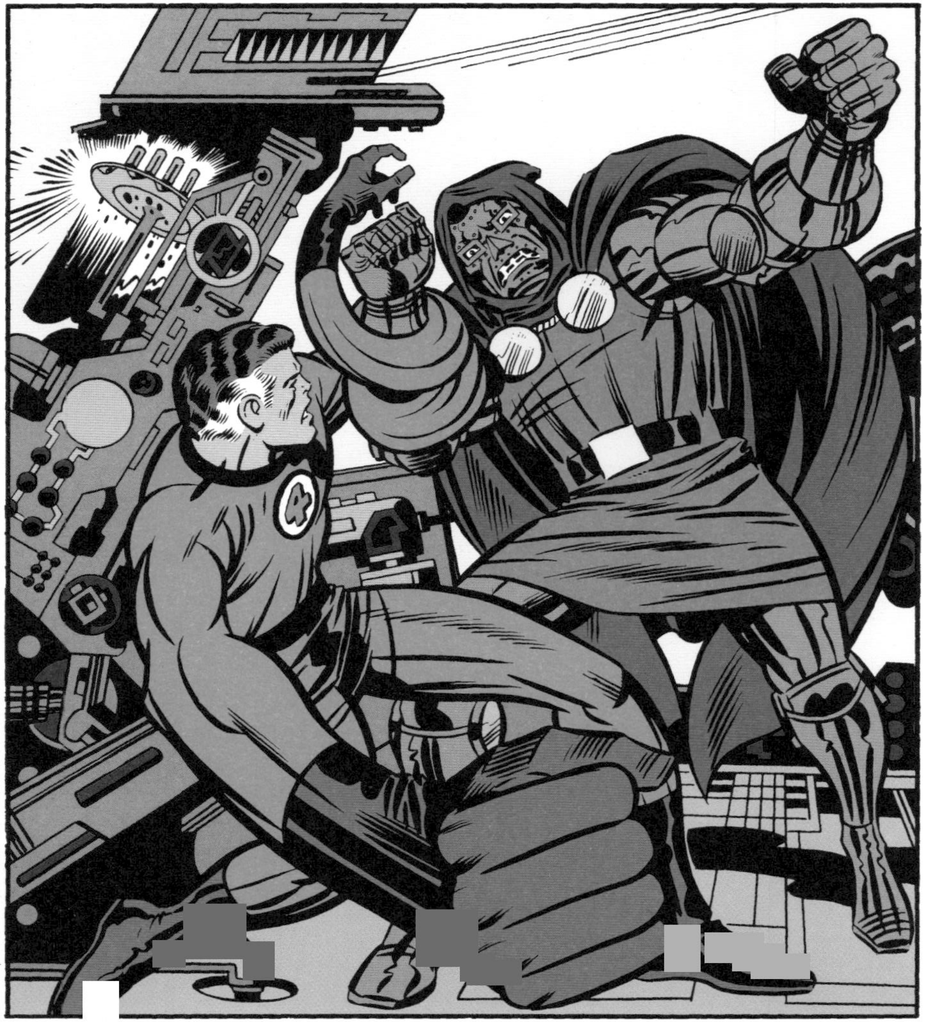

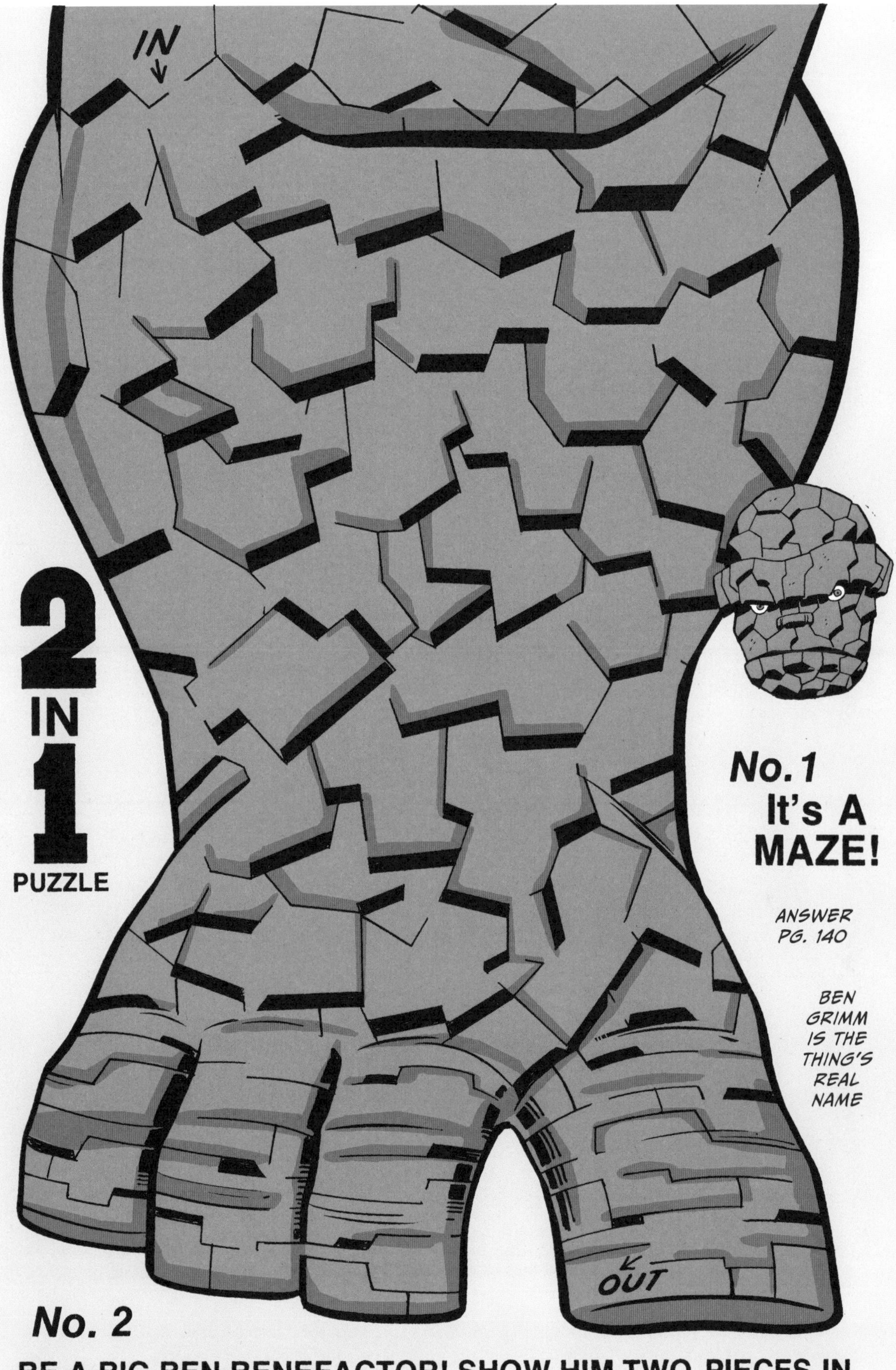
IN
OUT

# 2 IN 1 PUZZLE

## No. 1 It's A MAZE!

ANSWER PG. 140

BEN GRIMM IS THE THING'S REAL NAME

## No. 2

**BE A BIG BEN BENEFACTOR! SHOW HIM TWO PIECES IN THIS LUMBERING LIMB THAT ARE EXACTLY THE SAME!**

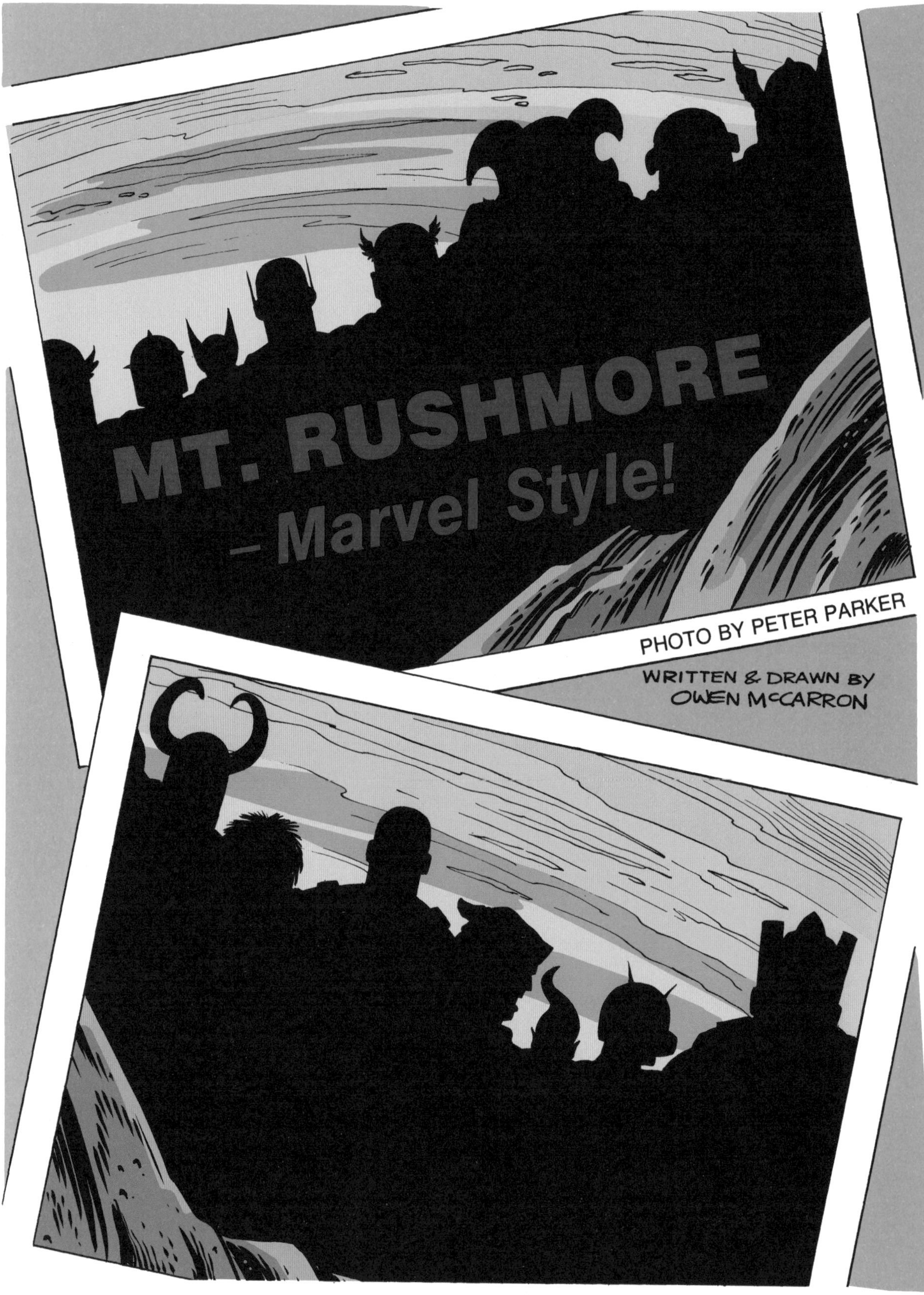
MT. RUSHMORE
– Marvel Style!
PHOTO BY PETER PARKER
WRITTEN & DRAWN BY
OWEN McCARRON

With his trusty camera slung over his shoulder, Peter Parker was out for a stroll . . . having a much-deserved rest from web-slinging. The sun was going down as he spotted a couple of mountain ranges that would look great in silhouette. When he developed them, he found that the rock formations looked like Marvel characters. Your job, mighty Marvel mountain-climber, is to tell us who those characters are.

ANSWER PG. 143

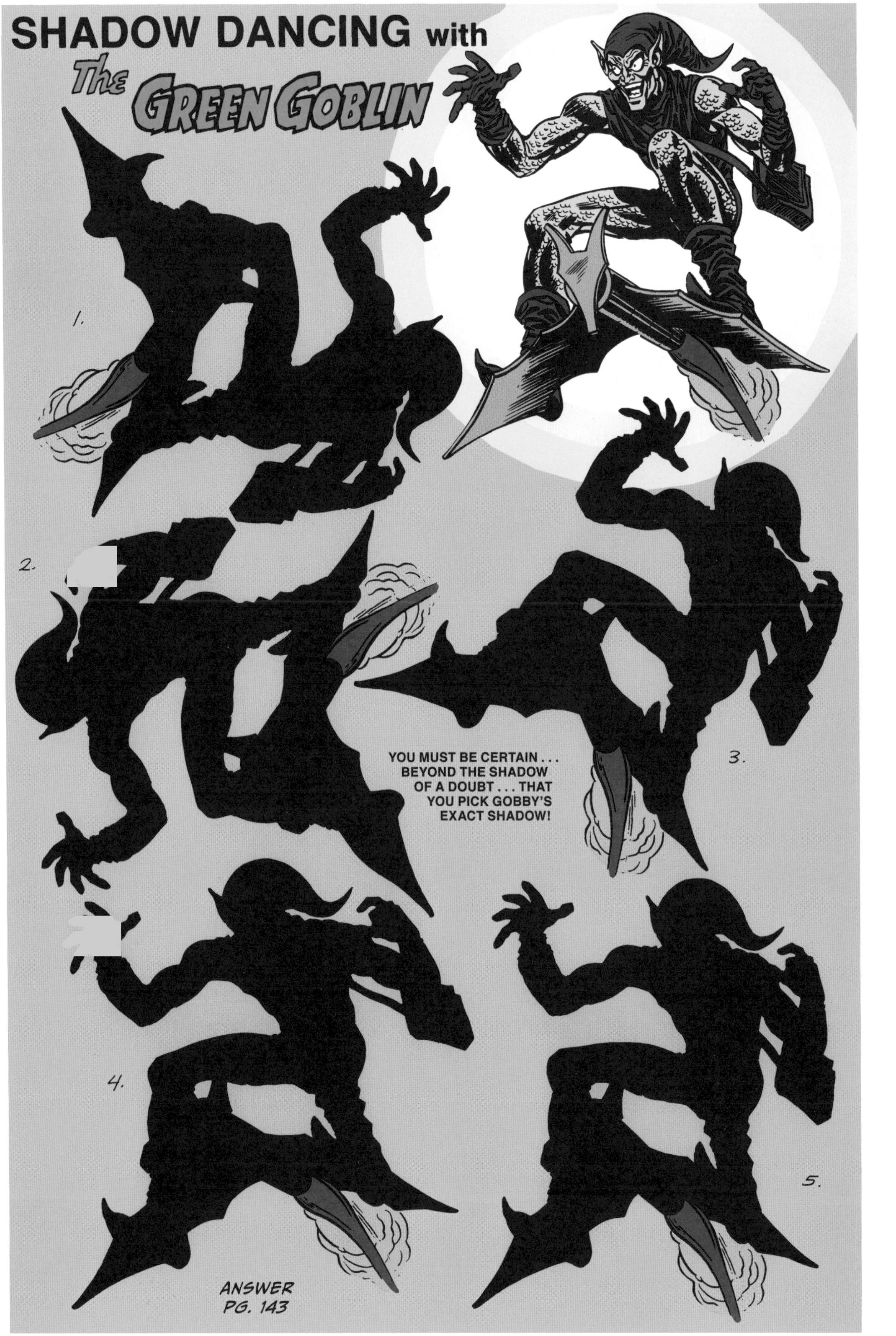
SHADOW DANCING with
The GREEN GOBLIN
1.
2.
YOU MUST BE CERTAIN . . . BEYOND THE SHADOW OF A DOUBT . . . THAT YOU PICK GOBBY'S EXACT SHADOW!
3.
4.
5.
ANSWER PG. 143

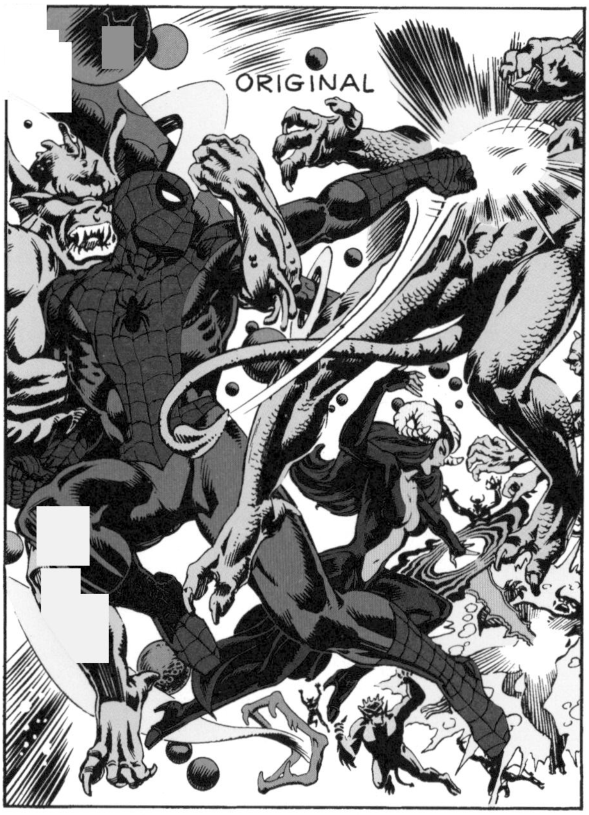
ORIGINAL

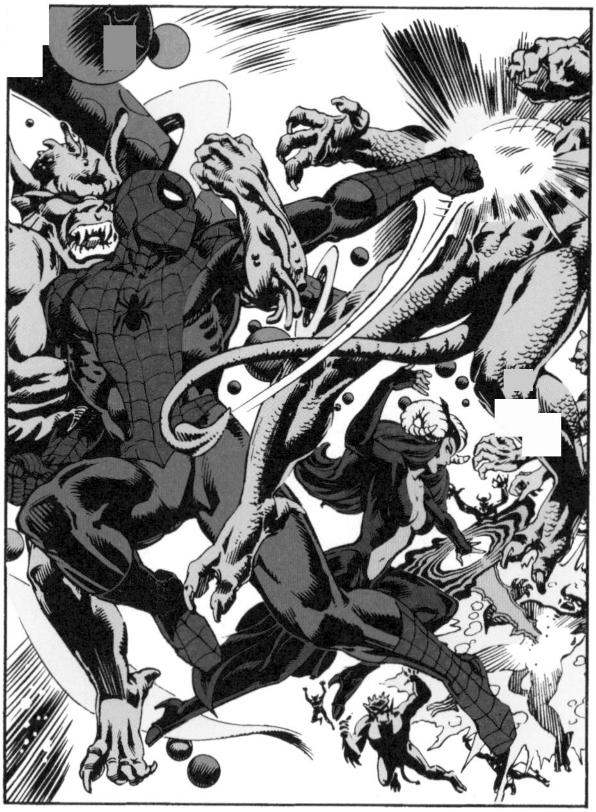

# WHAT'S MISSING?

Get out your magnifying glasses, mystery lover . . . it's time to solve another baffling mystery of WHAT'S MISSING. Study the pictures carefully against the one marked ORIGINAL, and let's see how many missing things you can find in each one. No fair to call Sherlock Holmes or the Pink Panther for help.

ANSWER PG. 141

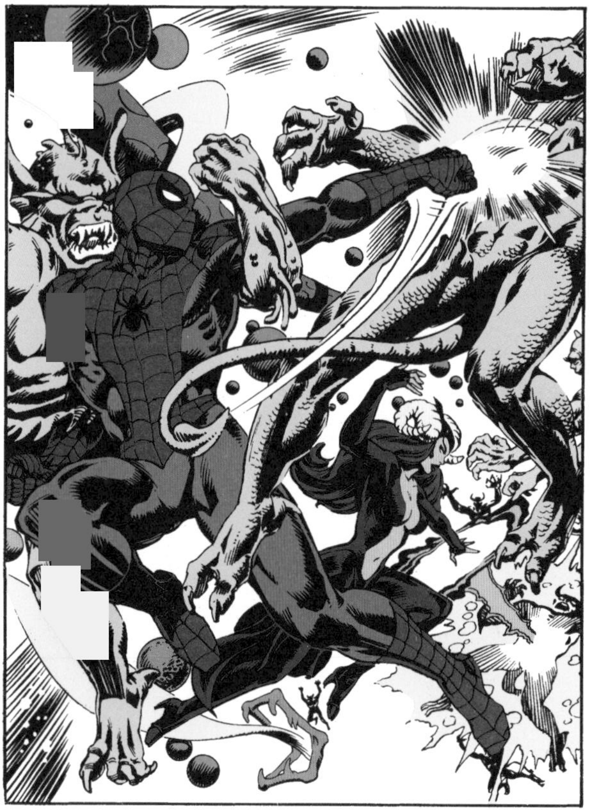

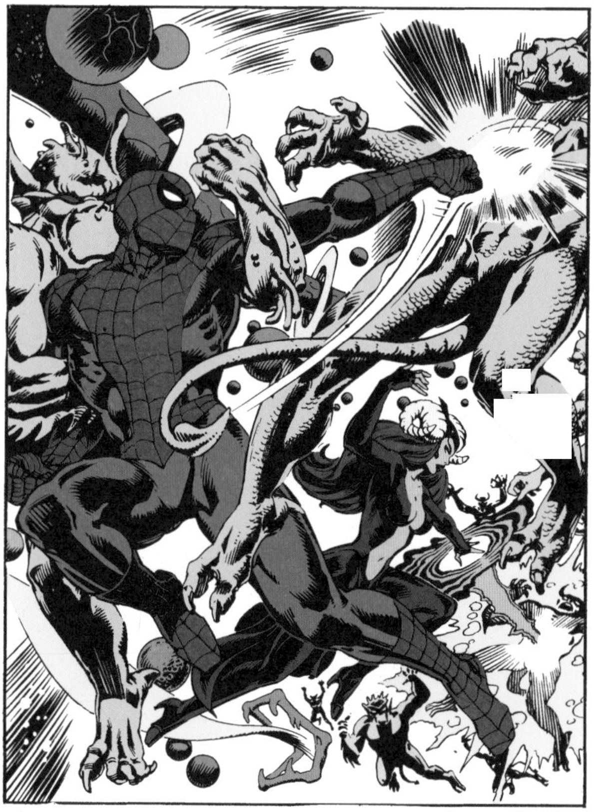

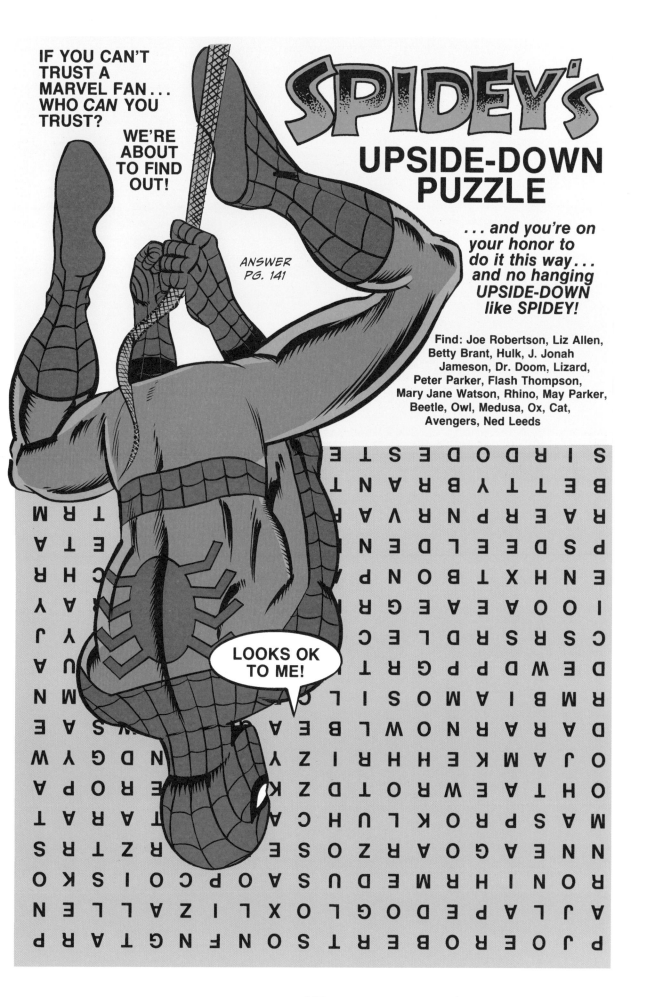

IF YOU CAN'T TRUST A MARVEL FAN... WHO *CAN* YOU TRUST?

WE'RE ABOUT TO FIND OUT!

# SPIDEY'S UPSIDE-DOWN PUZZLE

ANSWER PG. 141

*... and you're on your honor to do it this way... and no hanging UPSIDE-DOWN like SPIDEY!*

Find: Joe Robertson, Liz Allen, Betty Brant, Hulk, J. Jonah Jameson, Dr. Doom, Lizard, Peter Parker, Flash Thompson, Mary Jane Watson, Rhino, May Parker, Beetle, Owl, Medusa, Ox, Cat, Avengers, Ned Leeds

LOOKS OK TO ME!

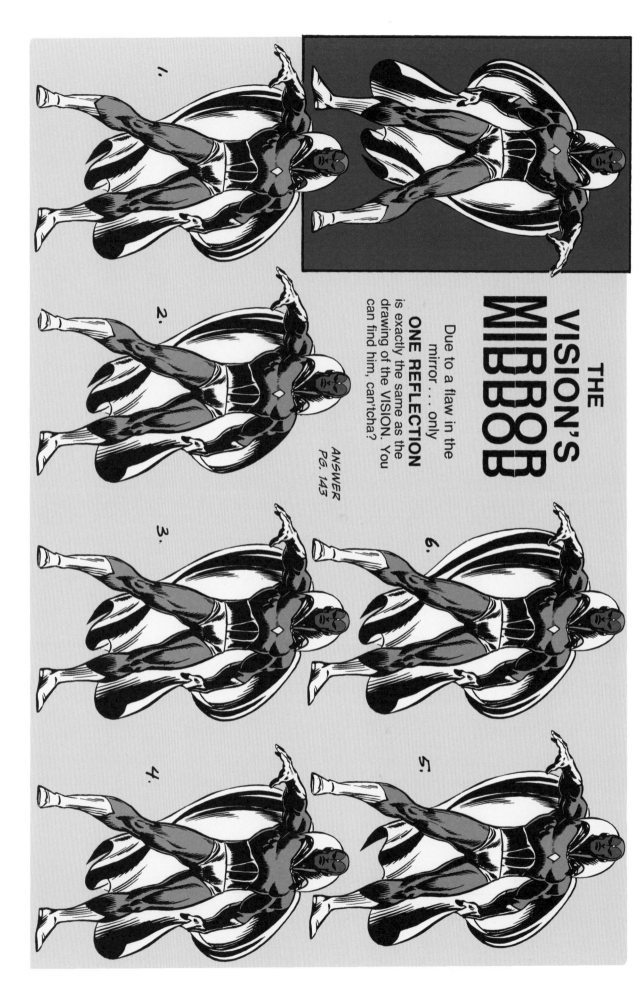

# THE VISION'S MIRROR

Due to a flaw in the mirror... only **ONE REFLECTION** is exactly the same as the drawing of the VISION. You can find him, can'tcha?

ANSWER PG. 143

1.

2.

3.

4.

5.

6.

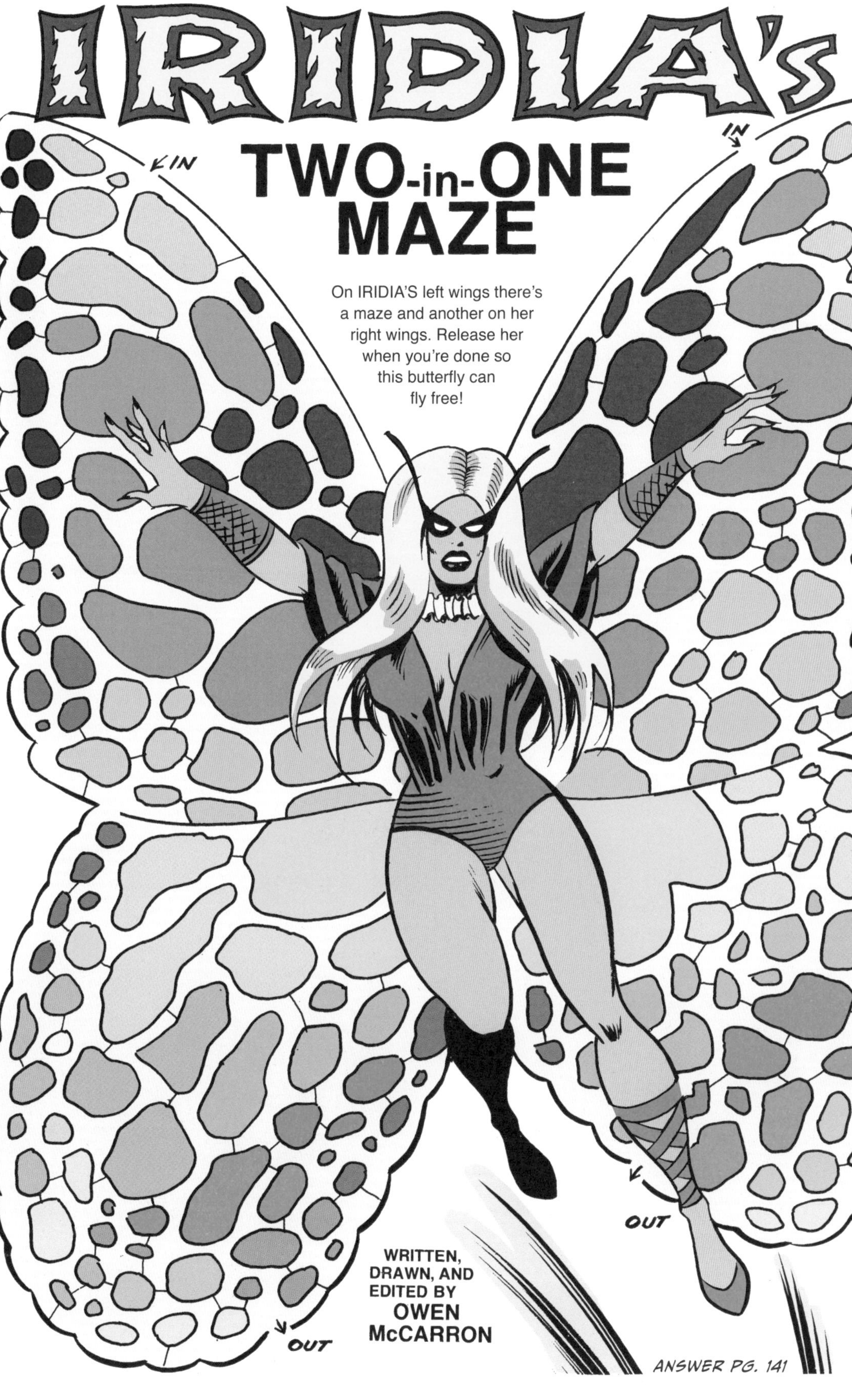
IRIDIA'S
TWO-in-ONE MAZE
On IRIDIA'S left wings there's a maze and another on her right wings. Release her when you're done so this butterfly can fly free!
IN
IN
OUT
OUT
WRITTEN, DRAWN, AND EDITED BY OWEN McCARRON
ANSWER PG. 141

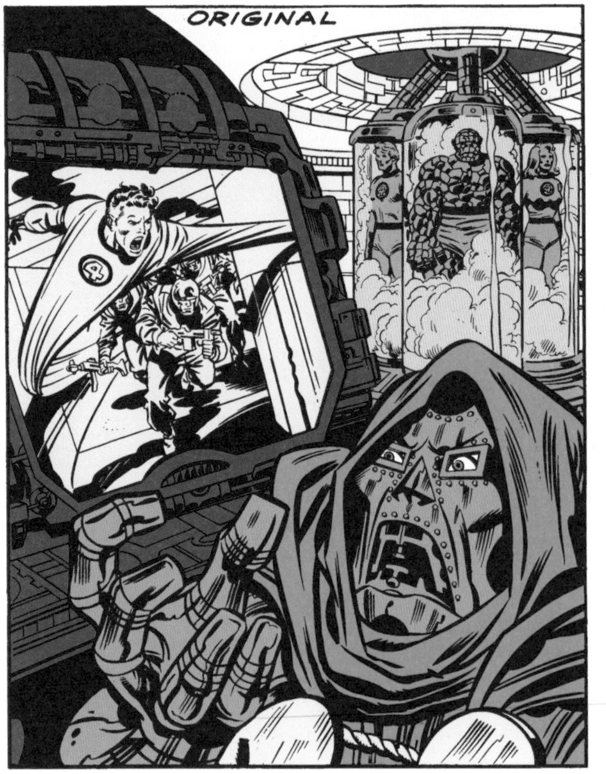
ORIGINAL

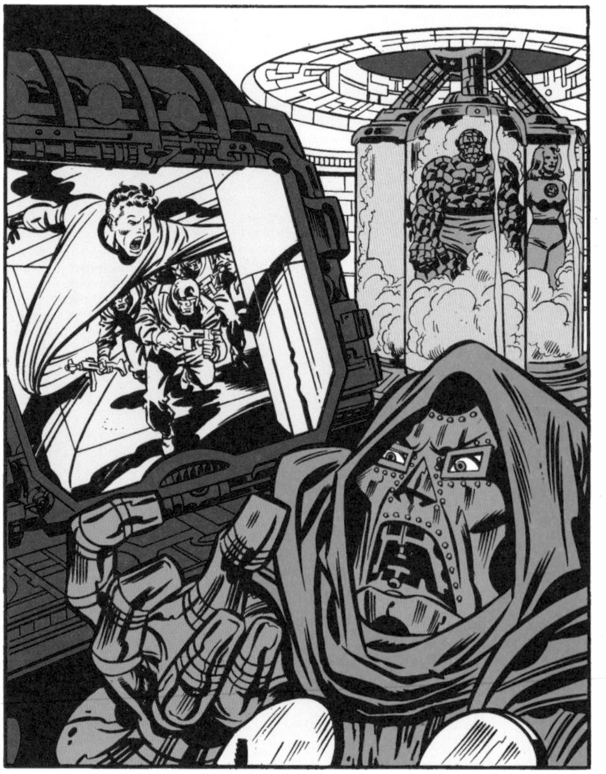

# WHAT'S MISSING?

Compare the three drawings against the one marked original and see what's missing. (Hint: there are several things missing in each one.)

ANSWER PG. 141

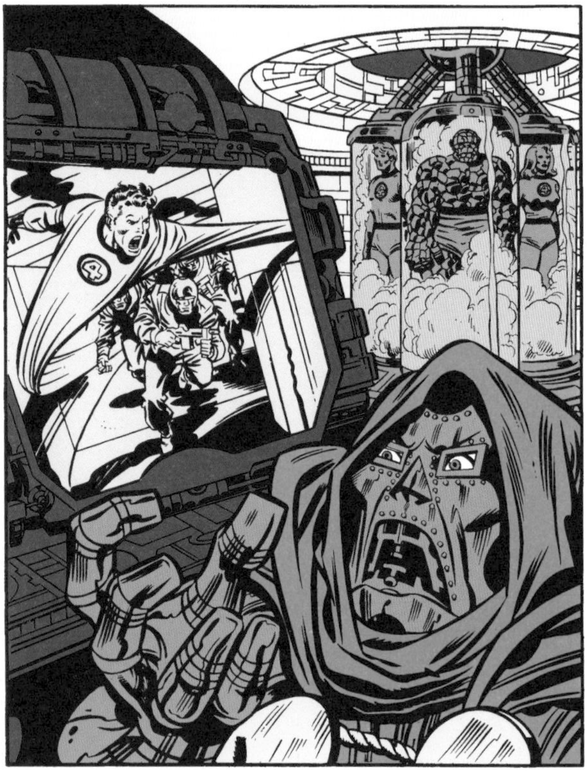

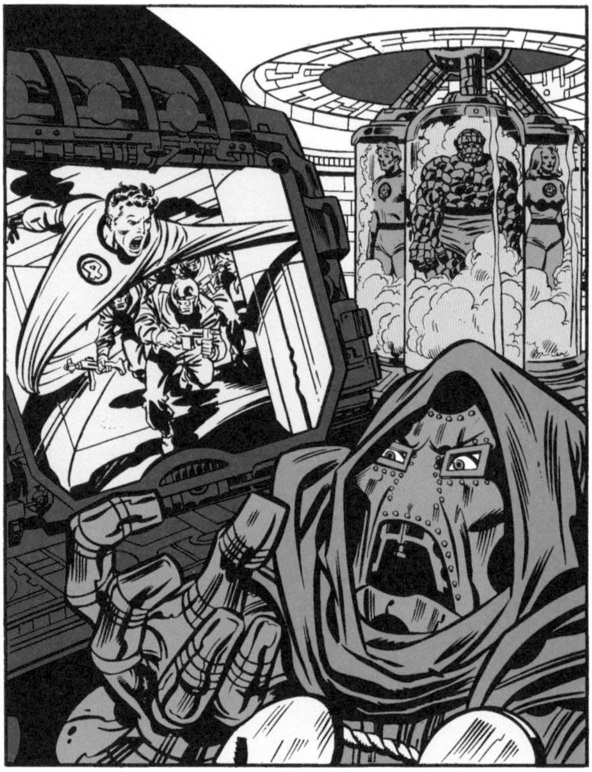

# LEARN TO DRAW
## MARVEL CHARACTERS*

# DOCTOR
# DOOM

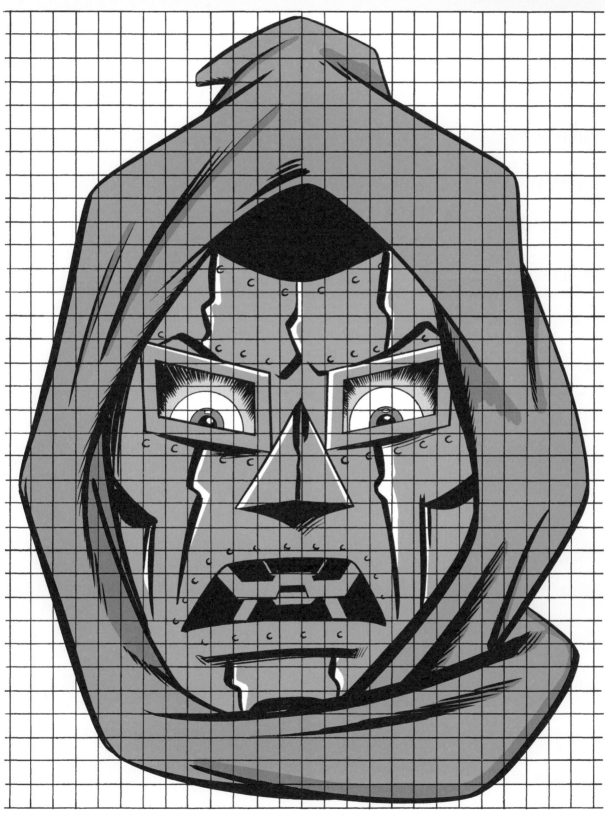

*GRAB SOME GRAPH PAPER TO DRAW LIKE THE PROS!

# ONLY MARVEL COULD COME UP WITH SUCH A MIND-BENDING PUZZLE CONCEPT!

# QUADRA · WORD FIND

**FIND EACH OF THE MARVEL SUPER HEROES SHOWN HERE FOUR TIMES**

Horizontal, vertical, diagonal, and backward, always in a straight line without skipping letters.

*ANSWER PG. 142*

```
T Y R O N Y R U F K C I N G K N O O M
H N R O O M H V A G L V H O Y G V A P
C I P U N O G A R D N O O M N H M O P
V C G O F O A G H O S T R I D E R H O
A K A H W K G D R T N I K C V W O O W
G F W V V R C A R D N O H A W K E Y E
H U O X Y W I I R E O O V R K A O P R
Y R P K R K D R N D E Y E K W A H V M
G Y L T W E E U Y F N N V N O A V M A
M A N H R Y I F V M O O N D R A G O N
V E O S O E R R V H A V O N O H V N N
O P O D O O Y U G V T A G M O A A A N
O G O V A L K Y R I E S A G K W Y M O
F H M W G C L V G Y O O R H E K L R P
P O W E R M A N E C R V D O G E R E G
N S G W V B V K N P I O N S H Y E W H
H T A O W G W A O O N N O V A E T O O
C R N P A A M H L O V O O W E N S R A
G I K I H R N I N K P V M O O N R P V
J D N H E G M E I R Y K L A V N O O M
L E A W N G O R E D I R T S O H G T S
C R O H A W K E V E G N I C K F U R Y
F P U R Y G H O S N A M R E W O P I N
```

DAREDEVIL'S **RADAR SENSE** HAS BECOME

# A MAZE OF TERROR

AS HE FACES THE UNSPEAKABLE FURY OF —?

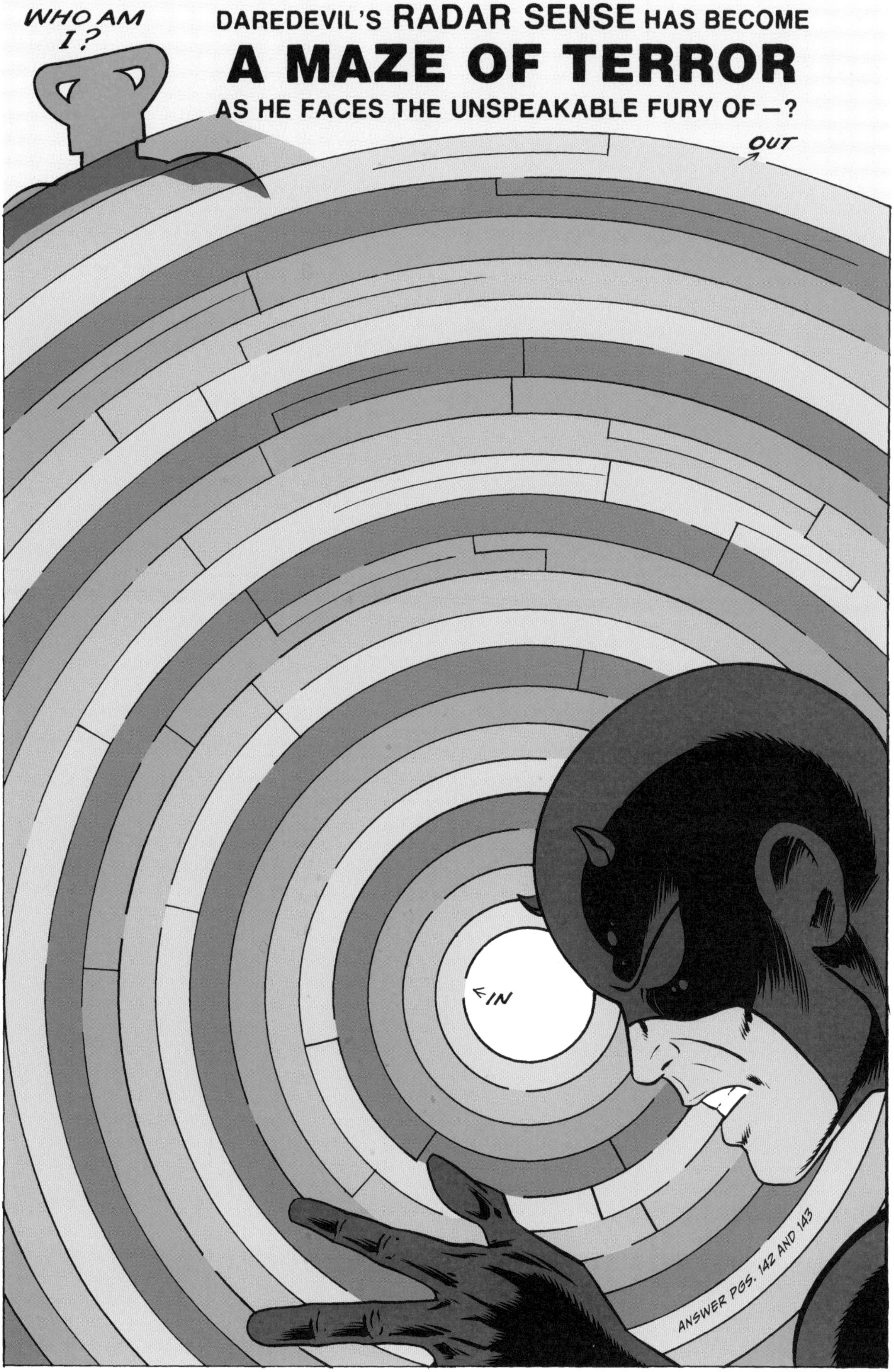
WHO AM I?
OUT
IN
ANSWER PGS. 142 AND 143

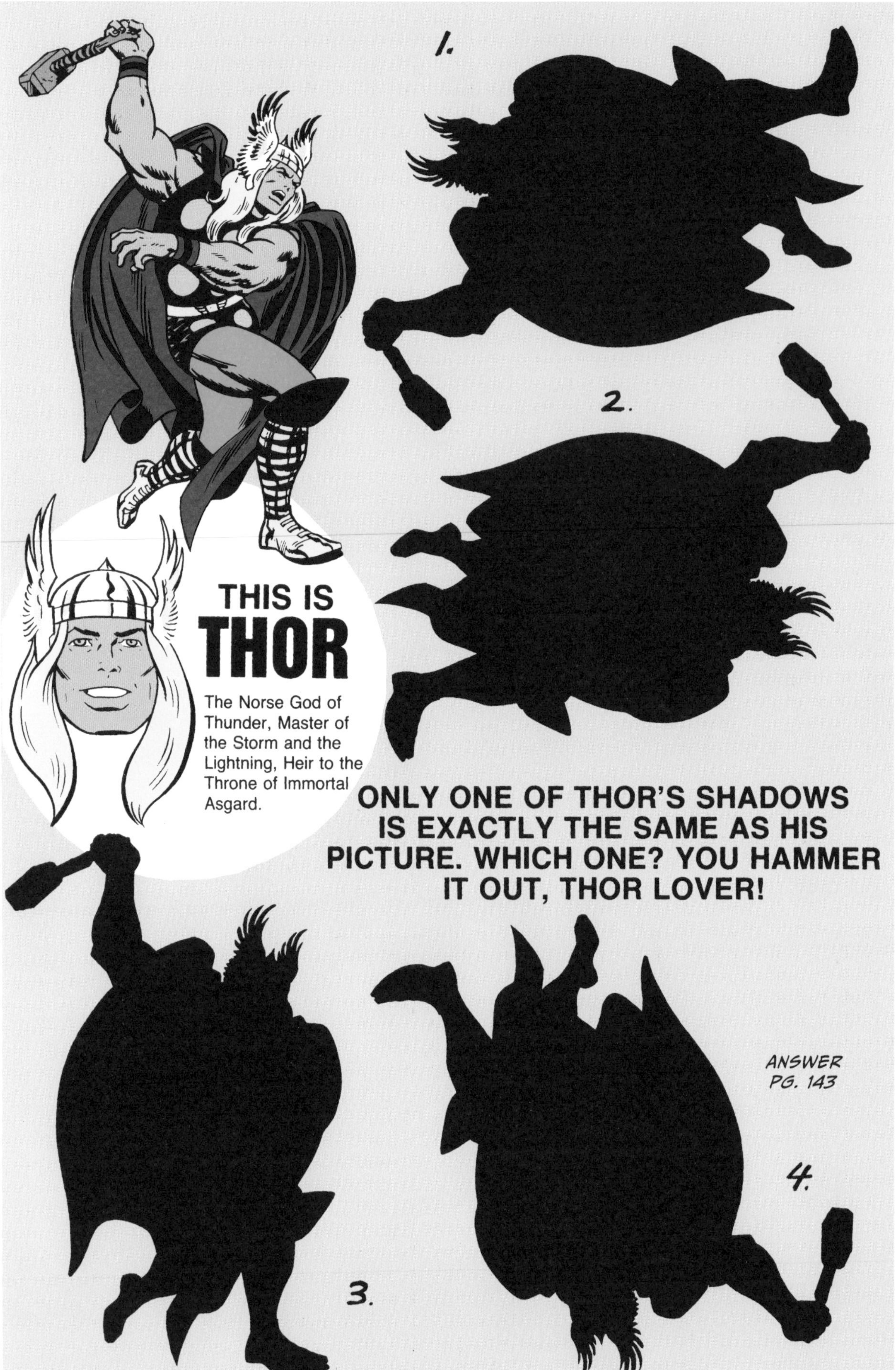
1.
2.
THIS IS
THOR
The Norse God of Thunder, Master of the Storm and the Lightning, Heir to the Throne of Immortal Asgard.
ONLY ONE OF THOR'S SHADOWS IS EXACTLY THE SAME AS HIS PICTURE. WHICH ONE? YOU HAMMER IT OUT, THOR LOVER!
ANSWER PG. 143
4.
3.

# THE JACK OF HEARTS CARD ATTACK!

**(JACK HART IS A YOUNG SUPER HERO WHO HAS PATTERNED HIS COSTUME ON A PLAYING CARD.)**

**THE JACK OF HEARTS TEAMS UP WITH THE FANTASTIC FOUR IN A CARD GAME FIGHT TO THE FINISH!**

## Here's how to play:

Firstly, you need a deck of regular playing cards, joker removed. Four players required.

From the deck of cards, the dealer, however declared, is to remove all the number four cards, and each player gets one.

After this is done, shuffle the rest of the deck and divide between the players, one card at a time. Each player should now have a total of 13 cards.

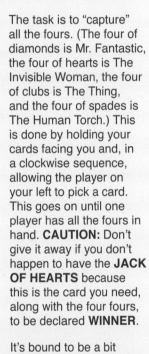

The task is to "capture" all the fours. (The four of diamonds is Mr. Fantastic, the four of hearts is The Invisible Woman, the four of clubs is The Thing, and the four of spades is The Human Torch.) This is done by holding your cards facing you and, in a clockwise sequence, allowing the player on your left to pick a card. This goes on until one player has all the fours in hand. **CAUTION:** Don't give it away if you don't happen to have the **JACK OF HEARTS** because this is the card you need, along with the four fours, to be declared **WINNER**.

It's bound to be a bit frustrating at times when you have all the fours but not the Jack of Hearts and someone picks one of your fours. Keep cool. It may take a little time to come up with the winning cards but remember: Victory is sweet. Have fun, fantastic foursome.

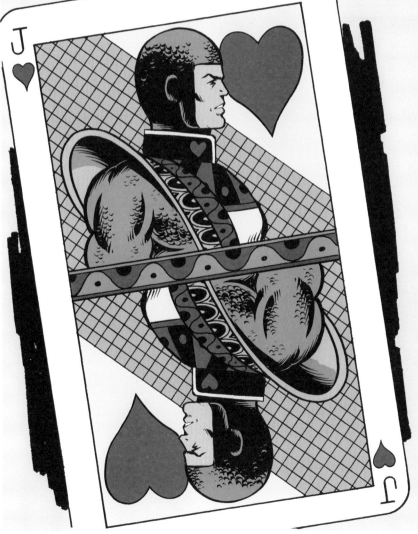

# WOLVERINE
## NEEDS YOUR HELP TO...

### FIND THE X-MEN!

**EXTRA!
FIND "OX"
7 TIMES!**

... and all these other Marvel characters who have an "X" in their names: Drexel Cord, Axonn-Karr, Phoenix, Alex, Factor X, Tryx, Xandu, Xander, Xartans, Xorr, Drax, Zaxton, Xemnu, Xemu, Terrax, Xeron, Agent Axis, Zzzax, Sphinx, Professor X, Maximus, Temax, Executioner, Triax, Martinex, Brother Ax, Texas Twister.

(WOLVERINE IS THE SHORT-TEMPERED MEMBER OF THE X-MEN.)

ANSWER PG. 142

```
T E S A X T W D A C D Q X I N E O H P S
T X A N D U X R N O R S R O Q C H A T E
E P Q S B N E A G E N T A X I S E T X P
X T R A U M E X D O B T H F J U Z E X T
P S P E L E Z N B R D C G O O M T B E R
R N O R E X A Z Z Z O W E N C I E R M D
O G R O N X X F R R E T C O G X R L A R
F R N I E O T R E T S I W T S A X E T E
E S H L P R O F E X R O R S X M G X T X
S P A J A X N C H A L T O A X L Q E P E
S X S T R C A X G O C R R P Z Y N C G L
O N R Z E P G I N T R E A S E Z R U L C
R V A O S Q X N R N H P C X A M E T R O
X X U A T A R A D T E M A Z I M U I E R
N J C W R C T E O R O M R L L E A O T D
C H X T H M A R T I N E X E O S L N E W
X E A N L C B F X X E C E A T E N E X S
R N P O C O G L G A X O N N K A R R T I
S A A L Q X I N E E H P G O T E S R X X
```

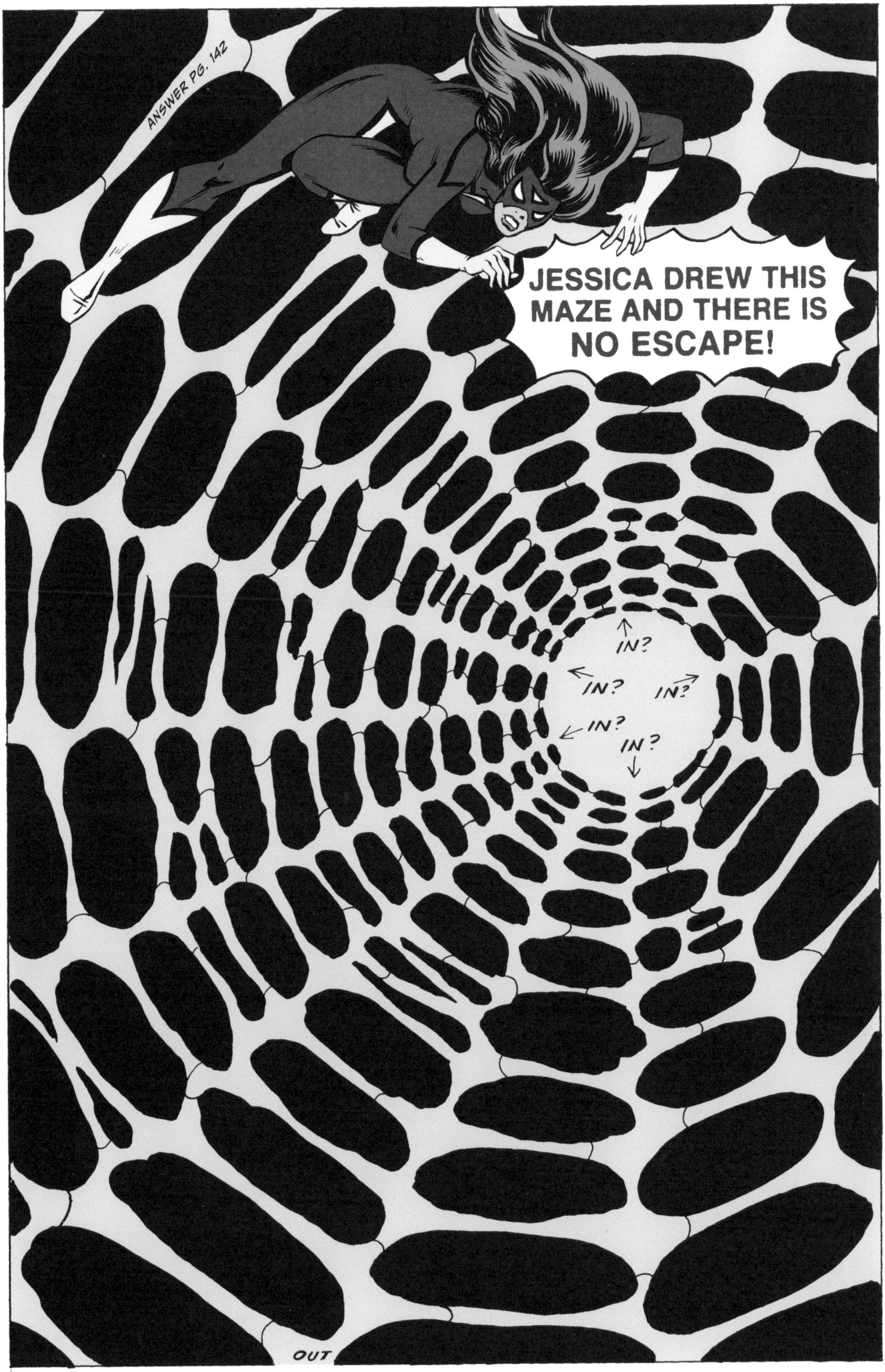
ANSWER PG. 142
JESSICA DREW THIS MAZE AND THERE IS NO ESCAPE!
IN?
IN?
IN?
IN?
IN?
OUT

**YOU DRAW THIS HALF OF IRON MAN**

*...and color it, too!*

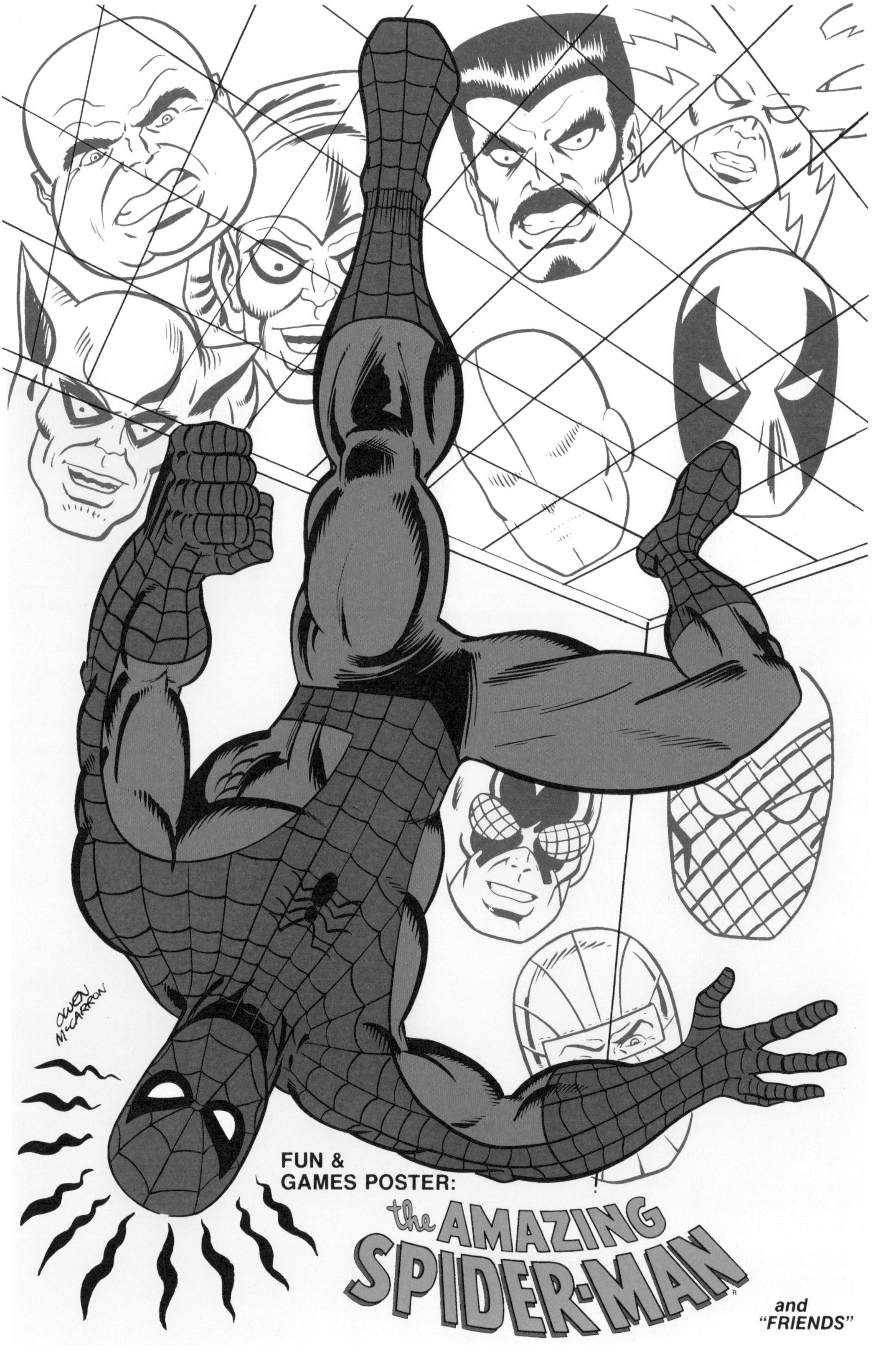
OWEN McCARRON
FUN &
GAMES POSTER:
the AMAZING
SPIDER-MAN
and
"FRIENDS"

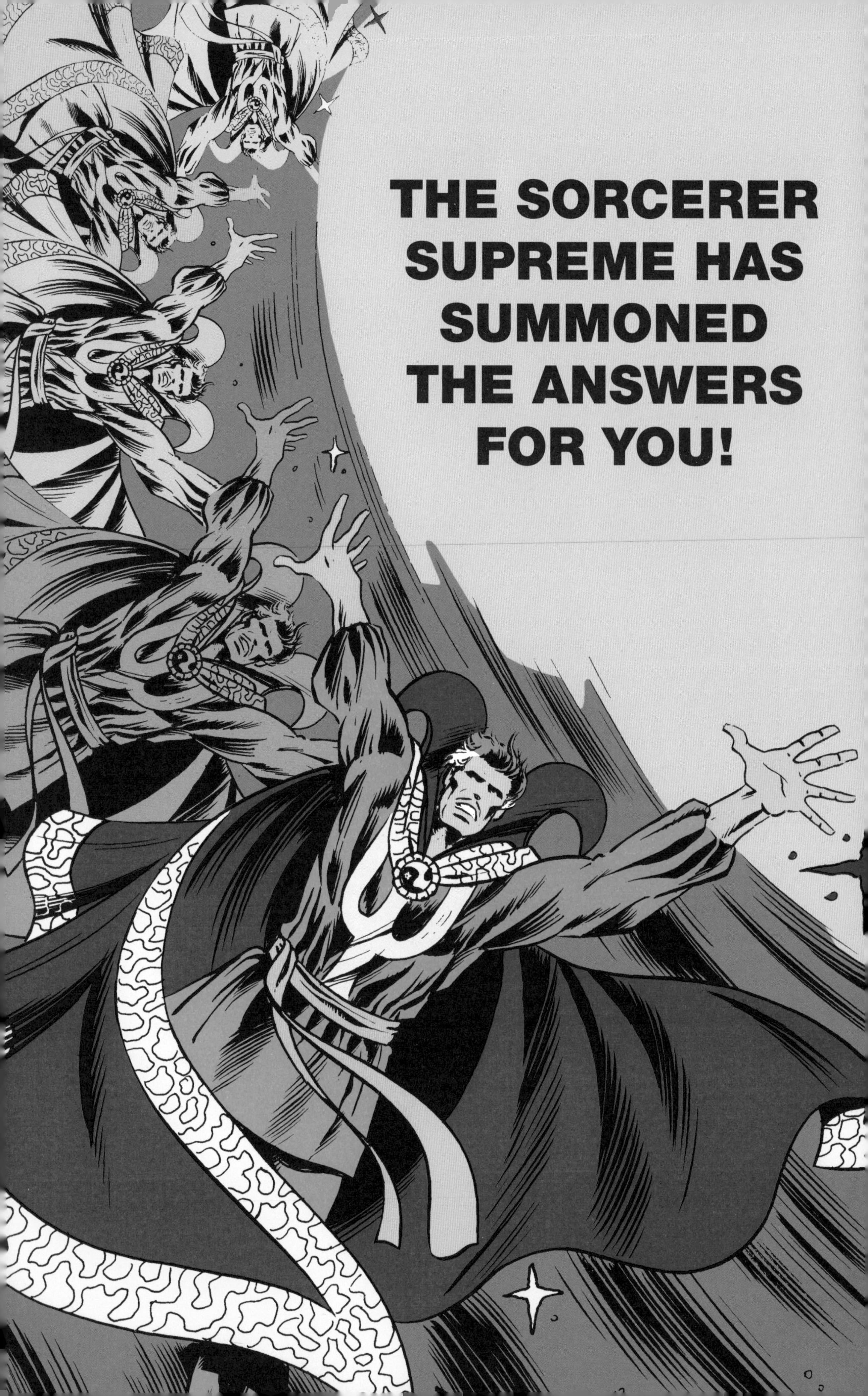
THE SORCERER SUPREME HAS SUMMONED THE ANSWERS FOR YOU!

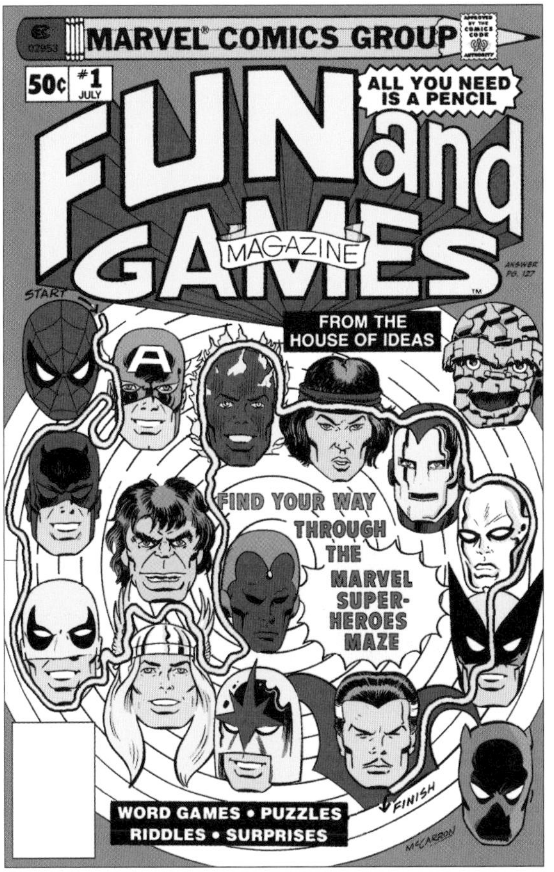
MARVEL COMICS GROUP
50¢
#1
JULY
ALL YOU NEED IS A PENCIL
FUN and GAMES
MAGAZINE
ANSWER PG. 127
START
FROM THE HOUSE OF IDEAS
FIND YOUR WAY THROUGH THE MARVEL SUPER-HEROES MAZE
FINISH
WORD GAMES • PUZZLES
RIDDLES • SURPRISES
McCARRON

4

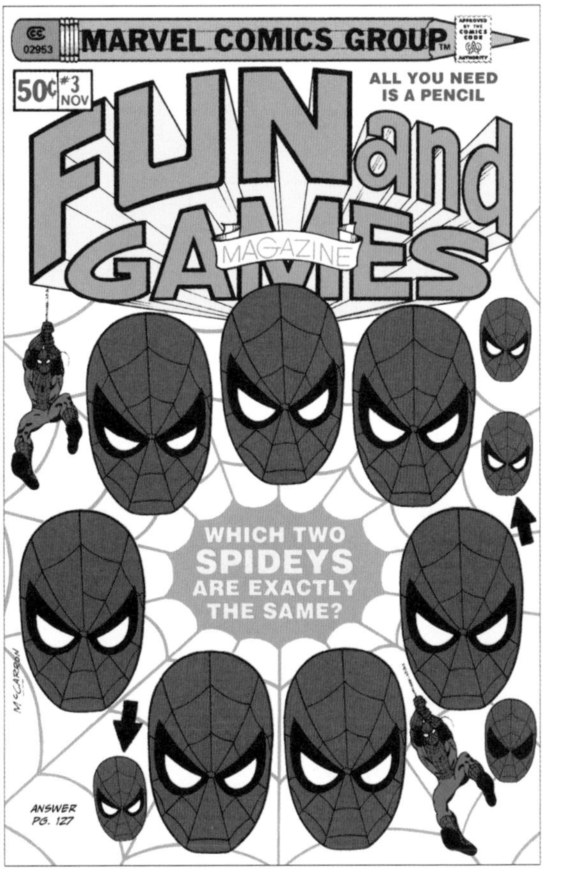
MARVEL COMICS GROUP
50¢
#3
NOV
ALL YOU NEED IS A PENCIL
FUN and GAMES
MAGAZINE
WHICH TWO SPIDEYS ARE EXACTLY THE SAME?
McCARRON
ANSWER PG. 127

6

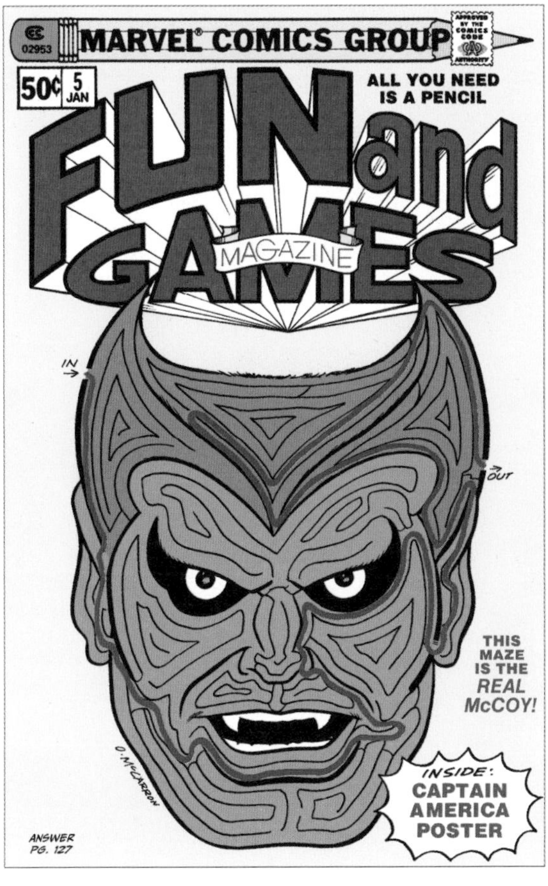
MARVEL COMICS GROUP
50¢
5
JAN
ALL YOU NEED IS A PENCIL
FUN and GAMES
MAGAZINE
IN
OUT
THIS MAZE IS THE REAL McCOY!
O. McCARRON
INSIDE: CAPTAIN AMERICA POSTER
ANSWER PG. 127

8

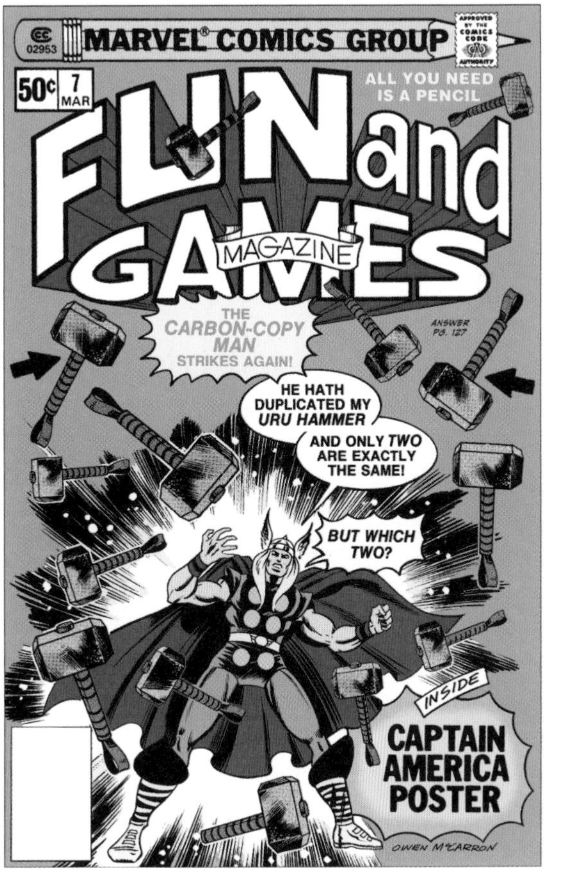
MARVEL COMICS GROUP
50¢
7
MAR
ALL YOU NEED IS A PENCIL
FUN and GAMES
MAGAZINE
THE CARBON-COPY MAN STRIKES AGAIN!
ANSWER PG. 127
HE HATH DUPLICATED MY URU HAMMER
AND ONLY TWO ARE EXACTLY THE SAME!
BUT WHICH TWO?
INSIDE
CAPTAIN AMERICA POSTER
OWEN McCARRON

10

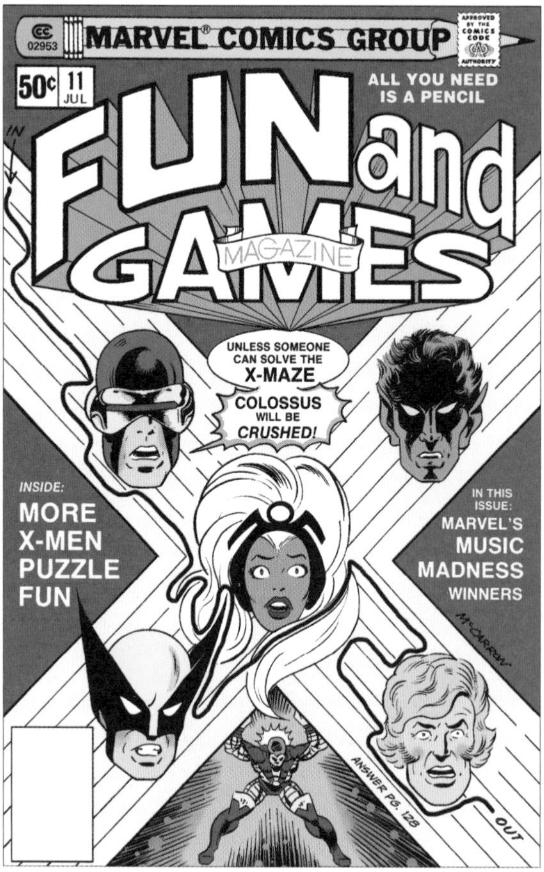
MARVEL COMICS GROUP
02953
50¢ 11 JUL
ALL YOU NEED IS A PENCIL
FUN and GAMES MAGAZINE
IN
UNLESS SOMEONE CAN SOLVE THE X-MAZE
COLOSSUS WILL BE CRUSHED!
INSIDE: MORE X-MEN PUZZLE FUN
IN THIS ISSUE: MARVEL'S MUSIC MADNESS WINNERS
ANSWER PG. 128
OUT

14

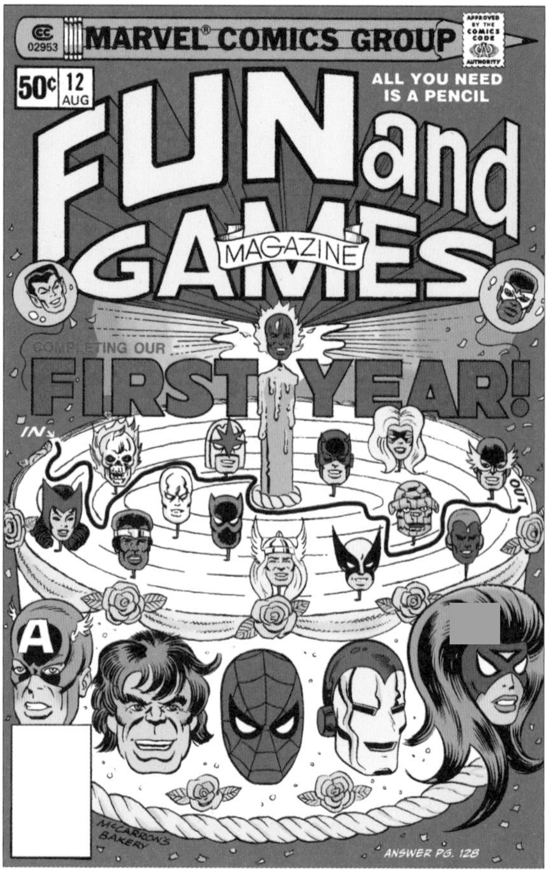
MARVEL COMICS GROUP
02953
50¢ 12 AUG
ALL YOU NEED IS A PENCIL
FUN and GAMES MAGAZINE
COMPLETING OUR FIRST YEAR!
IN
OUT
McCARRON'S BAKERY
ANSWER PG. 128

15

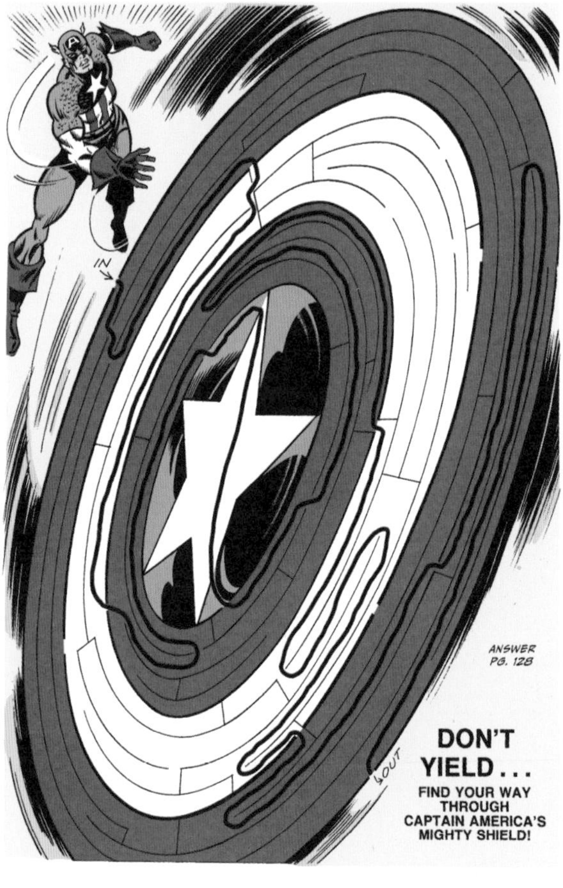
IN
ANSWER PG. 128
OUT
DON'T YIELD . . .
FIND YOUR WAY THROUGH CAPTAIN AMERICA'S MIGHTY SHIELD!

18

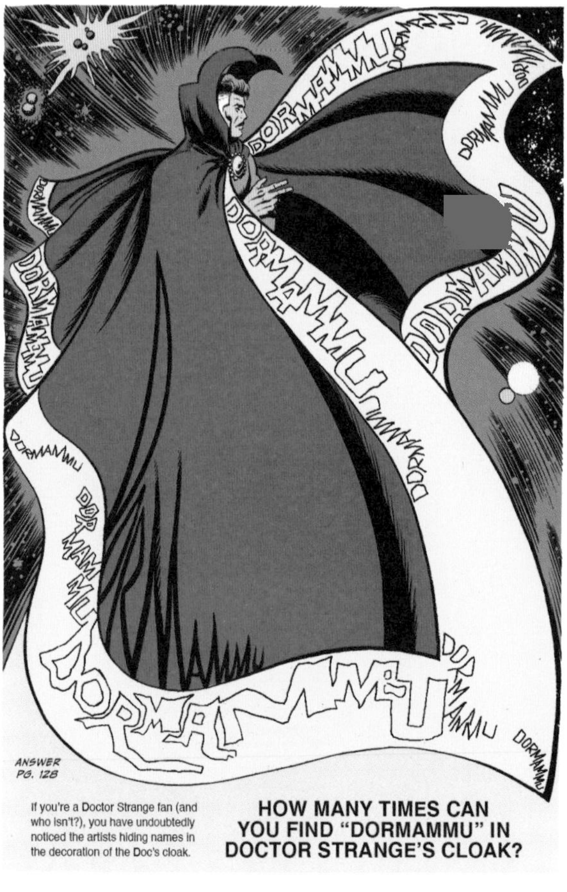
ANSWER PG. 128
If you're a Doctor Strange fan (and who isn't?), you have undoubtedly noticed the artists hiding names in the decoration of the Doc's cloak.
HOW MANY TIMES CAN YOU FIND "DORMAMMU" IN DOCTOR STRANGE'S CLOAK?

20

# MINI-MARVELS

While they're small in size, they're big in downright trickery. All you have to do is find the name of the Super Hero (pictured) as many times as you can in each of their own puzzles. Find them horizontal, vertical, diagonal, and backward in a straight line without skipping letters.

ANSWER ON PG. 129

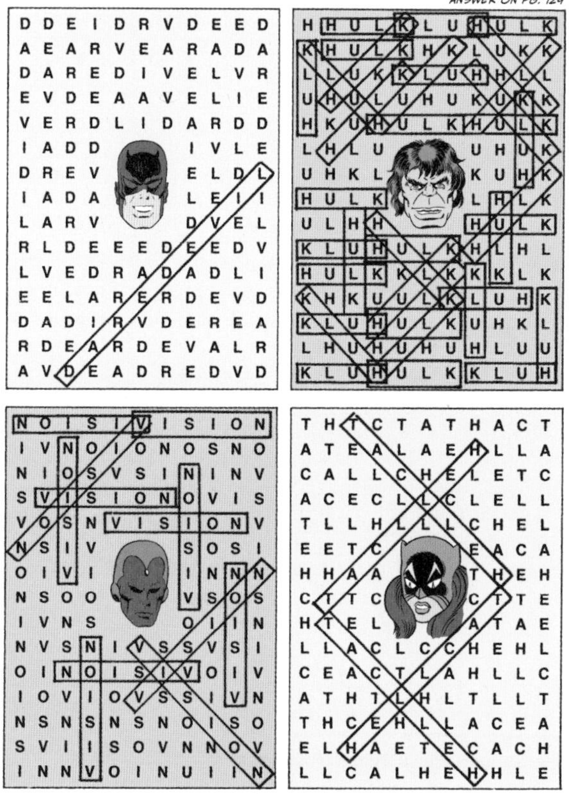

22

# WELCOME, NEW READERS!

Because you may be a new reader who has never before ventured into the world of MARVEL COMICS, we thought we should introduce you to the characters in our SECRET CODE BREAKER. We hope you get to know and love 'em all. Welcome aboard.

*- Stan Lee and Owen McCarron*

**A.** The Vision **B.** Human Torch **C.** Silver Surfer **D.** The Hulk **E.** Captain America **F.** Iron Man **G.** Black Panther **H.** Hellcat **I.** Thor **J.** Daredevil **K.** Captain Marvel **L.** Jack of Hearts **M.** The Thing **N.** Spider-Man **O.** Nighthawk **P.** Scarlet Witch **Q.** Ghost Rider **R.** Nova **S.** Storm **T.** Iron Fist **U.** Power Man (Luke Cage) **V.** Doctor Strange **W.** Sub-Mariner **X.** Shang-Chi **Y.** Wolverine **Z.** Spider-Woman

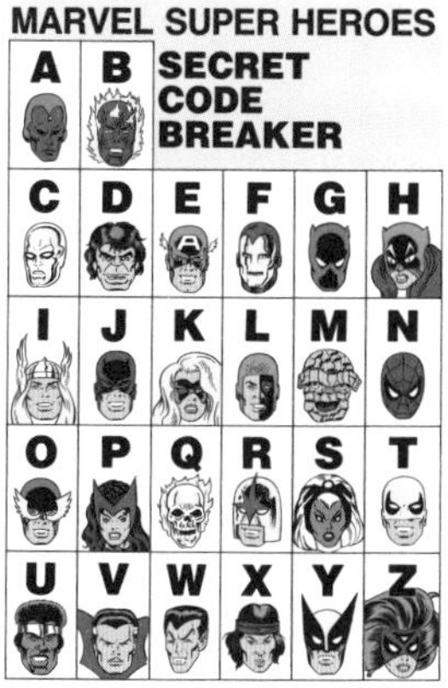
MARVEL SUPER HEROES
SECRET CODE BREAKER
A B C D E F G H I J K L M N O P Q R S T U V W X Y Z

24

# WHAT'S IN A NAME?

Here's our list:

| | |
|---|---|
| NORMAN | NAOMI |
| MARI | MOIRA |
| NAMOR | MONA |
| RONAN | RANI |
| OMAR | RAIN |
| NORA | NINA |
| NORMA | ANN |
| RAMON | RON |

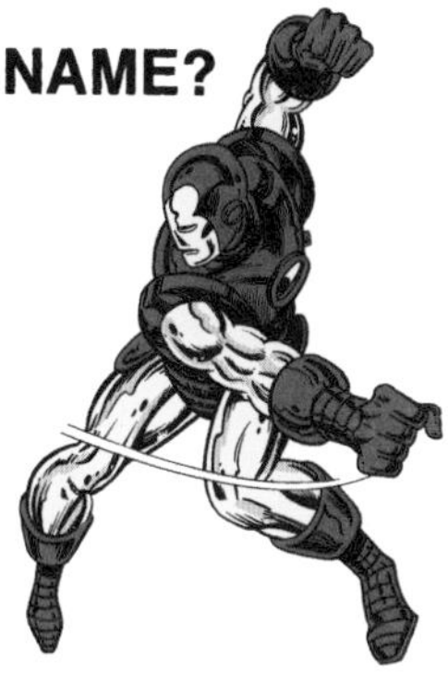

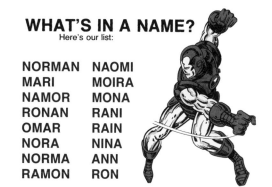

26

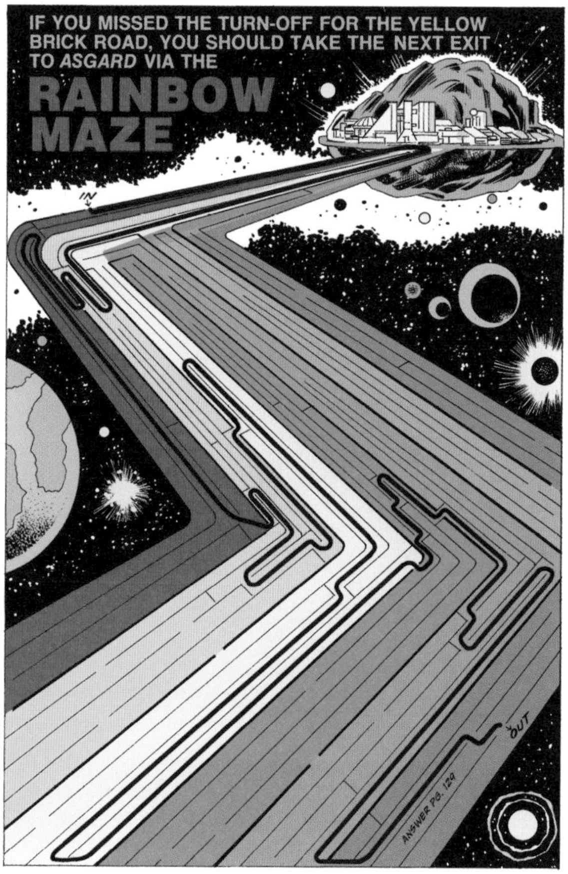
IF YOU MISSED THE TURN-OFF FOR THE YELLOW BRICK ROAD, YOU SHOULD TAKE THE NEXT EXIT TO ASGARD VIA THE
RAINBOW MAZE
IN
OUT
ANSWER PG. 129

27

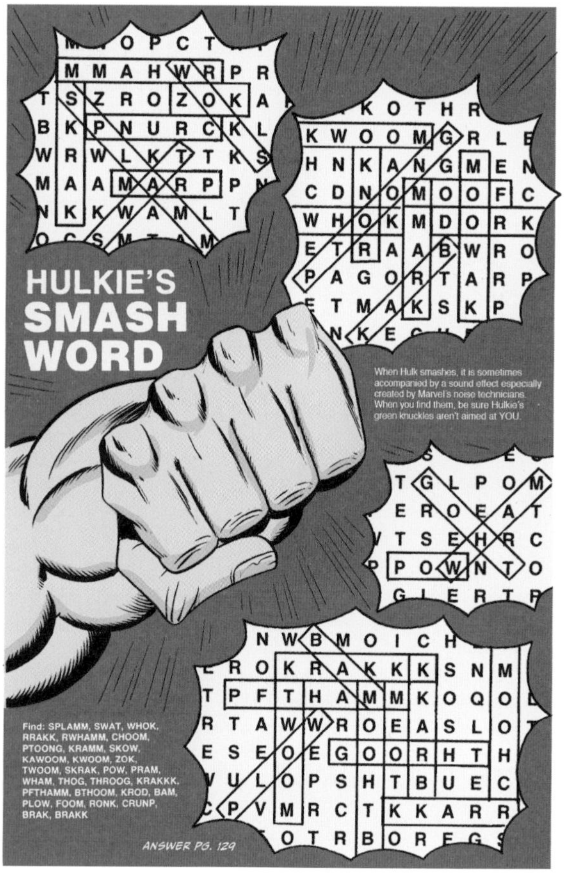
HULKIE'S SMASH WORD
When Hulk smashes, it is sometimes accompanied by a sound effect especially created by Marvel's noise technicians. When you find them, be sure Hulkie's green knuckles aren't aimed at YOU.
Find: SPLAMM, SWAT, WHOK, RRAKK, RWHAMM, CHOOM, PTOONG, KRAMM, SKOW, KAWOOM, KWOOM, ZOK, TWOOM, SKRAK, POW, PRAM, WHAM, THOG, THROOG, KRAKKK, PFTHAMM, BTHOOM, KROD, BAM, PLOW, FOOM, RONK, CRUNP, BRAK, BRAKK
ANSWER PG. 129

29

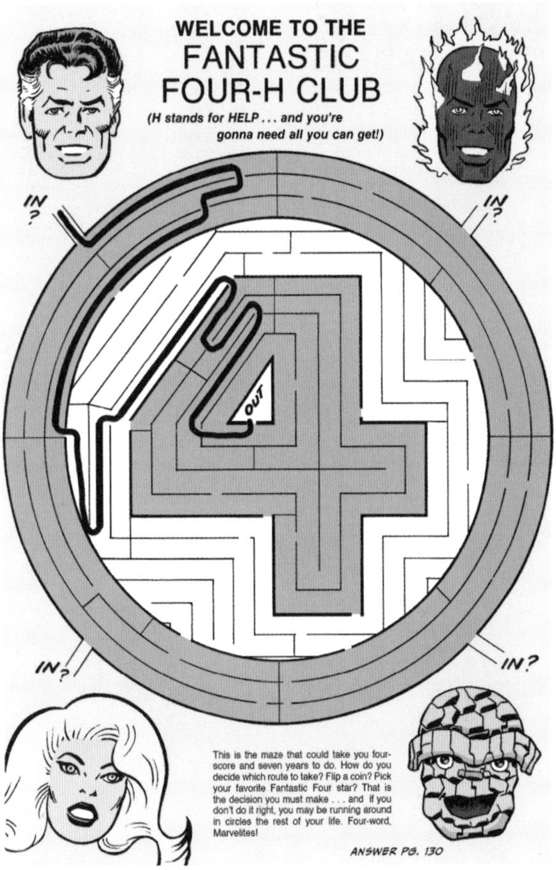
WELCOME TO THE
FANTASTIC
FOUR-H CLUB
(H stands for HELP . . . and you're gonna need all you can get!)
IN?
IN?
IN?
IN?
OUT
This is the maze that could take you four-score and seven years to do. How do you decide which route to take? Flip a coin? Pick your favorite Fantastic Four star? That is the decision you must make . . . and if you don't do it right, you may be running around in circles the rest of your life. Four-word, Marvelites!
ANSWER PG. 130

30

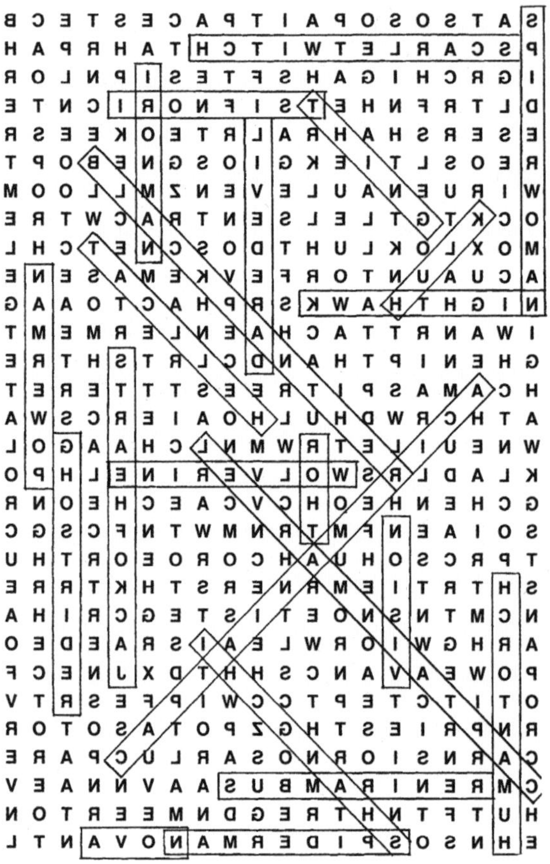

37

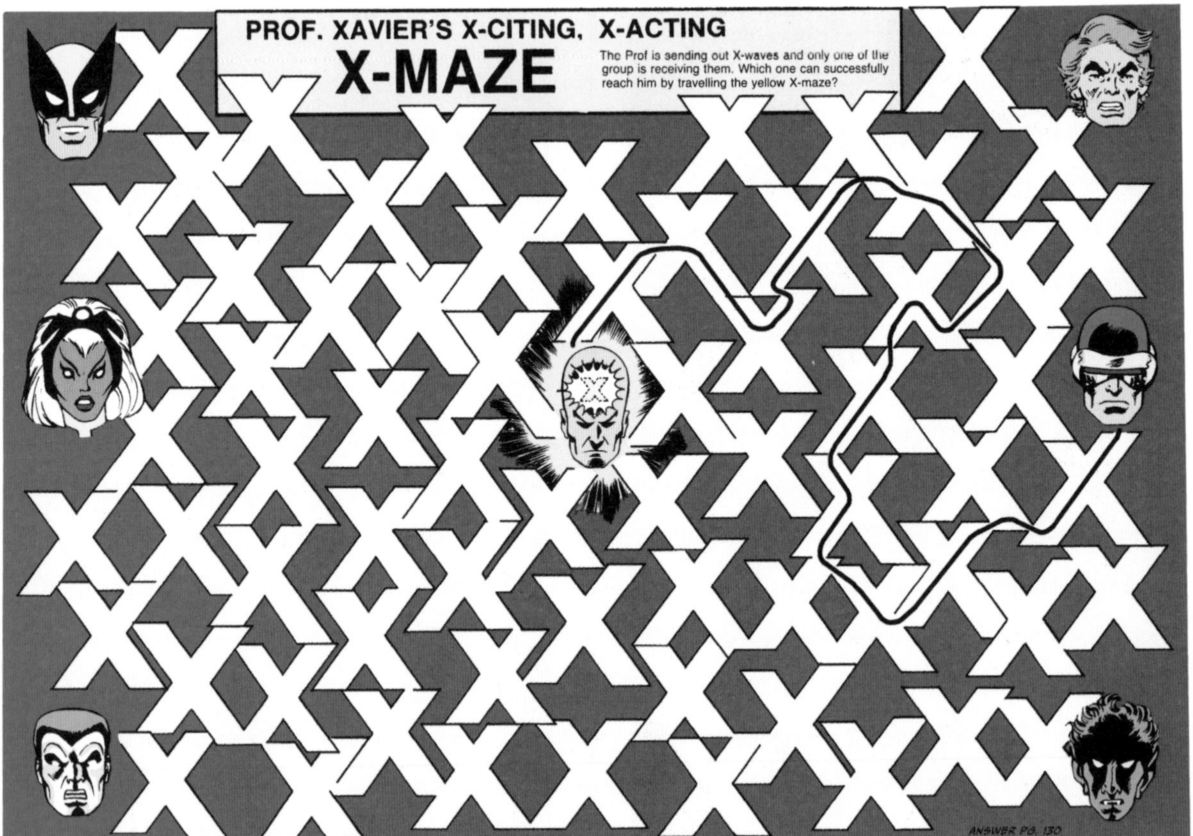
PROF. XAVIER'S X-CITING, X-ACTING
X-MAZE
The Prof is sending out X-waves and only one of the group is receiving them. Which one can successfully reach him by travelling the yellow X-maze?
ANSWER PG. 130

34–35

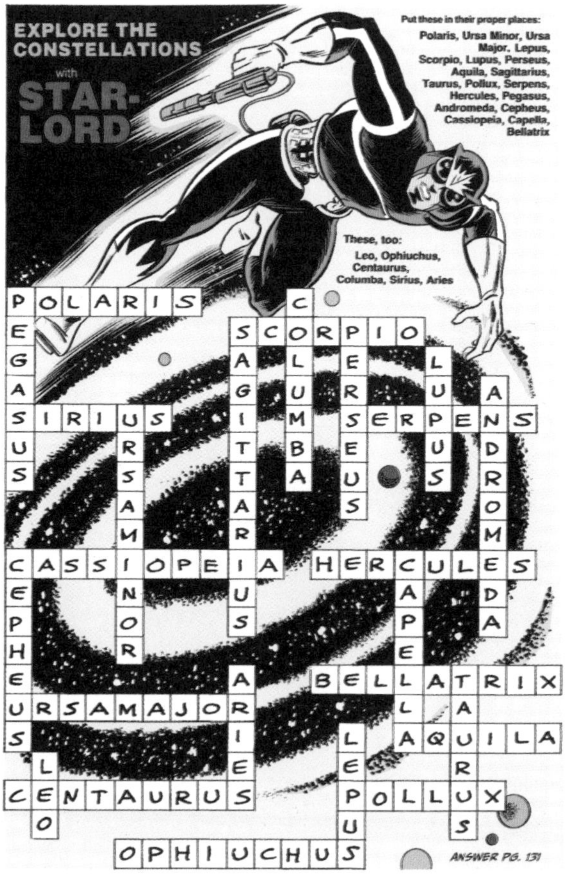
EXPLORE THE CONSTELLATIONS
with
STAR-LORD
Put these in their proper places:
Polaris, Ursa Minor, Ursa Major, Lepus, Scorpio, Lupus, Perseus, Aquila, Sagittarius, Taurus, Pollux, Serpens, Hercules, Pegasus, Andromeda, Cepheus, Cassiopeia, Capella, Bellatrix
These, too:
Leo, Ophiuchus, Centaurus, Columba, Sirius, Aries
POLARIS
PEGASUS
SCORPIO
SAGITTARIUS
COLUMBA
PERSEUS
LUPUS
SIRIUS
SERPENS
ANDROMEDA
URSA MINOR
CASSIOPEIA
HERCULES
CEPHEUS
CAPELLA
BELLATRIX
URSA MAJOR
ARIES
TAURUS
AQUILA
LEO
LEPUS
CENTAURUS
POLLUX
OPHIUCHUS
ANSWER PG. 131

38

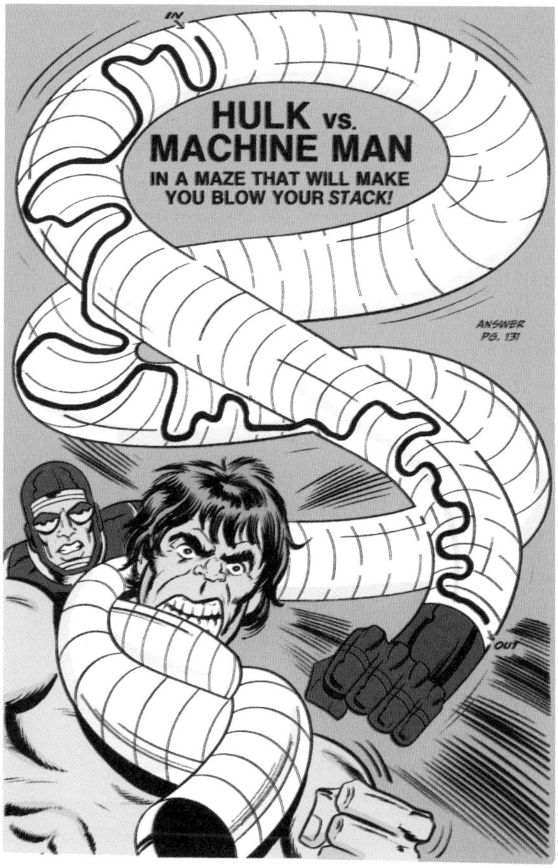
IN
HULK vs. MACHINE MAN
IN A MAZE THAT WILL MAKE YOU BLOW YOUR STACK!
ANSWER PG. 131
OUT

40

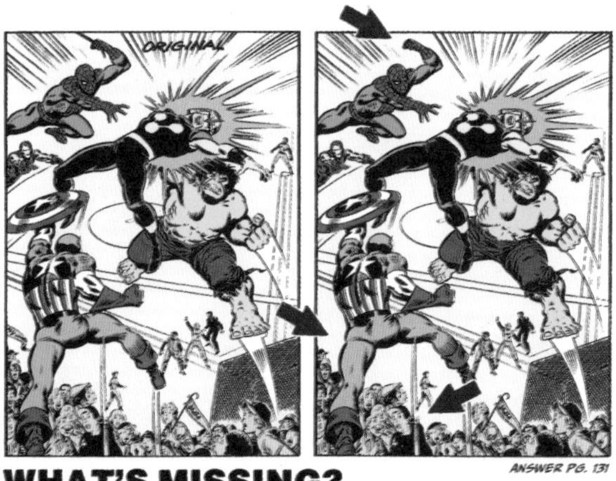
ORIGINAL
ANSWER PG. 131

## WHAT'S MISSING?

Captain America won't tell. Neither will Spider-Man, Nova, Hulk, or Iron Man. You're on your own, o searcher of missing things. Check the panels against the original and see for yourself. You can't find your pencil? OK, everyone, help this puzzle pal find their pencil. Now we've become a lost and found department. Sheesh!

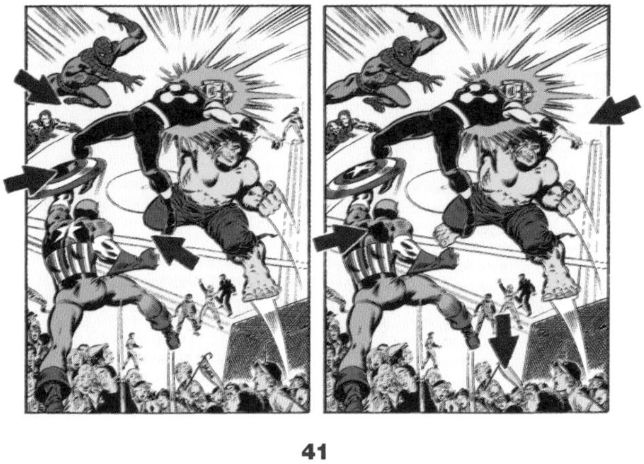

41

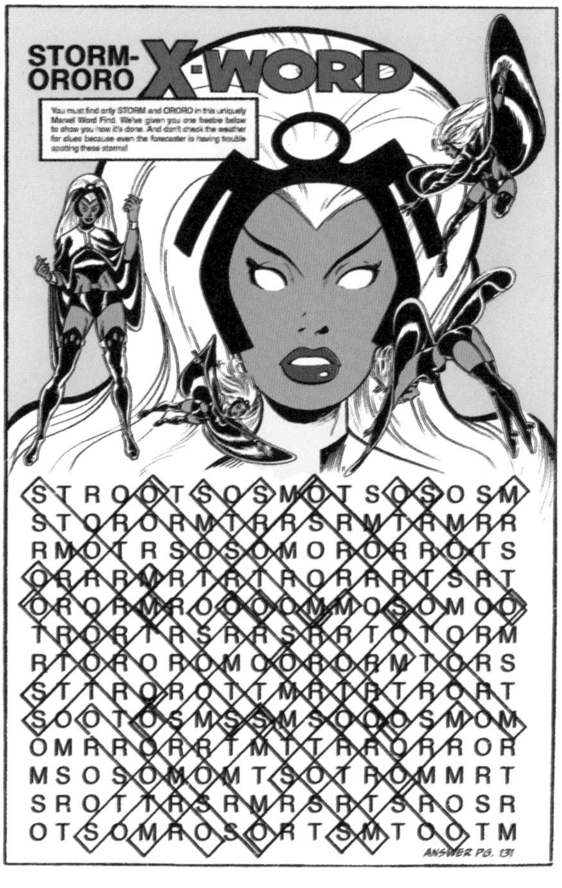
STORM-ORORO X-WORD
You must find only STORM and ORORO in this uniquely Marvel Word Find. We've given you one freebie below to show you how it's done. And don't check the weather for clues because even the forecaster is having trouble spotting these storms!
ANSWER PG. 131

42

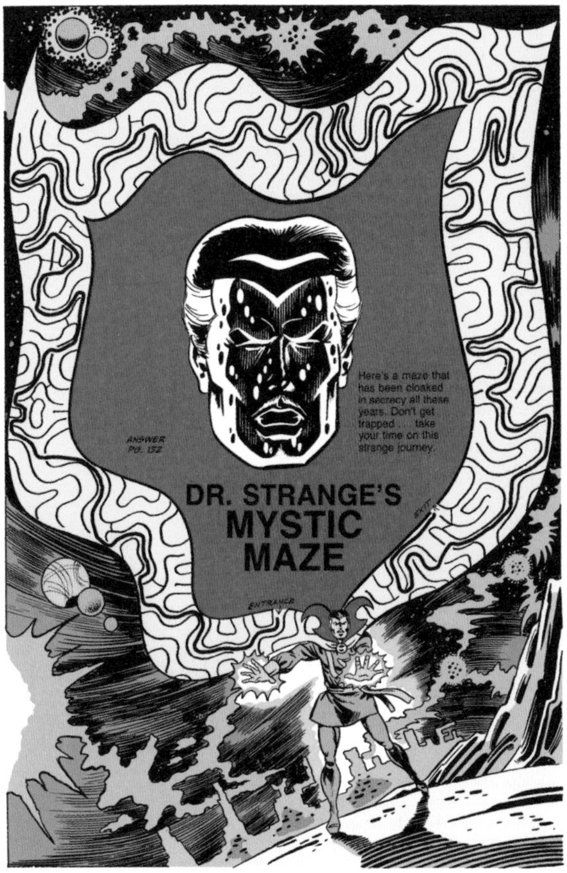
Here's a maze that has been cloaked in secrecy all these years. Don't get trapped . . . take your time on this strange journey.
ANSWER PG. 132
DR. STRANGE'S
MYSTIC
MAZE
ENTRANCE

44

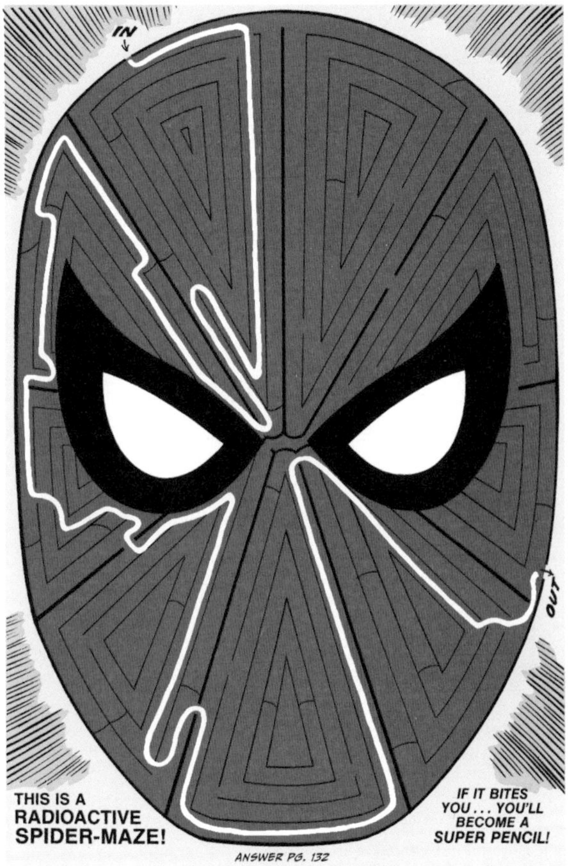
IN
OUT
THIS IS A RADIOACTIVE SPIDER-MAZE!
IF IT BITES YOU . . . YOU'LL BECOME A SUPER PENCIL!
ANSWER PG. 132

46

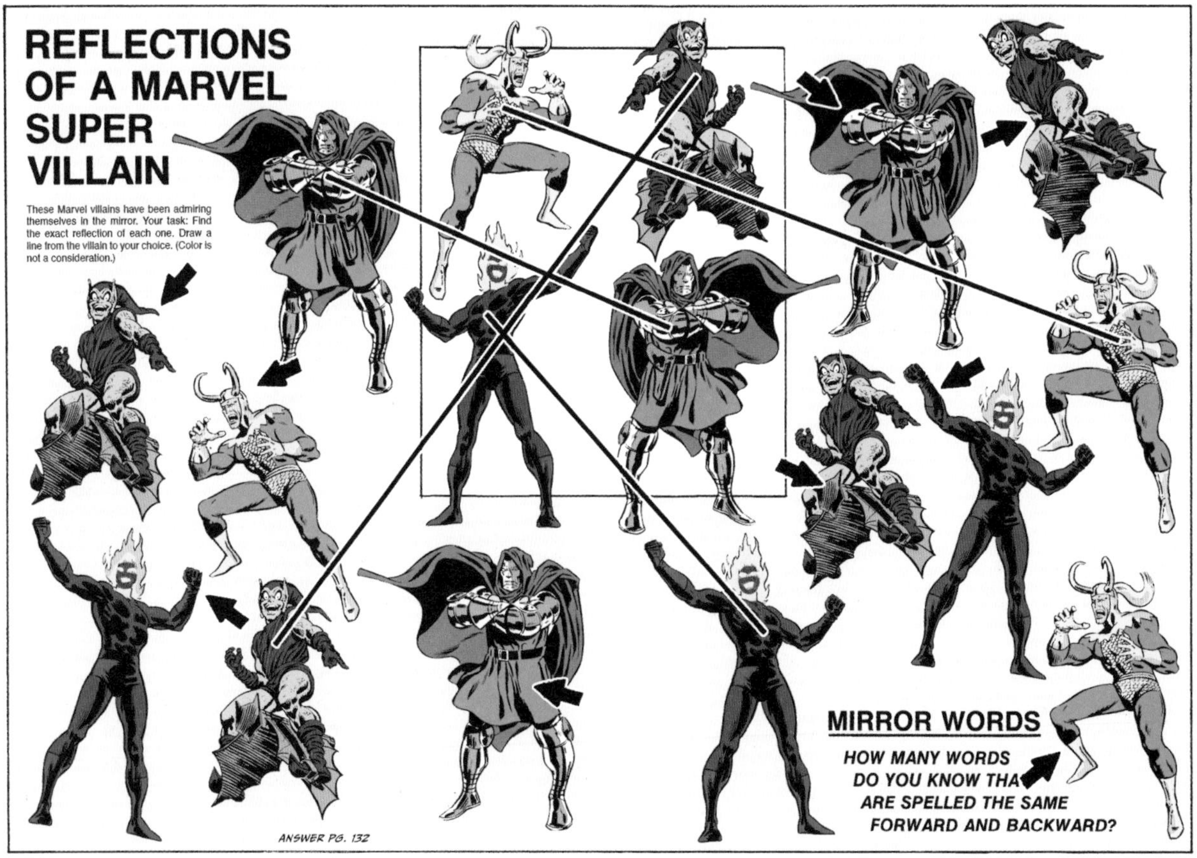
REFLECTIONS OF A MARVEL SUPER VILLAIN
These Marvel villains have been admiring themselves in the mirror. Your task: Find the exact reflection of each one. Draw a line from the villain to your choice. (Color is not a consideration.)
MIRROR WORDS
HOW MANY WORDS
DO YOU KNOW THA
ARE SPELLED THE SAME
FORWARD AND BACKWARD?
ANSWER PG. 132

48–49

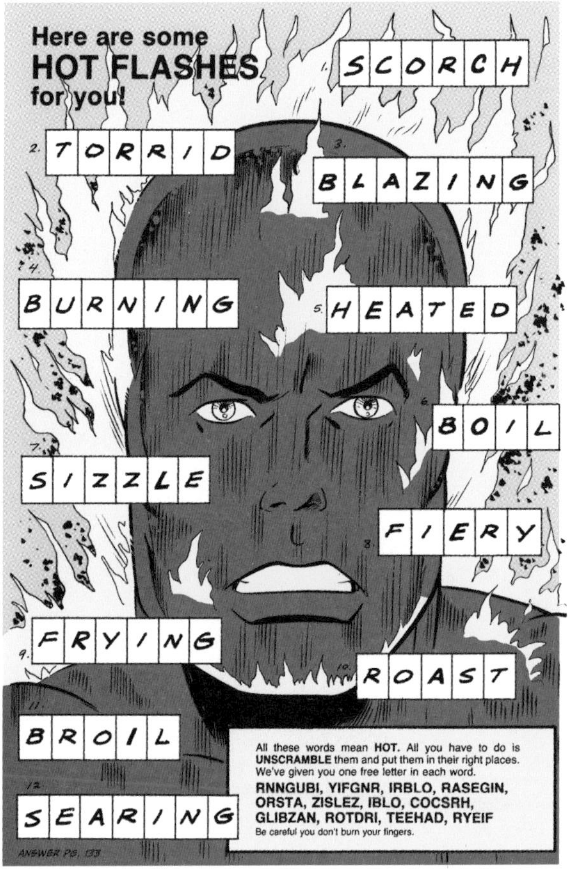

Here are some HOT FLASHES for you!
1. SCORCH
2. TORRID
3. BLAZING
4. BURNING
5. HEATED
6. BOIL
7. SIZZLE
8. FIERY
9. FRYING
10. ROAST
11. BROIL
12. SEARING
All these words mean HOT. All you have to do is UNSCRAMBLE them and put them in their right places. We've given you one free letter in each word.
RNNGUBI, YIFGNR, IRBLO, RASEGIN, ORSTA, ZISLEZ, IBLO, COCSRH, GLIBZAN, ROTDRI, TEEHAD, RYEIF
Be careful you don't burn your fingers.
ANSWER PG. 133


50

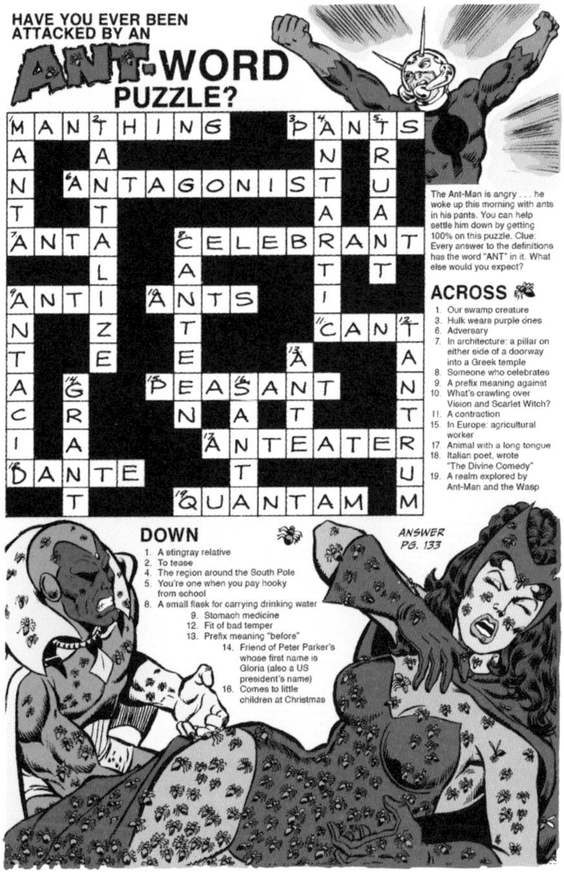

HAVE YOU EVER BEEN ATTACKED BY AN ANT-WORD PUZZLE?
MANTHING
PANTS
ANTAGONIST
ANTA
CELEBRANT
ANTI
ANTS
CANT
PEASANT
ANTEATER
DANTE
QUANTAM
MANTA
ANTAGONIZE
ANTARCTIC
TRUANT
ANTACID
DECANTER
ANTACID
PRENATAL
GRANT
ANTE
ANTIQUE
The Ant-Man is angry . . . he woke up this morning with ants in his pants. You can help settle him down by getting 100% on this puzzle. Clue: Every answer to the definitions has the word "ANT" in it. What else would you expect?
ACROSS
1. Our swamp creature
3. Hulk wears purple ones
6. Adversary
7. In architecture: a pillar on either side of a doorway into a Greek temple
8. Someone who celebrates
9. A prefix meaning against
10. What's crawling over Vision and Scarlet Witch?
11. A contraction
15. In Europe: agricultural worker
17. Animal with a long tongue
18. Italian poet, wrote "The Divine Comedy"
19. A realm explored by Ant-Man and the Wasp
DOWN
1. A stingray relative
2. To tease
4. The region around the South Pole
5. You're one when you pay hooky from school
8. A small flask for carrying drinking water
9. Stomach medicine
12. Fit of bad temper
13. Prefix meaning "before"
14. Friend of Peter Parker's whose first name is Gloria (also a US president's name)
16. Comes to little children at Christmas
ANSWER PG. 133


54

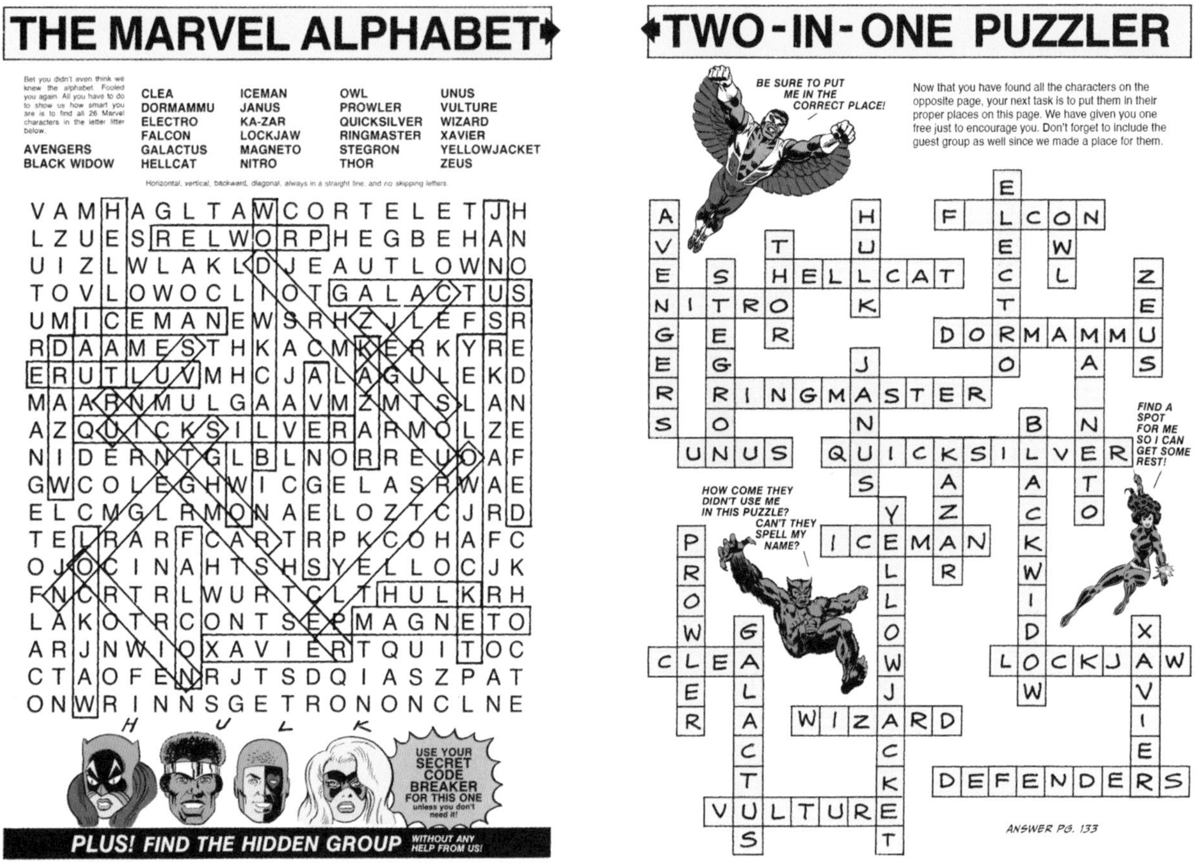

THE MARVEL ALPHABET
Bet you didn't even think we knew the alphabet. Fooled you again. All you have to do to show us how smart you are is to find all 26 Marvel characters in the letter litter below.
AVENGERS
BLACK WIDOW
CLEA
DORMAMMU
ELECTRO
FALCON
GALACTUS
HELLCAT
ICEMAN
JANUS
KA-ZAR
LOCKJAW
MAGNETO
NITRO
OWL
PROWLER
QUICKSILVER
RINGMASTER
STEGRON
THOR
UNUS
VULTURE
WIZARD
XAVIER
YELLOWJACKET
ZEUS
Horizontal, vertical, backward, diagonal, always in a straight line, and no skipping letters.
V A M H A G L T A W C O R T E L E T J H
L Z U E S R E L W O R P H E G B E H A N
U I Z L W L A K L D J E A U T L O W N O
T O V L O W O C L I O T G A L A C T U S
U M I C E M A N E W S R H Z J L E F S R
R D A A M E S T H K A C M K E R K Y R E
E R U T L U V M H C J A L A G U L E K D
M A A R N M U L G A A V M Z M T S L A N
A Z Q U I C K S I L V E R A R M O L Z E
N I D E R N T G L B L N O R R E U O A F
G W C O L E G H W I C G E L A S R W A E
E L C M G L R M O N A E L O Z T C J R D
T E L R A R F C A R T R P K C O H A F C
O J O C I N A H T S H S Y E L L O C J K
F N C R T R L W U R T C L T H U L K R H
L A K O T R C O N T S E P M A G N E T O
A R J N W I O X A V I E R T Q U I T O C
C T A O F E N R J T S D Q I A S Z P A T
O N W R I N N S G E T R O N O N C L N E
H U L K
USE YOUR SECRET CODE BREAKER FOR THIS ONE unless you don't need it!
PLUS! FIND THE HIDDEN GROUP WITHOUT ANY HELP FROM US!
TWO-IN-ONE PUZZLER
BE SURE TO PUT ME IN THE CORRECT PLACE!
Now that you have found all the characters on the opposite page, your next task is to put them in their proper places on this page. We have given you one free just to encourage you. Don't forget to include the guest group as well since we made a place for them.
AVENGERS
HULK
FALCON
ELECTRO
OWL
THOR
HELLCAT
ZEUS
NITRO
STEGRON
DORMAMMU
JANUS
RINGMASTER
MAGNETO
UNUS
QUICKSILVER
BLACKWIDOW
KAZAR
YELLOWJACKET
ICEMAN
PROWLER
GALACTUS
CLEA
LOCKJAW
XAVIER
WIZARD
DEFENDERS
VULTURE
FIND A SPOT FOR ME SO I CAN GET SOME REST!
HOW COME THEY DIDN'T USE ME IN THIS PUZZLE? CAN'T THEY SPELL MY NAME?
ANSWER PG. 133


52–53

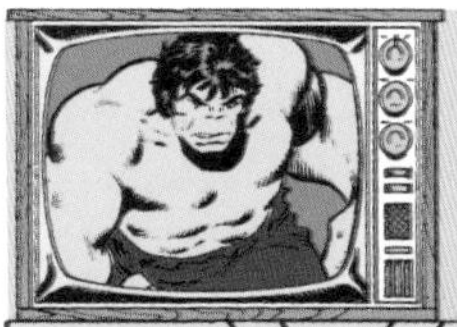

## HULK SMASHES THE SMALL SCREEN

Solve this maze before he gets angry . . . and hurry, before another commercial pops up!

ANSWER PG. 134

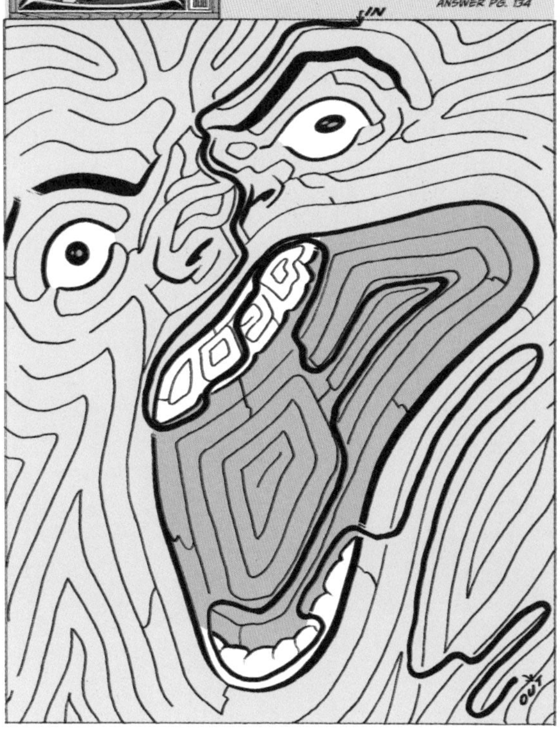
IN
OUT

56

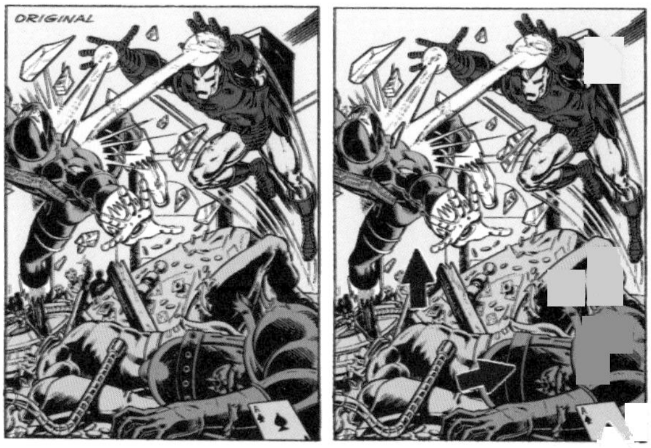
ORIGINAL

## WHAT'S MISSING ? ? ? ? ? ?

You're still working on WHAT'S MISS page 41? Either you've got your glas backward or you're using the wrong kind of private eye to help you. Why don't you call Jessica Jones . . . but be sure to ask her "how much" before she starts. After all, this could be the toughest case she ever tackled.

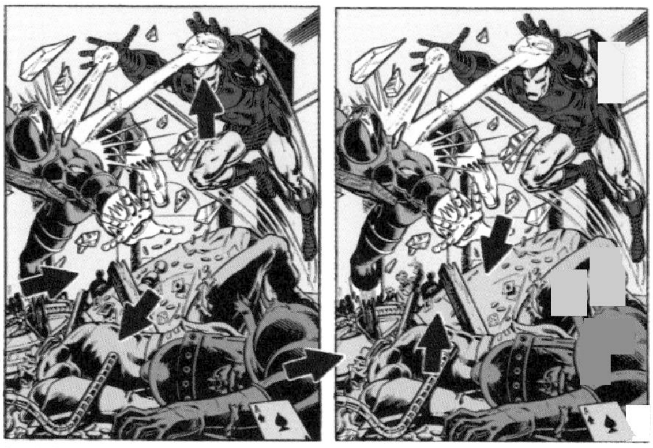

ANSWER PG. 134

58

## MINI-MARVELS

So. You're a Marvel Super Hero expert! OK, if you say so . . . but we wanna find out for sure. In each of these MINI-MARVELS, there are 10 villains carefully concealed who have met the Super Hero pictured in combat . . . usually the knuckle variety. Your job: Find them . . . before they find you. Lots of luck, expert. Ha!

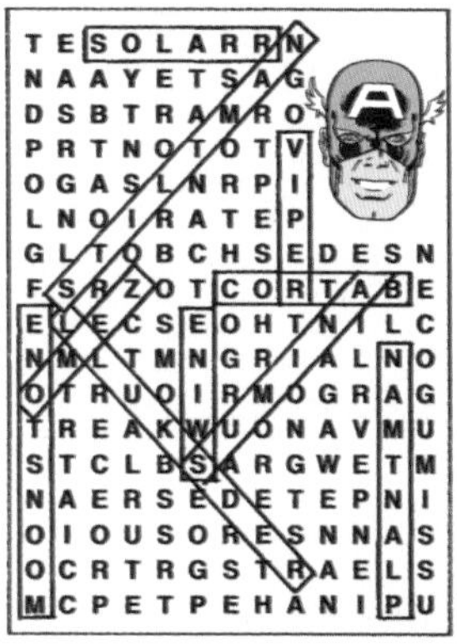

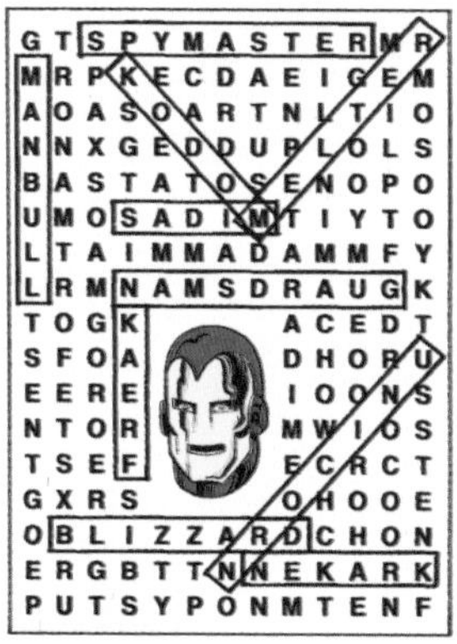

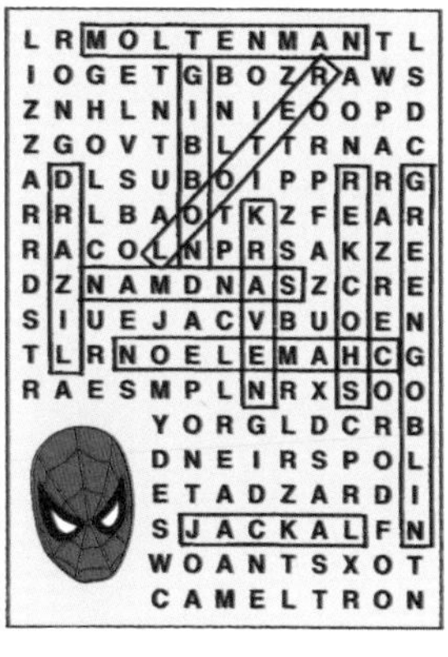

ANSWER PG. 134

59

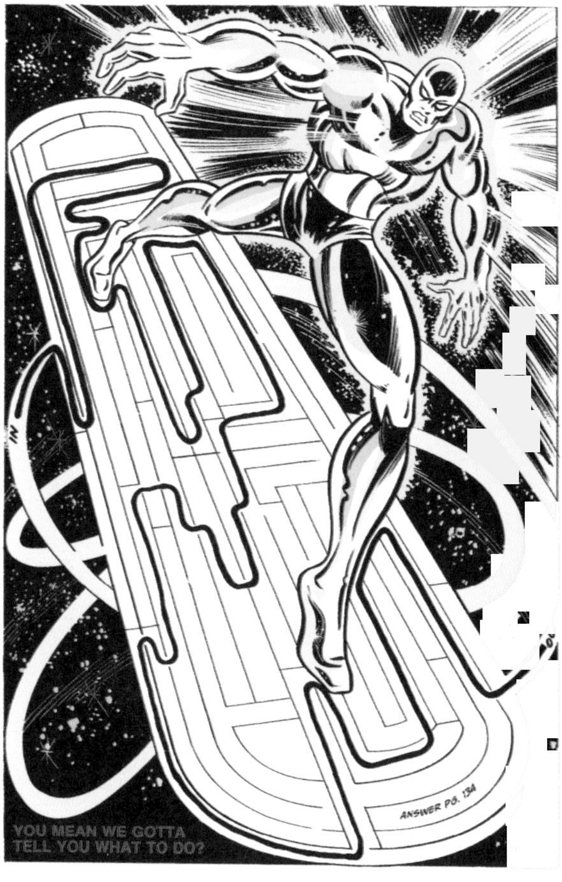
IN
ANSWER PG. 134
YOU MEAN WE GOTTA TELL YOU WHAT TO DO?

63

# THE EARLY BIRD GETS THE WORM!
## ... MINDWORM, *THAT IS!!*

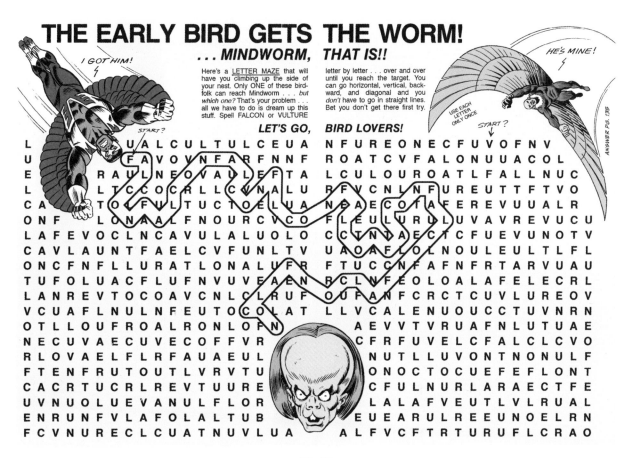

Here's a <u>LETTER MAZE</u> that will have you climbing up the side of your nest. Only ONE of these bird-folk can reach Mindworm . . . *but which one?* That's your problem . . . all we have to do is dream up this stuff. Spell FALCON or VULTURE

letter by letter . . . over and over until you reach the target. You can go horizontal, vertical, backward, and diagonal and you *don't* have to go in straight lines. Bet you don't get there first try.

### LET'S GO, BIRD LOVERS!

*I GOT HIM!*

*HE'S MINE!*

*USE EACH LETTER ONLY ONCE*

*START?*

*ANSWER PG. 135*

```
L U   U A L C U L T U L C E U A      N F U R E O N E C F U V O F N V
L U E   F A V O V N F A R F N N F    R O A T C V F A L O N U U A C O L
E       R A U L N E O V A U L E F T A L C U L O U R O A T L F A L L N U C
L C A   L T C C O C R L L C V N A L U R F V C N L N F U R E U T T F T V O
O N F   T O F U L T U C T O E L U A  N D A E C O T A F E R E V U U A L R
L A F E V O C L N C A V U L A L U O L O F L E U L U R U L U V A V R E V U C U
C A V L A U N T F A E L C V F U N L T V  C C T N D A E C T C F U E V U N O T V
O N C F N F L L U R A T L O N A L U F R  U A O A F L O L N O U L E U L T L F L
T U F O L U A C F L U F N V U V E A E N  F T U C C N F A F N F R T A R V U A U
L A N R E V T O C O A V C N L C L R U F  R C L N F E O L O A L A F E L E C R L
V C U A F L N U L N F E U T O C O L A T  O U F A N F C R C T C U V L U R E O V
O T L L O U F R O A L R O N L O F N     L L V C A L E N U O U C C T U V N R N
N E C U V A E C U V E C O F F V R        A E V V T V R U A F N L U T U A E
R L O V A E L F L R F A U A E U L        C F R F U V E L C F A L C L C V O
F T E N F R U T O U T L V R V T U        N U T L L U V O N T N O N U L F
C A C R T U C R L R E V T U U R E        O N O C T O C U E F E F L O N T
U V N U O L U E V A N U L F L O R        C F U L N U R L A R A E C T F E
E N R U N F V L A F O L A L T U B        L A L A F V E U T L V L R U A L
F C V N U R E C L C U A T N U V L U A    E U E A R U L R E E U N O E L R N
                                         A L F V C F T R T U R U F L C R A O
```

66–67

---

## WHAT'S MISSING?

A total of 6 things are different between these drawings. Compare one against the other, and you should have no problems. The Hulk took only 5 days to find them all. That's how easy it is.

*ANSWER PG. 135*

GREAT ACTION SHOTS LIKE THIS IN EVERY MARVEL COVER!

65

---

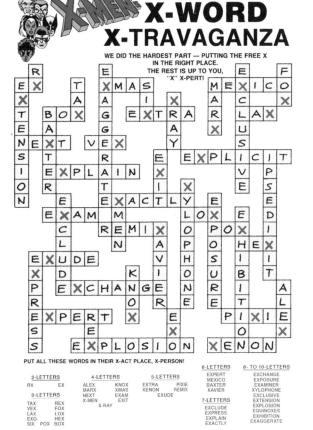

# X-WORD X-TRAVAGANZA

WE DID THE HARDEST PART — PUTTING THE FREE X IN THE RIGHT PLACE. THE REST IS UP TO YOU, "X" X-PERT!

**PUT ALL THESE WORDS IN THEIR X-ACT PLACE, X-PERSON!**

| 2-LETTERS | | 4-LETTERS | | 5-LETTERS | | 6-LETTERS | 8- TO 10-LETTERS |
|---|---|---|---|---|---|---|---|
| RX | EX | ALEX | KNOX | EXTRA | PIXIE | EXPERT | EXCHANGE |
| | | MARX | XMAS | XENON | REMIX | MEXICO | EXPOSURE |
| **3-LETTERS** | | NEXT | EXAM | EXUDE | | BAXTER | EXAMINER |
| TAX | REX | X-MEN | EXIT | | | XAVIER | XYLOPHONE |
| VEX | FOX | X-RAY | | | | | EXCLUSIVE |
| LAX | LOX | | | | | **7-LETTERS** | EXTENSION |
| EXO- | HEX | | | | | EXCLUDE | EXPLOSION |
| SIX POX | BOX | | | | | EXPRESS | EQUINOXES |
| | | | | | | EXPLAIN | EXHIBITION |
| | | | | | | EXACTLY | EXAGGERATE |

70

---

135

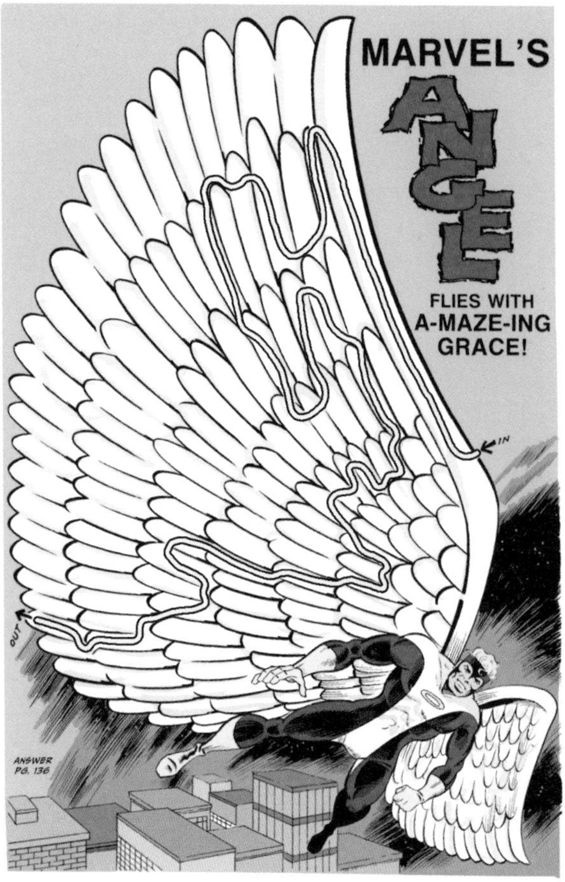
MARVEL'S
ANGEL
FLIES WITH
A-MAZE-ING
GRACE!
IN
OUT
ANSWER PG. 136

71

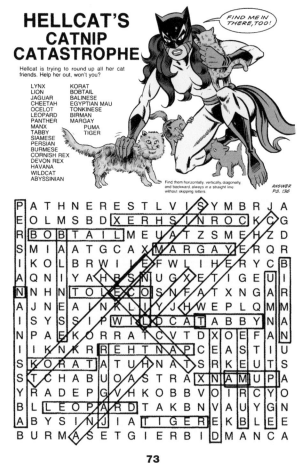

## HELLCAT'S CATNIP CATASTROPHE

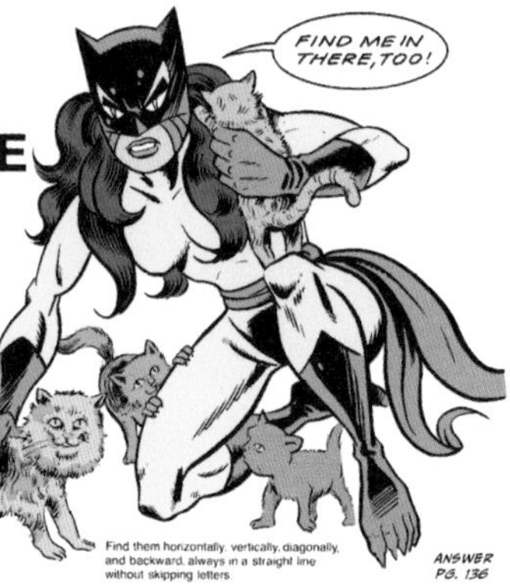
FIND ME IN THERE, TOO!

Hellcat is trying to round up all her cat friends. Help her out, won't you?

LYNX
LION
JAGUAR
CHEETAH
OCELOT
LEOPARD
PANTHER
MANX
TABBY
SIAMESE
PERSIAN
BURMESE
CORNISH REX
DEVON REX
HAVANA
WILDCAT
ABYSSINIAN
KORAT
BOBTAIL
BALINESE
EGYPTIAN MAU
TONKINESE
BIRMAN
MARGAY
PUMA
TIGER

Find them horizontally, vertically, diagonally, and backward, always in a straight line without skipping letters.

ANSWER PG. 136

| | | | | | | | | | | | | | | | | | | | |
|---|---|---|---|---|---|---|---|---|---|---|---|---|---|---|---|---|---|---|---|
| P | A | T | H | N | E | R | E | S | T | L | V | I | S | Y | M | B | R | J | A |
| E | O | L | M | S | B | D | X | E | R | H | S | I | N | R | O | C | K | C | G |
| R | B | O | B | T | A | I | L | M | E | U | A | T | Z | S | M | E | H | Z | D |
| S | M | I | A | A | T | G | C | A | X | M | A | R | G | A | Y | E | R | Q | R |
| I | K | O | L | B | R | W | I | L | E | F | W | L | I | H | E | R | Y | C | B |
| A | Q | N | I | Y | A | H | B | S | N | U | G | X | E | T | I | G | E | U | I |
| N | N | H | N | T | O | L | E | C | O | S | N | F | A | T | X | N | G | A | R |
| A | J | N | E | A | I | N | K | L | I | Y | J | H | W | E | P | L | Q | M | M |
| I | S | Y | S | S | I | P | W | I | L | D | C | A | T | A | B | B | Y | N | A |
| N | P | A | E | K | O | R | R | A | T | C | V | T | D | X | O | E | F | A | N |
| I | I | K | N | K | R | R | E | H | T | N | A | P | C | E | A | S | T | I | U |
| S | K | O | R | A | T | A | T | U | H | N | A | T | S | R | K | E | U | T | S |
| S | T | C | H | A | B | U | O | A | S | T | R | A | X | N | A | M | U | P | A |
| Y | R | A | D | E | P | G | V | H | K | O | B | B | V | O | I | R | C | Y | O |
| B | L | L | E | O | P | A | R | D | T | A | K | B | N | V | A | U | Y | G | N |
| A | B | Y | S | I | N | J | I | A | T | I | G | E | R | E | K | B | L | E | E |
| B | U | R | M | A | S | E | T | G | I | E | R | B | I | D | M | A | N | C | A |

73

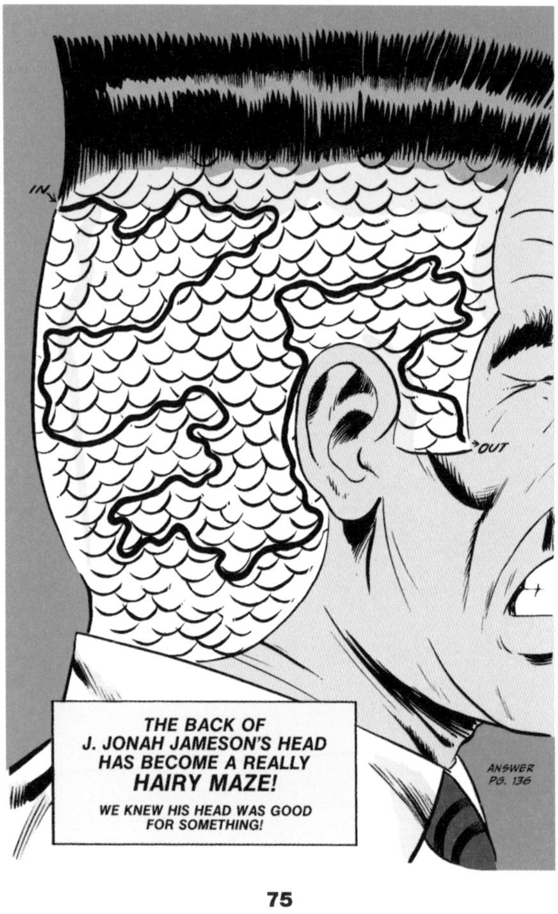
IN
OUT
THE BACK OF J. JONAH JAMESON'S HEAD HAS BECOME A REALLY HAIRY MAZE!
WE KNEW HIS HEAD WAS GOOD FOR SOMETHING!
ANSWER PG. 136

75

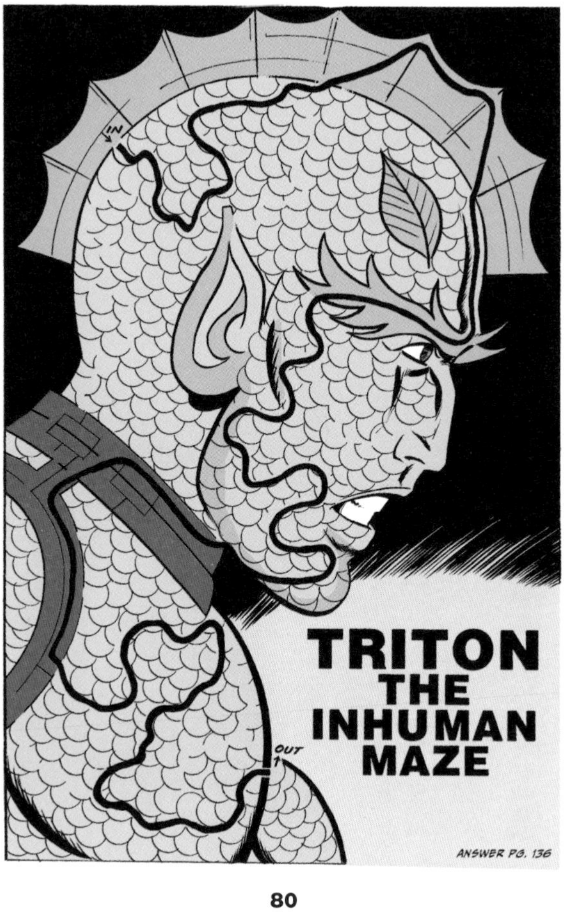
IN
TRITON
THE
INHUMAN
MAZE
OUT
ANSWER PG. 136

80

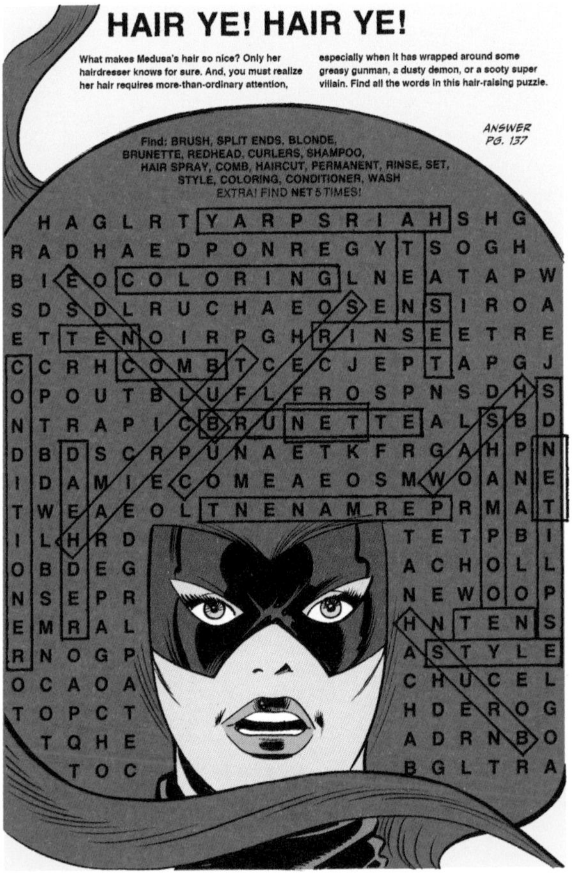
HAIR YE! HAIR YE!
What makes Medusa's hair so nice? Only her hairdresser knows for sure. And, you must realize her hair requires more-than-ordinary attention, especially when it has wrapped around some greasy gunman, a dusty demon, or a sooty super villain. Find all the words in this hair-raising puzzle.
ANSWER PG. 137
Find: BRUSH, SPLIT ENDS, BLONDE, BRUNETTE, REDHEAD, CURLERS, SHAMPOO, HAIR SPRAY, COMB, HAIRCUT, PERMANENT, RINSE, SET, STYLE, COLORING, CONDITIONER, WASH
EXTRA! FIND NET 5 TIMES!

81

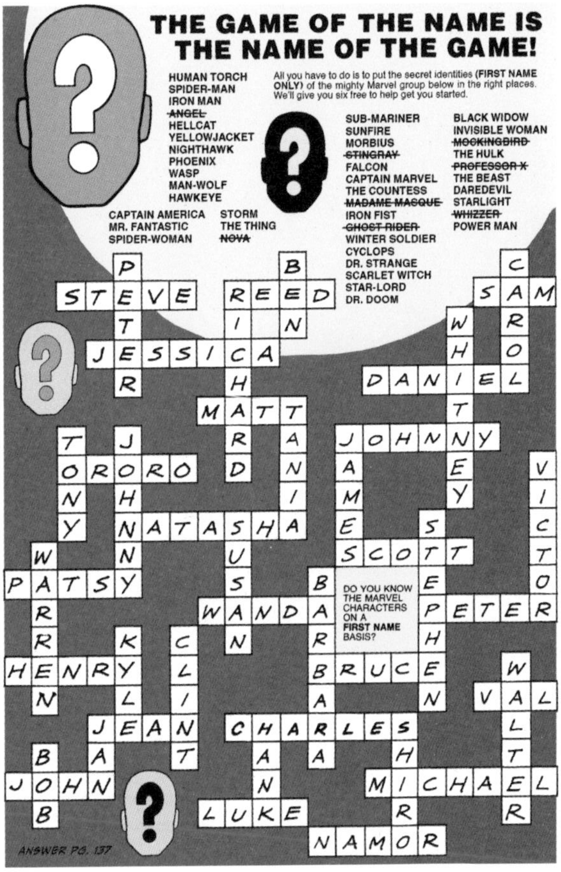
THE GAME OF THE NAME IS THE NAME OF THE GAME!
All you have to do is to put the secret identities (FIRST NAME ONLY) of the mighty Marvel group below in the right places. We'll give you six free to help get you started.
HUMAN TORCH
SPIDER-MAN
IRON MAN
ANGEL
HELLCAT
YELLOWJACKET
NIGHTHAWK
PHOENIX
WASP
MAN-WOLF
HAWKEYE
CAPTAIN AMERICA
MR. FANTASTIC
SPIDER-WOMAN
STORM
THE THING
NOVA
SUB-MARINER
SUNFIRE
MORBIUS
STINGRAY
FALCON
CAPTAIN MARVEL
THE COUNTESS
MADAME MASQUE
IRON FIST
GHOST RIDER
WINTER SOLDIER
CYCLOPS
DR. STRANGE
SCARLET WITCH
STAR-LORD
DR. DOOM
BLACK WIDOW
INVISIBLE WOMAN
MOCKINGBIRD
THE HULK
PROFESSOR X
THE BEAST
DAREDEVIL
STARLIGHT
WHIZZER
POWER MAN
DO YOU KNOW THE MARVEL CHARACTERS ON A FIRST NAME BASIS?
ANSWER PG. 137

84

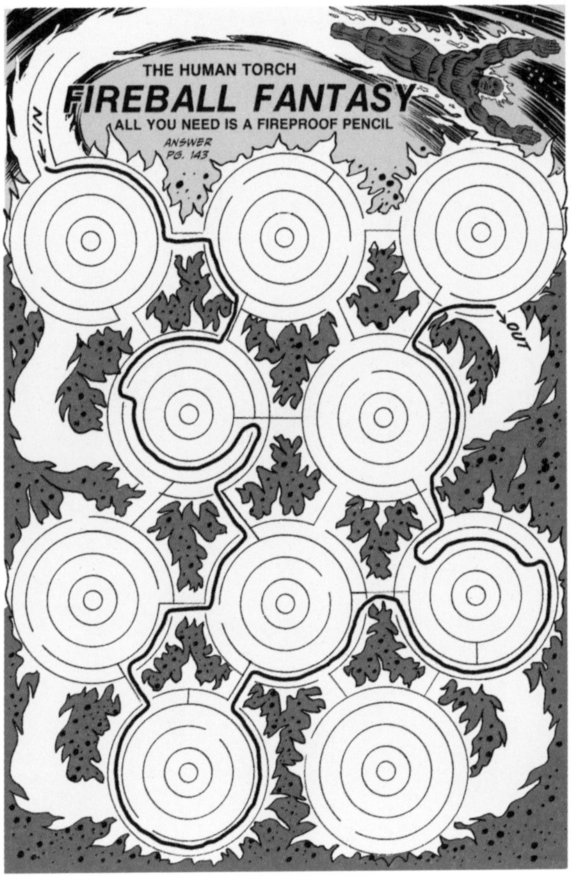
THE HUMAN TORCH
FIREBALL FANTASY
ALL YOU NEED IS A FIREPROOF PENCIL
ANSWER PG. 143
IN
OUT

85

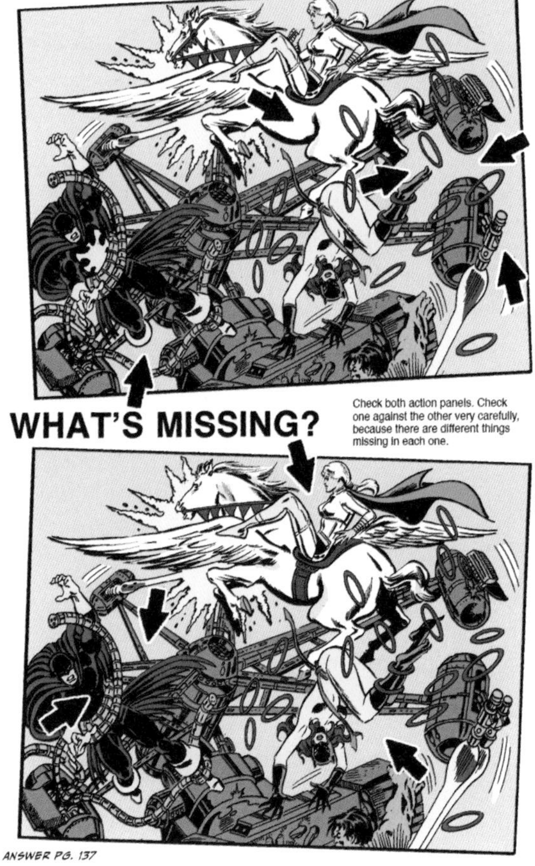
WHAT'S MISSING?
Check both action panels. Check one against the other very carefully, because there are different things missing in each one.
ANSWER PG. 137

86

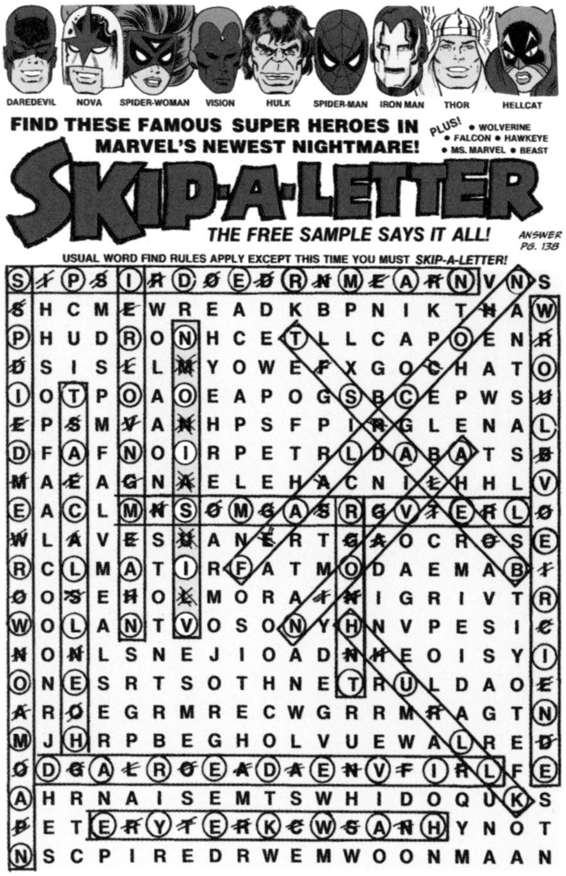
DAREDEVIL
NOVA
SPIDER-WOMAN
VISION
HULK
SPIDER-MAN
IRON MAN
THOR
HELLCAT
FIND THESE FAMOUS SUPER HEROES IN MARVEL'S NEWEST NIGHTMARE!
PLUS! • WOLVERINE • FALCON • HAWKEYE • MS. MARVEL • BEAST
SKIP-A-LETTER
THE FREE SAMPLE SAYS IT ALL!
ANSWER PG. 138
USUAL WORD FIND RULES APPLY EXCEPT THIS TIME YOU MUST SKIP-A-LETTER!

88

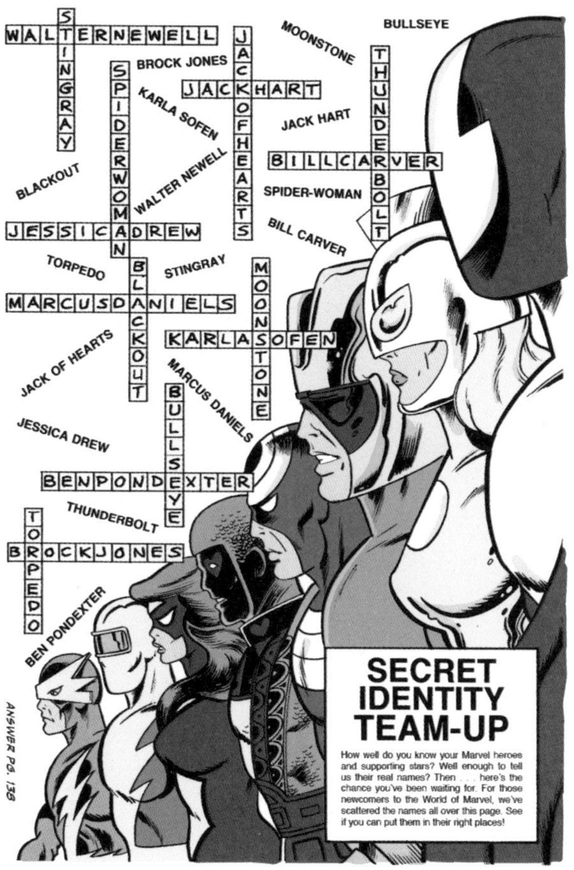
WALTERNEWELL
STINGRAY
SPIDERWOMAN
BROCK JONES
JACKHART
JACKOFHEARTS
MOONSTONE
BULLSEYE
THUNDERBOLT
KARLA SOFEN
JACK HART
BILLCARVER
BLACKOUT
WALTER NEWELL
SPIDER-WOMAN
JESSICADREW
BILL CARVER
TORPEDO
STINGRAY
BLACKOUT
MOONSTONE
MARCUSDANIELS
KARLASOFEN
JACK OF HEARTS
MARCUS DANIELS
BULLSEYE
JESSICA DREW
BENPONDEXTER
THUNDERBOLT
TORPEDO
BROCKJONES
BEN PONDEXTER
ANSWER PG. 138
SECRET IDENTITY TEAM-UP
How well do you know your Marvel heroes and supporting stars? Well enough to tell us their real names? Then . . . here's the chance you've been waiting for. For those newcomers to the World of Marvel, we've scattered the names all over this page. See if you can put them in their right places!

91

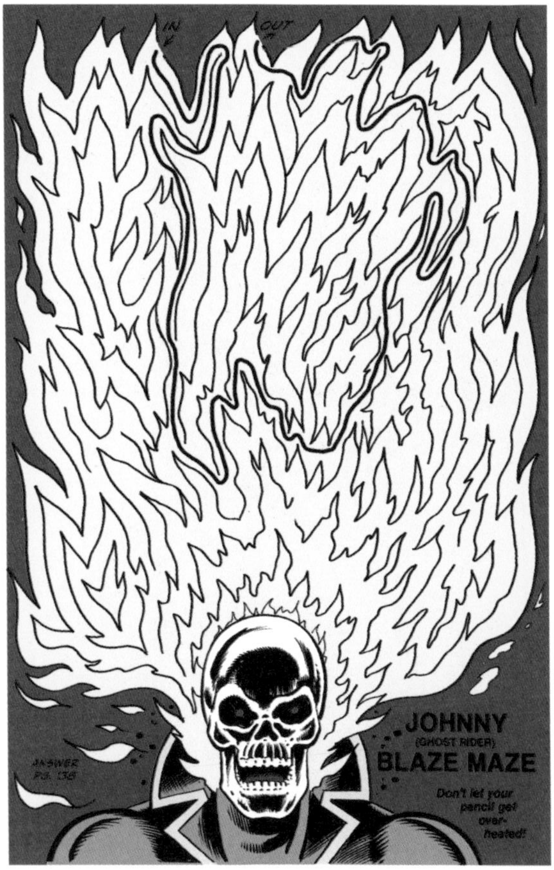
IN
OUT
JOHNNY (GHOST RIDER) BLAZE MAZE
Don't let your pencil get over-heated!
ANSWER PG. 138

93

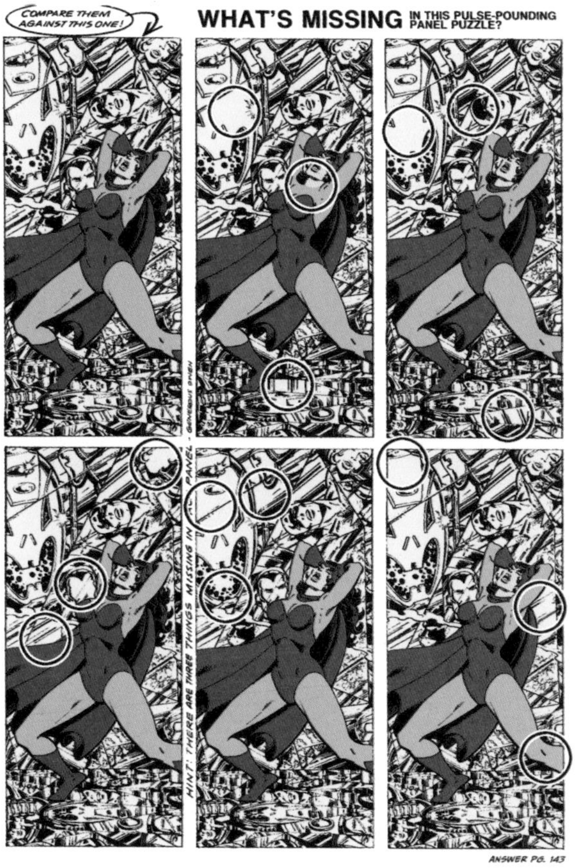
COMPARE THEM AGAINST THIS ONE!
WHAT'S MISSING IN THIS PULSE-POUNDING PANEL PUZZLE?
HINT: THERE ARE THREE THINGS MISSING IN EACH PANEL
ANSWER PG. 143

94

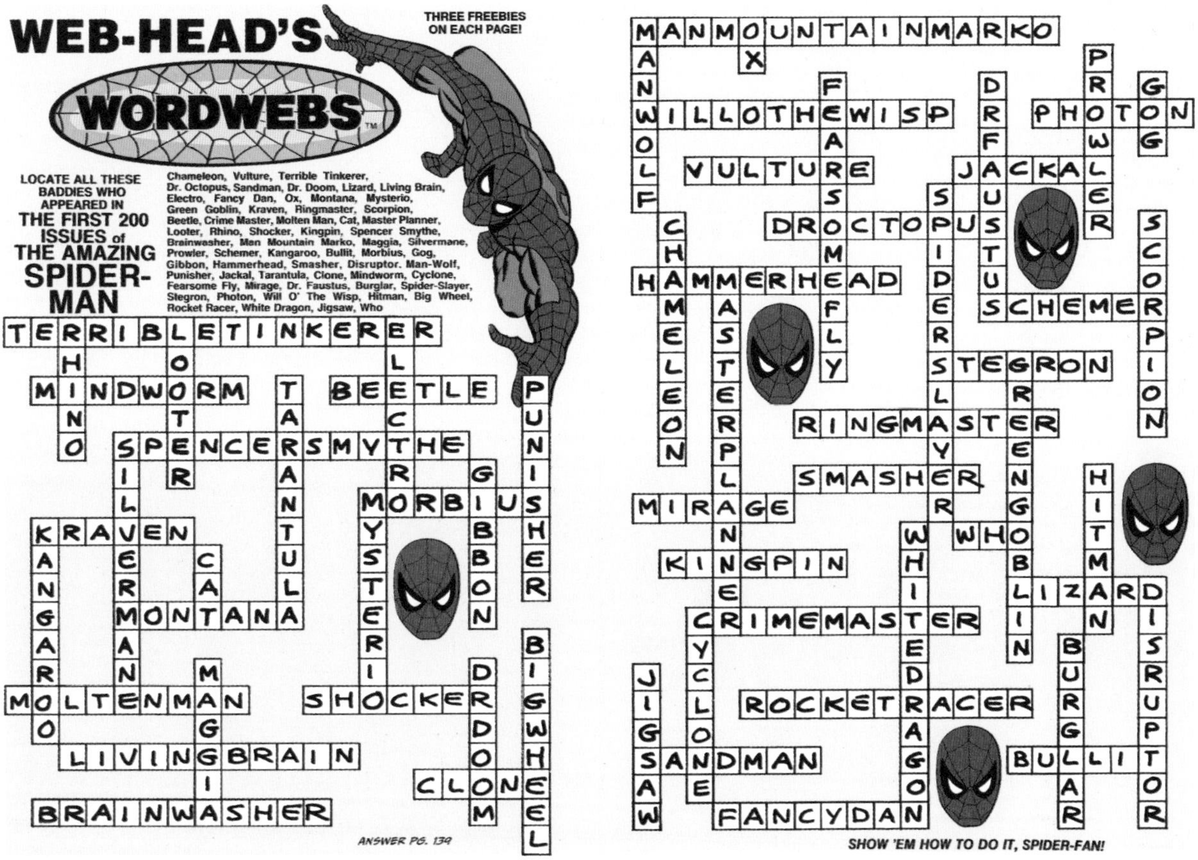
WEB-HEAD'S
WORDWEBS
THREE FREEBIES ON EACH PAGE!
LOCATE ALL THESE BADDIES WHO APPEARED IN THE FIRST 200 ISSUES of THE AMAZING SPIDER-MAN
Chameleon, Vulture, Terrible Tinkerer, Dr. Octopus, Sandman, Dr. Doom, Lizard, Living Brain, Electro, Fancy Dan, Ox, Montana, Mysterio, Green Goblin, Kraven, Ringmaster, Scorpion, Beetle, Crime Master, Molten Man, Cat, Master Planner, Looter, Rhino, Shocker, Kingpin, Spencer Smythe, Brainwasher, Man Mountain Marko, Maggia, Silvermane, Prowler, Schemer, Kangaroo, Bullit, Morbius, Gog, Gibbon, Hammerhead, Smasher, Disruptor, Man-Wolf, Punisher, Jackal, Tarantula, Clone, Mindworm, Cyclone, Fearsome Fly, Mirage, Dr. Faustus, Burglar, Spider-Slayer, Stegron, Photon, Will O' The Wisp, Hitman, Big Wheel, Rocket Racer, White Dragon, Jigsaw, Who
ANSWER PG. 139
SHOW 'EM HOW TO DO IT, SPIDER-FAN!

96–97

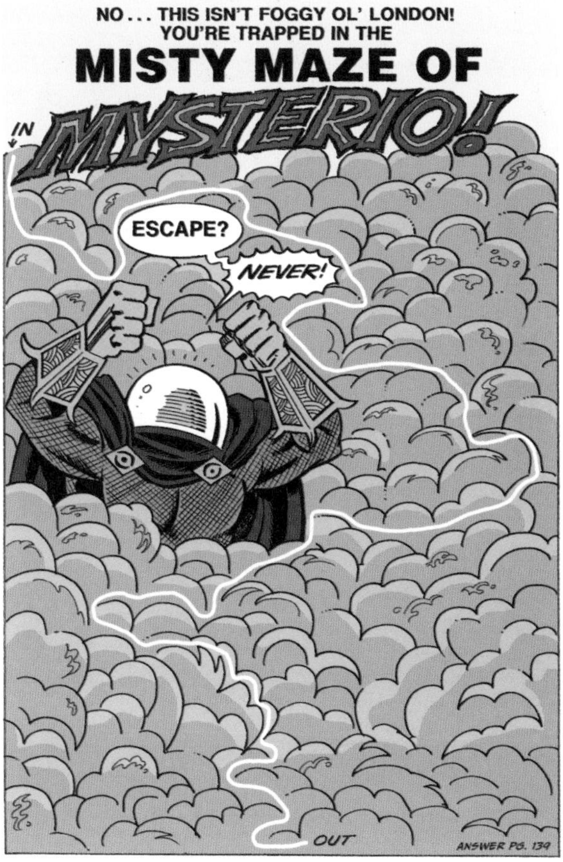
NO . . . THIS ISN'T FOGGY OL' LONDON! YOU'RE TRAPPED IN THE
MISTY MAZE OF
MYSTERIO!
IN
ESCAPE?
NEVER!
OUT
ANSWER PG. 139

99

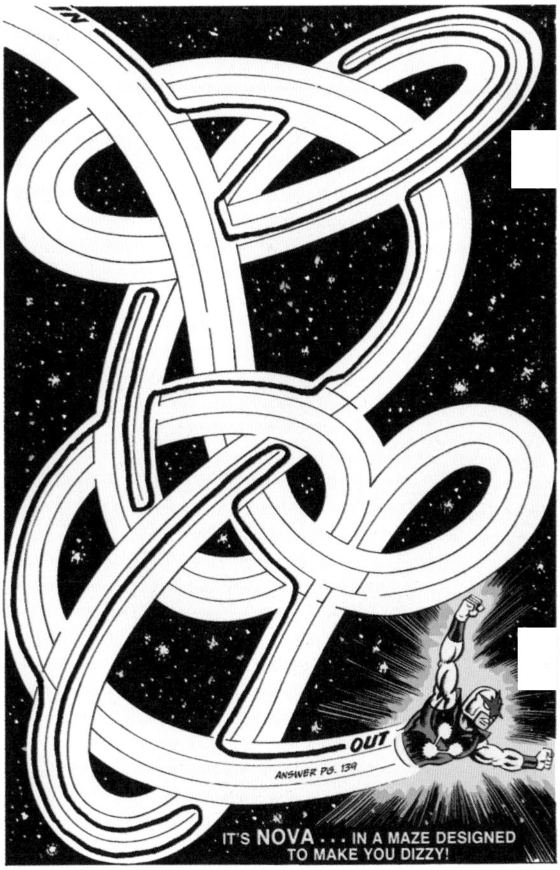
IN
OUT
ANSWER PG. 139
IT'S NOVA . . . IN A MAZE DESIGNED TO MAKE YOU DIZZY!

103

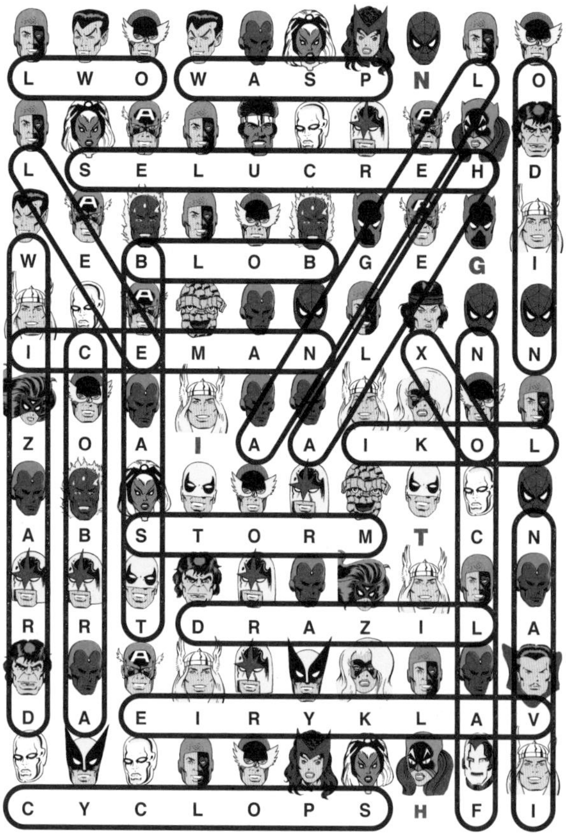

L W O W A S P N L O
L S E L U C R E H D
W E B L O B G E G I
I C E M A N L X N N
Z O A I A A I K O L
A B S T O R M T C N
R R T D R A Z I L A
D A E I R Y K L A V
C Y C L O P S H F I


104

# FAMILY REUNION TIME
## with SUB-MARINER

Believe it or not, the fish listed below are just a few that inhabit Subby's domain. Find them all, horizontal, vertical, diagonal, and backward without skipping letters and always in a straight line.

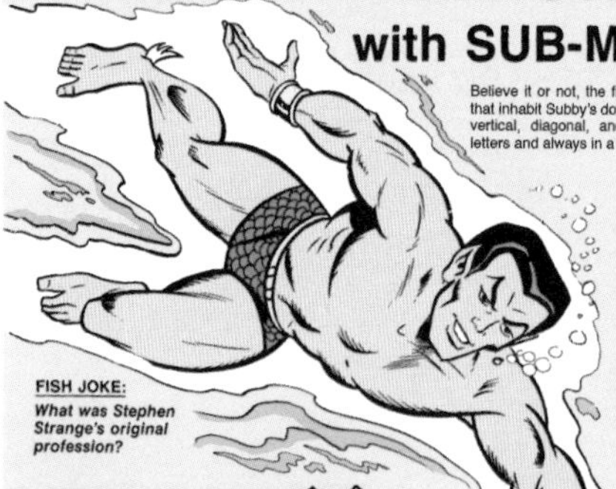

| | |
|---|---|
| BARRACUDA | STINGRAY |
| TUNA | SAWFISH |
| MACKEREL | CARP |
| PERCH | GAR |
| SUNFISH | TARPON |
| STURGEON | SMELT |
| HERRING | PIKE |
| TROUT | SEAHORSE |
| SALMON | GRUNION |
| FLATFISH | SAILFISH |
| COD | MOONFISH |
| EEL | BASS |
| MINNOW | GRUNT |
| SUCKER | PORGY |
| CATFISH | CHUB |
| TIGER SHARK | CROAKER |
| MANTA RAY | SCULPIN |

**FISH JOKE:**
*What was Stephen Strange's original profession?*

**FISH JOKE:**
*What was Subby's favorite Broadway show?*

ANSWER PGS. 140 AND 143

| | | | | | | | | | | | | | | | | | | | |
|---|---|---|---|---|---|---|---|---|---|---|---|---|---|---|---|---|---|---|---|
| N | I | P | L | U | C | S | H | P | H | H | | | | | | | | | |
| M | I | N | N | O | W | D | I | S | E | E | | | | | | | | | |
| O | N | O | P | A | T | K | T | R | I | C | | | | | | | | | |
| O | T | M | N | R | E | N | R | D | T | F | | | | | | | | | |
| N | M | L | I | M | E | I | O | C | D | L | W | H | C | H | H | P | B | U | C |
| F | B | A | R | R | A | C | U | D | A | E | O | A | S | L | S | M | E | L | T |
| I | T | S | E | G | K | C | T | S | M | N | I | T | S | I | I | C | O | T | N |
| S | I | U | S | I | R | A | K | W | O | H | N | D | A | C | F | D | U | K | U |
| H | G | C | R | O | N | U | O | E | L | C | U | O | B | A | T | N | R | O | R |
| Y | E | K | O | C | R | N | G | A | R | R | R | M | V | D | A | N | U | P | G |
| A | S | E | H | E | R | R | I | N | G | E | G | L | A | U | C | O | G | S | Y |
| R | H | R | A | S | U | P | L | N | T | P | L | A | C | N | E | P | R | M | S |
| G | A | P | E | T | K | R | A | H | S | R | E | G | I | T | T | R | U | R | P |
| N | R | P | S | I | C | A | R | K | B | R | E | R | R | A | B | A | N | E | O |
| I | K | W | H | S | P | C | G | R | U | N | I | O | N | K | E | T | R | K | R |
| T | S | F | I | A | E | S | G | L | H | H | S | I | F | T | A | L | F | A | G |
| S | A | I | L | F | I | S | H | E | C | R | O | A | K | E | R | O | W | E | Y |

105

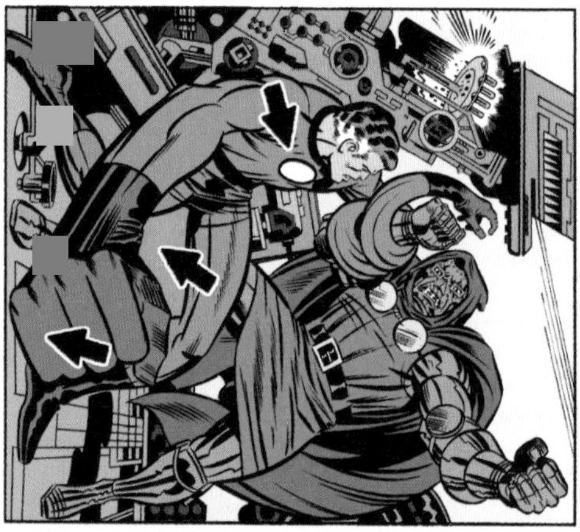

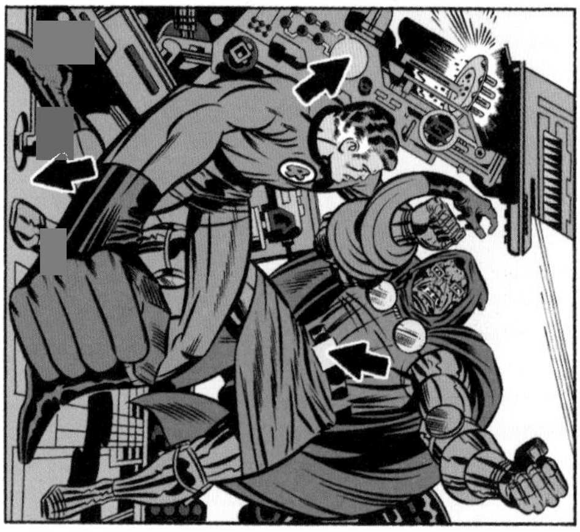

# WHAT'S MISSING?

There are 3 different things missing in each drawing. Compare them carefully against each other and you'll have no problem. We had special orders from Doctor Doom to go easy with this one . . . and when he speaks . . . guess who listens?

ANSWER PG. 140

108

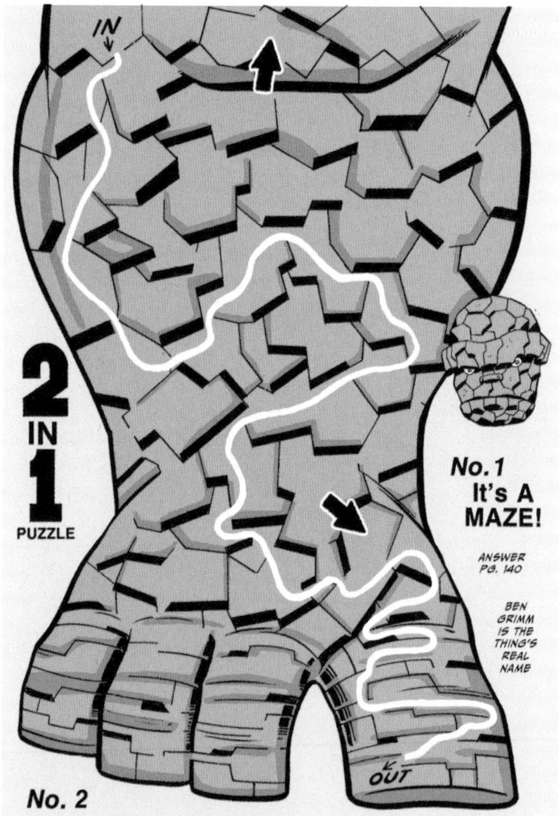

IN
OUT


**2 IN 1 PUZZLE**

**No. 1 It's A MAZE!**

ANSWER PG. 140

BEN GRIMM IS THE THING'S REAL NAME

**No. 2**

**BE A BIG BEN BENEFACTOR! SHOW HIM TWO PIECES IN THIS LUMBERING LIMB THAT ARE EXACTLY THE SAME!**

109

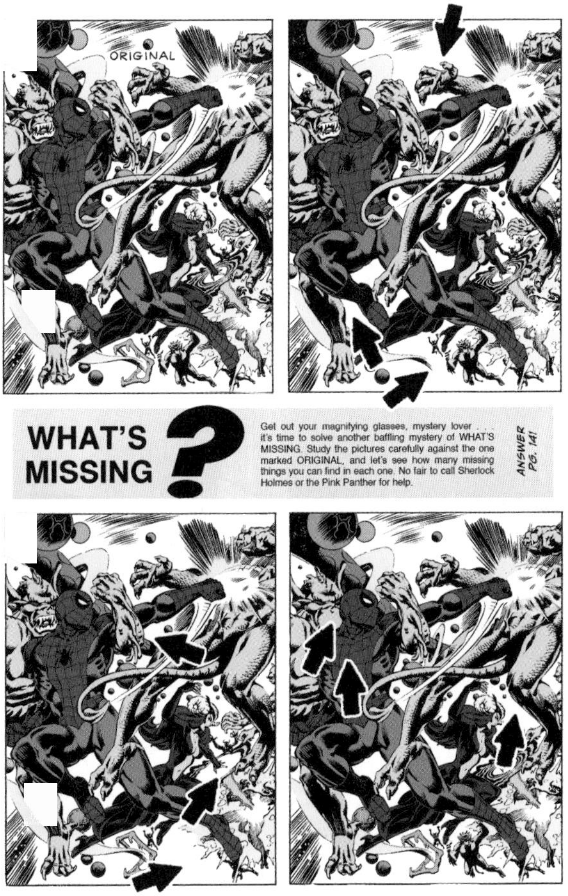
ORIGINAL
WHAT'S MISSING ?
Get out your magnifying glasses, mystery lover . . . it's time to solve another baffling mystery of WHAT'S MISSING. Study the pictures carefully against the one marked ORIGINAL, and let's see how many missing things you can find in each one. No fair to call Sherlock Holmes or the Pink Panther for help.
ANSWER PG. 141

112

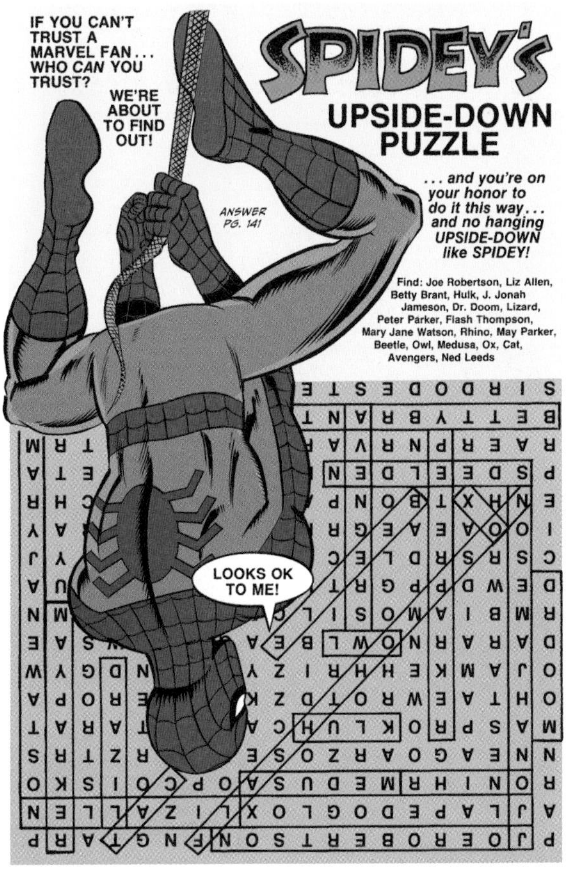
IF YOU CAN'T TRUST A MARVEL FAN . . . WHO CAN YOU TRUST?
WE'RE ABOUT TO FIND OUT!
SPIDEY's
UPSIDE-DOWN PUZZLE
. . . and you're on your honor to do it this way . . . and no hanging UPSIDE-DOWN like SPIDEY!
ANSWER PG. 141
Find: Joe Robertson, Liz Allen, Betty Brant, Hulk, J. Jonah Jameson, Dr. Doom, Lizard, Peter Parker, Flash Thompson, Mary Jane Watson, Rhino, May Parker, Beetle, Owl, Medusa, Ox, Cat, Avengers, Ned Leeds
LOOKS OK TO ME!

113

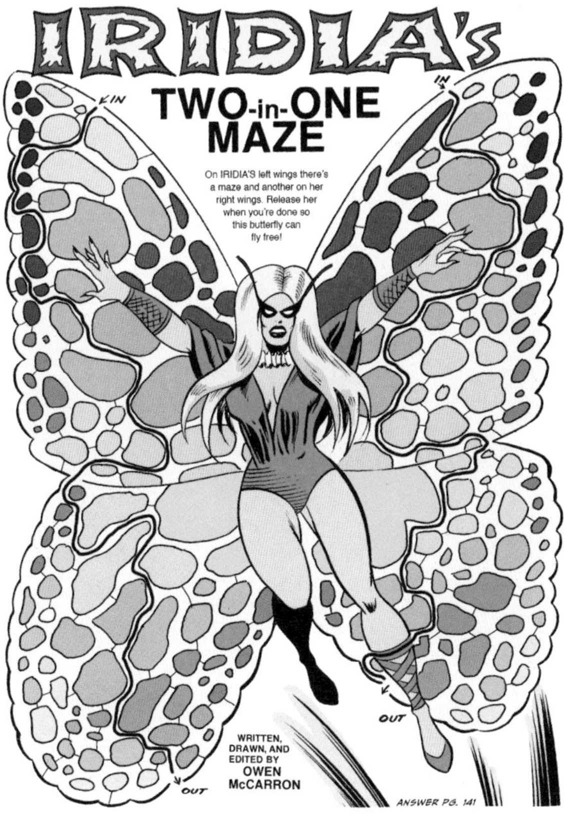
IRIDIA's
TWO-in-ONE MAZE
IN
IN
On IRIDIA'S left wings there's a maze and another on her right wings. Release her when you're done so this butterfly can fly free!
OUT
OUT
WRITTEN, DRAWN, AND EDITED BY OWEN McCARRON
ANSWER PG. 141

115

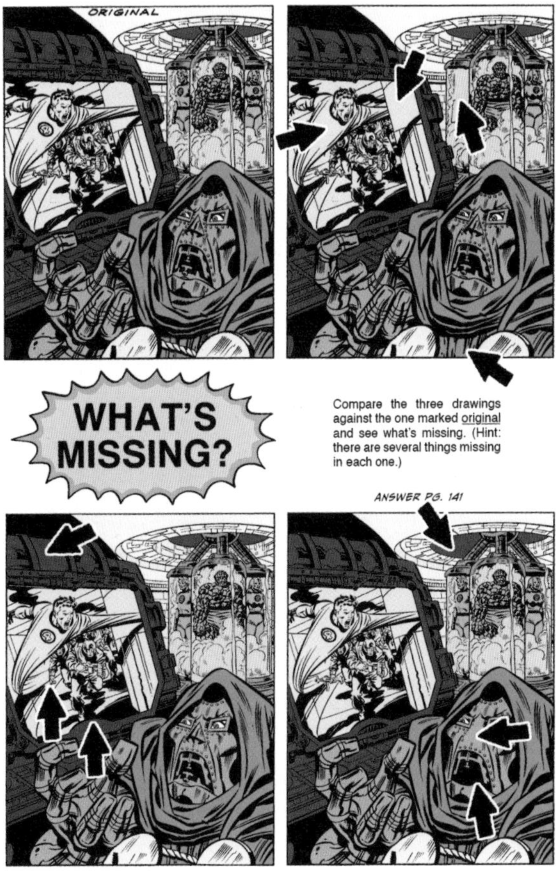
ORIGINAL
WHAT'S MISSING?
Compare the three drawings against the one marked original and see what's missing. (Hint: there are several things missing in each one.)
ANSWER PG. 141

116

# ONLY MARVEL COULD COME UP WITH SUCH A MIND-BENDING PUZZLE CONCEPT!

## QUADRA·WORD FIND

FIND EACH OF THE MARVEL SUPER HEROES SHOWN HERE **FOUR TIMES**

Horizontal, vertical, diagonal, and backward, always in a straight line without skipping letters.

ANSWER PG. 142

```
T Y R O N Y R U F K C I N G K N O O M
H N R O O M H V A G L V H O Y G V A P
C I P U N O G A R D N O O M N H M O P
V C G O F O A G H O S T R I D E R H O
A K A H W K G D R T N I K C V W O O W
G F W V V R C A R D N O H A W K E Y E
H U O X Y W I X R E O O V R K A O P R
Y R P K R K D R N D E Y E K W A H V M
G Y L T W E E U Y F N N V N O A V M A
M A N H R Y I F V M O O N D R A G O N
V E O S O E R R V H A V O N O H V N N
O P O D O O Y U G V T A G M O A A A N
O G O V A L K Y R I E S A G K W Y M O
F H M W G C L V G O O R H E K L R P
P O W E R M A N E C R V D O G E R E G
N S G W V B Y K N P I O N S H Y E W H
H T A O W G W A D O N N O V A E T O O
C R N P A A M H L O V O O W E N S R A
G I K I H R N I N K P V M O O N R P V
J D N H E G M E I R Y K L A V N O O M
L E A W N G O R E D I R T S O H G T S
C R O H A W K E V E G N I C K F U R Y
F P U R Y G H O S N A M R E W O P I N
```

---

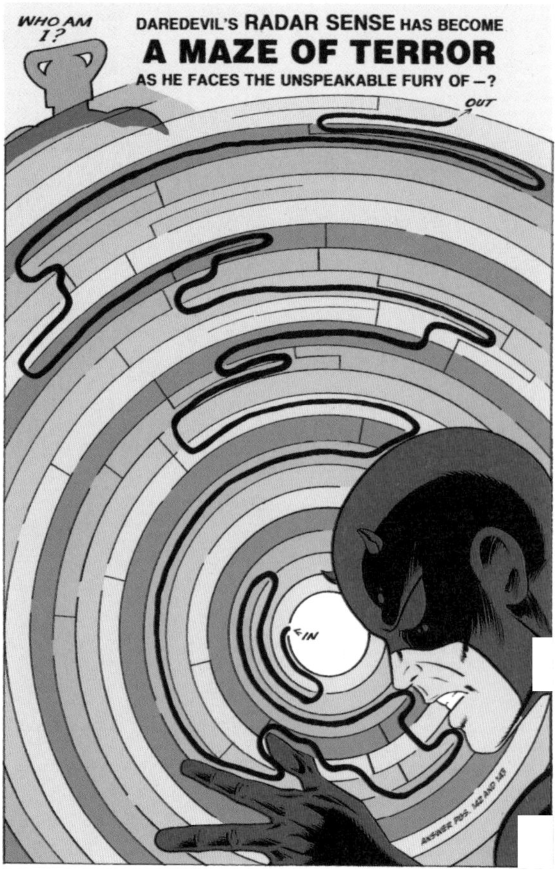

WHO AM I?

## DAREDEVIL'S RADAR SENSE HAS BECOME A MAZE OF TERROR

AS HE FACES THE UNSPEAKABLE FURY OF —?

OUT

IN

ANSWER PGS. 142 AND 143

**118** · **119**

---

# WOLVERINE NEEDS YOUR HELP TO...

## FIND THE X-MEN!

... and all these other Marvel characters who have an "X" in their names: Drexel Cord, Axonn-Karr, Phoenix, Alex, Factor X, Tryx, Xandu, Xander, Xartans, Xorr, Drax, Zaxton, Xemnu, Xemu, Terrax, Xeron, Agent Axis, Zzzax, Sphinx, Professor X, Maximus, Temax, Executioner, Triax, Martinex, Brother Ax, Texas Twister.

(WOLVERINE IS THE SHORT-TEMPERED MEMBER OF THE X-MEN.) ANSWER PG. 142

**EXTRA! FIND "OX" 7 TIMES!**

```
T E S A X T W D A C D Q X I N E O H P S
T X A N D U X R N O R S R O Q C H A T E
E P Q S B N E A G E N T A X I S E T X P
X T R A U M E X D O B T H F J U Z E X T
P S P E L E Z N B R D C G O O M T B E R
R N O R E X A Z Z Z O W E N C I E R M D
O G R O N X X F R R E T C O G X R L A R
F R N I E O T R E T S I W T S A X E T E
E S H L P R O F E X R O R S X M G X T X
S P A J A X N C H A L T O A X L Q E P E
S X S T R C A X G O C R R P Z Y N C G L
O N R Z E P G I N T R E A S E Z R U L C
R V A O S O X N R N H P C X A M E T R O
X X U A T A R A D T E M A Z I M U I E R
N J C W R C T E O R O M R L L E A O T D
C H X T H M A R T I N E X E O S L N E W
X E A N L C B F X X E C E A T E N E X S
R N P O C O G L G A X O N N K A R R T I
S A A L Q X I N E E H P G O T E S R X X
```

**122**

---

ANSWER PG. 142

JESSICA DREW THIS MAZE AND THERE IS NO ESCAPE!

IN? IN? IN? IN?

OUT

**123**

142

## 19: SPIDEY ON TELEVISION

No. 2 and 5 are the same.

## 21: HOW MANY SUPER HEROES?

12. They are: Nova, Thor, Spider-Man, Human Torch, Nighthawk, Captain America, Shang-Chi, Black Panther, Vision, Hulk, Iron Man, Daredevil.

## 25: UNSCRAMBLE THE MARVEL SUPER HEROES

1. Cyclops
2. Iron Fist
3. Power Man
4. Hellcat
5. Hawkeye
6. Spidey

## 28: DOC OCK'S MIRROR MYSTERY

No. 3 is correct

## 31: INVISIBLE WOMAN

Outline No. 1 is correct

## 33: SPIDEY'S ALPHABET ATTACK

Kraven, Kingpin, Beetle, Vulture, Lizard, Electro

## 43: NIGHTCRAWLER NAME-CALLER

Ace, Al, Alec, Ali, Angel, Angie, Archer, Archie, Ari, Aria, Ariel, Art, Cain, Cal, Carl, Carlie, Carrie, Carter, Cate, Celia, Celina, Charli, Charlie, Cher, Cian, Claire, Clint, Egan, Einar, Eli, Eric, Erica, Erich, Ethan, Gael, Gail, Gale, Galen, Garth, Gia, Gina, Glen, Grace, Grant, Greta, Gwen, Hal, Harriet, Helga, Henri, Ian, Ila, Ina, Ira, Laci, Lance, Lane, Lang, Lani, Lanie, Lea, Leah, Leigh, Lena, Lia, Liane, Lina, Lita, Nat, Nate, Neal, Neil, Nia, Nigel, Nita, Rachel, Rae, Rain, Raleigh, Rani, Regan, Regina, Rei, Ren, Rhea, Rian, Rich, Rita, Tai, Tegan, Teri, Thea, Tia, Tina, Trina, Twila, Wagner, Walt, Walter, Warner, Warren, Wilt, Wren

## 47: HOW MANY WORDS IN JESSICA DREW?

Draw, dew, war, wed, weed, car, care, card, cad, wear, ware, was, jaw, dress, dear, dare, sew, dice, case, side, sire, jar, sear, raise, raw, cease, disease, wire, acre, arc, crass, idea, red, dire, read, were, die, ear, said, ease, sir, acid, wide, ace, race, erase, crew, craw, weird, rad, rice, rise, wise . . . and so on.

## 55: WASP SHADOWS

No. 1 and 3, No. 2 and 5, No. 4 and 7, No. 6 and 8

## 60–61: PUNCHBOARD

1. HULK, Thanos 2. THE THING, Sandman 3. NICK FURY, Talos 4. LUKE CAGE, Dr. Doom 5. IRON MAN, Ultron 6. CAPT. MARVEL, Ronan 7. BLACK BOLT, Maximus 8. DR. DOOM, The Thing 9. SPIDER-MAN, Kraven 10. CAPT. AMERICA, Red Skull 11. FALCON, Zemo 12. MYSTERIO, Spider-Man 13. TIGER SHARK, Namor 14. THOR, Loki 15. SPIDER-WOMAN, Viper 16. BLACK PANTHER, Klaw

## 62: POETRY TIME

(Doctor Doom)
. . . and he'll sweep you up with his broom

(Reed Richards)
They play with their etch-a-sketch.

## 64: OPERATION: SUPER HERO

1. Geneva 2. Iran 3. Mumbai 4. Rome 5. Bolivia 6. Malta 7. China 8. Cuba

## 72: SECRET CODE BREAKER QUIZ

Question: Peter Parker is really The Hulk?
Answer: False

## 74: WORDS IN *DAILY BUGLE*

die, glue, bug, bed, leg, day, laid, lied, blue, lie, bail, age, ladle, lad, dale, lead, big, bag, dull, dab, deal, lug, lid, lib, bail, bad, gull, ail, ale, bull, gay, bay, lay, bulge, lube, bilge, badge, ball, gall, yield, glib, bell, able, bagel, daily, gill, glide, label, belly, dill, able, gel, gullible, etc.

## 76: SUB-MARINER WORDS

bus, near, sear, ream, mane, main, sin, sir, sire, sari, smear, urine, use, bar, mar, bin, brine, seam, bear, bare, burn, briar, barn, ban, bum, mine, miner, man, muse, rib, ram, mire, marine, ear, nib, rise, raise, name, base, remain, rim, brim, brain, and so on.

## 78: HOW MANY "THINGS"

22

## 79: PLAY CHARADES

Something Old, Something New, Something Borrowed, Something Blue.

## 82: SPIDEY'S SEVEN-LETTER NAMES

Shocker, Vulture, Kingpin, Prowler, Montana, Electro, Cyclone, Sandman, Carnage, Morbius, The Spot (and there could be many others).

## 89: COMPLETE THE RHYMES

This weird gent is called Drac.
He's often seen flat on his back
When he gets up, by heck,
He's after a neck
Then he crawls back to his sack.

Power Man's real name is Cage.
In a battle he'll always engage.
He was a hero for hire.
He never did tire
And he never made minimum wage.

## 90: WHAT DID HE SAY?

1. The early bird gets the worm.
2. Blood is thicker than water.
3. Don't bite off your nose to spite your face.
4. You're not the only pebble on the beach.
5. A miss is as good as a mile.
6. Hitch your wagon to a star.

## 92: CIRCLE WORD

1. Fantastic Four, 2. Black Panther, 3. Defenders, 4. Spider-Woman, 5. Captain America

Mystery Guest: Carol Danvers

## 98: SLIME-RHYME

Man thing, whose real name's Ted Sallis,
Had never wished anyone malice.
Without any pomp . . .
He fell in the swamp
And now he can play at "The Palace."

## 98: CRIME-RHYME

A villainous gent is Mysterio . . .
Crime seems to be his fortissimo.
His trademark's a mist—
He's a real masochist
But Spidey will make him quite wary-o.

## 100: MR. FANTASTIC

No. 5 is correct.

## 102: QUIZ-A-WHIZ

1. Daredevil
2. Steve Rogers
3. Kronus
4. Quicksilver
5. T'Challa
6. Seeker
7. Morbius
8. Impact

## 105: FAMILY REUNION WITH SUB-MARINER

Stephen Strange's original profession: He was a famous STURGEON.

Subby's favorite Broadway show: THE SEA LION KING.

## 110: MT. RUSHMORE

Top pic left to right: Nighthawk, Nova, Wolverine, Yellowjacket, Captain America, Dr. Strange, The Thing, Thor.

Bottom pic left to right: Loki, Hulk, Iron Man, Doctor Doom, Green Goblin, Ant Man, Galactus

## 111: SHADOW DANCING

No. 1 is the correct shadow.

## 114: VISION'S MIRROR

No. 3 is the one.

## 119: MAZE OF TERROR

Who is the villain: JACKHAMMER

## 120: THOR'S SHADOW

No. 1 is correct.

# MISSION ACCOMPLISHED!

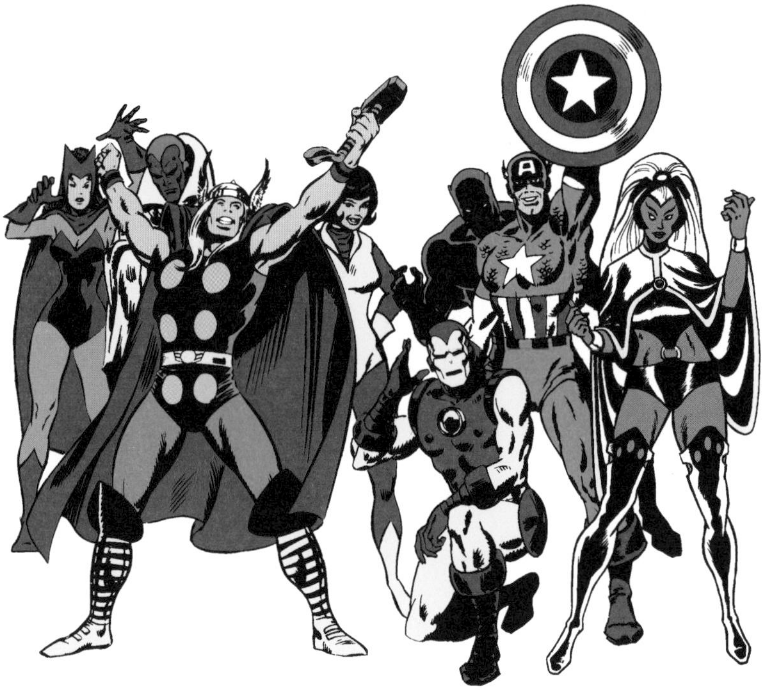

Bonus Answer: The Vision, Storm, Colossus, Human Torch, Spider-Man, Doctor Doom, Nova, Daredevil, Black Bolt, The Hulk, Nick Fury, Captain America, Scarlet Witch, Black Panther, The Thing, Power Man, Iron Man, Captain Marvel, Wolverine, Sub-Mariner, Silver Surfer, Thor, Mr. Fantastic, Iron Fist, Shang-Chi, Ghost Rider, Falcon, Nightcrawler, Doctor Strange, Hellcat, Nighthawk, Red Skull